Patristics and Catholic Social Thought

CATHOLIC SOCIAL TRADITION

Preface to the Series

In *Tertio millennio adveniente,* Pope John Paul II poses a hard question: "It must be asked how many Christians really know and put into practice the principles of the church's social doctrine." The American Catholic bishops share the pope's concern: "Catholic social teaching is a central and essential element of our faith . . . [and yet] our social heritage is unknown by many Catholics. Sadly, our social doctrine is not shared or taught in a consistent and comprehensive way in too many of our schools." This lack is critical because the "sharing of our social tradition is a defining measure of Catholic education and formation." A United States Catholic Conference task force on social teaching and education noted that within Catholic higher education "there appears to be little consistent attention given to incorporating gospel values and Catholic social teaching into general education courses or into departmental majors."

In response to this problem, the volumes in the Catholic Social Tradition series aspire to impart the best of what this tradition has to offer not only to Catholics but to all who face the social issues of our times. The volumes examine a wide variety of issues and problems within the Catholic social tradition and contemporary society, yet they share several characteristics. They are theologically and philosophically grounded, examining the deep structure of thought in modern culture. They are publicly argued, enhancing dialogue with other religious and nonreligious traditions. They are comprehensively engaged by a wide variety of disciplines such as theology, philosophy, political science, economics, history, law, management, and finance. Finally, they examine how the Catholic social tradition can be integrated on a practical level and embodied in institutions in which people live much of their lives. The Catholic Social Tradition series is about faith in action in daily life, providing ways of thinking and acting to those seeking a more humane world.

Michael J. Naughton
University of St. Thomas
Minnesota, USA

PATRISTICS
and Catholic Social Thought

Hermeneutical Models for a Dialogue

BRIAN MATZ

University of Notre Dame Press
Notre Dame, Indiana

Copyright © 2014 by University of Notre Dame
Notre Dame, Indiana 46556
undpress.nd.edu
All Rights Reserved

Manufactured in the United States of America

Library of Congress Cataloging-in-Publication Data

Matz, Brian J.
 Patristics and Catholic social thought :
hermeneutical models for a dialogue / Brian Matz.
     pages cm. — (Catholic social tradition)
 Includes bibliographical references and index.
 ISBN 978-0-268-03531-0 (pbk. : alk. paper) —
     ISBN 0-268-03531-8 (pbk. : alk. paper)
 1. Christian sociology—Catholic Church—History of
doctrines—Early church, ca. 30–600. 2. Fathers of the church.
3. Christian literature, Early—History and criticism.   I. Title.
           BX1753.M3545   2014
           261.8088'282—dc23
                2014001704

∞ *The paper in this book meets the guidelines for permanence and durability
of the Committee on Production Guidelines for Book Longevity of the
Council on Library Resources.*

For Heidi

Contents

Acknowledgments	ix
List of Abbreviations	xiii
List of Tables	xv
Introduction	1
Chapter 1 Patristic Sources and Catholic Social Teaching	7
Chapter 2 Themes in Patristic Social Thought	32
Chapter 3 An "Authorial Intent" Model	58
Chapter 4 A "Distanciation" Model	95
Chapter 5 A "Normativity of the Future" Model	122
Chapter 6 A "New Intellectual History" Model	141
Conclusion	160
Appendix 1. Asterius of Amasea's *Homily* 1	176
Appendix 2. Jerome's *Homily* 86	185
Notes	194
Bibliography	251
Index of Scriptural Passages	291
Index of Early Christian Sources	293

Acknowledgments

A work of this scale could not have come together without the participation and contribution of others. This study is the third of four volumes to be published from a research project directed by the Centre for Catholic Social Thought based at the Catholic University of Leuven in Belgium. The centre's work on social ethics in late antiquity spanned the period 2005 to 2009, and was funded by the Fund for Scientific Research of Flanders. I am grateful for their generous support of my research during this period.

That I was able to work on this project in the first place, and to do so in the beautiful environs of Leuven, is due to the generosity and encouragement of the project's two promoters, Johan Verstraeten and Johan Leemans (or, as I affectionately would note in my agenda when scheduling our quarterly meetings, "the Johans"). I suspect that it was during the time Johan Leemans began work on Gregory of Nyssa's social ideas several years ago that the project to explore the social ideas in the Greek Fathers first was conceived. Then, in conversations with Johan Verstraeten, an expert in Catholic social thought, who also has an interest in its historical roots, the two brought this research project to life. For my part, it remains clear that I have yet to plumb the depths of their combined expertise and wisdom in these fields of study. If the project has suffered from some oversight or a lapse of judgment, no doubt that comes from the limitations of this researcher. Nonetheless, it is hoped that together we have shed enough light on both the need for and the difficulties inherent in constructing a dialogue between patristic and modern

Christian social thought such that like-minded scholars may carry the work to even greater heights.

As for this particular text, it took shape during an important three days of conversation between members of our research staff and nearly twenty scholars invited to participate in a seminar in September 2007 at Catholic University of Leuven. I need not mention all their names here, for most of them later published revised versions of their remarks in the volume *Reading Patristic Texts on Social Ethics: Issues and Challenges for Twenty-First-Century Christian Social Thought*, ed. Johan Leemans, Brian J. Matz, and Johan Verstraeten, CUA Studies in Early Christianity (Washington, D.C.: Catholic University of America Press, 2011). In addition to these scholars, I have been grateful for conversations with colleagues both in ethics and in patristics at annual meetings of the Society of Christian Ethics and of the North American Patristics Society. I am also grateful to the assistance of the staff of the Maurits Sabbe Bibliotheek of the Faculty of Theology in Leuven and of the staff of the interlibrary loan desk at the Catholic University of Leuven Central Library. With the conclusion of this project, surely some measureable percentage of their workload over the past few years gave way to newfound time and energy for other researchers and their projects. I thank them very much.

Thanks are due to Michael Deckard, Colby Dickinson, and our weekly meetings together over cups of strong coffee at a local shop in Leuven during which we read together Gadamer's *Truth and Method* and Ricoeur's hermeneutical essays. They were remarkably patient with this novice in the field of twentieth-century hermeneutics. I am also grateful to Shawn Keough, with whom I shared an office at the Catholic University of Leuven. His near-religious zeal for unearthing hidden treasures for scholarly study among the many fields of oriental Christian studies was an inspiration, although I remain convinced he would have enjoyed his work more if he took many more coffee breaks with me. Thanks are due also to the many friends who gave me more than enough reasons to balance work with the pleasures of living in Europe. Thanks to Lucrèce de Becker, Jim and Krista Slagle, Jean Jacobs and Lies Vanoorle, John and Julia Dennis,

David Pratt, Michael and Julianne Funk Deckard, Shawn and Myrna Keough, Colby Dickinson, and Elisabeth Bayley. As well, thanks are due to my department chair at Carroll College, John Ries, who organized my teaching schedule during 2009–2010 in a way that enabled completion of this manuscript. Furthermore, thanks are due to Philip Gerard Holthaus, my copy editor for this book, whose many corrections improved the text very much, and to Taylor Stewart, my research assistant, who helped with the preparation of the indexes. Doubtless, errors remain for which I am entirely responsible.

Finally, I thank my wife Heidi for her understanding and support during the many hours of work that were required in order to complete this manuscript. Fellow parents of toddlers will know that she bore the brunt of the hard work needed to raise our boys during these delightful but challenging years. It is to her I dedicated this book.

List of Abbreviations

Other abbreviations are introduced in the text, such as titles of encyclicals.

ACW	Ancient Christian Writers: The Works of the Fathers in Translation
ANF	The Ante-Nicene Fathers, ed. Philip Schaff
ANL	Annua Nuntia Lovaniensia
BETL	Bibliotheca Ephemeridum Theologicarum Lovaniensium
CCSL	Corpus Christianorum Series Latina
CSEL	Corpus Scriptorum Ecclesiasticorum Latinorum
FOTC	The Fathers of the Church
GCS	Die griechischen christlichen Schriftsteller der ersten Jahrhunderte
GNO	*Gregorii Nysseni Opera*
LCL	Loeb Classical Library
NPNF	Nicene and Post-Nicene Fathers
PG	Patrologia Graeca, ed. J.-P. Migne
PL	Patrologia Latina, ed. J.-P. Migne
PTS	Patristische Texte und Studien
SC	Sources Chrétiennes
WSA	*Works of Saint Augustine: A Translation for the 21st Century*
WUNT	Wissenschaftliche Untersuchungen zum Neuen Testament

List of Tables

Table 1.	CST Documents and Their Patristic Sources: Summary	10
Table 2.	Patristic Sources in the CST Documents	11
Table 3.	Density of Patristic Source Citations in the CST Documents	17
Table 4.	Frequency of Rhetorical Function according to Citation Category	21
Table 5a.	Jerome's Dialogue, *Homily* 86, ll.110–24	115
Table 5b.	Jerome's Dialogue, *Homily* 86, ll. 110–14, a Contemporary Version	116

INTRODUCTION

Ever tried to place one ball on top of another? How about three balls, one on top of the other? Nearly impossible. This study attempts just such a feat in what some have deemed, well, if not altogether impossible, perhaps rather unnecessary or even inappropriate. Each of the three balls for this study represents a world of inquiry that seems to have nothing in common with the other two. One ball is the field of patristic studies. A second ball is the field of Christian social ethics. A third ball is the field of hermeneutics. Perhaps one may say that the first and third balls have something in common, for they share a concern with how to approach ancient texts. Likewise, perhaps the second and third balls have something in common. Each shares a concern with how to get out of those texts ideas with an impetus for action. Yet, can these three balls be stacked one on top of the other?

Indeed, I think they can be. What is more, I am not the first to try. The Catholic Church's social teaching documents have tried. These documents have tried to balance themselves on top of earlier Christian teaching on social ethics, including the writings of the Church Fathers. Yet, I argue, the Catholic Church has largely failed in its endeavor to appropriate these ancient sources for the benefit of audiences today. This is because the drafters of the social teaching documents never figured out how to position the third ball properly between themselves and the world of the Fathers.

BACKGROUND TO THE STUDY

This attempt to bring into dialogue with one another three worlds of scholarly inquiry began a few years ago with the recognition that the documents comprising Catholic social teaching (hereafter CST) had failed adequately to appropriate the voices of the Church Fathers on topics of socioethical concern.[1] For that matter, it may be argued they also failed to adequately appropriate the views of Scholastic writers, including Thomas Aquinas whom they quote with great interest and with relatively greater frequency compared to the Church Fathers. A summary of my research on this matter of CST's use of the Fathers comprises the first chapter of this study. However, the purpose there shall not be to highlight failure for its own sake; rather, I suggest that sins of omission, rather than commission, are responsible. Indeed, this study investigates several ways for Christian social thought in our day fruitfully to engage the social thought of Christians in late antiquity.

A complementary publication to this earlier study is a volume of essays from an expert seminar held in 2007 in Leuven on the theme of reading patristic texts for the benefit of Christian social thought.[2] The essays raise a variety of, for lack of a better phrase, "red flags" in reading patristic texts. Chief among these flags is the cultural dissonance between the world of late antiquity and the world of today. One cannot avoid the fact that patristic texts too often frame their arguments with an acceptance of the status quo of Greco-Roman social, economic, and political life. The changes patristic texts advocate are at the margins (e.g., encouraging the wealthy to cultivate a mindset of love for the poor). No patristic text proposes an alternative political scheme or a progressive tax scheme or the creation of a state welfare system. By the fourth century, few, if any, are the voices calling for a retreat from military endeavors despite the great strain it placed on the imperial treasury. By contrast, we live in a world in which individuals are not only free, but encouraged, to protest the actions of their governments and to cry out for justice. The patristic voices will be quite foreign in this regard.

The other red flags are similarly daunting. While scholars of Christianity in late antiquity have some degree of confidence about the authorship and date for many texts, it would be safe to say the majority of patristic texts cannot be safely dated, and many anonymous and pseudepigraphal texts are extant. Even for those texts whose authorship and date are known, it is not always entirely clear where or for whom they were written. This complicates enormously the task of applying hermeneutical models that emphasize authorial intent. Equally difficult is the task of teasing out redactions in texts. Some began their lives as homilies, but ended up becoming study aids for use in monastic circles.[3] Others have the form of an oration but may have been private letters. The provenance, audience, and author's intent of far too many texts is remarkably elusive. The Christian social ethicist interested in navigating the waters of patristic literature surely has his or her work cut out for him or her. Yet, as this study will demonstrate, there is much fruit to be gained by plying those waters nonetheless.

A further, complementary publication, still in progress, aims at assisting Christian social ethicists to do just that. It is a compendium of patristic socioethical texts in English translation. Over thirty texts are included within this volume, and bibliographic references point to many more. The texts are divided into four socioethical themes (justice and common good; private property; the poor; usury), and each theme is introduced with an accessible introduction to the late antique context, the patristic texts, and the secondary, academic literature. Then, each patristic text is introduced with some notes about the historical and/or literary context. This compendium will be a valuable tool not just for students of this topic, but also for Christian social thought specialists who wish to familiarize themselves with the social ideas of Christians in late antiquity.

NEED FOR THE STUDY

As has already been stated, although it deserves credit for having tried something in this regard on behalf of Christian social thought, CST does not evidence a clear understanding of *how to read* patristic texts for contemporary socioethical study. Far from being surprised or even disappointed by this, historians of Christianity in late antiquity should seize this opportunity to contribute to an important theological agenda. This agenda is to explain what role, if any, ancient Christian texts ought to have in the formation of twenty-first-century thinking about social ethics. On that score, this text is but one contribution.

This study suggests several factors are at work in any appropriation of an ancient text for a contemporary discussion. To begin with, there is the difficulty in identifying or even understanding the context in which many ancient Christian texts took shape. For a surprisingly large number of texts, one cannot be certain as to the author or the date of their composition. A second factor is the acknowledgment by the reader of an ancient text of his or her place in the assessment of the contribution of that ancient text to any contemporary discussion. A third factor is the challenge of bringing into dialogue with one another the worldviews of writers from very different cultures. In a word, then, the contribution of this study to that agenda is hermeneutics. That is to say, this study proposes that Christians today are best helped in their use of ancient texts for contemporary socioethical formation by a clear sense of options available to the reader for *how to read* ancient texts.

To that end, this study will propose four models. The first is an "authorial intent" model, articulated in the ideas of Friedrich Schleiermacher and Wilhelm Dilthey. The second is a "distanciation" model, relying here on the work of Hans-Georg Gadamer and Paul Ricoeur. The third model is "normativity of the future," so named by its proponents, Reimund Bieringer and Mary Elsbernd. The fourth model is "new intellectual history," which has in view contemporary literary-critical theories. Aware of the preponderance of voices contributing to this fourth model, this study considers the ideas of Elizabeth Clark, who herself is an eminent scholar of Christianity in late antiquity.

More will be said about this study's approach to and use of these models in a moment. For now, though, it is important to point out that a better understanding of models for reading patristic socioethical texts lends itself to a more informed approach to the use of such texts. For example, the models encourage readers to pay attention both to characteristic features of early Christian homilies and to the use of rhetorical devices such as hyperbole and extended imagery. Readers are warned against conflating the experiences of one Church Father with that of another. Similarly, readers are advised against dismissing important distinctions that the Fathers often draw between types of rich people and types of poor people.

This study's elaboration of four models for reading ancient texts not only lends itself to a more informed reading of those texts, but it also fosters constructive interdisciplinary dialogue. Scholars of Christianity in late antiquity are still only gradually awakening to a wider world of literary studies that can enrich their ability to communicate that heritage to a wider public. Scholars and practitioners of Christian social ethics are largely unaware of the voices from Christianity's distant past and yet this ignorance belies an eagerness to understand the contribution of these voices to their own work. The field of hermeneutics is the place where both communities can meet. Scholars of late antiquity can pull back the veil of what is an otherwise intimidating body of literature; social ethicists contribute the contemporary language and categories of thought by means of which the ideas of the Church Fathers are able to be translated to audiences today.

ORGANIZATION OF THE STUDY

The following chapters test the contribution of and unpack the implications for using each of the four hermeneutical models. As has already been stated, the first chapter reviews the place of patristic sources in CST, recognizing that CST is but one of many voices in the world of Christian social thought. CST serves as a test case for how Christian social thought today uses early Christian sources. It will be clear from this study that there is room for Christian social thought to mature in this regard. In the second chapter, our attention turns to the world of early Christian social thought. This chapter provides a wider context for understanding two case study texts upon which I rely throughout the remainder of the study. Having said that, the third chapter introduces my two case study texts as a control group for understanding how different hermeneutical models improve our reading of these sources. Both texts, Asterius of Amasea's *Homily* 1 and Jerome's *Homily* 86, are expositions of Luke 16:18–30, which is Jesus' parable of the rich man and Lazarus. The texts are introduced in this third chapter in the context of applying the first of my four models, the authorial intent model. So this chapter begins with an introduction to the authorial intent model and then applies it to each of my case study texts. The remaining three hermeneutical models are introduced and applied to my case study texts in chapters four through six. Each model reveals a different vision for how Christian social thought may fruitfully engage in a dialogue with patristic social thought. In my conclusion I compare and contrast the application of the four models to the control texts I argue there that, although each model holds promise, the normativity of the future model best takes account of the real concerns of Christian social thought when reading an ancient text. This model best translates the social thought of the Fathers into language most helpful to the social thought of Christians today. Finally, the appendices include an English translation of each of my case study texts. Readers will likely want to keep a tab on those pages as this study moves along.

In the final analysis, the study takes seriously the desire of Christians to balance the three balls of patristic studies, social ethics, and hermeneutics. If only in a metaphorical way, these three balls can, indeed, balance one on top of the other. Voices from the past have a way of refreshing us, helping us rethink what we do, believe, and say. Patristic voices are certainly not "it"; voices from other eras and also from other religious communities past and present deserve our attention. Yet, for the use of patristic voices, it is expected that this study offers some fruitful paths forward.

Chapter 1

PATRISTIC SOURCES AND CATHOLIC SOCIAL TEACHING

Deus Caritas Est (promulgated 2005; hereafter, *DCE*) set a new record for the penetration of patristic source materials into the fabric of a social encyclical. Of the encyclical's roughly 13,000 words, 1,030 of them (8 percent) are devoted to one patristic source or another. No other document of Catholic social teaching (CST) comes close (cf. table 3 below).[1] This raises several questions: what role do patristic sources play in the CST documents,[2] why are they not more frequently employed in the documents, and what may be done to raise their status within the texts if, in fact, they are deemed pertinent in the first place. This chapter explores some contours both of the CST documents and of the patristic sources that help one begin to address such questions.

The patristic era, encompassing at least the second through the seventh centuries,[3] is generally regarded as a time when the Church formulated its theology, narrowed its canon, and solidified its place in the social, cultural, and political contexts of the day. Theologically, the Church Fathers elucidated both Christianity's understanding of God as a trinity of coequal, consubstantial, and coeternal persons and its understanding of Christ as one person possessing in full both a divine and a human nature. These theologies were the foundation for additional considerations, including anthropology, ecclesiology, and eschatology.[4]

Important with regard to the CST documents are these expanded theological reflections. For instance, *Centesimus Annus (CA)* argued, "The guiding principle of . . . all of the church's social doctrine, is a correct view of the human person and of his unique value."[5] *CA* goes on to point out that a human person's unique value may be traced back directly to the *imago Dei* given to man at the creation of the world. God gave to man this *imago Dei* as a consequence of foreknowing that the Son of God would one day incarnate himself as a human. In other words, CST is built upon a notion of human dignity. This dignity is rooted in the gift of God to each person, a gift that is an outworking of the mutual love existing among the persons of the Trinity. Therefore, Christ would eventually redeem what had always been and will continue to be creatures in his own image. To the extent that the patristic world had correctly articulated the doctrine of the Trinity, of Christ and his two natures, of man and his need for redemption, and of the church's responsibility to pass along these truths to every new generation, then the CST documents owe an incalculable debt to its theological acumen.

It is precisely because of this theological debt that a study of patristic sources in the CST documents is warranted. I carried out just such an inquiry and summarize in the first part of this chapter that study's results.[6] From this inquiry it was clear CST's debt to patristic theology did not match its constructive use of patristic texts. Specifically, in this chapter I review six problems with how CST documents weave patristic texts into the fabric of their arguments. Then, the chapter turns to a consideration of the potential pitfalls and problems anyone would face in searching for *the social ethic* of the early church. Both a survey of the CST documents and of the patristic sources are important in order to appreciate what follows in this text: the consideration of four hermeneutical models for incorporating patristic sources into Christian socioethical discourse today.

PATRISTIC SOURCES IN CST

Table 1 lists the CST documents that were included in the study.[7] Looking to the table, the name of the CST document is given first, followed by a shorthand designation for it (to be used throughout this book). The third column identifies how many patristic source citations may be found in each document, and the final three columns break down that number in accordance with how those sources are presented in the body of the document. One category is the direct quotations of patristic sources in the CST documents. Quotations may or may not be accompanied by the patristic author's name or the name of the text from which the quotation comes. Quotations are generally associated with a footnote that supplies this data. A second category is the general references to patristic source material in the body of the CST document. One common example is, "The Church Fathers say. . . ." Such references may or may not be accompanied by a footnote to indicate what the drafter or drafters of the CST document had in mind. A third category is footnote-only references to patristic sources, where, were it not for the presence of a footnote, the body of the CST document gives no indication a patristic source is behind its thought. Four of the CST documents examined included no patristic sources. They are included in this list to let the reader know the extent of this study's search, but no further analysis as to their contents is given.

All told, 110 patristic source citations were identified in these CST documents. A detailed list of these 110 citations is given in table 2, which orders the citations in accordance with the place in the CST documents at which they are found. It identifies what type of citation each one is, a quotation (Q), a general reference (R), or a footnote-only reference (F). As well, it includes a final column identifying what the rhetorical function of each source is in the larger context of their respective CST documents.

Table 1. CST Documents and Their Patristic Sources: Summary

CST Text	Text Abbrev.	Total Number Patristic Sources	Quotations	References	Footnotes
Rerum Novarum (1891)	RN	2	2		
Quadragesimo Anno (1931)	QA	2	1	1	
Mater et Magistra (1961)	MM	3	2	1	
Pacem in Terris (1963)	PT	3	3		
Dignitatis Humanae (1965)	DH	8		8	
Gaudium et Spes (1965)	GS	18	1	6	11
Populorum Progressio (1967)	PP	2	1	1	
Medellin Documents (1969)	Medellin	0			
Octogesima Adveniens (1971)	OA	0			
Iustitia in Mundo (1971)	IM	0			
Evangelii Nuntiandi (1975)	EN	15	6	3	6
Puebla Documents (1979)	Puebla	2		2	
Laborem Exercens (1981)	LE	0			
Familiaris Consortio (1981)	FC	4	3	1	
The Challenge of Peace (1983)	ChP	5	3	1	1
Economic Justice for All (1986)	EJA	2	1	1	
Sollicitudo Rei Socialis (1987)	SRS	6		6	
Centesimus Annus (1991)	CA	1	1		
Santo Domingo Docs. (1992)	SDomingo	2		1	1
Compendium of CST (2004)	ComCST	19	5	5	9
Deus Caritas Est (2005)	DCE	16	6	9	1
TOTALS		110	35	46	29

Table 2. Patristic Sources in the CST Documents

(Sorted by CST Document)

Source No.[1]	CST Text	Patristic Source	Patristic Text	Citation Type[2]	Rhetorical Function[3]
1	RN 19	Gregory the Great	*Homily on the Gospel* 9.7	Q	1
2	RN 24	Tertullian	*Apology* 39	Q	4
3	QA 16	Ambrose	*On the Passing of Satyrus* I.44	Q	1
4	QA 50	"Church Fathers"		R	2
5	MM 119	Gregory the Great	*Homily on the Gospel* 9.7	Q	1
6	MM 214	Augustine	*Confessions* I.1	Q	1
7	MM 235	"Ascetical tradition"		R	2
8	PT 46	John Chrysostom	*Comm. on Rom., Hom. XXIII* 13.1	Q	4
9	PT 92	Augustine	*City of God* 4.4	Q	3
10	PT 165	Augustine	*Sermon LIII A* 12	Q	4
11	DH 10	Lactantius	*Divine Institutions* V.19	R	2
12	DH 10	Ambrose	*Letter to the Emperor Valentinian* 21	R	2
13	DH 10	Augustine	*Contra Litteras Petiliani* II.83	R	2
14	DH 10	Augustine	*Letter* 23	R	2
15	DH 10	Augustine	*Letter* 34	R	2
16	DH 10	Augustine	*Letter* 35	R	2
17	DH 10	Gregory the Great	*Letter to Virgil and Theodore*	R	2
18	DH 10	Gregory the Great	*Letter to John of Constantinople*	R	2
19	GS 21	Augustine	*Confessions* I.1	Q	1
20	GS 22	Tertullian	*The Resurrection of the Body* 6	F	3
21	GS 22	Council – Const. II	*Canon* 7	F	3

Table 2. Patristic Sources in the CST Documents (continued)

(Sorted by CST Document)

Source No.[1]	CST Text	Patristic Source	Patristic Text	Citation Type[2]	Rhetorical Function[3]
22	GS 22	Council – Const. III		F	3
23	GS 22	Council – Chalcedon		F	3
24	GS 22	Council – Const. III		F	3
25	GS 39	Irenaeus (Lyon)	*Against Heresies* V.36	F	3
26	GS 43	Ambrose	*On Virginity* Ch. 8, Art. 48	F	3
27	GS 44	Justin Martyr	*Dialogue with Trypho* Ch. 110	F	2
28	GS 44	Tertullian	*Apology* 50.13	F	2
29	GS 48	Augustine	*On the Good of Marriage* 2–5, 23–24	F	3
30	GS 57	Irenaeus (Lyon)	*Against Heresies* III.1.2	F	3
31	GS 69	Basil (Caesarea)	*Homily VII* 2	R	4
32	GS 69	Lactantius	*Divine Institutions* V.5	R	4
33	GS 69	Augustine	*On John* Ev. Tr. 50, Art. 6	R	4
34	GS 69	Augustine	*Enarrationes in Psalmos* 147	R	4
35	GS 69	Gregory the Great	*Homily on the Gospel* 20.10–11	R	3, 4
36	GS 69	Gregory the Great	*Rules for Pastors* III.21	R	3
37	PP 23	Ambrose	*On Naboth* 12.53	Q	4
38	PP 23	"Church Fathers"		R	1
39	EN 15	Augustine	*Sermon XLVI, De Pastoribus*, 1–2	F	4
40	EN 16	Cyprian (Carthage)	*On the Unity of the Church* 14	F	2
41	EN 16	Augustine	*Enarrationes in Psalmos* 88, II.14	F	3
42	EN 16	John Chrysostom	*Homily on the Capture of Eutropius* 6	F	2
43	EN 21	Minucius Felix	*Octavius* 19 and 31	F	4

44	EN 21	Tertullian	Apology 39	F	4
45	EN 53	Justin Martyr	Apology, Book I 46.1–4	Q	2
46	EN 53	Justin Martyr	Apology, Book II 7.1–4; 10.1–3; 13.3–4	Q	2
47	EN 53	Clement (Alex.)	Stromata I.19.91, 94	Q	2
48	EN 53	Eusebius (Caesarea)	Preparatio evangelica I.1	Q	2
49	EN 59	Augustine	Enarrationes in Psalmos 44.23	Q	3
50	EN 61	Didache	Didache 9.1	R	1
51	EN 61	Gregory the Great	Homily on the Gospel 19.1	R	1
52	EN 67	Leo I	Sermons 69.3; 70.1–3; 94.3; 95.2	R	2
53	EN 71	John Chrysostom	Hom. on Genesis VI.2; VII.1	Q	2
54	Puebla II.1.1	"Church Councils"		R	2
55	Puebla II.2.4	"Church Fathers"		R	2
56	FC 6	Augustine	City of God 14.28	Q	3
57	FC 13	Tertullian	Ad Uxorem II.8.6–8	Q	4
58	FC 16	John Chrysostom	On Virginity 10	Q	1
59	FC 25	Ambrose	Hexameron V.7.19	Q	4
60	ChP 81	Augustine	City of God IV.15	R	2
61	ChP 112	Justin Martyr	Dialogue with Trypho Ch. 110	Q	3
62	ChP 112	Justin Martyr	Apology, Book I 14 and 39	F	3
63	ChP 113	Cyprian (Carthage)	Letter to Cornelius 60.2	Q	1
64	ChP 114	Sulpicius Severus	Life of St. Martin 4.3	Q	1
65	EJA II.34	Cyprian (Carthage)	On Works and Almsgiving 25	Q	3
66	EJA II.57	"Church Fathers"		R	2
67	SRS 31	Basil (Caesarea)	Longer Rules Q. 37, 1–2	R	4
68	SRS 31	Theodoret (Cyrus)	Concerning Providence Or. 7	R	3
69	SRS 31	Augustine	City of God 19.17	R	4
70	SRS 31	John Chrysostom	On the Gospel of St. Matthew 50.3–4	R	4

Table 2. Patristic Sources in the CST Documents (continued)

(Sorted by CST Document)

Source No.[1]	CST Text	Patristic Source	Patristic Text	Citation Type[2]	Rhetorical Function[3]
71	SRS 31	Ambrose	On the Work of Ministry II, 28.136–40	R	4
72	SRS 31	Possidius	Life of St. Augustine 24	R	3
73	CA 3	Irenaeus (Lyon)	Against Heresies I.10.1 and III.4.1	Q	1
74	SDomingo I.1.9	Epistle to Diognetus	Epistle to Diognetus 8	F	4
75	SDomingo II.1.4.3	Council – Const. I	Nicene-Constantinopolitan Creed	R	4
76	ComCST 53	"Church Fathers"		F	2
77	ComCST 87	"Church Fathers"		R	4
78	ComCST 114	Augustine	Confessions I.1	Q	1
79	ComCST 135	Gregory (Nyssa)	Life of Moses 2.2–3	F	3
80	ComCST 142	Augustine	Confessions II.4.9	F	2
81	ComCST 184	Gregory the Great	Rules for Pastors III.21	Q	3, 4
82	ComCST 265	John Chrysostom	Homilies on Acts 35.3	F	2
83	ComCST 265	Basil (Caesarea)	Longer Rules Q. 42	F	2
84	ComCST 265	Athanasius (Alex.)	Life of St. Antony 3	F	3
85	ComCST 265	Ambrose	On the Death of Valentinus 62	R	2
86	ComCST 266	Irenaeus (Lyon)	Against Heresies V.32.2	F	3, 4
87	ComCST 266	Theodoret (Cyrus)	Concerning Providence Ors. 5–7	F	3
88	ComCST 328	"Church Fathers"		R	2
89	ComCST 329	Hermas	The Shepherd III.1	F	4
90	ComCST 329	Clement (Alex.)	Homily, Quis dives salvetur 13	Q	4
91	ComCST 329	John Chrysostom	21 Homilies "On the Statues" 2.6–8	R	2
92	ComCST 329	Basil (Caesarea)	Homily VII 5	Q	4

93	ComCST 329	Gregory the Great	*Rules for Pastors* III.21	R	2
94	ComCST 582	John Chrysostom	*Homily on Perfect Love* 1.2	Q	3
95	DCE 7	"Church Fathers"		R	2
96	DCE 7	Gregory the Great	*Rules for Pastors* II.5	Q	4
97	DCE 9	Ps. Dionysius	*Divine Names* IV.12–14	F	2
98	DCE 17	Augustine	*Confessions* III.6.11	Q	4
99	DCE 19	Augustine	*On the Trinity* VIII.8.12	Q	3
100	DCE 22	Justin Martyr	*Apology, Book I* 67	R	4
101	DCE 22	Tertullian	*Apology* 39.7	R	4
102	DCE 22	Ignatius of Antioch	*Letter to the Romans*	Q	2
103	DCE 23	4th–6th centuries Egypt		R	4
104	DCE 23	Gregory the Great	*Letter to John of Italy*	R	4
105	DCE 23	Ambrose	*On the Work of Ministry* II.28.140–43	R	4
106	DCE 24	Julian the Apostate	*Letter 83*	R	4
107	DCE 28	Augustine	*City of God* 4.4	Q	1
108	DCE 38	Augustine	*Sermon LII* 16	Q	3
109	DCE 40	Sulpicius Severus	*Life of St. Martin* 3.1–3	R	4
110	DCE 40	Antony/Early monastics		R	1

1. The column "Source No." assigns to each patristic source a unique number, used to refer to the patristic source citations throughout the chapter.
2. The column "Citation Type" indicates how the patristic source is presented in the CST document:
   Q = a direct quotation in the body of the CST document;
   R = a general reference in the body of the CST document;
   F = a footnote-only reference in the CST document.
3. The column "Rhetorical Function" indicates the following use for each patristic source citation:
   1 = an ornament to the main argument of the document;
   2 = an appeal to authority for the main argument of the CST text;
   3 = a further, theological elaboration of the document's main point;
   4 = a further, practical elaboration of the document's main point.

A close examination of the 110 patristic source citations in the CST documents reveals an inconsistent approach to the use of patristic sources in CST documents. Below, I identify six major problem areas in this regard. Each problem area is illustrated either by a summary table or by a detailed example. In some cases I provide a list of further examples of the problem by directing the reader to source numbers in appendices 1 and 2.

Frequency of Use

First, in numerical terms, the patristic sources are hardly noticeable amid the sea of words that comprise the CST documents. The opening paragraph of this chapter highlighted the uniqueness of *DCE* in this regard, but table 3 makes the point quite clear. Besides the fact that five of the CST documents include no patristic sources at all, the patristic sources comprise 1 percent or less of the text for most of the remaining sixteen CST documents. Table 3 lists the total number of words in each CST document, including footnotes, and the total number of those words used for the patristic source citations.

Of the 110 citations, sixty-eight (62 percent) are found in just four documents. It is not the case that these four documents are the longest; indeed, *DCE* is among the shortest and it has the third highest number of patristic source citations. Nearly 8 percent of *DCE*'s total word count is devoted to patristic source material. Thus, there is very little correlation between the size of a CST document and the density of its patristic citations. The same is true with respect to the average word count for each patristic citation in the CST documents. *ChP* cites only five patristic sources, but, on average, each one is accorded generous space in the text. *GS*, by contrast, has the second highest number of patristic citations, but, on average, accords each one very little space in the text. Again, no significant correlation exists between average word counts for the citations and either the size of the texts or the number of sources.

An examination of table 2 reveals an imbalance between Greek and Latin patristic sources. Of the 110 citations, eighty-six allow for such a distinction to be made.[8] Of the eighty-six, twenty-two are Greek sources (26 percent), sixty-four are Latin sources (74 percent).

Table 3. Density of Patristic Source Citations in the CST Documents

CST Text	Total Word Count[1]	Word Count for Patristic Citations	Density of Citations (%)	Total Number Patristic Citations	Avg Words per Citation
RN	10,385	77	0.74%	2	38.5
QA	15,133	63	0.42%	2	31.5
MM	18,606	56	0.30%	3	18.7
PT	12,505	115	0.92%	3	38.3
DH	4,084	137	3.35%	8	17.1
GS	27,357	368	1.34%	18	20.4
PP	11,478	126	1.10%	2	63.0
EN	17,181	358	2.08%	15	23.9
Puebla	--	--	--	--	--
FC	27,642	239	0.86%	4	59.7
ChP	40,909	549	1.34%	5	109.8
EJA	56,929	152	0.27%	2	76.0
SRS	19,760	232	1.17%	6	38.7
CA	18,374	57	0.31%	1	57.0
SDomingo	--	--	--	--	--
ComCST	129,238	1,097	0.85%	19	57.7
DCE	12,934	1,030	7.96%	16	64.4
TOTALS	422,515	4,656	1.10%	106	43.9

1. The numbers in the second and third columns were determined by applying Microsoft Word's "Word Count" tool to the document's original-language text (i.e., Latin for most documents). This study makes no claim that these calculations are exact.

Despite an imbalance in the number of citations, the number of authors cited is relatively more balanced. From the Latin side, eleven authors are cited; from the Greek side, ten are cited. What this means is that some Latin authors are cited with greater frequency than others. Indeed, some of the same patristic texts are cited multiple times (e.g., Augustine's *City of God*). This may be evidence that the drafters of CST documents often relied on earlier CST documents for their identification of patristic sources.

Context Oversight

Only two of the seventeen CST documents, *ChP* and *DCE,* consciously framed their patristic source citations within their historical or literary contexts.[9] *ChP* and *DCE* were careful to include both a reference to the time during which the patristic writers lived and a summary of the literary context in which the citation is found. These are critical pieces of information to help the reader assess the contribution of each patristic source to the wider argument of the CST document. The lack of such helpful contextualization of the patristic sources outside *ChP* and *DCE* is a record of missed opportunities for the CST documents. The contribution of the patristic sources is limited in the other texts. Having said that, it would be wrong to claim the patristic sources themselves were beholden to the original contexts of the documents, biblical or otherwise, that they had cited. The Church Fathers regularly extracted earlier sources from their own historical, literary, and theological contexts to create new ones. Still, the CST documents emerged in an age that paid greater attention to contextualization. Arguably, readers approach these documents expecting not to be misled by manipulated sources. A modern reader expects the CST documents to more faithfully represent the original contexts of the historical sources to which they turn.

Context Mismatch

Third, and perhaps as one explanation for the previous problem, the CST documents often incorporated the patristic sources into a context that did not match their own original context. This restricted the full effect of the patristic sources by either not incorporating the fullness of their arguments or by substantially changing the arguments those patristic sources had made. Consider, for example, source numbers 27 and 28, whose ideas about what constitute threats to the church were supplanted by the CST document's own ideas. *GS* argued those who oppose the church might nevertheless play a role in supporting it, as far as the church itself is concerned, when such opposition leads to self-reflection and improvement.[10] Yet, it cites here Justin Martyr and Tertullian,[11] whose texts acknowledged the value to the church not of those who oppose it, but of those whose work was directly intended to *undermine* it. A Christian in the second century faced very physical consequences, for the Christian belief system was viewed as a threat to the cultural and political fabric of society. *GS*, by contrast, addressed a world where opposition had a more intellectually or politically dismissive character, where it was possible simply to avoid the church while living within a pluralistic cultural and political framework. It is curious, then, that *GS* mixed these two contexts. Similar such examples may be seen in source numbers 37, 67, 68, 69, 80, and 92. In short, the CST documents all too often misapply the original contexts of the patristic sources to their own.

(Mis-)Quotation

Fourth, and related to the previous point, the CST documents modified quotations of patristic sources in order that, at times, those quotations might better fit the new context. Such changes were documented in source numbers 1, 2, 6, 8, 9, 49, 56, and 57. To be fair, the changes rarely altered the meaning of the patristic source, and, in some cases, the changes appear to be honest scribal errors. In the handful of cases where alteration of the quote did change the meaning (source numbers 1 and 9, perhaps also 49), it is clear that the CST document did so to match the argument it had already established and was trying to avoid the larger context of the original patristic source.

Patristic Sources Not Socioethical Sources

A fifth problem area is that the CST documents rarely included patristic sources that were themselves interested in socioethical themes. This concern is a bit more difficult to tease out, for, on the one hand, many patristic sources were employed to undergird theological points (e.g., anthropology, Christology, eschatology, or ecclesiology), which, one could argue, are important to any construction of a socioethical argument. That is to say, the CST documents cannot encourage development efforts for the common good if they have not first taken the time to explain that every person has inherent dignity on account of the *imago Dei* within them and that Christ (the God-Man) had come to redeem them. Patristic sources are certainly helpful on these points. On the other hand, far too many of the patristic sources were used for these purposes and not for emphasizing or explaining, to keep the current example, what development for the common good looks like. In a broad sense, any biblical passage or any patristic source citation could be woven into an argument in such a way that makes it appear to be concerned with social ethics. Yet, one wonders how appropriate is, for example, Augustine's statement in *Confessions* I.1, "our hearts are restless until they rest in you" to social ethics. It is a helpful text for many reasons, but it is not, per se, a socioethical text. The same could be said for many other patristic source citations in the CST documents (cf. source numbers 3, 8, 11–18, 20–25, 26, 29, 30, 39, 40–41, 45–48, 49, 50–51, 52, 58, 73, 79, 94, and 99, and all the general references to the "Church Fathers").

Uneven Contribution to CST Rhetoric

This last problem area for patristic sources concerns the general unevenness in how the drafters of the CST documents understood what could be the rhetorical function of patristic sources in the CST documents. To speak positively, the CST documents more often than not used the patristic sources for theological or practical extensions of their own arguments rather than employing them simply for ornamental or authoritative purposes. However, most of these beneficial extensions to CST arguments were buried in footnotes or otherwise presented in a manner that limited their effectiveness.

To back up, an examination was made of the rhetorical function of each patristic source in the CST documents (cf. table 2's rightmost column). The patristic sources were able to be divided into four rhetorical categories. The first was ornamental speech, which is to say the patristic source did not add to or detract from the argument of the text, but repeated the argument in different words. The second was an appeal to authority. In this case, the patristic citation did not add to or detract from the argument of the CST document, but was called upon to buttress the argument by showing it was not a new idea. A third rhetorical function was theological elaboration. The patristic citation extended the argument of the CST document by giving a theological defense for it or by drawing out its theological implications (e.g., Augustine's eschatology is operating behind the language of the CST document). The fourth rhetorical category was practical or pastoral elaboration. In this case, the patristic source extended the argument of the CST document by offering an illustration of its implications or by explaining what may be expected of a person who agrees or disagrees with it (e.g., what rich people ought to do to care for the poor). In three cases, interestingly enough, the rhetorical function of the patristic source extended the argument of the CST document both in theological and practical ways.

Table 4. Frequency of Rhetorical Function according to Citation Category

Rhetorical Function	Quotations	References	Footnote-only	TOTAL
Ornamental (1)	11	4	0	15
Historical Authority (2)	6	20	9	35
Theological (3)	9	4	15	28
Practical/Pastoral (4)	11	18	6	35

The data in table 2 has been summarized in table 4, which lists the number of times the different rhetorical functions are used in accordance with the three citation types (i.e., quotations, references, and footnote-only citations). The numbers (1) through (4) in the first column refer to the numbers used in the column "Rhetorical Function" in table 2. Table 4 makes clear that the rhetorical function of a majority of the citations (63 out of 113; 56 percent) was to extend the argument of the CST document in theological or practical terms. The citations in these categories are evenly split as quotations (20), references (22), and footnotes-only (21). Thus, the CST documentary tradition does not privilege one form of incorporating a patristic text over another in terms of how that patristic text functions rhetorically. Arguably, the footnote-only references will escape the attention of the common reader, and this limits their effect in extending the arguments. Related to this, table 3 also makes clear that more than half of the footnote-only citations are theological elaborations, and most of the theological elaborations of the CST arguments found in patristic sources are relegated to footnote-only citations. Thus, when a CST document relied on a patristic source to explain its theological arguments, it chose not to do so in the main body of the text.

In brief, an examination of the rhetorical function of the patristic source citations does not reveal any particularly interesting patterns or trajectories. Yet, this is a noteworthy point in and of itself. Each document truly is its own rhetorical tour de force. The decision to select certain patristic texts and not others, and the decision on how to incorporate those texts was the responsibility of those who drafted the CST documents. Certainly, some drafters looked back at earlier documents to mine them for patristic source material, but there is no indication they did so with an interest in correcting perceived woes or in following good examples, rhetorically.

PATRISTIC SOCIAL THOUGHT

The six problems discussed above raise an admittedly thorny problem of whether or not it is possible to ask ancient texts to address contemporary concerns. On the one hand, it does not seem altogether inappropriate to ask of ancient texts what they have to say on matters of modern concern, so long as we do not expect that those ancient texts answer the questions in ways that are natural to a modern text. It is to be expected that moderns wish to know upon what their ethical heritage might rest or on what issues they need not entirely reinvent the wheel. In the process, one will discover some historical starting points for contemporary reflection. Having said that, the potential exists for being hopelessly lost in a struggle against imposing not only one's own socioethical categories on ancient texts, but also one's own ideas about when those ancient texts do and do not address those concerns.

Perhaps there are two ways of resolving this dilemma. First, one may limit the scope of one's investigation almost exclusively to homiletic material from the Fathers. Homilies are, by nature, texts that move in and out of theory and praxis in the lives of people. We accept homilies as texts that have a context, and so are able to approach them from the outset as texts from which we pick and choose what is helpful to us as members of the homily's extended audience.[12] Importantly, one would not want to include the offhand remarks about social concerns common in other types of patristic texts. Rather, it is best to concentrate one's research on those texts that construct a socioethical argument in light of biblical or philosophical themes or in reaction to a contemporary event.

Second, one may pay careful attention to the particular historical context for each ancient text. This is because the Fathers may make little reference in their homilies to the particular problems in their communities, but nevertheless it is clear that, in view of the time and the place in which they were written, the points they do make bear on pertinent social issues. Take, for example, Gregory Nazianzen's *Oration* 6.[13] Traces of evidence from within the homily reveal Gregory wrote it in reaction to a theological dispute between Gregory's father, then bishop in Nazianzus, and a local community of monks. We can surmise what may have been the nature of the dispute from the assurances Gregory gives to the monks that his father is a true "Nicene."[14] Nevertheless, the theological dispute gave rise to an occasion for

Gregory to offer a picture of the inner-Trinitarian life as a model for solidarity among humans.[15] Thus, at first glance, this homily seemingly unrelated to social ethics because of its intention to settle a local doctrinal dispute ends up becoming important for our purposes here due to its contribution to our understanding of the common good.

Students of patristic social thought quickly discover that much of the material rich in regards to social ethics emerged in the post-Constantinian era. There are a number of possible explanations for this. Among them, we should rightly accept that most of the homiletic material of the preachers prior to the fourth century has been hopelessly lost to the dustbins of history. Most homilies are extemporaneous works, and in the absence of funds to afford scribes—and this next to impossible for all but the wealthiest bishoprics—the preacher could only hope that his words effected change in his own congregants' hearts and minds, not that his words would be recorded for posterity. Another possible explanation may lie in the fact that preachers in the pre-Constantinian era were substantially less burdened with imperial legislation to carry the social burden of a city's masses.[16] We know from Justin Martyr, Tertullian, and Minucius Felix, at least, that Christians were very much engaged in charitable relief work among their Christian and non-Christian neighbors alike.[17] However, this charitable work emerged in a vacuum of government support and in response to the Gospel's call and the call in Paul letter's to the Romans (cf. Rom 12) for self-sacrificial living. By the mid-fourth century, imperial legislation had drawn the Christian bishops and their clergy into a more organized system of poor relief.[18] This kept the issue at the forefront of the Christian leaders' minds, and thus it may well have played a role in ensuring that social themes were a regular part of the homilies.

Although the selection of three themes to be discussed below may seem limited, combined they bring readers into a great appreciation for the complexity of patristic social thought. The Fathers did not offer simplistic answers to social problems. In broad strokes, we may affirm that the chief end of patristic social thought was the cultivation of virtue. Virtue for the rich. Virtue for the poor. Virtue through almsgiving. Virtue through detachment from worldly goods.

Virtue expressed by *apatheia*.[19] This concern for virtue and its ethical implications had Stoic precedents, so no one should read patristic social thought without Seneca, among others, in mind.[20]

Yet, it would be unfair to the Fathers to characterize their thought as simply a repackaging of Stoic thought. Indeed, patristic social thought had a number of distinctive theological underpinnings that are discussed in the next section of this chapter. One important theological support was Christology. Since the second century, Christians taught that a recapitulation of the world order was initiated with the Incarnation.[21] There is nothing to be left untouched by the restorative hand of Christ and of his servants. There is to be no separation between *homo spiritualis* and *homo politicus,* or between *homo spiritualis* and *homo oeconomicus.* All of life is to be in concert with the restorative work of Christ, and at its most basic level is care for the poor and the sick. The poor were seen as embodiments of Christ, in accordance with Matthew 25. There could be no greater testimony to one's love for Christ than one's love and care for the poor and needy.

Another theological support for the Fathers was their anthropology. A common refrain in the Fathers is that the poor are "fellow slaves" with those who are not poor. Clement of Alexandria argued that rich and poor persons share a common humanity since both come from a mother and a father. It could be argued this was just a nice platitude, a repackaging of Paul's claim in Galatians that in Christ there is "no Jew or Gentile, no slave or free, no male or female" (Gal 3:28). True, this passage comes up often in the Fathers. However, the Fathers embraced this anthropology not because of a scriptural maxim, but because of their eschatology. Christians looked ahead to a new world order, one in which the prelapsarian state of humanity would be restored.[22] The incarnation was understood to be a significant step forward in the movement of God's plan for that restoration, revealing some of what the glorified state would be, but the expectation of the *eschaton* demanded a certain set of responsibilities in the present age. The Fathers taught Christians to live in accordance with God's commands and his ultimate design for humanity. This meant not being so attached to worldly goods, to the politics of this world, to *this* world at all.²³ The distinctions humans make among themselves are the making of *this* world, not of the world God intended or of what he has planned in the eschaton. For this reason, Christians best express their hope in a resurrection and in the eschaton when they make no distinction between persons in the present age.

It is also clear that the Fathers' concern with the eschaton went deeper than expressing their anthropology. It also revealed their understanding of divine judgment. For those who love this world, who are attached to this world, and who live as though there is no eschaton or day of judgment, the Fathers were unequivocal in their promise of divine judgment and associated wrath.²⁴ God will vindicate in the eschaton those Christians who watched their neighbors grabbing whatever they could as they moved with reckless abandon through the economic, judicial, social, and political fields of this life. Ultimate justice is to be found only in the eschaton, for only then will God rule directly over a new heaven and a new earth. Until that time, Christians are to be defined by patience, contentment, and self-discipline.²⁵

We may also surmise that Christian ecclesiology functioned as a helpful, although less obvious theological, underpinning to patristic social thought. Of course, the Fathers' teaching was generally distributed to the Christian masses in the form of preaching, a constitutive element of the weekly services. However, the earliest Christian apologies reveal that Christians gathered not only to hear apostolic teaching, but also to receive the eucharist and to prepare a financial collection. From the example of Paul's collection for the poor believers in Jerusalem (1 Cor 16:1–2), Christians by the late second century had begun collecting funds for their poor fellow Christians as well as their poor non-Christian neighbors. Christians did not collect funds in those early days to pay a salary for their ministers, or to maintain youth programs, or to run summer camps. Instead, they collected funds in order to distribute them to the widows, orphans, and poor, and for the burial expenses of those who could not afford them.²⁶ In the third and fourth centuries, funds began to be set aside for maintenance of priests and of monks and virgins, but by and large the emphasis remained on collecting funds for distribution to those with needs. Christians were reminded of their responsibility to the poor every week at the time of the collection. Christians also knew to whom among the clergy or among the bishops' staff they must turn if they required some of those funds for their own survival. The Christian church had embedded itself within the lives of not only its own members, but also within the lives of the non-Christians in the community by virtue of its weekly collection of offerings.

The above notwithstanding, there are some areas in which the Fathers' social ideas lacked appropriate sophistication. For one, some Fathers (e.g., Basil, Chrysostom) understood the economic benefits associated with the constant rotation of money within an economic system.[27] Despite this, there are regular denouncements in the Fathers' texts against certain types of employment and certain types of frivolous spending (e.g., Asterius identifies as such money spent on horse breeders, jugglers, actors, and prodigal flatterers).[28] What is missing in the Fathers' writings is an appreciation for the fact that the spending of money on frivolous things keeps people employed in those professions. There is a distribution of wealth that happens when people with means spend their income even on frivolous things. Money circulates. Unemployment rates are lower. With the possible exception of the flatterers, maybe those so employed earned an honest living off the frivolous spending of the rich. One may conclude the Fathers believed some forms of money earning and money spending are unjustified no matter the economic benefits. Money simply should be earned by or spent on less ethically unquestionable activities.[29] However, one wishes that the Fathers had at least acknowledged the economic and employment realities associated with their existence and had given a more sophisticated defense for their positions.

Also with respect to monetary policies, the Fathers did not appreciate the possibility that money could be loaned at interest to those who would use the loan wisely. For example, a tradesperson could take out a loan to purchase equipment that would enable him or her to increase his or her productive capacity. Everything would depend, of course, on the terms of the loan, but it would be possible in such a circumstance for the debtor to repay the loan and its interest while also raising his or her standard of living. It may also be possible for such a tradesperson to use the increased production capacity as a reason to hire additional workers, thereby extending the economic benefit of the original loan. This is how regular loans are understood to operate in our contemporary society. It is not entirely clear that this was not in the minds of some of the people who took out loans in late antiquity. The economic realities of that time, including especially the exorbitant rates of interest, were, of course, stacked against anyone pursuing a loan, but this does not mean the Fathers could not have at least acknowledged the possibility that loans could expand production capacity within an economic system.

A third issue concerning which the Fathers' writings lacked appropriate sophistication is the area of politics. The educated elite among the bishops of the fourth and fifth centuries had access to Plato's *Republic* and *Laws*, Aristotle's *Politics*, and Cicero's *De legibus*. They were aware of alternative political arrangements to the imperial system. For reasons unbeknown to us, the ideas in these texts simply fell on deaf ears. In the main, the Fathers do not discuss political theory.[30] They were keenly aware of both the pitfalls and the benefits that came with the religious propensities of a particular emperor, but that never translated into suggestions for how a society ought to be managed. We are left to glean what they might have thought about this from a variety of texts. For example, from Gregory Nazianzen *Or.* 43 we learn about the intention and the design of Basil's *Basileia*, almost a city unto itself dedicated to care for the poor, the dying, and the road-weary travelers and pilgrims.[31] We have Eusebius of Caesarea's praise for the life and Christian service of Emperor Constantine.[32] Again from Gregory Nazianzen we have denouncements of the type of imperial policies put forward by the apostate emperor Julian.[33] We have Augustine's explanation of the moral debauchery and misplaced pride that characterized the history of Rome and its empire.[34] There are almost countless letters from bishops to civil officials addressing particular matters such as local taxes or a particular judicial judgment. Yet, considering the Fathers' decided opinions about the problems afflicting the poor, about usury, and about the excesses of wealth, one cannot help but wonder why the Fathers did not advocate or, at least, advance alternative forms of governing such that economic disparities were not so pronounced. It seems that, via their classical training, the Fathers had access to tools that would enable them to imagine other possible worlds, but for some reason they left those thoughts behind as topics better suited to the idealistic bubble that shrouded their school days.[35] Nevertheless, having said all of this, perhaps we should be more sympathetic to the Fathers on this point. Perhaps political talk really was a luxury best afforded to school-age young men. The daily life of a pastor or of a bishop was simply about many other more pressing things. Still, one might wish that, given the opportunity, a pastor or bishop might recall his former school days on this subject of politics for the benefit of his congregation, even if was to be nothing more than a display of eloquence and erudition. From what has come down to our day, that occasion must have been so rare or the speech so inglorious that it was hardly worth writing down and remembering.

What may we conclude from these three issues about which we have expressed some concern in studying patristic social thought? We may conclude the world of late antiquity was not geared around or toward entrepreneurism. (Wealthy families in late antiquity may have been opportunistic, but to call them entrepreneurial would do a disservice to most of today's entrepreneurs.) The economic, philosophical, and cultural tools of analysis were at the disposal of the Fathers and of the educated elite of late antiquity, but they simply never took the bait. The Fathers never entertained the possibility that life could be other than what it was, save for their understanding of the eschaton. The reason for all of this is tied to what was mentioned above: the Fathers were far more interested in the cultivation of virtue—individual virtue—than they were in social change. It is this feature of the Fathers' writings and of the whole of late antiquity that creates the greatest distance for moderns who approach their texts and ask what they might have to teach us. Today's Christians may be too democratic and too entrepreneurial to find much of the Fathers' concrete ideas of any help. For this reason, it is the theology and the ways of reading the Bible in these early Christian homilies and texts that holds the greater possibility of bearing fruit for Christian social thought today.

CHAPTER SUMMARY

Indeed, both a study of the patristic sources in CST and the potential pitfalls in reading patristic texts on social ethics suggest a carefully nuanced approach is warranted. One aspect of this approach is to situate patristic source citations within their literary and historical contexts, or at least to acknowledge when the contexts are different. This concern emerges from a presumption that most readers of the CST documents do not know the history of early Christianity, including the names, the places, or the key events that shaped it. Devoid of context, readers may dismiss ancient source citations as quaint. Footnote-only references to patristic sources are particularly troubling in this regard. Instead, future CST documents ought to incorporate the author and argument of the patristic source into the main argument of the text, and leave to footnotes only the details pertaining to references for the relevant passages. Again, *DCE* illustrates well this component to a new vision. To a certain extent, this will restrict the freedom of CST documents to use patristic texts in a merely ornamental or authoritative fashion; however, the theological and pastoral proclivities of the patristic texts may reinvigorate CST and give it a powerful, newfound voice.

Another aspect is for CST documents to incorporate a narrative approach to ethics. The Christian story of God's compassion for the poor and marginalized as expressed in various biblical pericopes (i.e., the historical narrative) demands to be told and retold in every generation. That story, when read in light of one's present situation (the present narrative) requires a response: either engage in social action or consciously decide not to do so. The patristic authors often recalled the same biblical pericopes (e.g., Mt 25, Lk 16) in expositing their vision for Christian social justice (including, e.g., the poor are the ones truly rich before God; the wealthy are obliged to transfer their excess to the poor; yet, the rich are not specifically denounced for being such, and poverty is accepted as part of the necessary balance between people), and this served to preserve the historical narrative for action in the present narrative of their hearers. The same must be done in Catholic social thought of today.[36] Some have suggested such an approach will contribute (happily) to a further shift away from a natural law framework[37] and, instead, toward a theological approach in which Christians share in the life of the poor Christ. It is suggested further this shift demands either separate documents or arguments for the church's two audiences (i.e., Christians and "all people of goodwill"). Perhaps, but particular Christian teachings need not be exclusivist. They may, in fact, help formulate new universal ways of thinking that future societies will deem "natural."[38] What is said to Christians now may well be of value to "all people of goodwill" in the future.

In sum, the point is not to fill future CST documents with *more* references to patristic sources, but to include within them *better* references to patristic sources. The goal is to protect the freshness of pastoral teaching that is the CST documents and not to burden them with academic footnoting. They should invite the reader into the world of Christianity's past for an understanding of its contribution to the present and future. CST should unsettle its readers and disrupt society's complacent attitude toward social injustices. I believe the world wants to hear from the church; even more importantly, it wants to see the church draw from its unique historical well in support of this agenda.

As this study begins, it is clear that at least one subset of Christian social thought, the CST documents, desires to incorporate but remarkably mishandles the patristic source material at its disposal. The root of the problem is a good understanding of how best to incorporate patristic texts into contemporary, socioethical discourse. What is the best way to "read" (or, to interpret) patristic socioethical texts such that they may fruitfully engage the world of Christian social thought? The next chapter moves us forward in this project with a more detailed examination of three important themes in patristic social thought: common good, private property, and the poor.

Chapter 2

THEMES IN PATRISTIC SOCIAL THOUGHT

To this point, it has been argued that CST has an interest in incorporating patristic social thought into its mix of variables. It has also been shown that CST has had difficulty joining its message to that of patristic socioethical texts. Moreover, it was suggested that much of this problem is due to the difficulty of applying a text from so foreign a context as the world of late antiquity to the world we inhabit. This chapter pulls back further some of the veil shrouding the foreign context of patristic social thought. It surveys three prominent ethical themes in early Christian texts: common good, private property, and the poor.[1] Certainly, the patristic writers spoke of other concerns such as slavery, land rights, and nonviolence, but these concerns only dot patristic texts rather than constituting the particular focus of any one text's argument. We are on safer ground staying with those themes that were prominent within the patristic texts themselves. In anticipation of my examination of two patristic homilies in the following chapters of this book, it behooves the reader to have some sense both of the wider context out of which these texts emerged—both Greco-Roman and Christian—and of the questions that preoccupied early Christians at the time. For each topic, the reader is introduced first to the wider, Greco-Roman context into which the early Christians inserted their own ideas. Then, the particular ideas of the early Christians are summarized, with particular attention paid to the developments of the concept during the second through fifth centuries.

COMMON GOOD

To speak of "common good" is to speak of a social reality in which all members of a society possess the wherewithall to be fulfilled.[2] This sounds elusive. Admittedly, it is a definition that itself demands further definition. We may ask how a society creates a common good, and we may ask what is the responsibility of each member of a society for the maintenance of the common good once achieved. Yet, these questions reveal a gut-level instinct within each person that societies ought to pursue the common good, however that may be defined.

In the history of Christian ethical reflection on the common good, the seminal figure is Thomas Aquinas. In the thirteenth century, he incorporated earlier Greek philosophical and political discourse about the common good into his own reflections on justice. Since Aquinas's role in discussions about the common good is so dominant, it is nearly impossible to explore patristic ideas about the common good without being anachronistic. We cannot help but "discover" in patristic writings words and ideas that relate to Christian ideas of the common good that the patristic writers themselves were not consciously trying to articulate. Put another way, while we should be careful not to read the ideas of Aquinas or modern Christian writers on the common good back into the patristic writers, we cannot help but do so to the extent that the ideas of Aquinas and others aid our search for what might be relevant texts from the patristic world.[3]

Before we turn to an examination of some historical details, the reader should first be aware that there are a number of Greek and

Latin expressions for "common good." Consequently, any research into the field demands due attention to the nuances that each expression lends to the idea. In Greek, the most natural expression would be ἀγαθόν κοινόν, but, surprisingly, it is quite uncommon. Similarly, the phrase κοινόν συμφέρον ("common advantage"), which lends itself to a materialistic notion, is nearly as rare. Somewhat more common is the expression κοινόν λυσιτέλουν ("common profit/advantage"), which is what is typically used by Aristotle and is found occasionally in the Greek Fathers. Most common in the Greek Fathers is κοινόν ὠφέλεια and the crasis κοινωφελής ("common profit or benefit"). This construction lends itself to a variety of contexts for the Fathers, to include the Christian as well as the political community. Anything that contributes to health or stability in those communities may be deemed for κοινωφελής.[4] On the Latin side, Cicero used two expressions, *salus populi* ("health of the people") and *utilitatis communione* ("community of interests"). These expressions lend themselves to intangible, rather than materialistic, ideas of what is the common good. Not dissimilarly, Augustine used the expression *bonum commune* when talking about what is the type of life offered to citizens in the city of God, as opposed to the inhumanity and discontent found in the earthly city. It is Augustine's expression that we find in Aquinas's writings, although Aquinas substitutes Aristotle's political and judicial rhetoric for Augustine's spiritual rhetoric.

Common Good in the Greek and Roman Contexts

One may begin the study of common good in history with Plato and Aristotle. Indeed, Aquinas borrowed from Aristotle in expressing his own views on the matter. Taking them in chronological order, we begin with Plato. Significantly, in his *Republic,* Plato explains that the best life, the happy life, is one oriented toward the Good. It stands to reason, then, that the common good is a set of conditions whereby all the members of a community are educated in knowledge of the Good. The presence of the common good is, for Plato, the presence of justice, which is wisdom and virtue among all in the community and a barometer of the community's health (*Republic* I.351a–54c). Thus, Plato organizes his political philosophy around how just such a common good may be achieved. Within his organizational scheme for a community, he posits the existence of philosopher-kings (or Guardians), who alone among the citizenry are most aware of and instructed in the Good. To Plato, it is the Guardians' responsibility to provide leadership, administration, and judicial functions over other citizens in order to facilitate the common good (*Republic* V.462–64). Later in life, in his last dialogue, *Laws*, Plato seems to ameliorate his demand for such an elite group of philosophers; in their place he inserts laws and a community of citizens whose roles within the community are precisely defined, highly regimented, and numerically controlled. Nonetheless, even in this revised political philosophy, Plato reiterates and furthers key points of his understanding of the common good. For instance, Plato writes, "The whole point of our legislation was to allow the citizens to live supremely happy lives in the greatest possible mutual friendship" (*Laws* V.743c). Plato, and Aristotle later, link the happiness of individuals to expressions of friendship. This is not unimportant insofar as it helps us understand that the good of a community is the ability for all in the community to be happy, that is, to be oriented toward the Good. Yet, friendships can all too quickly be disrupted when there are disputes over property and money, and Plato was not oblivious to this problem. He wrote, "For a number of reasons, and especially because the state offers equality of opportunity, there must be graded property-classes, to ensure that offices and taxes and grants may be arranged on the basis of what a man is worth" (*Laws* V.744b). Plato's references here to progressive tax policies and the need for ensuring equality of opportunity stress the responsibility of government and the laws of a community to facilitate the common good.

Aristotle's ideas about the common good are expressed well in his treatise *Politics*, although this treatise itself looks back to his *Ethics* for its language about the chief aim of human existence: happiness. *Ethics* X.10 (1179b–1180a) argues that the happy life presupposes life in common; thus, it is a small step to connect the happy life with politics. This connection implies the ultimate good of human life is inseparable from the common advantage of a *polis*. Indeed, Aristotle defines the common good of a society this way. "All those governments which have a common good in view are rightly established and strictly just" (*Politics* 1297a), he writes, and then later adds, "A city is a society of people joining together with their families and their children to live agreeably for the sake of having their lives as happy and as independent as possible . . . so that the end then for which a city is established is that the inhabitants of it may live happy" (*Politics* 1280b).[5] Just as the chief aim for each individual is a life of happiness, so too the chief aim of a community is happiness. Thus, the common good of such a community is the establishment and maintenance of conditions that foster each person's and each family's pursuit of happiness. It is not a happiness defined in materialistic terms, but it is the product of everyone seeking the good for others, which, again tying *Politics* back to *Ethics,* is a consequence of true friendship. Aristotle elaborates on some of the conditions that contribute to the common good. He commends democracies over other forms of government; he commends property laws that protect private ownership without, at the same time, discouraging the sharing of some goods in common; as well, he commends contentment with one's resources and moderation with respect to further acquisitions of land, all of which contribute to peaceful relations between cities. Most importantly, Aristotle commends qualifications for citizenship, which leaves open the possibility that Aristotle also commended limiting extensions of friendship only to fellow citizens within a city. It is this last feature that marks some of the boundaries many in later centuries and many still today find with respect to the value of Aristotle's work. The growth both in trade and in communication networks in the centuries following Aristotle increasingly diminished the likelihood any one city would be content merely with its own resources.

Indeed, Stoic ideas about the common good were something of a departure from Aristotle. They were not content to confine the common good to a community of citizens or to a community of those deemed to be one's friends. Rather, some, like Cicero, argued that all humans share a common nature; thus, there is no defensible reason to think that the common good extends to any community less than that of the entire human race. Cicero, in *De officiis* III. 28, makes just this point.

> Now surely it is absurd to say, as some do, that they would not deprive a parent or brother of anything for their own advantage, but that there is another rationale for the rest of the citizens. Such men decree that no justice and no fellowship exist among citizens for the sake of common benefit, an opinion that breaks up all fellowship in the city. There are others again who say that account should be taken of other citizens, but deny it in the case of foreigners; such men tear apart the common fellowship of the human race.[6]

Fellowship among all humans was intended by the gods, argued Cicero, so it is a slap in the face of the gods to place one's own advantages against the interests of others, including those of foreigners and even of those who are deemed useless to society (e.g., those nearing death and tyrants; see *De officiis* III.29–30).[7] Although Cicero's universal ideas were an improvement over Aristotle's, and we find a thread of his ideas in the later Christian writers,[8] his position too was deemed a bit extreme by his near contemporaries. Some ameliorated it to suggest that there are human contexts—be they political or otherwise—that shape and refine our contributions to the common good of all humans.[9] Hybrid views like this take stock of the reality of human life without giving up on the ideal of a common good built around universal common humanity.

Common Good in Christian Teaching and Its Context

There are at least three ways in which the Fathers incorporated language about the common good into their discourse. The first, not surprisingly, is into discussions about the common good of the Christian community. Romans 12:4–5 (cf. also 1 Cor 12:12) compares the Christian community to a body, and each member of the community has an obligation to support the other parts. Theodoret of Cyrus, in his commentary on this passage in Romans, says that the support each member gives to the community contributes to the common good (κοινόν ὠφέλεια). Moreover, this unity of the Christian community is a consequence of the grace of God, a grace which itself is acknowledged to be a gift given by God for the common good of all people.[10] Ephrem, a notable hymn writer in the Syriac tradition, was praised for seeking after the common good of the Christian community.[11] It was a constitutive expression of Ephrem's piety, Gregory pointed out. Similarly, preachers were aware of the fine line they walked between preaching in a way that affirmed the intellectual integrity of their work while also being of benefit to all in the community. Origen, in his *Contra Celsum* VII.59–60, exposed as elitist those whose preaching did not invite all types of persons into a dialogue with the truths of Scripture.[12] Gregory of Nyssa, in *On Virginity* 2, similarly denounced as pompous the speech writing and delivery intended for the benefit only of the elite. By contrast, he wished to speak about virginity in a simple way, that it might be for "common benefit" (κοινόν λυσιτέλουν).[13] A pseudo-Chrysostom sermon, *On the Parable of the Prodigal Son,* begins by exclaiming that a sermon such as it is delivered for "common benefit" (κοινόν ὠφέλεια).[14]

Within this same category of the common good of the Christian community, one should not overlook those passages that arose out of polemical contexts. That is to say, some texts express the common good of the Christian community in terms of shared orthodox theology. Basil of Caesarea, in a letter to some Egyptian bishops, praises their zeal for refuting the theology of the Apollinarians. With their orthodox theology the Egyptian bishops "furnish the means which are of common benefit [κοινωφελῆς] and indispensable to salvation."[15] John Chrysostom, too, with a clear debt to Romans 12:4–5, argues, "[N]othing is so pleasing to God as to live for the common advantage [κοινωφελῆς]. For this end God gave us speech, and hands, and feet, and strength of body, and mind, and understanding, that we might use all these things, both for our own salvation, and for our neighbors' advantage."[16] In sum, the Christian message is most effectively distributed for common benefit to the world after the Christian community itself is in theological agreement.

Second, patristic writers spoke about the common good in economic terms. On this point, the Fathers understood that healthy economic activity was built around the continuous movement of capital: from buyers to merchants, merchants to producers, and producers to employees, the employees themselves being buyers again. In this way, everyone has a share in the common good of an economic system. Basil of Caesarea, in his *Homily* 6, condemned stockpiling. He wrote, "Riches grow useless left idle and unused in any place; but moved about, passing from one person to another, they serve the common good [κοινωφελῆς] and bear fruit."[17] The context for Basil's homily is the appropriate disposition of an abundant harvest, but the homily had in view redemptive almsgiving. This is significant, for it reveals that Basil understood that the poorest citizens and the feeble were not equal participants in the constant rotation of money within an economic system. They were unlikely to be earning a regular wage; thus, it was the obligation of those with greater financial means to inject more of their financial capital into the economic system via direct, financial assistance to those on the economic fringe. In this way, both the rich and the poor may more equally share in the economic common good.[18] Chrysostom, too, was aware that healthy economic systems depended on everyone participating to the extent they can in sharing what they possess with others. One way this is accomplished is expressed in his *Homilies on 1 Corinthians* 10, in which he argues that the common good is fostered when each person shares his or her skills with others: the wealthy share their wealth; the poor share their labor; the sailors share the goods from their journeys; the soldiers share their honors earned in battle; and the teachers share their knowledge. Everyone has something that is able to be distributed to others.[19] The bottom line for Chrysostom, which he pointed out in *Homilies on John* 15.3, is that the pursuit of the common good is nothing less than a reduction of the inequities, particularly economic inequities, in this life.[20]

Third, and in line with the classical tradition, the patristic writers incorporated common good language into their political discourse.[21] Although we do not have texts from the Fathers like that of Plato's *Republic*, the Fathers were certainly aware of the political realities of their day, and they wrote about them. Admittedly, their comments are often brief, and one should not approach them as harbingers of historical accuracy. Even so, one may be impressed at the depth of understanding found in Gregory Nazianzen's remarks about the "common benefit" (κοινόν ὠφέλεια) derived from a "government administered with moderation, the lowering of taxes, the judicious choice of magistrates, [and] the punishment of embezzlers."[22] Similarly, we read a lengthy diatribe about the effect of oppressive taxation on the good of communities (particularly on the artisans, tradespeople, and the poor within the communities) in Salvian of Marseille's mid-fifth-century text *Concerning the Governance of God*.[23] More widely known is Augustine's *City of God*. Augustine situates language about the common good within the framework of pride. The hallmark of the heavenly city is the common good, for in that city there is no pride.[24] The earthly city could also exhibit the common good, but pride obscures the earthly city's politics. Citizens, especially the rulers, of the earthly city take credit for any successes rather than acknowledging every good thing as a gift of God; consequently, according to Augustine, they make private what ought to be common and so diminish any hope of bringing about a common good.[25] This contrast between private and common goods that Augustine raises is also found in earlier writers. Basil of Caesarea, in *Homily* 12, praises the biblical king Solomon for his goodness, a goodness that manifests itself in his looking out for the common good rather than his own private good.[26]

Having said that, there are also writings of some Fathers that resemble the classical writers and already anticipate some of the judicial language that will flower in the Scholastic age. For example, Irenaeus of Lyon, in *Against Heresies* V.24, writes, "Earthly rule ... has been appointed by God for the benefit of nations, ... conducting themselves after a quiet manner, so that under the fear of human rule, men may not eat each other up like fishes; but that, by means of the establishment of laws, they may keep down an excess of wickedness among the nations."[27] Irenaeus's reflection here on the teaching of Romans 13 underscores the contribution of the state to fostering the common good. It is realistic that many people are not content with their own goods, but desire—and more than that, acquire unjustly—the goods of others. The state has a role in quelling such misbehavior and restoring good order. This is true as much for "intranational" conflicts as it is for "international" ones. Similarly, Clement of Alexandria, in his *Stromateis* I.27, likens society to a person's body which, when sick, must subject itself to certain, short-term pains at the hands of a physician in order to bring about long-term healing. Thus, a society made sick by wickedness and injustice must have, in order to protect the common good, laws that punish evildoers and, if necessary, enforce capital punishment on the worst of society's offenders. "It is the highest and most perfect good," Clement writes, "when one is able to lead back any one from the practice of evil to virtue and well-doing, which is the very function of law."[28] Judicial language is also found in John Chrysostom, *Homilies on the Acts of the Apostles* 5.4.[29] He remarked that laws and good government constitute a "common benefit" (κοινόν ὠφέλεια), and everyone is happy to submit to laws when they are written by fellow citizens rather than by foreigners. But Chrysostom uses this brief remark in order to make a theological point: since people so readily submit to human laws, he expresses confusion as to why so many harbor distaste for his preaching about divine laws. To his mind, God's laws should also be seen as a "common benefit" for the construction of healthy societies, and they should be received with greater joy than those written by humans.

PRIVATE PROPERTY

Private property poses a significant challenge to Christian ethics. On the one hand, people may not require to sustain their existence as much property and wealth as they think they do and the attachment to property by its owner may reflect a lack of appreciation for God's providential care of the created realm (cf. Mt 6). On the other hand, private property gives its owner dignity, meaning, and a sense of purpose in life. It is a reward for their investment of time, labor, or money. Christian ethics aims to strike a balance between a person's material desires and the dignity that comes from private ownership. Consequently, a Christian ethic of private property invites those who invest their labor into producing a good to consider the possibility that the good they have produced may be better used by someone who did not labor to produce it. Put another way, Christian ethics asks whether or not one's sense of dignity, meaning, and purpose in life may come *both* from keeping some property (what one needs) *and* from giving the rest away to those with needs.

Private Property in the Greek and Roman Contexts

Even a cursory review of the ideas about private property in the Greco-Roman and Christian milieu reveals the difficulty everyone felt about the topic. Private property was understood to be a social problem, but forcibly redistributing property had few, if any, supporters. With respect to the classical writers, some suggestions for how to solve the private property dilemma emerged. In the fourth century B.C.E. there were calls for the creation of a common stock of property from which every citizen could draw in order to satisfy his needs. The playwright Aristophanes suggested women would be the best managers of such a common stock, which would include land, money, and most goods.[30] Plato's teaching on the role of Guardians is strikingly similar to Aristophanes' promotion of women as better managers of civic affairs.[31] In the wrong hands, according to Plato, property undermines social unity.[32] Consequently, Guardians will oversee a common stock of property and, in so doing, preserve the good of the city.[33] Nevertheless, neither Aristophanes nor Plato denounced the right of people to own different amounts of private property. Plato suggested the goal is not for everyone to be happy in the sense of possessing many things; everyone is to be happy with the goods appropriate to their position within the city (421b–d).[34] In another of Aristophanes' plays, *Ploutos* (388),[35] the character Chremylus sets off to heal the sight of Ploutos, the god of wealth, in order that wealth might begin to come only to those who are virtuous. Along the way, Chremylus meets Poverty, who informs Chremylus that he is embarking on an ill-concieved plan, for once everyone becomes rich, no one will have anything. This is because no one will be willing to work long hours at trades; there will be no bakers or harvesters. Everyone will want someone else to do it, and no one will agree to do it. Poverty, she argues, alone fosters a productive society. Some deprivation of wealth actually is good for the soul (ll. 507–89).[36]

A different approach to the problem of private property is that of Xenophon and, later, of Aristotle. They advocated a distinction between "use" and "ownership" of property, a distinction which meant that laws that protect private property ownership may continue to exist, but the better instincts of people should draw them to a sharing of property based on use. Xenophon (c.429–c.357 B.C.E.), in his *Education of Cyrus,* writes of a particular episode of Cyrus's schooling in which Cyrus was asked to judge between two boys of different heights who each owned coats that were better suited to the height of the other boy.[37] Cyrus judged that use, rather than ownership, of property was a better arbiter for the distribution of goods. Consequently, he ordered the boys to switch coats. Yet, for this he was severely reprimanded by his teachers. To keep the application of justice simple and fair, Cyrus's teachers said, ownership is the more just means of deciding who should possess what. Aristotle seems to be in agreement with Cyrus's first instincts, but he too comes down on the side of maintaining property rights based on current ownership.[38] To his mind, human depravity would never allow the lifelong sharing of goods from a common stock, no matter how useful a particular piece of property was to a person at any given time.[39] Thus, despite their misgivings, Xenophon and Aristotle accepted the status quo as that which would cause the least amount of injustice. This basic understanding is behind Cicero's later insistence that the taking of the goods of another—whether by force of law or of banditry—is an injustice. In agreement with the Stoics, he argued that the goods of the earth belong to all and exist for the benefit of all persons.[40] Private property, then, is an aberration of Nature and so the ideal is for all things to be held in common. However, private property exists and so it is a matter of *justice* that humans respect existing private property rights. Justice in the present trumps a reordering of society in accordance with Nature for the future.[41]

Somewhat in contrast to Xenophon and Aristotle (also Cicero, though an anachronism) are the ideas articulated by their contemporary Menander in his play *Dyskolos*.[42] On the one hand, Menander agreed with their discontent that laws protect property rights based on ownership rather than use. On the other hand, he believed there was a solution: distinguish between needs and superfluities with respect to private property. Laws may then protect a person's right to own needed, or useful, property, but not property that is superfluous to needs. He based this distinction on the fact that property is temporary, and so people may safely detach themselves from it. If nothing else, the short span of human life will mark out the limits of one's ability to "own" property.[43] This detachment view of private property will later find an articulate proponent in Seneca who, a substantially wealthy court official himself, in the mid-first century C.E. composed the treatise *De vita beata,* in which it is argued that the man who possesses virtue possesses the only thing that is truly good.[44] Consequently, the accumulation of goods, land, and money and the frivolous spending subsequent to it are no adequate measure of pleasure.[45] Moreover, property and wealth are fleeting, so any virtue tied to things temporary will always put true happiness in jeopardy. Far better, in Seneca's view, to hold property and wealth at a distance. One may possess wealth and property, but their acquisition should be by just means.[46] In the end, *indifferentia* (equivalent to the Stoic ἀδιάφορα) is the goal (xxii.4), and thus riches may be despised whether one has them or not. It is the ideas of Menander and of Seneca that will aquire great currency in the later teachings of the Fathers.

To conclude this brief examination of the notion of detachment from private property in the Greco-Roman context, two points should be borne in mind. On the one hand, the classical texts reveal a general unease over the right of a person to private property, for it seems that each assumes the acquisition of private property by one necessarily involves the deprivation of another. On the other hand, they accept as a fact of life the obligation of governments to protect every citizen's legal right to private property. As a principle, the notion of detachment from private property functions as a measure of virtue. The "true" philosopher, the number of whom the classical authors understand will always be small, direct their thoughts to the soul and not to things temporary, to include property as much as the body. Having said that, we may turn our attention to the writings of the Fathers. Although in their writings we move away from legalistic arguments, the right to private property is largely unchallenged.

Private Property in Christian Teaching and Its Contexts

Jesus, in Mark 10:21, taught the rich young ruler to "sell all that you have and give the proceeds to the poor." This suggests Jesus called for a lifestyle of renunciation, and, in the second century, some Christian writings taught as much with respect to private property. The *Epistle of Barnabas* 19, for example, exhorted its readers, "Treat as common all things with your neighbor, and do not say things are 'one's own,' for if you are sharers in incorruptible things, how much more ought you to be sharers in corruptible things!"[47] The command not to call things "one's own" is also found in *Didache* 4.8, a late first- or second-century document, although it is less clear in *Didache* that the author held strictly to a renunciation view.[48]

At least two works in the second century signaled a definite shift away from renunciation: Irenaeus's *Against Heresies* IV.30.1–3 and *Shepherd of Hermas,* especially Parables (or, Similitudes) 1–2.[49] Irenaeus accepted property's inherent moral neutrality. Echoing Xenophon and Aristotle, property itself was not to blame; rather, one's use of property was to be the subject of any scrutiny. To Irenaeus, the possession of property was not a right following upon the spending of one's own labor to acquire it. This is because all property is the result of someone else's earlier labor. Thus, property could never really be considered "private" because no one person could ever claim to have produced it.[50] For his part, Hermas framed the need for detachment in terms of a need for Christians to be aware that earth is not their home.[51] Yearning for earthly goods is an affront to God.

In the third century this detachment view was picked up by Clement of Alexandria in his *Quis dives salvetur.* Clement applied a spiritual style of exegesis to his reading of Mark 10 that had gained some currency by that time. Clement argued that Jesus could not have meant for every person to be without property, for such a situation would mean that no one would have anything to give to the poor.⁵² From this starting point, Clement articulates a different vision for private property, one in which a person may freely possess what he or she needs or is useful to him or her, but all that is superfluous must be given to the poor or otherwise needy.⁵³ This recalls the necessities/superfluities distinction of Menander. Thus, with Clement, a more fruitful course of inquiry about private property has been opened: How much is *enough*?⁵⁴

From that point, it seems that the Fathers were in agreement with a detachment, as opposed to a renunciation, view of property.⁵⁵ This is not to say the renunciation view had disappeared,⁵⁶ for Epiphanius, in the mid-fourth century still found adherents to a renunciation view deserving of condemnation in his *Panarion*⁵⁷ and a fifth-century text by an adherent to Pelagius's views argued for renunciation as well.⁵⁸ The Pelagian text insisted that only renunciation of property and wealth would ensure elimination of poverty for others. Yet, the detachment view was articulated by more and more of the ecclesiastical elite. One of Clement's early successors in Alexandria, Peter, also preached on the need for detachment from property in his sermon *On Riches*.⁵⁹ Peter argued that God makes a separation between the rich person and the *merciless* rich person (§14–15). The former gives little thought to his wealth and shares it liberally with the poor; the latter is consumed with thoughts of wealth and despises the needs of the poor. More pronounced in Peter than in Clement, though, is the encouragement of the rich to give alms. Peter encouraged the merciless rich person to give thought to the afterlife, and to the negative consequences due to come for having dismissed the plight of the poor (§16–29). To Peter's mind, the distribution of alms to the poor is the starting point for those with relatively greater financial means who wish to ensure their wealth is not a hindrance to their relationship with God. So, too, Lactantius derided Plato for his naiveté or, worse, stupidity, in calling for a rejection of money. Such people who follow Plato, "could have acquired a great name for liberality, but they throw the means away, earning neither distinction nor gratitude."⁶⁰

Gregory Nazianzen preached a homily encouraging love for the poor, particularly those with serious health problems. He observed in this homily that disordered affection for property was responsible for the strife between persons and between nations.[61] Love for the poor begins, in part, with a recognition that property truly belongs only to God.[62] Similarly, Asterius of Amasea, in his homily *The Unjust Steward*, balanced a concern for the temporariness of property with each person's responsibility toward God for his or her use of property.[63] Everyone will be obliged one day to give an account of his or her use of property before God.[64]

Bridging the fourth and fifth centuries is the homiletic career of John Chrysostom. The wealth of socioethical teachings attributed to him is best explained by the sheer volume of his writings coupled with increasing imperial legislation that shifted the burden for poor relief ever more into the hands of the Christian church during this period.[65] In several homilies Chrysostom framed the entire property question this way: property exists to test human virtue, and whether or not we are virtuous is determined by the extent to which we willingly give of our possessions to the poor.[66] Consider, for example, his *Homilies on Matthew* 77, a homily that explores how people ought to treat wealth and property in light of the fact that unknown to everyone is both the time of Christ's second advent and the time of their own death, whichever will come first. Consequently, one's attitude toward property must take into account the need to use wisely during the short span of life the resources God has placed at one's disposal. In combination with every Christian's responsibility to his or her fellow humans, Chrysostom can then suggest that the sharing of possessions fosters love between people.[67] Giving to the poor is, in fact, giving to them what was already theirs in the first place. God had simply entrusted the rich with the responsibility to dispense it. In the final analysis, and somewhat surprisingly, Chrysostom suggested that pursuing the good of one's neighbor is a calling even more important than martyrdom![68]

John Chrysostom defined superfluous property as all things that go beyond what is needed to live healthfully and respectably.[69] He exhorted his hearers not to spend their money on unnecessary things, for such things are not really theirs at all insofar as they ultimately belong to God and to his designated heirs, the poor.[70] Furthermore, he taught that a gradual reduction in one's concern for the body will lead to a gradual reduction in one's acquisition of superfluous property and, correspondingly, a gradual increase in one's willingness to give alms.[71] Even more to the point, Chrysostom argues that wealth helps humans on their way to eternal punishment, whereas thankfulness and contentment aid in the remission of our sins.[72]

In the Syriac Christian world, Rabbula, bishop of Edessa in the mid-fifth century, was remembered not only for the depth of his own detachment from private property but also for the many exhortations he gave and rules he put in place for priests and monks to disassociate themselves from private ownership of property.[73] Rabbula's was a profound model for, indeed, throughout late antiquity, a rich person who did not want to divest himself of wealth (to enter a monastery) but wanted still to serve the church could take a vow of celibacy and become a priest. By the same token, it would be premature to conclude that the early monasteries were poor by virtue of the fact that the monks who entered them divested themselves of all possessions prior to entering. Indeed, the monasteries seem to have been quite wealthy. There is a significant correlation between the wealth of monasteries and the wealth of those who sought the monastic life.[74]

In sum, several points are important to keep in mind with respect to the Fathers' ideas about private property. First, they appreciated the temporariness of private property, and this temporariness was further highlighted by humanity's own temporariness on the earth. Second, and corresponding to the first, they recognized that, in the eschaton, God will require of those with property and wealth an account of how they managed that wealth for the benefit of the needy. Third, the Fathers acknowledged that all creation was intended by God to be for the benefit of all. They believed God intended for the rich and poor to share with one another—the rich share their superfluous goods and the poor share their nearness to God.[75] Perhaps few of these ideas will resonate with many Christians today. Indeed, one wonders if Christians today might benefit not from particular, patristic teachings regarding private property but instead from an awareness of some theological categories that drove the patristic authors to think as they did about social ethics.

THE POOR

To enter a study of the poor in early Christian texts is to grapple with several problems at the same time. First, there is the problem of knowing to what part of the socioeconomic ladder the poor person is assigned. There were several different levels of poor people, much as in our own day.[76] Second, there is the problem of analyzing the rhetorical function of the poor person within the Christian text. More often than not, it seems poor persons function as literary foils for the protagonists, the wealthier members of the congregation.[77] At other times, the concern with their plight is genuine, so one wonders what was actually expected of the audience when Greco-Roman society was not geared around programs of social welfare. Third, there is the challenge of understanding what to do with the Fathers' seeming lack of eagerness to call for systemic changes in the structures that created widespread poverty. Readers today not only expect more out of their religious leaders, but expect more out of their governments and transnational institutions.

The problems of poverty were quite real then as they are now,[78] but the analysis of the problems and the proposed solutions found in patristic texts may take the reader aback. One profitable course would be to appreciate the richness and depth to the Fathers' arguments when they connect the lives of the poor with the life of Christ. Similarly, that the Fathers addressed the poor in their texts at all was a countercultural move that itself deserves credit.[79] Their texts are an invitation to us to consider where our churches have failed to raise the flag on today's social injustices.

The Poor in the Greek and Roman Contexts

In Hesiod's *Works and Days,* Hesiod exhorted his brother, Perses, to strive for goodness through honest labor.[80] To Hesiod, it is not good to be poor, for poverty is really just a product of laziness or idleness. Consequently, the poor person is the one who deservedly has little or no food. A less dismissive presentation of poor persons is found in

Aristophanes' play *Wealth*. The main character Chremylus sets out to heal the sight of Wealth, for, Chremylus believed, if Wealth could see again, then it would be possible for him to give wealth only to those persons who are righteous. Along the way, Chremylus meets Poverty. Poverty warns him not to fulfill his plan, for it was necessary that poverty exist in the world. To be sure, Poverty (πενής) distinguishes herself from beggars (πτωχεια), the former of whom are artisans or craftsmen, the latter of whom are without either the ability or the willingness to work. In any case, Poverty argues that if every person was rich, then no one would want to work as a servant, none would want to be bakers or blacksmiths or labor in any of the trades. Everyone would want someone else to work. Worse, if wealth passed only to the righteous, then the righteous would be at the mercy of unscrupulous individuals laboring in the trades. No, according to Poverty, it is better to keep the current system of socioeconomic inequality than to have everyone be rich or to be reliant on the services of unscrupulous persons.

Although different in their treatment of the poor, both Hesiod and Aristophanes depict poverty in a negative light. There is nothing righteous about being poor. To the extent possible, poor people are expected to work and to pull themselves up out of their difficulties. This attitude continues well into the common era. Seneca, in his text *On Providence*, promotes hard work, self-discipline, and cultivation of virtues. Poverty is a good thing, since it motivates the right kind of people to become good. The only people it fails to motivate are those who are, by nature, lazy.

> "Why, however," do you ask, "was God so unjust in his allotment of destiny as to assign to good men poverty, wounds, and painful death?" It is impossible for the moulder to alter matter; to this law it has submitted. Certain qualities cannot be separated from certain others; they cling together, are indivisible. Natures that are listless, that are prone to sleep, or to a kind of wakefulness that closely resembles sleep, are composed of sluggish elements. It takes sterner stuff to make a man who deserves to be mentioned with consideration.[81]

With this, it is becoming clear that poverty is good—rather, a good—but the poor are neither good nor a good for the construction of a better society.

Plotinus, the Neoplatonist philosopher of the third century, connected this idea to metaphysics. "But if one considers that things external to the soul are evils, illness or poverty for instance, how will one trace them back to the nature of matter? . . . [P]overty is lack and deprivation of things which we need because of the matter with which we are coupled, whose very nature is to be need."[82] To Plotinus, poverty can be transcended even if it remains a constant, physical reality, but it certainly is a dreaded weight on our body and intensifies the need for contemplation.

Although not a philosphical text, we find a practical outworking of what Plotinus has said in the second-century text *The Dream*, by Lucian of Samosata. In it, Lucian describes a choice he had as a young boy to pursue training in the craft of sculpting or in the craft of rhetoric. During a dream in which this choice is played out, "Culture" tells him of the hard life of labor and occasional poverty he will endure as a sculptor. "Living in obscurity you will have meagre and sordid returns and an abject spirit; you will count for nothing in public, neither sought after by your friends nor feared by your enemies nor envied by your fellow citizens—just a workman and one of the masses, cowering before your superiors and paying court to the eloquent."[83] This Nietzschean picture expresses well the lot of the poor in late antiquity. They were "the masses," the nobodies of society.

With the expansion of Christianity, awareness of the poor grew. According to the *Codex Theodosianus* (*CT*), two laws from 382 addressed the plight of poor people. In *CT* 14.18.1, able-bodied beggars were obliged to work in the public services in exchange for rations of food or a sleeping mat near the porticoes. *CT* 16.2.6 stipulated one of the obligations associated with tax-exempt status for churches. It required churches to use their financial resources, buildings, and landholdings to support the needs of the poor. The burden for poor relief shifted increasingly toward the churches during the late fourth and fifth centuries.[84] Even in the mid-fourth century, the breadth of the Christian church's philanthropy programs had attracted the attention of the emperor, Julian, who obliged the priests of the state cults also to distribute rations of food, oil, and wine to widows and the poor.[85]

To sum up, there seems to have been a fairly remarkable shift from the classical to the late periods of antiquity. In the classical period, the poor were derided as lazy and idle, justly deserving of their hunger. By late antiquity, the poor were seen as objects of sympathy, deserving of the financial resources available to the church and to the state. It is likely this transition had something to do with rhetorical shifts in what it meant to be a "friend" of a poor person. Aristotle had argued in his *Ethics* that some relationships constituted true friendship (between equals) and others constituted patron–client friendships. The formal, almost contractual patron–client relationships between "friends" in the classical world gave way to an openness to true friendship with the poor in late antiquity.[86]

The Poor in Christian Teaching and Its Contexts

It has already been suggested that the increased attention to the poor in Christian texts of late antiquity is due, in part, to the tax-exempt status Christian clergy increasingly enjoyed. By most measures, the Church Fathers took this responsibility seriously. One way in which they did so was to raise an awareness of the plight of the poor—especially the poorest of the poor—in their homilies. In one example of this, John Chrysostom quantified for his congregants the number of those who are beggars in contrast to the rest of the population. He suggested that 10 percent of the population was among the truly poor and 10 percent among the truly rich.[87] This leaves a vast middle, 80 percent of the population, who from one year to the next might see themselves move in or out of what some are now referring to as "shallow poverty."[88] That is to say, any one medical crisis, any one crop failure, any one famine, or any period of temporary unemployment could move them from "Poverty" to "Begging," to use Aristophanes' distinction, much as any one good year for their crops or their trade would ensure they could meet the needs of themselves, their families, and even strangers.[89]

More recent scholarship on poverty in the Roman Empire refines Chrysostom's offhand estimate. On the one hand, it confirms Chrysostom's estimate that only 10 percent of the population was "rich" by documenting that 90 percent of the population lived at or below subsistence wages.[90] On the other hand, the picture is a good bit more complex for those in the lower 90 percent. Twenty-eight percent of the residents were definitively below subsistence level. Serious disease and early death were ever-present realities for this group that included widows, orphans, prisoners, unskilled day laborers, and some farm families. Then, a staggering 40 percent lived at subsistence level, but their situation was so precarious that they often fell below it. This included skilled and unskilled laborers, employed artisans, most merchants, and small shop owners. Another 22 percent also lived at subsistence level but less precariously so. This typically included some merchants, traders, artisans, regularly-employed workers, and large shop owners. That leaves only a mere 10 percent of the population with surplus resources that would allow them to ride out temporary financial setbacks. This group included, not surprisingly, members of the senatorial and decurial classes, whose land wealth was substantial. It also included those merchants, traders, and artisans whose businesses were sufficiently large as to employ others.

Consequently, we should expect to find particular references to the plight of the 90 percent, especially the lowest 28 percent, in the literature of the Fathers during the second through fifth centuries. Indeed, the homily "Against Covetousness" preached by Asterius of Amasea in the last decade of the fourth century is one such text. It paints a bleak picture both of the "shallow poverty" in which most of the population found itself and of the travails of the poorest in society. With respect to those in shallow poverty, consider this remark from the homily in which Asterius looks out at the world from the perspective of the wealthy person:

> These men [i.e., the wealthy people] are profoundly depressed by general prosperity and delighted by general distress. They pray that intolerable burdens of taxation may be imposed by public proclamation that they may increase their money by usury. They want to see their neighbors throttled by money-lenders, in order

that they may secure for themselves their farms, their chattels, or live stock, when through necessity they are thrown on the market at a low price....[If] they see any portent of any calamity threatening to fall on the community at large, they rejoice over it.[91]

According to Asterius, the livelihoods of those in shallow poverty are always at the mercy of a good crop yield, good weather, or sustained employment. Later in the homily, Asterius will comment on the plight of the poorest segment of the population. He contrasts the living conditions of the wealthy and the poor. After describing the richly ornamented homes under whose roofs the wealthy find shelter, Asterius then said, "[O]thers [i.e., the poor] have not the shelter of two boards. When they cannot live in open air, they either take refuge beside the furnaces of the baths, or, finding the attendants of the baths inhospitable, they dig into the dung like swine, and so contrive to get for themselves the needful warmth."[92] To Asterius, the poorest of the population largely consisted of those who had to beg even for shelter. The two references to the plight of the poor in this homily by Asterius suggest at least two different categories of poor people: one with land, crops, and money to lose, the other with no permanent shelter of any kind. It is important that readers of patristic homilies in which there are references to the plight of the poor be mindful of the distinctions between levels of "poverty" in late antique society so as not to conflate references to one group with references to the other(s). Indeed, the question of "the poor" is still very much one about which scholars have more to learn.[93]

In addition to the tax exempt status issue, perhaps another reason the Church Fathers paid greater attention to the plight of the poor is due to their own growing political prominence. They began to assume the classical role of public benefactor (εὐεργέτης).[94] For instance, there was earlier discussion of Basil's new city for the poor. It seemed to raise Basil's status within the region, as Gregory Nazianzen's encomium for Basil suggests.[95] Naturally, we should expect also that preaching about "the poor" and about the plight of the poor was part of the strategy the Fathers had for ensuring their philanthropic institutions moved from the drawing board to reality, and for ensuring the contributions needed to sustain them were forthcoming.[96]

Behind projects such as hostels, hospitals, and *diaconia* was monasticism. The fifth-century *Lausiac History* by Palladius recalled the life and work of many desert monks, including the lengths to which several went in caring for the poor and beggars.[97] With respect to the encouragement for Christians to found, to build, or to otherwise support the development of institutional structures that would alleviate the sufferings of the poor, Palladius relates at least two important accounts. One of these is that of Ephraem, a deacon in Edessa. Like Basil after him, Ephraem came to the rescue of his fellow citizens during an extended famine. We are told that Ephraem went to the wealthy citizens and asked, "Why do you not have pity on the people who are perishing, instead of letting your wealth rot for the condemnation of your souls?"[98] After several of the wealthy contributed to his relief efforts, Palladius tells us, "[Ephraem] divided up the porticoes, and he put up about three hundred beds and cared for the famished ones. The dead he buried, and he took care of those who had hope of life, and as a matter of fact he daily provided nourishment and help to all those who came to him each day because of the famine; and this he did with the money allotted to him."[99] Ephraem's decision to use the money given to him to feed and to house the poor and to bury the dead was an already long-established Christian charitable response. The use of the porticoes of the church for sheltering the homeless became more common from Ephraem's day onward as Christian churches grew both in number and in size.

Palladius provides us with a second account in his *History* of the institutionalizing of poor relief. He wrote of a time when Macarius of Alexandria took some of the wealth of a woman committed to virginity for the construction of a hospital. Macarius had told the virgin she would receive jewels in exchange for the money, but the only "jewels" she was ever shown were the lives of the poor women and men being cared for in the hospital. This calls to mind the popularly known story of St. Lawrence who, in Rome, presented the poor people receiving financial support from his church to those who had demanded he turn over the church's wealth.[100] Thus, in addition to exhortations for personal contributions of alms or of labor to the poor, the Fathers of the third through fifth centuries both taught the need for and implemented the construction and maintenance of institutional structures for alleviating economic injustice.

In sum, during the fourth and fifth centuries, the Fathers raised the status of the poorest of the poor in the eyes of the rest of the community. Identifying the poor as "athletes" or "gladiators" or repeatedly identifying them with the poor Christ of Matthew 25 signaled the bishops' awareness of and identification with the poor.[101] Cyril of Alexandria even connected his and his congregants' love for the poor with bringing about the common good.[102] In most every case, the point was Christocentric, for loving the poor meant both loving and mimicking the life of Christ, who himself became poor for our sake.[103] Every time Christians partake in the eucharist, they are asked to remember the poor Christ. It was not a major leap for the Fathers to ask their audiences to move from the presence of Christ in the eucharist to an appreciation for the presence of Christ in the lives of the poor. In this shift, both the poor and society's obligations toward the poor become larger than life itself.

CHAPTER SUMMARY

The two case study texts we will consider in the remaining chapters of this monograph are concerned with precisely the issues that have occupied our attention here. The reader takes with him or her into the study of Asterius's *Homily* 1 and Jerome's *Homily* 86 an awareness that the common good was as much if not more a theological concern as it was an economic or political one in the Fathers. The reader also is aware that Asterius and Jerome inherited Clement of Alexandria's turn from a renunciation to a detachment view of private property. The voices for renunciation were few by the time Asterius and Jerome were preaching, even within monastic circles. So, too, does the reader take with him or her into the reading of our case study texts the awareness that the poor were a more or less invisible aspect of early Christian texts. To be sure, they were there, but most often as a tool to influence the behavior of those with wealth or resources. The extent to which Asterius and Jerome conform to or break from this mind-set will be discussed in the following chapter. Guiding our reading of these two texts will be the interests of Christian social thought to profitably recover this tradition for its own benefit. To that end, we begin in the next chapter to analyze our two case study texts from an authorial-intent model, the first of four hermeneutical models evaluated in this study.

Chapter 3

AN "AUTHORIAL INTENT" MODEL

To this point, it has been argued that Christian social thought has an interest in incorporating patristic social thought into its mix of variables. It has also been argued that Catholic social teaching, one part of the Christian social thought spectrum, has had difficulty joining its message to that of patristic socioethical texts. Much of this problem is due to the difficulty of applying a text from so foreign a context as the world of late antiquity to the world we inhabit. That was why, in the previous chapter, I surveyed three major themes in patristic social thought. Early Christian ideas of the common good, private property, and the poor each had an influence on the authors and on the construction of the two case study texts that occupy our attention for the remainder of this study.

In this chapter I turn to the first of four hermeneutical models that may lend themselves to a fruitful dialogue between Christian social thought in our day and patristic social thought. This chapter will explore an "authorial intent" model, particularly as it was expressed in the hermeneutical ideas of Friedrich Schleiermacher (1768–1834) and Wilhelm Dilthey (1833–1911). As the name implies, this model argues that the locus of interpretation for any text is the intention of the author in writing it, an intention that presumes some interest on the part of a particular audience in the author's mind. This engagement between the author and the audience created a need for textual unity, and so authorial intent is connected with the inherent unity of a text. After elucidating the contours of this model, I turn to an application of the model to both case study texts. For each text, special attention will be paid to the various connections the authorial intent model fosters between our case study texts and Christian social thought.

SURVEY OF THE "AUTHORIAL INTENT" MODEL

The authorial intent model developed during the early nineteenth century, its chief exponent at that time being Friedrich Schleiermacher. His major work, upon which I rely here, *Hermeneutik und Kritik*, was published posthumously in 1838.[1] Schleiermacher defines at the very beginning of the work the scientific concept of hermeneutics as "the art of understanding another person's utterance correctly."[2] The rest of the work unpacks the two parts of this definition. There is a need both to understand "the utterance as derived from language" and to understand that utterance "as a fact in the thinker."[3] In other words, understanding is both grammatical and psychological. The grammar and word choices of an author are contextually determined, a context that is both literary and historical (i.e., social, temporal, linguistic, philosophic, etc.).[4] Ancient texts, such as the New Testament, which was Schleiermacher's concern in this work, are further complicated by their translation into a modern language, which adds an entirely new layer to the texts. This is so even for the reader who knows the ancient language (e.g., the Greek of the New Testament), for the reader still translates, if only in his or her mind, the words and ideas of the ancient text into his or her own language. The use of lexica in preparing a translation also complicates matters, for, as Schleiermacher notes, the author of the lexicon knows only a selection of ancient material; thus, the definitions found in a lexicon are conditioned by that knowledge and so may or may not be appropriate to the texts we today might wish to read.[5]

Schleiermacher divided *Hermeneutik und Kritik* into two parts for the two parts of understanding: grammatical and psychological. The first part takes aim at the myriad of issues surrounding grammatical interpretation, and he organizes the material around two so-called canons (*Kanon*) of grammatical interpretation. The first canon says, "Everything in a given utterance which requires a more precise determination may only be determined from the language area which is common to the author and his original audience."[6] Put another way, the original author and his audience of a text give a text its meaning. Schleiermacher even says that such a study helps the interpreter know the author of a text better than he or she knows him- or herself, for the author wrote unconsciously of things about which interpreters today must become conscious.[7] To wit, words have multiple meanings, and when they are used idiomatically or figuratively, the interpreter's artistic ability—the ability to decide upon the range of possible meanings and to limit that list to those that are most probable in light of the author's intent or the audience's understanding—comes to the fore.[8]

Schleiermacher's second canon of grammatical interpretation says, "The sense of every word in a given location must be determined according to its being-together with those that surround it."[9] In this part of the work, Schleiermacher talks about the significance for the interpretive art of the many different parts of a sentence: subject, predicate, independent clauses, subordinate clauses, prepositions, prepositional phrases, direct objects, indirect objects, etc. This is as much a grammatical aid as it is a work on interpretation. The point he makes repeatedly throughout is that, for the meaning of a text as a whole, the interpreter is to be concerned about whole sentences and independent clauses, but for determining the meaning of an individual word, that word's syntactical function is crucial. Sentences and independent clauses establish contrasts and continuities between ideas within the text as a whole.[10] They build an argument. There is something decidedly circular about the whole process, too—

indeed, it is called a "hermeneutic circle"[11]—for one cannot identify the arguments of the sentences without first translating the sentences, but one cannot translate the sentences correctly until one has a sense of the text as a whole. It seems, then, that the interpreter who is good at his or her art knows of his or her responsibility to return to a text many times, recognizing that every interpretation is subject to revision when the words of the text are read again.

The second part of Schleiermacher's work unpacked psychological interpretation, the second element in understanding. Psychological interpretation is just as much an art as grammatical interpretation; here, the concern is not with understanding of the words and arguments of the text, but with the unity of the work. Schleiermacher explained it this way: "[T]he unity of the work, the theme, is here regarded as the principle which moves the writer, and the basic characteristics of the composition as his individual nature which reveals itself in that movement."[12] Put another way, the interpreter wants not only to know why an author wrote a text but also to pay attention to how that reason dictated the use (or nonuse) of elements in the text. At a basic level, authors choose a genre for their text based upon the situation that led to their writing. Genres have a prehistory to an author, so the interpreter will want to know the prehistory of genres such as epigrams, poetry, and prose before interpreting a particular text written in one of those genres.[13] From basic issues such as this, Schleiermacher proceeds to talk about the unity of a text within the author's thought. Authors write with intention; they choose a rhetorical style that best communicates their intention. And, of course, authors may have primary and secondary intentions. Interpreters are obliged to distinguish between the two in any work in order to stay focused on the former while also deciding what the latter contribute to the work's overall unity.[14] Incidentally, this matter of secondary intentions already foreshadows some of what we will find in the postcolonial model, although in the later model there is no presumption of textual unity.

To this point, it is clear that both grammatical and psychological interpretation are essential to understanding a text. In the *Kritik* part of *Hermeneutik und Kritik*, Schleiermacher walks the student of hermeneutics through the several ways in which a particular text may not represent the author or the author's intention. For one, in nearly every case, interpreters do not work with autographs, but instead have recourse only to later copies or to editions (in the case of the NT). Copies of texts are often flawed through accidental and sometimes intentional scribal errors. It is also the case that we no longer know the author of some texts, or the reputed author is one about whom we ought to be skeptical. Sometimes stories are collected by later individuals and then presented in a manner that does not represent the mind of the original author of the story. These are just a few of Schleiermacher's examples, under what are called different types of criticism—form, source, redaction, etc. The point is that interpreters must be wary of the many difficulties associated with texts, particularly those difficulties that might limit access to the historical context or to an identification of the unity of a text.

One has entered, it seems, into a remarkably tricky business interpreting ancient texts. One may not presume to have understood the word choices and grammar of a text until one has come to know the author him- or herself. This, of course, would require acquainting oneself with other works by the same author. It would also demand an acquaintance with texts by other authors on the same theme, preferably written around the same period of time, in order to assess the meaning of words in a wider, social context. Also, texts have meaning precisely because they are written to a particular audience, and so some knowledge about the audience and/or the historical context in which the text was written is also important. Finally, all of this is compounded by the difficulty of making sense of texts that must be translated into a contemporary language, expressing ideas from a context not one's own in words that make sense within a context that is one's own. Yet, none of this suggested to Schleiermacher the type of pessimism that one finds in the theories of this book's later chapters. To be sure, Schleiermacher pleaded for the exercise of humility.[15] Hermeneutics is an art, after all. Nevertheless, he believed, once an interpreter was aware of the pitfalls, the interpreter could successfully avoid them.[16] Knowledge of what one does not know is, in this case, power to declare with force what one knows.

Wilhelm Dilthey expanded upon the work of Schleiermacher, in particular, by widening the notion of a hermeneutic circle to include *Verstehen* of the lived experience of the author, which is possible only after *Verstehen* of one's own lived experience. Dilthey sought to explain what distinguishes humane studies from the physical sciences. In the latter one tests hypotheses in controlled conditions; in the former, one tests hypotheses of understanding within an appreciation for the many factors that affect human life, that change the direction of or otherwise influence human thought and behavior.[17] Dilthey wrote of several features of human life concerning which the interpreter is obliged to pay careful attention. First, every expression of a person has meaning to others when that expression is set within a common background. Take the example of a child, as Dilthey does, who "grows up among the regular life and habits of a family. . . . Before it learns to speak, it is already deeply immersed in the medium of a common background."[18] Corresponding to this, a person's objective mind possesses an ordered arrangement that enables it to make sense of the particular expressions in a common background. An author's common background with an audience, then, is common because the author can rely on the ordered arrangement of his or her audience's mind and so express things in particular ways. The later interpreter, then, has an obligation to become a part of that common background in order to benefit fully from the particular expressions of an author. That is the role of *Verstehen,* as the interpreter enters more and more into the common background of the author and his or her audience.

Second, and related to what has just been said, the interpreter is conscious that he or she is working backward in time whereas the author of the text under study has moved forward in time. According to Dilthey, this situation makes it possible for the author to actually extend the horizons before him or her without indicating as much to the later interpreter. Unless the interpreter knew well the common background of the author's world, the interpreter would not be sufficiently prepared to recognize movements in new directions taken by an author. Dilthey wrote, "In the operation of understanding as such the direction of the life-process is reversed. But a perfect sharing of life is only possible if our understanding moves forward along the actual line of events. Constantly striding forward, it advances with the life-process itself. In this way the process of self-projection or transposition widens out."[19] This notion of "common background" becomes the thorn in the side of every interpreter. Perhaps that is why Dilthey summarizes the connection between *Verstehen* and interpretation this way, "Understanding only becomes interpretation which achieves validity when confronted with linguistic records.... It is to counteract the constant irruption of romantic whim and skeptical subjectivity into the realm of history by laying the historical foundations of valid interpretation on which all certainty in history rests."[20] Understanding of the common background is tied to the understanding of texts, for, in the end, texts are what we can know the best. Thus, with Dilthey, one cultivates a more sophisticated psychological interpretation apparatus than that found in Schleiermacher. Also, like Schleiermacher, Dilthey has an optimistic view of the entire *Verstehen* enterprise, which encourages interpreters to continue to ply their trade with much reward in sight.[21]

From the preceding, and for the purposes of this study, the authorial intent hermeneutical model encourages attention to four elements of patristic socioethical texts. First and foremost, the interpreter is required to know the life situation of a text's author. As was mentioned in the previous chapter, that will not always be possible, for questions of authorship are far from resolved with respect to every text. Even if an author is known, the date of composition of a text may not be known, so it will be difficult to know for which audience a text was prepared. Second, the interpreter is to cultivate an understanding of the common background of the author and his or her audience. If the audience is a parish congregation, then some knowledge of that city, its residents, its Christian population, and its demographics will be helpful. If the audience is a monastic one, then it will be helpful to know under which *Rule,* if any, the community lives. The demographics of the monastery or convent would be equally helpful, as would knowing something about the location, the climate, the type of work in which the monks or nuns engaged, and also about the general economic health of the institution. Third, since the

Fathers' socioethical texts are often homiletic in nature, the interpreter is interested to know what are the ecclesiastical, doctrinal, and biblical-theological influences upon the texts. Questions such as during what time of the church year the homily was delivered or against whom or against which heresy a homily was constructed shall be important considerations. Fourth and finally, the interpreter shall be careful to dissect the text, with all its particular expressions, in order to ascertain its main and subsidiary points. To give but one example, the Fathers' socioethical texts are filled with stories of their own creation alongside exegesis of the biblical pericopes. This lends itself to making some determination about the place of these stories in the trajectory of each text's overall argument, be they rhetorical embellishments or reinterpretations of the biblical text. I now turn to an application of the authorial intent model to our two case study texts.

APPLICATION OF THE MODEL TO ASTERIUS OF AMASEA'S *HOMILY* 1

We know very little about Asterius. He came of age in the mid-fourth century and, by the early 390s was preaching in Amasea, a city in the Pontus region (along the south-central coast of the Black Sea in modern-day Turkey). Sixteen homilies are attributed to him today, although some had earlier been misattributed and some additional homilies previously passed down under Asterius's name are now correctly assigned to others.[22] The highly rhetorical style of most of his homilies suggests he had an extensive education, and we should expect that he had some contact with other Cappadocian luminaries of the late-fourth century (e.g., Gregory of Nazianzus, Gregory of Nyssa, Amphilochius of Iconium).[23]

Date and Setting of the Homily

We consider here Asterius's first homily, entitled "The Rich Man and Lazarus." As with all but one of Asterius's homilies, we have nothing in this or other texts to help us identify a date for its delivery. Since it is an exposition of Luke 16, it may be this was preached during the Lenten season, similar to Jerome's homily discussed later in this chapter. Also, Asterius no doubt was aware that by preaching on the topic of loving the poor, he was helping fulfill the government's mandate that Christian churches and clergy come to the aid of the poor with their resources in exchange for the various tax exemptions they received.[24] Indeed, evidence of this concern abounds in the many extant homilies concerned with the plight of the poor among preachers across the Roman Empire. Thus, Asterius likely preached this homily both out of his concern to fulfill his duty as bishop (as protector of the poor), and also out of his civic obligation to care for the poor in exchange for decurial and imperial tax exemptions.

Summary of the Homily

Homily 1.1

Asterius's homily may be divided into four parts. Asterius opened the homily with a challenge for the audience to match their words of Christian instruction with their deeds of service. This is itself an important socioethical point insofar as our lives are to mimic the life of Christ. Asterius praised Christ for having taught by both word and deed. The words to which Asterius referred were Jesus' commands to his disciples to love others. Surprisingly, however, the deeds Asterius had in mind were not the works and behaviors of Jesus toward others, as one might expect, but instead were the *stories about deeds* told by Jesus to the crowds and to his followers. This is a convenient definition for introducing his homily on Jesus' parable about the rich man and Lazarus. To Asterius, words and deeds must go together, and this is no less true in how Jesus taught us. In mimicking Jesus, then, Asterius set himself to the task both of expositing what Jesus had done (i.e., uses words) and of expanding Jesus' teachings with additional stories or further details about the story (i.e., deeds).

If one may label the words/deeds explanation as Asterius's practical or pastoral argument, what he says next, and what he develops throughout the remainder of the homily, may be deemed his socioethical argument. A distinction is to be drawn between a righteous and an unrighteous mentality with respect to wealth. As the homily will eventually explain, rich people can be either righteous or unrighteous, and so, too, may poor people. What will also become clear is that there is a connection between one's words/deeds and one's status as a righteous person. So, the two arguments merge as the homily progresses. In any case, Jesus' parable of the rich man and Lazarus elucidates this distinction, and so it is to an exposition of this story that Asterius will now turn.

Homily 1.2–5
Parts two through four of the homily are easily distinguished from one another due to the fact that Asterius began each of them with a quote from the biblical text leading us into a new part of the parable. This second part of the homily begins with the words of the parable, "There was a man who was rich and clothed in purple and fine linen."[25] What Asterius argued in this part may be summed up in this sentence, "It is the dwelling-place and nature of the ones taking hold of an ordered and frugal life to measure use to the need for necessary things."[26] Asterius evokes a traditional wordplay (equally exploited by other Greek patristic writers on the topic of wealth and poverty) on the cognates *chrêsis* and *chreia*. This idea of measuring what, among perhaps many needful things, is both necessary and needful at any given moment is what escapes rich people. When you have more wealth than you need, you stop being concerned about where the money is spent. Consequently, you end up spending money on things you think are needful, but, in fact, are far from this.

This was precisely the direction Asterius went. He explained the problem with two examples. The first concerned unnecessary expenditures on clothing. According to Luke 16:19, the rich man clothed himself with costly garments (i.e., "purple" and "fine linen": πορφύραν and βύσσον). Whereas garments made either from sheep's wool or from flax are satisfactory to cover one's body, rich people are unsatisfied with these presumably pedestrian fabrics. A consideration of the socioethical implications of Asterius's reference to sheep's wool and to flax (both renewable resources) will be taken up below. For now, it suffices to continue a review of Asterius's example.

Wealth inclines people to desire softer fabrics, he argued, such as silk (connected to βύσσον in Luke 16:19), and dyed fabrics (πορφύραν) that require the destruction of the life of shellfish, for example, in order to use their blood in the creation of a dye. Wealth thinks nothing of the great expense involved in acquiring the silk threads from abroad and in hiring a fisherman to extract the shellfish from the sea. Men who do this, according to Asterius, are "womanish" (θηλυδρίας).

This, however, is not all. Using the comparative, μᾶλλον, Asterius argued that the problem is much worse. Not only does wealth engender a love for softer and dyed fabrics, it also desires that these fabrics be decorated with pictures. Wealthy people enjoy the attention of others, and decorated clothing was one such way of attracting it. So, again, Asterius wondered whether or not such a rich person thought seriously about where and how his money was being spent. He suggested such people act contrary to the teaching of Paul with respect to clothing (likely an allusion to 1 Tim 2:9–10). Paul's words about modest clothing are not matched by the deeds of wealthy people, according to Asterius, which recalls his words/deeds correspondence from the first part of the homily.

Surprisingly, the problem with clothing gets worse. For, not only does this love for decorative clothing afflict the wealthy, it afflicts the *Christian* wealthy, too. So-called pious rich people (πλουτούντων εὐλαβέστεροι) weave biblical images onto their clothing. Yet, rather than depicting stories about Jesus caring for sick and poor people, why not care for the sick and poor people yourself, wondered Asterius. This nonsense jeopardizes the rich person's soul. Far better it is to sell the clothes with images of Christ on them and to honor the living image of God, one's soul. "Do not depict Christ [i.e., on your garments] . . . but, bearing understanding, carry around the incorporeal Word upon your soul."[27] No detail of the biblical text is unprofitable. From these two words, πορφύραν and βύσσον, a world of arrogance has been exposed. For this reason, suggested Asterius, "The haughty clothing of the rich man benefits us."[28]

Clothing was not the rich man's only problem, however. Jesus' parable also critiqued his love for lavish celebrations (εὐφραινόμενος λαμπρῶς). Hyperbolically, they were said to take place daily (καθ' ἡμέραν). Asterius's critique followed what he has expressed now several times: this is "unmeasured, or excessive" (ἀμέτρου).[29] Underlying this term is the idea of excess versus balance (vice vs. virtue) in Greek philosophy and humoristic (Galenist) medicine, in which excess = imbalance = sickness. Virtue resides in balancing use with necessity. Asterius's rich people know neither what is needful, how much is needful, nor when it is needful. They do not measure; they do not take account. There is no end to the luxuries rich people seek, and all of this comes at the expense of the widows, orphans, and poor people whose needs may otherwise have been met with these funds. Indeed, for Asterius, "all the poor are robbed! And all the orphans are mistreated!"[30] Repeating an observation common among the Fathers at that time, Asterius noted that luxurious living is for the idle, it cultivates vice rather than virtue.[31] In sum, in this second part of the homily Asterius argued that a wealthy person's excessiveness, displayed in, perhaps among other ways, fine clothing and food for all to witness, are symptomatic of a disease that runs particularly deep into his or her character.

Homily 1.6–8
In the third movement, Asterius turned his attention to the miserable life of Lazarus. The biblical text painted a picture of a man diseased, starving, homeless, and dying. At this point, one would suspect that Asterius would expand upon these descriptions of Lazarus with stories of contemporary displays of abject poverty, much as he had supplemented the biblical description of the rich man with stories of displays of opulent wealth. Yet, this is not what Asterius does. Now, briefly, Asterius elaborated on the physical and mental suffering Lazarus no doubt experienced. Recalling Lazarus's leprosy, Asterius surmised Lazarus had by then lost his feet, since otherwise Lazarus surely would have long ago left this unkind, rich man's gate. Also likely, Lazarus had lost his hands, for he asked not for alms, but that crumbs of leftover food be given to him. However, these brief comments do not rise to the same level of the stories of rich people told by Asterius in the previous part. Instead, Lazarus's role here in the parable is to direct us back again to the rich man. Asterius wrote,

"And very carefully the beneficial aspects of the narrative on the final circumstances of the beggar [were written], in order that the hardness of the one who had no mercy might be recorded."³² The ἵνα clause (translated "in order that . . . ") reveals that Asterius thought Lazarus was little more than a literary foil to expose further the rich man's depraved character. Thus, in the main, this part of the homily further castigates the rich man. He was an "unreasoning animal" (ἄλογον); in fact, he was even worse than an animal, since even animals take compassion on those within their species, according to Asterius. This again ties in closely with the earlier notion of excess = illness, based on the Platonic understanding of the soul, in which the intellect ought to control the emotive faculties of the soul. In the case of Asterius's rich man, the passions rule in place of reason. The result is unreason (ἄλογον). The rich man paid no heed to the *imago Dei* coursing through Lazarus's soul. The rich man offered no dignity to the pitiable sight of Lazarus's human flesh.

Asterius concluded this section with a complaint about the injustice, the inequality of it all. The poor man Lazarus is impoverished further by the heartlessness of the rich man. The rich man not only holds onto his wealth, but he flaunts it in unseemly, public ways. "But since the remaining things are good for the audience, passing up the groanings, o poor man, be cheerful in what follows."³³ What follows, Asterius promised, is the restoration of justice by God in the afterlife. There, every person receives his or her due reward.

Before turning to this final section, it is worth pointing out an interesting feature of the homily so far. Asterius has not been consistent in his use of language for Lazarus. Recall that in the previous chapter, under the section describing the poor, it was noted that Greek had two words for poor people, πένης and πτωχός, the former a reference to the working poor, the latter a reference to the begging poor. The biblical text consistently refers to Lazarus as πτωχός, but Asterius alternated between the two terms. He used πτωχός in paragraph six and wherever he quotes the biblical text, but every other time he referred to Lazarus he used the term πένης. This might suggest the two terms had lost some of their distinctive edge in the region around Amasea by the late fourth century, and thus Asterius could use both terms without confusing his audience. This may have been true for all of Cappadocia, too, since Gregory of Nazianzus similarly conflates the terms in his homily on loving the poor (*Or.* 14).[34] However, to be sure, a full, lexicographic study should be done of this, but that cannot be done here. In light of the fact that the one time Asterius used πτωχός apart from the biblical quotations he did so in the sentence immediately following citation of the biblical text, suggests it is equally possible this was a slip on Asterius's part. That is to say, despite his awareness of the difference between the two terms, his insistence on using πένης may mean that his intended audience was not one that included πτωχοί. Perhaps his congregation was somewhat better off, financially, and so his pastoral work largely dealt with the working poor. Lazarus, though a beggar, is raised to the status of a working poor person in order to make the distinction between the rich and working poor in Amasea more concrete in the text of Jesus' parable.

Homily 1.9–12
In the final part of the homily, Asterius turned to the disconcerting future facing those rich people who do not have a proper disposition toward the needy. As with the previous two sections, this section too opened with a citation of the biblical text. "And it came to be that the poor man died and was carried up into the bosom of Abraham by the angels" (Lk 16:22).[35] The "bosom of Abraham" presented to Asterius a problem. If every just person was sent to Abraham's side, he reasoned, there would scarcely be room for more than one adult or two children. "The idea presents itself to us that what is guiding the interpretation is the image of the material bosom [changed] to the mental bosom."[36] There must be another explanation, an allegorical one.[37]

Allegorical interpretation is a nice recourse when dealing with problematic texts, particularly those where the connection to Christ is difficult to ascertain from the words of the text themselves. Here, though, Asterius was preaching a parable, so he might just have easily dismissed this interpretive problem as a feature of storytelling—akin to S. T. Coleridge's dictum, "the willing suspension of disbelief."[38] Yet, Asterius did not dismiss the problem. In fact, he spent so much time in this last part of the homily trying to explain it away that one wonders if Asterius actually believed he was preaching a parable at all! He may well have believed this was a *real* story about *real* people about whose lives and fortunes Jesus took time one day to discourse.

Asterius explained the textual difficulty in the following way. First, he established that Abraham was considered "of God" (οὗτος γεγένηται τοῦ Θεοῦ), and this as a result of having been graced through a visit from the Trinity to announce the birth of Isaac and the impending destruction of Soddom and Gomorrah (see Gen 18). In light of what follows, this first part of the argument seems important only to the extent that one can say being with Abraham is more or less the same as being with God himself. That is why, second, Asterius argued that the biblical text suggests Abraham's bosom is a resting place for the weary and afflicted. Christ, too, has that reputation. Thus, in fact, "Abraham's bosom" is nothing other than the presence of Christ, "being the judge and the one who rewards virtue and the one who calls the righteous with a gentle voice."[39]

Having resolved this dilemma, Asterius turned finally, from paragraphs ten through twelve, to the eternal fates of the rich man and Lazarus. Asterius even repeated the text of Luke 16:22 he had cited at the beginning of this part, so there is a feeling that Asterius has "rebooted" the homily to get back on track with the main point of the text. First, he argues for a distinction between righteous and unrighteous poor people. "Therefore, not every poor person is righteous, but those who are [like] Lazarus."[40] This is because some poor people are not content with their lot in life. Some steal. Some kidnap. What they do not do is bear their suffering with "a philosophic mind" (φιλοσόφῳ ψυχῇ). As was mentioned in the previous chapter under Christian attitudes toward private property, what Asterius means here is the Stoic virtue of treating all things as ἀδιαφορία. Unrighteous poor persons harbor bitterness—perhaps toward society or perhaps toward God—when they cannot have as much as they want.

The reverse situation is also true. There are rich people who are not generous with their wealth. They presume upon it as security for this life. Wealth replaces God for them. They are not worried about eternal consequences, because they doubt there is a God in charge of any eternal existence. These are unrighteous rich people. Unlike Job, who maintained virtue both when he was rich and when he had lost nearly everything, unrighteous rich people despair of misfortune. "And one does not despair of every rich man, but [one despairs of] the one with the conduct of such living, such as he who was contemporaneous with Lazarus had."[41]

In the afterlife, there is a reversal of fortunes. The righteous poor are carried to a place of rest. The unrighteous rich die and are buried. Torment afflicts the unrighteous rich both with respect to their bodies in the grave and with respect to their souls in Hades, according to Asterius. There is no escaping this judgment. All appeals for mercy will be denied by God. For Asterius, that is the entire point of the chasm metaphor. It separates people according to the decisions they have made in their earthly life. Since it is not possible to go back and live that earthly life again, it is not possible to change the decision of God to place a person one side or another of the chasm. The decision to live righteously must be made while one still has the opportunity to influence the judgment of God.

Social Thought of the Homily

Asterius's homily raises a number of issues with which the authorial intent model would be concerned. We may begin at the level of the text itself. In the summary of the homily provided above, it was evident that Asterius devoted a disproportionate amount of space to the foibles of and dangers facing wealthy people compared to the plight of poor people such as Lazarus. This imbalance may simply reflect the makeup of his audience. This is not unusual in early Christian social preaching; the poor are rarely the subject of any special inquiry. To be sure, there is regular mention of "the poor" or "the needy," but in only a handful of cases does one actually get a glimpse into what life might be like for the poor person of late antiquity.[42]

As noted above, Asterius did not deem poverty to be, of its own accord, a characteristic of a life of righteousness, and neither did the secular society give the poor people more than a passing glance. Understandably, Asterius probably believed keeping the focus on the wealthy and powerful individuals of Amasea would be the most expedient course of action toward social justice. Yet, one may conclude the imbalance belies a deeper belief that wealthy people hold enough of the cards to control how the game of life plays out for everyone else. Check the pride and ostentatious living of the wealthy, and you restore justice to the poor, or so Asterius's thinking may have run. As was noted in the previous chapter, the rhetoric of patristic social thought aimed at one or both of castigating the wealthy either for their opulent living or for their lack of charitable giving. Asterius chose the former course, for hardly a mention is found in the homily regarding transfers of wealth to the poor. This raises some concerns for incorporating Asterius's homily into contemporary Christian social thought, a point to which we shall turn in a few moments.

Second, another textual issue noted above, was that Asterius used the terms πένης and πτωχόν interchangeably when describing Lazarus. This is despite the fact the terms designated different groups in late antiquity. In any case, if Asterius could see in the face of Lazarus both the beggars and the working poor, so too may Christian social thought take stock of the challenges facing both groups in our day. It is not widely understood that poverty and need afflicts those who are steadily employed and their children. Too often one has in mind only beggars or those on the welfare rolls.

Third, Asterius condemned an unrighteous disposition toward wealth. Asterius wrote, "[Jesus] turns away from the overbearing and haughty man of wealth, and loves a kindly disposition, and poverty when united to righteousness."[43] Like most Church Fathers of his and earlier generations, the status of the wealthy person in the church was dubious. For the wealthy Christian, everything depended on his or her disposition both toward wealth and, for that matter, toward those who were in need of their kindness. By the same token, the quote above also reminded the audience that the poor person is not automatically accepted as being more spiritual. Poverty is to be "united to righteousness." Asterius also stated in this homily that some poor people inappropriately rationalize acts of thievery with the excuse that it meets an immediate, financial need. For Asterius, poverty is not a good thing, but it certainly is to be borne with dignity by those whose lot in life it is.

One of Asterius's critiques of wealth was that it led people to believe they were entitled to freedom from entanglements with the poor. Large houses, numerous attendants, and exquisite cuisines were part and parcel of the lifestyle that separated wealthy people from poor people that Asterius condemned. There is a social-environmental ethic at work here that plays well into the concerns of Christian social thought in our day.[44] A divinely given, shared human nature is something that we experience as much if not more than something we intellectually assess. Asterius's critiques fit well, for example, the New Urbanist city planning models that incorporate mixed-use (i.e., residential and commercial) zoning rules and public transport networks to increase population densities and to bring different types of people together.[45] Asterius likely would condemn gated residential communities, exurban shopping centers, and long commutes by single-passenger vehicles from distant suburbs. Such things are of particular concern in our day as countries with large populations such as India and China experience rising standards of living that correspond to increasing demands for food, energy, and consumer goods.

This social-environmental ethic also extends to Asterius's critique of wealthy people's propensity to misuse the natural goods of the earth. Sheep's wool, leather, and flax are renewable resources provided by God for clothing; the sun, rain, and land are gifts for growing simple food. Unfortunately, wealthy people want to be different from everyone else. They destroy animals to make silk and fabric dyes. Their palettes are satisfied only when simple foods are dressed up with exotic, imported spices. Christian social thought in our day encourages movements such as "slow food" and "buy local," which support food and goods producers in a local area.[46] It also embraces a simple living ethos described in recent literature as the "new monasticism."[47] Asterius certainly encouraged this type of heightened concern for ecological balance in the ways human persons interact with the natural world.

Also part of this critique of wealth was Asterius's insistence that need was the proper measure of wealth.[48] Every person should ask him- or herself the question "What do I need?" Sufficient wealth is what one needs to survive plus enough to be hospitable toward others.[49] The rich man in Jesus' parable indulged in unmeasured wastefulness with his resources, and this is to be contrasted with what should be the proper orientation of Christians: "It is the dwelling-place and nature of the ones taking hold of an ordered and frugal life to measure use to the need for necessary things."[50]

One example of excess was the wealthy's love for decorative clothing. Wealthy people spurn clothing fabrics from natural resources (flax and sheep's wool); instead, they demand threads drawn from Persian worms that have been dyed in colors made with the blood of shellfish. Then, as if love for the dyes was not enough damage to the wealthy person's soul, they require pictures be woven into or painted upon the fabrics. Christians who tried to act piously by incorporating into their clothing pictures of biblical scenes or of the person of Jesus exposed their avarice all the more.

Although this matter of clothing seems strange to us today (the proliferation of gaudy Christian clothing notwithstanding), there were at least two truths at stake in this for Asterius. First, when people spurn natural fabrics for specialty fabrics and dyes, in effect they are denouncing God's gift of the natural world. This goes back to the creation narrative. God had given to Adam and Eve the rest of the created realm to meet their physical needs. Sheep are one of many universal gifts of God, and they are a renewable resource. You sheer the sheep for their wool to make clothing, and then the wool grows back to provide new clothing at a later time. Persian worms were made by God for purposes other than for providing silk threads. Shellfish were made by God for purposes other than for humans to kill them in order to extract their blood for fabric dyes. To think and to behave otherwise in this way is, to Asterius, "to abuse life."[51] God intended that we use the renewable resources that he has made available to all humans (other Church Fathers will point to God's provision of the sun, rain, arable land, and wind as other universal goods) to meet our physical needs.

There is yet another truth at stake in this complaint about how wealthy Christians misuse their clothing, and this goes back to Asterius's earlier distinction between words and deeds. The biblical images wealthy Christians portray on their garments are merely "words," but deeds bring the words to life. If wealthy Christians would feed the hungry instead of picturing the baskets of bread left over from the miraculous feeding of the crowd, according to one of Asterius's examples, then their deeds would bring the words (i.e., the pictures) to life and tutor others in the faith. Asterius's social thought placed a premium on deeds rather than words, for needy people required real help and not just the sympathy of those who passed by or were near to them.

Fourth, Asterius taught not only that people are to make a *just use* of their wealth, but also that they are to maintain *just ownership* of their wealth. Recall earlier that Asterius had said that "all the poor are robbed! And all the orphans are mistreated!"[52] when the rich withhold their resources. Once a wealthy person has met his "needs," such a person actually ceases to be the owner of the additional wealth now in his or her possession. That wealth belongs instead to those with immediate financial or hunger needs. By the same token, Asterius did not agree the poor should take by force what the wealthy refuse to give to them. Yet, it hardly seems consistent to exclude that as one reasonable course of action. Apparently, many had done precisely that, for Asterius characterized such poor people as incorrigible. "[T]he poverty of those who are in extreme want, and have at the same time an unmanageable or incorrigible disposition, leads to many evil deeds of daring."[53] It would be far better, in his view, that the poor bear their hardships with a Stoic disposition. In Christian social thought today, this is very much a disputed question: Just how far may the poor go in demanding that a rich person's superfluous resources be handed over to relieve their suffering?[54] Wealthy Christians should never let matters reach that point of despair, but if they are unwilling to honor God and give their superfluous goods to the needy, what is a Christian poor person to do?

Fifth, Asterius emphasized both the redemptive and the punitive aspects of the eschaton. God will in the afterlife restore justice. Poor and oppressed peoples are obliged to bear their suffering with dignity and with faith in God. This requires patience, a virtue which ties in well to Asterius's distinctions between the righteous and unrighteous rich and poor. This is because whatever joys or pleasures are associated with wealth in this life are short-lived. Certainly, they will be exchanged for pain and torment without end in the next life. Equally important, no amount of pleading for forgiveness in the next life will be met by God with the ability to leave that torment and enter heaven.

There is no hope of repentance at that point. Like the Hebrew psalmist who lamented unchecked injustices (Ps 18), so too did Asterius suggest that, if Jesus had ended the parable with the stories of Lazarus's and the rich man's death, without telling of the afterlife, then he too would have cried foul (*Hom.* 1.6). Fortunately, that was not how the story ended. There was a reversal of fortunes for the rich man and Lazarus. This is Asterius's final, pastoral card. If the wealthy are moved to help the needy neither by appeals to their greed (i.e., God will reward you a hundredfold for giving to the needy), nor by appeals to their soul (i.e., the dire life condition of needy persons), nor by appeals to their conscience (i.e., the wealthy are responsible for the plight of the needy), then perhaps they will be moved by appeals to their self-interest (i.e., do what you ought to do now before death makes it too late). Belief in the reality of punishment for the damned in the afterlife was a consistent theme in many early Christian social homilies. Like those, Asterius was in this homily not afraid of drawing on the entirety of Scripture's resources in calling his congregants to repentance.

In the final analysis, Asterius's concern with the mentality and behavior of wealthy people is helpful, but the important question today would be whether or not it can be scaled to larger, relational structures. Like Jesus' parable, Asterius limited his comments to the sphere of individuals. It made sense for him to have done so in the context of a worldview concerned with individual, as opposed to corporate, virtue. To Asterius, since the cause of economic inequality lies in the individual abuse of wealth, then redress too must focus on the individual. Individual behavior affects the redistribution (or lack thereof) of wealth, which in turn affects the well-being of all in the economic community. Today, we recognize something quite different. Individual, poor persons suffer at the hands of institutions, be they financial, industrial, political, or transnational.[55] One wonders if Asterius would not articulate today the connections that exist between the decisions of large institutions and the effect those decisions have on poor people. Asterius might help his congregants understand the connections that exist between their decisions on what to buy and where to buy and the salaries paid to the laborers involved in the production and sale of those goods. So, too, he might help his congregants appreciate the complexities of global labor markets, of agricultural subsidies paid to farmers in the developed world, and of the financial instruments sold to developing nations by organizations like the World Bank. This would not dismiss the biblical challenge for those with superfluous wealth to transfer that to individual, needy persons (e.g., via organizations like Compassion International or World Vision), but it does put the problems that the poor face in wider perspective.

Summary

Asterius has walked us through a delightful forest of biblical and social ideas. One nearly forgets, in fact, that Asterius is preaching a *parable,* for the homily regularly treats the characters in Jesus' story as if the people and the events were real. Preaching the parable in this way, Asterius's audience—and we may include ourselves here as a part of the extended audience[56]—comes to grip both with the dangers associated with luxurious living and the seriousness of a callous disregard for the plight of poor people. The rich people Asterius condemns are those who misuse their superfluous wealth. They deny the goodness of God by misusing or appropriating for private use the goods God created and intended for use by all humans for the maintenance of life. Worse, they assume that their wealth entitles them to a life free of entanglements with the needy. Moreover, they harbor a fundamental disdain for the truths of Scripture in that even after death they arrogantly demand that their pleas for forgiveness be met by God with mercy. Asterius has indeed covered a lot of ground with such a short, biblical pericope. We turn now to Jerome's exposition and to his consideration of the socioethical issues at stake in preaching Luke 16.

APPLICATION OF THE MODEL TO JEROME'S *HOMILY* 86

To pick up Jerome's *Homily* 86[57] is to be confronted immediately with the grand place he holds in Christian history—he is a leading, theological light of the Western world in the late fourth and early fifth centuries and a translator of the Bible into the vernacular of his day, Latin. His service to the Christian church began in Rome, as a member of the bishop's staff, continued during travels to Trier and Aquileia, until finally he settled in Bethlehem. There, he built a monastery and his travel companion and patron, Paula, also built there a convent.[58] Jerome remained in Bethlehem from 398 until his death in 419 or 420, although he occasionally traveled to visit other monasteries and to learn of their ways of life, including especially those of Pachomius in Egypt, but also at Caesarea and on the outskirts of Jerusalem. Nearly all Jerome's homilies were preached during his latter years, most probably after 400, after the founding of his monastery in proximity to the Church of the Nativity.

Date and Setting of the Homily

Jerome preached often at the Bethlehem church, usually on Sundays but at least once on a Wednesday (filling in for an ill priest).[59] Also, from comments in some of his homilies, he occasionally was invited to preach alongside the bishop, John, in Jerusalem.[60] Every Sunday, the monks of Jerome's monastery and the nuns at Paula's neighboring convent were expected to be in attendance. Judging by the rough estimates given of the sizes of their respective communities, the two communities alone may have contributed nearly one hundred congregants for mass.[61] Naturally, one expects to find in Jerome's homilies—apparently all delivered extemporaneously—evidence of his concern to address their experiences.

This homily offers hints in this direction, so one suspects *Homily* 86 was one of those delivered to a predominantly monastic audience at the Church of the Nativity in Bethlehem. Assigning a year to the homily, however, is all but impossible. Jerome says in the homily only that he was delivering it during the early days of Lent, and that Psalm 103 was read together that Sunday with the Luke passage.[62]

Summary of the Homily

This homily is a thorough reworking of the biblical text into a drama set as often in the fifth-century context of his audience as it is within the first-century context in which Jesus related it. Jerome frequently changed persona, alternatively (1) speaking the words of the biblical text; (2) giving voice to the rich man's interior thoughts; (3) enjoining his audience to condemn the rich man; (4) playing the role of Abraham; (5) narrating with word-pictures the scenes of Hades experienced by Lazarus and the rich man; and (6) pastorally exhorting his audience to avoid the sins of the rich man. Often the dialogue is short, presented in staccato fashion in the text, but it may not be that Jerome delivered it this way. Since he apparently taught ex tempore, what we have today is what a scribe was able to record while Jerome spoke.[63] We have the *ipsissima vox* of Jerome, but probably not the *ipsissima verba*. Even so, the dramatic interpretation of the passage is vibrant and engaging. One can imagine the audience hanging on Jerome's every word.

Homily 86.1–57
Structurally, we may divide Jerome's homily into four parts.[64] Jerome opened his homily with the suggestion that this parable of Jesus was not, in fact, a parable at all. Instead, it was a story about real people and real events, a possible feature of Asterius's homily, too, as was noted earlier. According to Jerome, there were too many names of real people in the story for it to be a parable. "A parable poses an example, but suppresses identification. Where Abraham is mentioned by name, and Lazarus, the prophets, and Moses, there Lazarus is genuine; if Abraham is a true person, so also is Lazarus.... [F]iction is not congruent with the actual."[65] It will be shown later that, toward the end of the homily, this view of Jerome's about the verity of the story inevitably forced him into a difficult, interpretive corner when he tried to connect the timing of this parable to the timing of Jesus' release of the captives in Hades.

Also in this first part, Jerome identified pride as the rich man's problem. Jerome pointed out that Jesus' parable nowhere critiques the rich man for greed, for theft, or adultery; rather, the rich man's problem was that he presumed that he was too important to stoop to care for the physical needs of another person. "Most wretched of men, you see a member of your own body lying there outside at your gate, and have you no compassion?"[66] Jerome here addressed the rich man in the story as if Jerome himself had been on the scene, part of the dramatic act that runs throughout this homily. It is noteworthy that Lazarus is said to be a "member of your own body." Rich and poor alike share a common humanity. This bond ought to be stronger than whatever bonds the rich man might desire with others for socioeconomic advantage. Shockingly, according to Jerome, it was the rich man's dogs that deigned to do what this fellow human would not do, to touch Lazarus, to lick the sores on Lazarus's body (ll. 55–57).

Jerome also described Lazarus's suffering. "He lay there full of ulcers . . . he did not have just one sore, his whole body was sores. . . . There is some relief to sickness if one has resources, but if you add poverty to extreme weakness the infirmity is doubled"[67] The rhetorical benefit is to expose further the disdain the rich man showed to this member of his own body. If we take seriously Jerome's view that this was a story about real people and real events, it would seem, then, we also ought to take seriously Jerome's opinion here that Lazarus was intentional in choosing the gate that he did. "'Who lay at his gate.' He was lying at the gate *in order to* draw attention to the cruelty paid to his body and to prevent the rich man from saying, 'I did not notice him.'"[68] Lazarus may have been suffering physically, but he must not have lost his ability to think clearly. However, this only confounds the text further, for one may rightly wonder why Lazarus had not chosen the gate of a more hospitable man's home. What benefit could possibly derive from exposing the rich man's cruelty? This would make greater sense if Jerome accepted the story as a parable, for then it would be natural that Jesus, not Lazarus, injected such a meaning into the events.

Homily 86.58–138

Jerome expounds upon the separate experiences of Lazarus and the rich man in Hades in the second part of the homily. It is in this section we discover the greatest number of dialogue exchanges. The first few lines were devoted to the experience of Lazarus in Hades. Angels attended to this one who suffered so greatly in life. "Every angel rejoices to touch so precious a burden. With pleasure, they [i.e., angels] bear such burdens in order to conduct men into the kingdom of heaven."[69] That he was taken to the bosom of Abraham rather than the side of Abraham is also significant to Jerome. Being taken into the bosom depicts Abraham as a "most compassionate father" (*clementissimus pater*) who restores life to Lazarus. He who clung to life on earth now has it to the full in the next life.

Such was not true for the rich man. The remainder of this second part of the homily unpacked his suffering, torment, and emotional pain. Indeed, like Asterius's homily, Jerome's homily was almost entirely concerned with the plight of the rich man. Lazarus was rather more a literary foil. The rich man's problems began in earnest with his death and entrance into the *inferno* (= ᾅδη).[70] There, he witnessed Lazarus enjoying happiness. Seeing Abraham so far away compounded the pain. "The riches of others are torments to those who are in poverty."[71] Also like Asterius, Jerome has articulated the great reversal of fortunes that befell Lazarus and the rich man. The rich man is now the one in poverty; Lazarus enjoys newfound riches, though of a spiritual rather than an earthly kind.

Jerome interjects here this question, "Someone may say to me, 'Is Paradise in Hades?'"[72] It is a reasonable question, for it is strange to imagine that a person being tormented in Hades may also see Lazarus and Abraham in Paradise. Are not the two completely *other*? Admittedly unsatisfactorily, Jerome answered the question by saying the bosom of any saint is a type of paradise. So, there are paradises in the bosoms of saints, but these should not be confused with Paradise. Lazarus, for the time being, knows only the former and not yet the latter. Yet again, one finds the strangeness of the need to treat issues such as this, but it is driven in part by the decision of Jerome's not to treat this biblical text in the genre of a parable, but in the genre of a historical account. As well, it alerts us to his concern more with a literal exegesis than with an allegorical exegesis of the text. That is so up to the point the text demands an allegorical explanation, as he will later suggest another part of the parable does.[73]

Next, Jerome addressed the rich man's requests. He wanted Abraham to pity him. Jerome, however, suspected pity was not an emotion one could feel in the afterlife (l. 108). Only God pities. God pities humans, for that was why he sent the Son to restore humanity. But, Jerome recalls, the Son had to go because no human could do what needed to be done. As far as Jerome was concerned, what this suggests, then, is that true pity is the provenance of God alone. The pity humans have for one another is of a lesser sort; it does not save. Thus, Abraham could pity the rich man, but it would not be the type of pity the rich man really needed. That type of pity needed to come from God, but, as will be clear later in the homily, God decided not to extend this pity once those like the rich man enter Hades. There is a finality to the judgment of God.

Perhaps it was for this reason the rich man's next request was for Lazarus to assuage his torment with a drink of cool water. Here, too, though, the rich man ran into problems. Jerome sarcastically remarked, "You long for water, who formerly were so fastidious at the mere sight of smeary and spattered dishes."[74] The reversal of fortune theme returned at this point in the homily, as Jerome reminded the rich man that he had enjoyed good things, such as water, while on earth. Now, it was Lazarus's turn to enjoy them. Jerome incorporated, too, a Platonic framework for thinking about what is "good." He said, addressing his audience, "Be sure you know what he [i.e., the rich man] means: good things to you, but they are not good. You have received what you thought were good, but you cannot have been a lord upon earth and reign here too."[75] Wealth on earth *seems* good, but it is in fact *not* good. Jerome does not say here what is good, but one presumes he means righteousness or being in a right relationship with God. In fact, the reverse of the rich man's problem is Jerome's pastoral exhortation to his (monastic) audience: "If ever we are sick, if we are beggars, if we are wasting away in sickness, if we are perishing from the cold, if there is no hospitality for us, let us be glad and rejoice."[76] These seemingly evil things—indeed, they are evil things, to Jerome—are not to be a cause for dejection; on the contrary, suffering them with gladness will lead Jerome's audience to the Good. The caveat "with gladness" was important, for it reminded the audience the eternal consequences are different for the righteous and the unrighteous poor.

In the final analysis, the torments of Hades for the rich man were so great that Jerome concluded the rich man's desire to leave Hades had more to do with escaping them than with any newfound love for Lazarus. The rich man wanted to leave Hades, but for the wrong reason. That, in fact, is what makes the torments of Hades all the more painful, according to Jerome. Once in the midst of them you realize you will never escape from them.

Homily 86.139–231
Having found no pity for his soul and no drink for his body, the rich man appeals for the salvation of his brothers (Lk 16:28). This forms the third movement of the homily. Jerome interpreted the rich man's request allegorically; the man's five brothers were better understood as his five senses.[77] Jerome earlier expressed that he did not believe the rich man was repentant in Hades for the right reason. Here he explained this was because the man's five senses still had a love for earthly things and not for the things of Christ. "These brothers of yours loved wealth; they had no eye for poverty."[78] Then, in the following sentence, this remarkable phrase was added, "They cannot be saved unless they die."[79] Based upon what had already been said and upon what Jerome will say later about the chasm metaphor, it does not seem likely that he meant the same type of salvation that Lazarus now knew. This must be a different type of salvation, one that does not result in an end to the torments. Indeed, Jerome said of the rich man he is "fixed in punishment" (*in poenis constitutus*).

One suspects, instead, this salvation is rather more a purification, a refining fire, a new clarity of the Good. The type of salvation Hades offers is truth, which is to say, among other things, the truth of who God is, of how the spiritual and material worlds relate to one another, of the reality of ultimate judgment for human sin, and of the need for loving the needy. For Jerome, then, if one will not come to the truth (i.e., be saved) during one's earthly life through reading Moses and the prophets, one will come to the truth in Hades. Yet, part of the truth one learns at that point is that God has decreed judgment for failing to come to that truth during the earthly life.

While this terrible truth settled into the man's consciousness, Jerome continued with the man's appeal that it not be so. As the biblical text recorded, the man insisted the brothers would repent if only someone went to them from the dead (Lk 16:30). Jerome then said, "Here, a dogma is being revealed without our realizing it. One thing is said, another is foreshadowed."[80] Rather than taking up the man's appeal, Jerome instead turned to the question of whether or not it can be substantiated from the biblical texts that Jesus had, in fact, sought to save human sense organs. Jerome articulated the following proof texts: (1) Matthew 6:22, on hearing; (2) Matthew 11:15, on sight; (3) 2 Corinthians 2:15, on smell; (4) Psalm 33:9, on taste; and (5) 1 John 1:1, on touch. These texts reveal how our senses were called to pay heed to the person and work of Jesus.

Now, since the rich man had apparently died before Jesus' resurrection, Jerome found it necessary to argue that the Hebrew Bible predicts the coming and the resurrection of Christ. He wrote, "The brothers were in us, also, before our Lord rose from the dead."[81] Jerome digressed into a recollection of the many errors of his own senses from his days as a youth, particularly those involving improper relationships with women (a nod to his monastic audience, perhaps).[82] He wrote that his senses needed to die in order that they might live "in the Spirit" (*ut viverent spiritu*). The senses, then, being a part of human life before and after knowledge of Christ, were akin to the presence of Christ both in the Old and the New Testaments.

Jerome did not pass up the opportunity to use this idea as a challenge to the heresies of Marcion and of Mani. The former had sought to divide the testaments as representing two very different gods, with deference to the god of the Christian texts. The latter had presumed he received direct messages from God's spirit, and so the biblical texts were ancillary to these direct messages. Jerome instructed his audience to believe that the two testaments are a unity. Reading the Hebrew Bible is nothing less than listening to the words of Christ.

Homily 86.232–327
Jerome concludes his homily in this fourth part with several pastoral exhortations. First, "Let it suffice to hear about Lazarus, or rather, to hear that he was the rich man."[83] Second, "May the torments of the rich man be a restraint upon us and the example of the poor man an incentive to us."[84] Third and finally, "The Christian soul, the soul of the monk, the soul of him who naked follows the naked Christ, when it looks with envy upon a rich man . . . may it call to mind the rich man; may it ponder well his voice as he cries out and begs for the touch of Lazarus' finger."[85] The reversal of fortunes theme returns here. Jerome's homily intended to reframe his audience's way of thinking about the world. The only action to which he called his audience was to think—both to think differently and to think better. People like Lazarus are actually the rich ones. The love for riches is a fast-track to eternal torments. The less one possesses, the better one is able to follow Christ.

At this point, one expects the homily to end, but Jerome suddenly remembered that he had not completed what he started discussing at the beginning of the homily. This was the matter of the time of the story in human history. Jerome earlier declared that the events Jesus described were happening *at that very time*. In this last part of the homily Jerome wondered about the connection between these events and the final judgment Christ predicted was to come at the end of the age (cf. Mt 25). Believing, as Jerome did, that the resurrection of Christ must precede the final judgment, then the events of Luke 16 were taking place *prior to* the final judgment.

By the same token, it is not until Jesus dies and then rises from the dead that he will lead from Hades into Paradise the saints of old. "[B]efore Christ died, no one had ascended into heaven, not even the thief. That flaming, flashing sword was keeping Paradise safe; no one would open the gates Christ had closed."[86] It is the post-resurrection Christ who asks the angel with the flaming sword to stand down from guarding the entrance to Paradise. Christ had earlier closed the entrance, according to Jerome, which suggests he connected the reference to Paradise with the decision to close off access to Eden (cf. Gen 3). After the resurrection, Christ shall reopen it and the saints may go in. Thus, according to Jerome, the events of the story took place in Hades, where Abraham, Moses, and the prophets still then resided. Lazarus had found a place of rest in the bosom of Abraham while in Hades. The rich man had found no one to comfort him there, and so was tormented.

Yet, now, suffice it to say, Jerome had gotten himself into an interpretation of the biblical passage that is unduly constraining. He is obliged to explain how the rich man and Lazarus can be experiencing different realities in Hades even while being able to see and talk with one another. Also, if Jerome is right, ought we not to expect that the rich man's torments will only *increase* after the final judgment day when he moves from Hades to Hell? The rich man seems to be suffering so much right now, but Jerome's interpretation required the audience to conclude the rich man will suffer even more once he has been formally judged and condemned.

This play with the time elements invites Jerome to offer a parable of his own making to explain the truth of the rich man's pre- and postjudgment day torments. He told the story of a thief awaiting trial in prison. Jerome explained prisoners like such a thief already suffer the torments of life in prison—"the darkness, filth, hunger, creaking of chains, groaning of the fettered, weeping of those who are with him."[87] Jerome then added that, although the torments of prison are bad enough, they only served to prepare the thief for the worse punishments to come following his trial and condemnation by a judge. The thief dreads the future torments for he knows that they will be worse than what he is experiencing now. This, according to Jerome, was the state of the rich man in Hades. He was tormented by the fear of the punishments that surely awaited him following the day of judgment. The pains of this torment were so bad, in fact, that the rich man already in Hades asked for relief from the hand of Lazarus. Having completed now what he started at the beginning of the homily, Jerome was satisfied that he had said enough and concluded the homily.

Social Thought of the Homily

In the course of the homily, Jerome made at least three socioethical arguments. First and foremost, he promoted the right use of superfluous wealth. Like Asterius, Jerome believed that it was okay to have wealth so long as a person willingly distributed to the needy that which is superfluous, although his definition of superfluous was more narrowly defined than what was discussed in the previous chapter.[88] Whereas other authors, Asterius included, had argued that superfluous wealth is that which is *beyond what you need,* Jerome here suggested superfluous wealth is that which *you would otherwise waste*. Jerome told his audience, "Why do you save what is superfluous to your pleasures? Give in alms to your own member what you waste. I am not telling you to throw away your wealth. What you throw out, the crumbs from your table, offer as alms."[89] To Jerome, the heart of the rich man's problem was pride. To a prideful man, there is no such thing as superfluous wealth; all wealth is merited. Pride in one's wealth and social standing manifests itself in disdain for the lives and fortunes of others. Pride looks down on those who do not achieve similar or proportional levels of success. It disdains those who try to meet their needs in ways (e.g., by begging) other than the ways in which the rich person met his or her needs. Moreover, this disdain takes no account of the abilities or disabilities of those who are the objects of scorn. The rich man paid heed neither to Lazarus's hunger nor to his incapacitating illness, both of which surely prevented his ability to work. Besides all this, the social ideas at the time all but doomed beggars like Lazarus to an early death, and this fact alone probably comforted the rich man in knowing that he would not have to bear Lazarus's appeals for help for too long.

What this immediately suggests to our context is that there is no particular need for individuals to dispense with superfluous wealth. Rather, there is need to dispense with pride. If dispensing with superfluous wealth is necessary for that to happen, then so be it. Certainly, one may dispute what is or is not superfluous wealth, but Jerome's definition unnecessarily blurs the line further. A debate over what is or is not wasteful spending of one's wealth can easily digress into class warfare. Besides that, wasteful spending of one's wealth can easily have the beneficent effect of employing many people in crafts, trades, and service industries. Christian social thought would be well advised to steer clear of this difficulty by articulating superfluous wealth in terms of just use and just ownership of goods. Put another way, those like the rich man in Jesus' parable are obliged to take account of the common good; in this way, pride yields to humility and the considerations of others.

This is why Jerome put forward his second argument, that the antidote for pride is compassion. Addressing the rich man, Jerome said, "Most wretched of men, you see a member of your own body lying there outside at your gate, and have you no compassion?"[90] Jerome did not let the rich man off the hook for suggesting he did not notice him or that no one made his presence known. Lack of compassion prevented the rich man from seeing those around him with needs. Underlying Jerome's argument for compassion is the Christian anthropology of inherent dignity for all who bear the *imago Dei*. Lazarus is referred to as a brother (*fratrem;* ll. 150–53) to the rich man, notwithstanding Jerome's allegory about the rich man's five brothers. Lazarus is also called "a member of your own body" (*partem corporis tui;* l. 29). Giving alms to a person such as Lazarus is nothing less than giving them to your own flesh (l. 33).[91] In a way, then, the charge to be compassionate bears within it the seeds of its own, self-centered rewards. If you are compassionate toward others, God will be compassionate toward you in the life to come. Jerome has reiterated this biblical concept in such a way that his audience can now see the inversely proportional relationship between pride and compassion, with charity being the tipping point leading to divine rewards.

Jerome's third socioethical argument in this homily was that the poor are obliged to suffer their indignities in this life. For whatever reason, God had seen fit to allow the events of this world to take their course. The rich seem to get richer at the expense of ever greater numbers of poor people. While oppressed people have to wait until the afterlife to find relief for their suffering, Jerome was satisfied that the proud will have their day in God's court soon enough. He wrote,

"If ever we are sick, if we are beggars, if we are wasting away in sickness, if we are perishing from the cold, if there is no hospitality for us, let us be glad and rejoice; let us receive evil things in our lifetime. When the crushing weight of infirmity and sickness bears down upon us, let us think of Lazarus."[92] There is a long-standing debate in liberation theology circles about just how far those who are oppressed may go to remove the yoke of their oppressors.[93] It was safe for Jerome to preach that the poor and oppressed ought to look to Lazarus and to suffer their indignities with honor in this life. As well, it was certainly the case that the Christian Church played a significant role in mitigating the suffering of many in late antiquity, but *mitigating* the suffering was all it was prepared (and perhaps able) to do.[94] Jerome and others in his day trusted that God would restore the fortunes of the righteous poor in the afterlife.

Fourth, Jerome, like Asterius, distinguished between the righteous and the unrighteous poor. Whether one is righteous or not depends upon a willingness to bear the burden of poverty with dignity, accepting it as a gift from the Lord. Jerome went so far as to call Lazarus the rich man (l. 240), as evidenced by the eternal rest with Abraham he received. Thus, to be righteous is to be truly rich. Translated into the modern context, then, Jerome invites Christian social thought to emphasize the cultivation of virtues, particularly patience (for the poor) and charity (for the wealthy). Injustice, one may conclude, is not systemic, but a result of the poor behavior of a few.

Fifth, and perhaps most prominently, Jerome emphasized the eschatological implications of social concern. The difficulty here, of course, is that most audiences today have little understanding both of eschatology and of what happens to people in the afterlife, to say nothing of the disagreement among Christians whether or not anyone would be judged "evil" by God and so sent to an eternal hell. Having said that, one suspects Jerome would argue with some success that there are eternal consequences (without being specific as to what those consequences are) for how one treats the poor in this life. It is a matter of self-interest to rectify one's relationship with God now by altering one's disposition toward wealth before it becomes too late. Not only this, Jerome could articulate the sense of freedom that comes from detachment (ἀπαθεία). Particularly in a Western context, one values the opportunity to remake oneself, to rebuild one's image, to start over. Jerome's eschatological concern offers this opportunity, a new way of living and of being human.

Summary

We have seen that Jerome shares with Asterius a deep disdain for the corruption of the soul, the profligate lifestyle, and the neglect of the poor associated with superfluous wealth. Since pride lay at the root of this problem, compassion is the necessary antidote. Also like Asterius, Jerome encouraged the poor to bear their burden with dignity and to await God's restoration in the afterlife. Jerome's play with elements of time in the parable seemed to justify his free construction of a new dialogue between the characters of the story, inserting himself and his audience into the mix. This also influenced Jerome's interpretation of the chasm metaphor. Jerome's call for his audience to get right with God now suggests that the chasm separates not only saints and sinners in Hades, but also the present life and the afterlife. Moreover, the reason the chasm is a chasm at all is because the disposition of a human soul remains fixed once crossing into the afterlife. The torments of the afterlife keep the unrepentant soul in a state of wishing to repent, but for all the wrong reasons.

Perhaps we may even add another point to the discussion: Jerome constructed a world his audience then could imagine inhabiting. The rich man's groanings, yearnings, wailings, and pains all resonate with a human person's own search for rest in God. Jerome's audience was able to draw from the rich man's story both admonition and consolation, reminders about the fragility of life, and encouragement to be faithful.

CHAPTER SUMMARY

This chapter began with a survey of the authorial intent model, taking its cues from the work of Friedrich Schleiermacher and Wilhelm Dilthey. The model aimed at interpreting a text with a view to its author's intention in writing it. Especially in Schleiermacher's text, it was clear the model was especially concerned to raise questions about just how much one can know about a text, about its author, and about the author's context. Yet knowing the potential problems was deemed to be, in fact, half the battle of interpretation. Being conscious of what you do not know actually is a step in the right direction.

The authorial intent model was then applied to the first numbered homily in the extant collection of Asterius, bishop of Amasea in the late fourth and early fifth centuries. We know precious little about the author, but the text of the homily still yielded several insights about the author's intent. Addressing what was likely an audience comprised of wealthy and working-poor people (likely none who were πτωχοὶ), Asterius's intent was to encourage a "measured" approach to wealth, one devoid of excess. His audience was asked to live in accordance with their needs and not their wants, to measure the use for necessary things at any given time, and to measure their attitude toward both wealth and need. Also, it was important to measure life and the value of the created world. Wealthy people who kill silkworms and shellfish to create fanciful clothing, for example, have exceeded necessity. They have violated the natural resources God had given to humanity. This and other critiques of improper measurement, alongside proposals for what Asterius might consider better uses of wealth, were teased out in the final segment summarizing Asterius's socioethical ideas for the benefit of contemporary, Christian social thought.

Next, the authorial intent model was applied to Jerome's *Homily 86*, which, like Asterius's homily, was an exposition of Luke 16:18–30 and preached during either the later years of the fourth century or the early part of the fifth century. Jerome likely preached this homily to a largely, but not exclusively, monastic audience in Bethlehem. Jerome's intent with the homily was to encourage an eschatological orientation in his audience's attitude toward wealth. The overwhelming majority of the homily, in fact, was concerned with the torments of the rich man in Hades for having neglected the needs of the poor while on earth. This eschatological orientation to wealth conforms to few of our modern sensibilities, so Jerome's homily invites Christian social thought to rethink its privileging of justice in our context over ultimate justice in the age to come.

It is precisely because of limitations such as the one just mentioned that Christian social thought might be a bit leary of the benefits ultimately derived from patristic texts with an authorial intent hermeneutic. There are other hermeneutical models that take greater stock of modern sensibilities in their reading of ancient texts such as these by Asterius and Jerome. The following chapters explore the potential benefits of the second model in this study, a hermeneutic of distanciation.

Chapter 4

A "DISTANCIATION" MODEL

The previous chapter both introduced the two case study texts for this book and applied to them an "authorial intent" model of interpretation. The chapter also teased out the contributions of these texts' socioethical ideas to Christian social thought in our day, chief among them being a renewed concern among individuals for those with needs in our societies. This chapter turns from the "authorial intent" model to a "distanciation" model. The model comes from the hermeneutical ideas of Paul Ricoeur, a French philosopher of the second half of the twentieth century. The chapter begins with a summary of the distanciation model. Then, following the pattern laid down in the previous chapter, the distanciation model will be applied to each of the two case study texts. One final note: it bears repeating that the survey of this and the other models in this book are just that—surveys. Experts of Ricoeur's thought, for example, will no doubt wish that something had been phrased differently, that some other text or passage of his had been cited than those below, or that one or more additional ideas had been explained. Nevertheless, it is hoped that what is said in summary fashion below faithfully represents an outline of Ricoeur's ideas about distanciation.

SURVEY OF THE "DISTANCIATION" MODEL

Since we are transitioning here from an authorial intent model to a model that consciously distances itself from the author of a text, it should be said at the outset that a growing body of literature on "structuralism" had grown up during the early to mid-twentieth century that aided this transition. Structuralism clarified the role of symbols in language as a tool for analysis of narratives, be they textual or cultural.[1] This includes, among other things, paying attention to tropes, oppositions, and mimesis (i.e., the representations of reality) in texts. The fascination with structuralism in language led proponents not only of the distanciation model but also of the two models discussed in the following chapters to consider texts as having a voice independent of an author. Paul Ricoeur, following upon the heels of Hans-Georg Gadamer in this respect, accepted structuralism's invitation. However, at the end of the day, both Gadamer and Ricoeur were skeptical of structuralism's project of detaching the meaning of symbols from the author of the narrative, and thereby detaching them from having some *particular* meaning. The very fact that an author constructed a text in the first place gives the symbols within that text meaning. At the same time, Gadamer and Ricoeur were quick to point out that these meanings quickly move beyond, or distance themselves from, those intended by the author when the text is read outside that author's own context. To unpack this distanciation idea, we review first the contribution of Gadamer, and then turn to some texts of Ricoeur.

Gadamer's magnum opus *Truth and Method* may be better titled "Truth is not found in method."[2] This is because truth is not discovered by any particular method. Gadamer wrote his dissertation on Plato, so it should not be surprising that he affirmed the existence of the Good. Yet, a person's access to the Good is shrouded by the limitations of human finitude. Gadamer accepts that some access to the Good is available in every part of creation; consequently, texts—themselves created works—are one access point to the Good. However, in saying they are one access point, it is acknowledged that there exist many access points. If it were theoretically possible to inquire about the Good along every access point (including more than just texts), then it may be the case that the Good can be known. However, Gadamer harbors a justifiably deep skepticism of humans so availing themselves.

In *Truth and Method,* this skepticism plays out in his clarifying what is the distinctive contribution of the human sciences vis-à-vis the natural sciences. The natural sciences refine the task of observation. The human sciences refine the task of interpretation. Gadamer takes to task the ideas of Spinoza, Schleiermacher, Dilthey, Ranke, and others for their unwarranted positivism about human ability in the task of interpretation.[3] For Gadamer, the intention of an author of a work of art (i.e., texts as well as paintings, music, and other works of art) is unknowable. Traditions that have built up around works of art are helpful to us only to the extent that they serve to clarify our understanding of the present.

Thus, for Gadamer, readers of written texts, for texts are our concern here rather than other works of art, must assume several responsibilities. One responsibility is to have a correct understanding of texts.[4] We acquire representations of texts within our consciousness, but these are not dictated to us by the original composer of the text. Not only is it entirely impossible to know with certainty the mind of the original composer, even if we could know it, what we would know would be unhelpful to readers living outside that context. Yet, Gadamer was quick to point out that this does not entirely free written texts for any reading whatsoever. We may be free to read texts into different contexts, but at one point every text was the product of a creative act and so is limited by what was *not* done in its production. To be clear, then, Gadamer argues that interpretation of texts by readers is re-creation, but not of the creative act that brought the text into existence but of the created work that infuses meaning into a context.

Another responsibility is to appreciate the difference between interpretation and historical study.[5] Historical study explores the world behind the text in order to discover something about the past.[6] The one engaged in historical study is not interested in applying the text to him- or herself. He or she does not see him- or herself as the text's addressee. The task of interpretation, on the other hand, places the reader in the text's line-of-sight. The reader sees him- or herself as the text's addressee, and so is responsible to bring the written text into dialogue with his or her own context.

Still another responsibility is to place on the table for review the reader's entire worldview.[7] Gadamer suggested there must be a "prejudice against prejudice" (Vorurteil gegen die Vorurteile).[8] "The recognition that all understanding inevitably involves some prejudice gives the hermeneutical problem its real thrust," he wrote.[9] Readers are obliged to raise their prejudices to a conscious level. This allows the prejudices to be checked and so to exclude anything that prevents the reader from understanding the text. There will, of course, remain hidden prejudices, but this actually invites the reader to ever expand the community of readers with whom he or she reads a text. Indeed, a text may—and perhaps ought to—be read more than once with increasing fruitfulness.

In that spirit, there is at least one further responsibility, and this is really a culmination of the earlier ones: the responsibility to develop a "hermeneutical consciousness."[10] Principally, this is acquired by asking questions, attempting answers to questions, and asking what is behind those answers. Questions expose prejudices, move us beyond mere historical inquiry, and challenge accepted authoritative interpretations. Openness to reading a text in wider and more diverse communities is one feature of this development. According to Gadamer, a hermeneutical consciousness culminates in a readiness for experience, for new and more experiences.[11] The reader understands that he or she needs such experiences to be a more adept interpreter.

All of this is important for our investigation into the reading of patristic homilies. On the one hand, patristic homilies are texts that lend themselves to interpretation. On the other hand, the texts purport to connect the reader rather directly to Truth, to the Good, that is, to God. They draw links between who God is and God's work in the world. They outline paths along which Christians may travel to connect with God. For that reason, the patristic homilist does not see himself as providing only one access point among many to Truth,[12] and, even if he did, he would not accept the idea that Truth still eludes the listener. Indeed, the homilist and the laity alike recognize that God, in his essence, remains to some extent unknowable, but this is not the same as saying that one cannot be sure God as Truth is ever known at all. The listener is sure that he has been taught by the homilist *some* Truth, has been given *some clear* understanding of Truth, all the while acknowledging there is still more to learn.

I suggest that, for the patristic homilist's audience, then as now, they believe themselves to have sidestepped some of Gadamer's concerns about human confidence in being able to know God. Yet, Gadamer anticipated this maneuver when he incorporated into his discussion an analysis of the role of homiletic proclamation, at least by Protestant ministers.[13] A Protestant audience makes an immediate separation between the words of the preacher and the words of Scripture with respect to authority, he suggested. The preacher is trusted to give applications but never to be the voice of Truth. The audience ascribes to another text, the Bible, inherent authority in proclaiming Truth. For Gadamer, this reveals a fore-understanding (*Vorverständnis*) provided by faith, and so places it outside the realm of the human sciences.[14] For this reason, the entire religious enterprise, not unlike the judicial one, is outside the realm of the human sciences for Gadamer.

Nevertheless, one wonders what would happen if patristic homily audiences carried into their hearing or reading of the homily the hermeneutical task of the human sciences. That is to say, what would happen if we today read patristic homilies without a fore-understanding that either they or the biblical texts on which they are based teach *some* Truth or *some clear* understanding of Truth? What if, instead, they are accepted as dialogue partners about what *might be* Truth? Specifically, one may ask what can be gained from them with respect to our construction of social ethics. It seems this may obviate Gadamer's concerns.

Gadamer brought to the foreground in discussions about hermeneutics the problem of human finitude and the need for a skepticism about our ability to have discovered either Truth itself or some clear understanding of it through any particular method. After Gadamer,

Truth may no longer be found in method, but perhaps that only qualifies the Truth side of the equation. A valid method or methods remain very much in play. On this score, we may turn to the hermeneutical ideas of Paul Ricoeur. Methodological considerations and questions fill most of his texts. In what follows, this study summarizes these methodology considerations and questions in terms of his concern with a text's genre, his concern with a community's reception of its past (in this case, Christian social thought's reception of its past, patristic social thought), then his understanding of the interpretive task itself, and, finally, his understanding of Christian contributions to social ethics.

Before interpretation begins in earnest, Ricoeur believed it was vital to determine the genre of the text with which one is working. Genre is a means of production, for it is created the moment an author composes a text.[15] Since our concern here is with homilies, we are reading texts within a community of faith that operates at the limits of thought. In his work *Conflict of Interpretations,* Ricoeur argued *arche* and *telos* are the limits of thought.[16] Between these two points, we operate with reason. Texts that go beyond the *telos* or turn back beyond the *arche* take us away from reason and aim instead toward what Ricoeur called "conviction."[17] The Bible is just such a text. It asks its reader to move beyond reason to conviction, which then moves the reader into action.[18] Christian homilies, like our case study texts, straddle reason and conviction; this is because they form arguments about the biblical text with reason, presenting the ideas of the biblical texts as more or less obvious when read with the lens of the Christian community's faith. Yet, because they recognize the biblical texts are read correctly only with the faith of the community, homilies help their audiences grasp the conviction(s) to which the biblical narratives point. Homilies lead their audiences into a better grasp of the narratives. More to the point, homilies instruct Christian audiences in how to write themselves into the biblical narratives.

Although Ricoeur did not, as far as I can tell, reflect on the place of patristic homilies in the Christian tradition, one senses that he would find them to be similarly capable of teaching us how to write ourselves into the biblical narratives. The problem, however, is that they come from a very different time and place than our own. So, this entire project is about inviting Christian social thought today to bring back material it has nearly forgotten. Ricoeur's *Memory, History, Forgetting* provides us some guidance in this task.[19] The search of one's or a collective's memory of a past is not always successful, but when it is successful, the aim is to create from it what Ricoeur called "happy memory."[20] Ricoeur agreed with Husserl that there is a break between presentation of an event to our minds (i.e., what we saw, heard, etc.) and the presentification of a memory of the event in our minds (i.e., what we would say we saw, heard, etc., if asked about it in, for example, a police investigation).[21] The difference between what was presented to our minds and what is the presentification of the memory of the event recalled to our minds is the role of imagination. Ricoeur acknowledged imagination fills in gaps in the wider context of events that we thought we remembered as they actually were.[22] Yet, recollection is a process of searching for the truth. Faithfulness of memories is the goal of recollection, so humans likely would be remiss if they felt too much of their memory was imagination.[23]

What is called for, then, is the regular exercise of memory. Memory is exercised in two ways. At a cognitive level, there is the welcoming or the reception of an image from the past. Sometimes those images are received spontaneously (which the Greeks called μνήμη); other times the images are recalled after great effort (what the Greeks called ἀναμνήσις), since memories may have been "forgotten."[24] It is the search for memories that is of particular concern here, for such effort confronts the problem of memories that have been repressed.[25] We repress memories for a variety of reasons—sometimes political (e.g., amnesty programs), other times personal (e.g., child abuse)—but Ricoeur argued repression harms the entire project of the duty of memory, of the duty of faithfulness in recollection, and that is justice.[26] It is at this point that one senses the connection between this project on memory and the concern of my project here.

Tying together the idea that the goal of recollection is to create a "happy memory" and that the duty of memory is justice, the move toward happy memory is a move toward justice. Not all memories are, of course, happy ones, in the usual sense of the term. However, that is not Ricoeur's point. His point was that recollection ought to *create* happy memory. That is to say, the search of memory and the restoration of repressed memories create something new in the mind of a person or of a community. Meaning is then constructed from that recollection. When that meaning suggests something particularly sinister, such as abuse, genocide, or political repression (examples Ricoeur mentioned), then it is the task of the person or of the community to attach to that meaning a new action: forgiveness.[27] Forgiveness is what creates happy memory out of the recollection of decidedly unhappy events in one's memory. Forgiveness is precisely forgiveness because it has not forgotten the events of the past, but because it has remembered them, has identified them for what they are, has ascribed meaning to them, and now is ready to move beyond them. The unhappy past has not changed, but our memory of that past will now be conjoined to a memory of forgiveness for that past.[28]

To connect what has been said thus far with our project of reading patristic socioethical texts, one begins by noting, as I did in the first chapter of this study, that patristic social thought is a lost, or perhaps we may say now a repressed, memory to Christian social thought in our day. The aim is to recollect that memory, to create from it happy memory. There are, of course, unhappy aspects of the patristic past, so Christian social thought today may join forgiveness to its recollection. Together, recollection and forgiveness help to reconcile Christian social thought to its patristic past. Thus, we may say not only is the aim of Christian social thought justice for our world, but the aim of Christian social thought's happy memory of its patristic past is justice in how that past is treated.

Since appropriation of ancient texts, such as our case study texts, into contemporary discourse is a necessary stage in interpretation, we turn now to a consideration of Ricoeur's particular ideas about the hermeneutical task. In three different collections of essays Ricoeur organized his thoughts about the questions of hermeneutics.[29] One overarching idea that emerges from these texts is the problem of distanciation, which is that aspect of our engagement with a text that accepts its otherness, especially with respect to its situatedness in another time and space. Ricoeur wrote of distanciation that it "is constitutive of the phenomenon of the text as writing . . . it is the condition of interpretation."[30] The very fact that someone writes anything down at all belies their own acceptance of this distanciation. We wish for our ideas to have life at a later time, even if it is something as simple as writing down a grocery list for later use. We want our texts to outlive the precise time and space in which they were written. This is actually a positive aspect of texts, as Ricoeur notes: "The dominant problematic is that of the text, which reintroduces a positive and, if I may say so, productive notion of distanciation. In my view, the text . . . is the paradigm of distanciation in communication. As such it displays a fundamental characteristic of the very historicity of human experience, namely, that it is communication in and through distance."[31] As one methodical consideration, then, recognition of distanciation ought to be at the forefront. It is this that begins the disruption of any inclination we might have to bond with the intent of the text's author.[32] Once free from this inclination, there opens before us what Ricoeur calls a "surplus of meaning."

Ricoeur argued that this surplus of meaning emerges from the "world of the text," which is "the central category, both for philosophical hermeneutics and for biblical hermeneutics."[33] The world of the text is the locus of interpretation. The text has meaning. It unfolds a world before the reader, or before a community of readers. The new meanings created add to the distance between author and reader, which in turn validates the capacity of a text to create meaning in the first place.

Breaking with authorial intent in favor of textual meaning, readers are free to construct meanings that make sense in their own contexts. Moreover, textual meaning grows as a text is read and received over time within a community. So, whether a reader is aware of it or not, he or she constructs "new" meaning(s) for a text with the benefit of a community's experience of reading the text. One thinks here especially of biblical texts, which have this role within the Jewish and Christian faith traditions, but also of patristic texts, for they have had a long life of being read and interpreted within the Christian community. It would be rare, indeed, to discover a text that one is the first ever to interpret. And not only within communities is this the case, but also across communities to which a text may appeal and within the lifetime of a single reader. The ability for a text to speak to different situations in different communities or at different times in the life of a person attests to the surplus of meanings accessible from every text.[34]

Ricoeur organizes his explanation about how readers construct new meanings in terms of three parts of a hermeneutic circle: naïve understanding, configuration, and appropriation.[35] These three parts seem to correlate with Ricoeur's three parts of a narrativity circle, which he called *mimeses*.[36] What we glean from both the hermeneutic and narrativity circles is that readers must first come to terms with their predispositions, prejudgments, and prejudices. Following that, readers are obliged to pay attention to the many details of a text, especially to any stylistic elements that provoke the reader's imagination (a nod to structuralism). Finally, readers are to bring the ideas the text called to mind into dialogue with the reader's own context (i.e., there is to be a fusion of two horizons: that of the text and that of the reader). At this final stage the reader asks what about his or her own context must be reexamined, rethought, or reconfigured in light of the ideas called to mind by the text.[37]

As it turns out, we do not have to wonder at what Ricoeur thought about a fusing of the horizons between early Christian texts and Christian social thought today on the topic of social ethics, for he wrote an article on just this topic published in 1966, "Le projet d'une morale sociale."[38] In this article, Ricouer evaluated the contribution of the Christian tradition to the construction of social ethics. He argued there are no longer universal norms either that may be elicited via exegesis from the biblical texts or from the history of Western culture that may be construed as a social ethic. What is more, even if there were, Ricoeur argued that the culture has already disbanded any notion that such norms are helpful. Although the world today values humanity as the unique subject of history, it seeks to personalize relations that otherwise would remain anonymous in an industrial society. Thus, people today both want and need particulars, they want and need analyses of concrete problems, they want correctives for local problems. From this perspective, Ricoeur argues, the Christian tradition is not at all in a weak position; on the contrary, it has a wealth of concretizations, particulars, and analyses of local problems in its biblical stories and in its preaching of the stories. Ricoeur summarized the argument of the article this way:

> On the one hand, it is necessary to look in social reality for the discontinuous, unstable, and varying points of insertion for Christian preaching. On the other hand, it is necessary to start from the work of specialists bearing on such well determined points as work, business undertakings, information, and so forth, and not to look for their insertion in a system—in a whole—but to disengage their most concrete and historic affinities with biblical teaching. In short it is necessary *to place the biblical concrete in direct contact with the social exact.*[39]

To translate this into the terms of this project, the exegesis of many patristic texts would not then suggest to us a grand socioethical narrative. That ship sailed long ago. Even if it had not, though, today's society would find it remarkably unhelpful. Instead, one should focus on patristic social preaching's practice of applying concrete biblical texts to concrete local situations. Might not the patristic texts invite us to imagine the application of these biblical texts in new ways? The proposal seems promising.

To conclude this section, the distanciation model invites us to read texts in a completely different way than we encountered with the authorial intent model. The distanciation model begins with the text itself, not the author of the text, and the world of the text, not the world of the author, is the locus of interpretation. Furthermore, no text is off limits in a distanciation model, including especially those readers have sought to repress, since out of the reading of every text may come happy memory. In fact, recollection of the past yields justice, even if forgiveness is needed for some parts of the past. In any case, openness to recollection moves the reader forward into some more technical aspects of the reading task. Specifically, the distanciation model calls upon the reader to maintain a prejudice against prejudice, which is to say the reader must come to terms with his or her prejudices, prejudgments, and presuppositions. The reader then cultivates a "hermeneutical consciousness," which is the reader's awareness of his or her responsibility to question the text, to pay attention to its details—in short, to play with the text. Playing with the text and letting the text play with oneself creates a fusion of horizons. As a result, new meanings emerge, and the more one engages in this play the greater the opportunities for creating ever new meanings. Thus, for our patristic texts, the more frequently Christian social thought is willing to play with the texts in light of concrete, contemporary concerns, the greater the opportunities for the patristic texts to generate new meaning.

APPLICATION OF THE MODEL TO ASTERIUS OF AMASEA'S *HOMILY* 1

Turning first to Asterius's homily, the distanciation hermeneutical model highlights this text's propensity to bring the biblical account to life with elaborate stories and images from everyday life. Through these stories and images, one is convicted of the many times and many ways in which one, like the rich man, lives for this world, revels in its unacknowledged pettiness, and pays no heed to what shall be one's disposition in the life to come. For having accomplished this, the homily gives the parable new urgency. The homily invites the reader to consider the truth about what he or she really values in this life, something most people would rather not be asked to do.

This is aided, to some extent, by the fact that the homily has collapsed two aspects of the biblical story's "otherness." In the first place, and this was noted in the previous chapter, the homily treats the story not as a parable, but as one about real events with real people. Already, then, the homily brings the lives of Lazarus and the rich man into closer proximity to our own by treating them as real rather than fictional people. In the second place, the homily collapses the time that separates their lives from our own. At §9.3, where Asterius wrestled with the true identity of Abraham's bosom, Asterius said, "Why then, wonderful Luke—for I will speak as if you are both visible and present—[do you speak of Abraham's bosom rather than the bosom of other saints]?"[40] The author of the biblical narrative is no longer a person from a four-hundred-year-old past, but he may be said to be among Asterius's audience at the time of the homily itself. Thus, at the same time as we become cognizant of our distance from the author of the homily, we become equally aware of the homily's desire to collapse whatever time separates us from the biblical event (since it is not seen as fiction) itself. Having said this, we may turn now to several of the stories and images used in the homily that suggest to us paths upon which we may write ourselves back into the biblical story.

First, the homily has constructed new stories about what it means to live like the rich man. In the previous chapter, it was noted that Asterius spoke of how rich people love fancy clothing, eat expensive food, and throw lavish, unseemly parties. Beyond the technical and rhetorical aspects of these descriptions for embellishing the biblical texts, a distanciation hermeneutical model would have us pay special attention to the ways in which these texts reveal something deeper about ourselves. For instance, in relating the stories about fanciful clothing worn by the rich, Asterius acknowledged that the reason the rich do this is because it attracts to them the attention and awe of the crowd.[41] Asterius's intention was to highlight the rich man's pride, and that is as far as the authorial intent model would take us. Yet, a distanciation model invites us to see the story equally as a critique of the nonrich. This is because such people give the rich people exactly what they desire: attention and awe, and they do this precisely because, deep within themselves, they wish that it was they who could wear such clothing. They wish that it was they who were the objects of attention and awe. So, the problem of the rich man is a problem of every person. It is only the case that some have the means to carry their sin of pride to its fullest measure. In this way of thinking, the lack of wealth may actually become a cause for rejoicing among the nonrich. Once the sin of pride within them has been exposed, the nonrich may rejoice that their lack of wealth limits their commission of further sin.

Likewise, when rich people wear their "power suits" around town they are, according to the homily, "playing the part, but not being serious."[42] Clothing becomes a distraction not only to the nonrich, but also to the wearers of the garments themselves. One imagines such a person admiring him- or herself in the mirror for a long period of time, fancying him- or herself to be more important than he or she is. They attend business meetings and presume that their expensive suit, rather than the quality of their product or service, will impress a client. The rich person may even train him- or herself to talk in ways that match the quality of the suit, but, again, all of it comes out of a prideful heart and not a genuine love or respect for others. Eventually, the ruse will be exposed, much as everything came crashing down for the rich man once in Hades.

Second, the homily's stories of the poor man, Lazarus, equally generate new ways of thinking about the biblical text. The homily told of his illnesses, his homelessness, his exposure to the weather, and the physical deformities that were a result of his leprosy. Lazarus called out but was not heard. Lazarus asked only for crumbs from the table but was ignored. To Asterius, this was evidence of the justness of the rich man's condemnation. Asterius said of the rich man that he treated Lazarus "as if he were a stone."[43] Yet, Lazarus was, for all intents and purposes, treated as a stone by Asterius, too, for Lazarus was deemed little more than a literary foil to expose the rich man's problems. Asterius nowhere examined why there are people like Lazarus in the first place. He nowhere asked how it can be that a baby born into a family, weaned and nurtured by a mother, and dwelling under the roof of a family home ends up leading a life like that led by Lazarus. No doubt there were many devastating events that led to this fate. Though it rightly described the plight of the poor man at the point in time in which he encountered the rich man, Asterius's homily did not turn back the clock to a consideration of these earlier events. Instead, it reveled in the justice Lazarus discovered when the clock moved forward to the point of his death. The avoidance of such concerns exploits prejudices in the reader, too. Thus, there is an opportunity for Christian social thought to overcome both the problem of the rich man and the problem of Asterius's homily, that of treating poor people like stones. It may turn back the clock from the starting point of the biblical parable and treat the ailments of Lazarus's earlier life. It may explore the difficult childhood of people like Lazarus, the poverty of his parents, the lack of a proper education, the failure of a healthcare system that allowed his ailments to go untreated leading inexorably to leprosy, the discrimination he experienced in finding a job, the loss of his home to usurious debts he could never repay, and the abandonment by his friends. Asterius rightly cued our interest in the poor man's present condition, but the chain of causes that led to it deserves equal treatment.

Third, another story Asterius told was of the poor people he had seen in the judicial courts. "Every time, whenever I approach a ruler's judgement-seat, I have seen that all persons who break into homes and kidnappers, even thieves and robbers and murderers, too, were wanderers, houseless and homeless."[44] These are the unrighteous poor people, destined for eternal judgment like the rich man in the parable. Asterius's homily, then, invites Christian social thought to turn from any romantic naiveté of poverty in the biblical text but to know the world as it is. There are righteous and unrighteous poor people in the world, and our sympathies are to lie with the former. In particular for those who work alongside of and on behalf of the needs of poor people, Christian social thought certainly is aware of the complexities, and is not tempted to dilute the problems of criminal behavior among the poor. However, Asterius spoke of poor people he met at a particular point in their lives: standing before a magistrate being judged for their crimes. The circumstances of poverty that led to their behavior do not appear to mitigate either his or the magistrate's view. Christian social thought would do well to continue Asterius's vigilance against naiveté, but it would do well also to move beyond Asterius's interest in the one-time encounters with such poor people. Importantly, one wonders if such poor people are truly unrighteous. Perhaps the conviction of a crime and the punishment of a jail sentence are what is needed to turn the lives of these individuals around. One wonders if even one year later they might not be just as likely to convert to Christianity and be active members of a local congregation. The point is, Asterius confidently expressed a judgment on the lives of some poor people based on one, chance encounter. Christian social thought should develop a longer time horizon and be less inclined to pass judgment based upon any one single event in a poor person's life.

Fourth, Asterius's homily invites Christian social thought to revel in the torments of the rich man, for they signal the restoration of justice. Asterius suggested several directions this might take. One is the celebration of the rich man's death. He had "lowered that honored nature [i.e., his spiritual nature] to be in sympathy with the flesh that is from raw matter,"[45] and "did not leave behind a worthy memorial of his own life."[46] He, "dying the death of beasts," according to Asterius, was "covered in disgraceful forgetfulness."[47] Simply put, it was time for the rich man to go. Society was much better off without him. Another is the joy at the rich man's newfound poverty. It was sheer folly for the rich man to have ever believed that the wealth of the earth mattered. In Hades, it was all taken away, "as a beaten slave is deprived of possessions."[48] In Hades the rich man is "deeply humiliated... uttering complaints like a lamenting old woman."[49] There is no mourning the rich man, for he in Hades receives his due. Still another is the satisfaction of watching his cries for mercy go unheeded. Asterius wrote, "He seeks mercy, which he had not given when he had the power of benefiting another.... Such is the thoughtlessness of those who love the body. This is the end of those who love wealth and pleasure."[50] Then later, "Neither any confession of the justice of the judgment lightens the punishment, nor does pity for the one in torment lessen the penalty ordained."[51] This is the dark tone on which the homily draws to a close. Even if the damned repent and acknowledge their punishment is just, the punishment remains. Even if others pity the damned, the punishment remains. This eschatological approach has long been a part of the Christian tradition. For some in the community of Christian social thought, it is one of those aspects of the tradition from which it seems difficult to build a happy memory. For others, the permission to rejoice at the death and eternal torments of an oppressor or violator of justice is a fresh start to healing and peace. Such rejoicing fosters harmony between what one feels and what one is allowed to say. Acknowledging a victim's right to express his or her pain may encourage the victim then to take steps toward forgiveness and to create from the experience a better memory.

In keeping with the distanciation model's concern for genre, the study of Asterius's homily should ask in what ways it helps us write ourselves into the biblical narrative, to create new meaning out of the biblical text. At the end of the day, that is what Christian social thought desires for its readers. It wants its readers to find new meaning in the biblical texts; it wants to know how to employ the patristic texts as a tool in that endeavor. As we saw in the first chapter of this study, CST struggles at precisely this point. Thus, the distanciation model is particularly helpful since it encourages readers to look for the ways in which homilies like Asterius's write their readers back into the biblical stories. On this point, we have not been disappointed. The homily collapsed two "otherness" aspects of the biblical texts that brought it immediately to life. First, the parable was said to be about real people and real events. Second, the story's author, Luke, was questioned as though present with the reader. Lazarus, the rich man, Abraham in the afterlife—each one speaks to us, challenges us to live in a way that is pleasing to God. The homily also created new stories from current events. Each story exposed prejudices, arrogance, and pride within us. We find ourselves yearning to be more compassionate people for having read the homily. In sum, the distanciation model has moved us in a particularly helpful direction with respect to the overall project of Christian social thought.

APPLICATION OF THE MODEL TO JEROME'S *HOMILY* 86

Turning next to Jerome's *Homily* 86, the distanciation model opens several new ways of thinking about the biblical text and about particular problems in the field of social ethics. First, it is a text deeply concerned about the eschatological ramifications for decisions here on earth. There are two worlds of justice—the one visible to us now, which is rather more an experience of injustice, and the one that will be visible to us in the life to come, which this text leads us to believe will be a rather more shocking experience of justice. The finality of justice in the afterlife is not what we are comfortable hearing. This is probably due to the fact that, while we want justice in our world, we also are people who believe in second, third, and many further chances. We are uncomfortable with finality.

Concretizing the prospects for socioethical intervention, as Ricoeur would have us do, consider that in the United States many states during the mid-1990s adopted what are called "three strikes and you're out" laws (an analogy taken from American baseball).[52] After a third felony conviction, a person is sentenced to life in prison without the possibility of parole. So, a person will get a second chance, and even a third chance, but after that society is done with this repeat offender. Beginning in the mid-2000s, many Americans grew weary of the large numbers of people being caught up in this law, especially for felony offenses that most Americans are willing to pardon more than three times (including especially felony drug possession charges). So, what we have ended up with is nationwide attempts, most being successful, in repealing the "three strikes and you're out" laws. Americans want justice, but they want a justice that always leaves open the possibility of pardon and hope. *Homily* 86 leaves us with the uncomfortable feeling that a day is coming when that type of justice is no more. This is part of the "otherness" quality of this homily, but it suggests that, while we can, we let ourselves be who we are, be human and offer multiple chances to the penitent. Equally so, we may leave to God whatever he will decide to do in the life to come, nevertheless wishing that even then God will offer multiple chances to penitent offenders.

Second, the homily invites us to delight in a play with the two testaments of the Bible. Consider, for example, the homily's play with the connections between Lazarus and the lives of Moses and other Hebrew prophets (ll. 161–78).[53] Moses and the prophets wore rough clothing, lived in caves and holes in the ground, were poor, and suffered dangers and hunger throughout their lives. Moses and the prophets *were* Lazarus; Lazarus is every poor man who ever loved God. Later, the homily connects the love for poverty as love for

Christ (ll. 209–14). So, Lazarus stands for Christ. The parable, then, may be construed as a choice between loving wealth and the goods of the earth or loving Christ. From this one may draw further connections between this parable and the Hebrew Bible. For instance, Qohelet attacked wealth for its inability to make a person happy. So, too, Proverbs repeatedly subjugates wealth to the acquisition of wisdom. The fool who despises wisdom is the rich man who despised Lazarus. Genesis 3 was a choice between a love for the things of this earth and a love for the truths of God. Adam and Eve confronted Lazarus in the one restriction God had placed upon them: not to eat from the Tree of the Knowledge of Good and Evil. The point here is that *Homily* 86 has only just begun to open the door to our convergence of stories from across the testaments.

This play with biblical texts is matched, third, by the homily's equal intention to play with the dialogue of the parable itself. The biblical text is little more than a cue card to an extemporaneous speech. One is reminded here of Ricoeur's second stage of *mimesis*.[54] The biblical text's meaning is by no means fixed; the compactness of its narrative demands (nay, cries out for) an expansion into a dialogue with contemporary referents. Consider the following passage:

> "Send Lazarus to dip the tip of his finger in water." "Send Lazarus." You are mistaken, miserable man; Abraham cannot send, but he can receive. "To dip the tip of his finger in water." Recall your lifetime, rich man; you did not condescend to see Lazarus and now you are longing for the tip of his finger. "Send Lazarus." You should have done that for him while he lived. "To dip the tip of his finger in water." See the conscience of the sinner; he does not dare ask for the whole finger. "Cool my tongue, for I am tormented in this flame." Cool my tongue, for it has uttered many a proud word. Where there is sin, there is also the penalty for sin. "To cool my tongue, for I am tormented in this flame." How evil the tongue can be, James has told us in his Letter: "The tongue also is a little member, but it boasts mightily." The more it has sinned, the more it is tortured. You long for water, who formerly were so fastidious at the mere sight of smeary and spattered dishes.[55]

We may reorganize the same passage into four columns (see table 5a): (1) Jerome's citation of the biblical passage; (2) Jerome's dialogue with the rich man; (3) Jerome pretending he is the rich man; and (4) Jerome's pastoral exhortations to his audience. This is a delightful play with the biblical text. Not only had Jerome recited the biblical text and consequently addressed his audience as their pastor, but he has also inserted himself into the story both as Abraham addressing the rich man and, most interesting of all, as the rich man himself(!) explaining why he had behaved so poorly in his earthly life. Elsewhere in the homily Jerome played the role of Lazarus, so we have yet a fifth persona in other passages. To wit, one can imagine Jerome constantly changing his stance as he shifts between the many roles in which he cast himself for this homiletic play. In Jerome's way of thinking, the biblical text's meaning is by no means fixed; the compactness of its narrative demands (nay, cries out for) an expansion into a dialogue with contemporary referents. Indeed, one may imagine something like the version in table 5b. One could go on with this, but the point is clear. Jerome's homily invites Christian social thought to construct a play of its own with the characters in the biblical story. Every voice and line in the biblical story may be shifted around to create a new story worthy of a contemporary audience's sensibilities.

Fourth, in addition to this play with the dialogue of the biblical text, *Homily* 86 further plays with time elements in the biblical text. It does this while explaining one of the key metaphors of Luke 16, that of a chasm that separates sinners and saints in the netherworld. Our text first quotes the relevant biblical text, then exposits it, saying, "'Besides all that, between us and you a great gulf is fixed.' It cannot be bridged, removed, or leveled. We can see it, but cannot cross it. We see what we have escaped; you see what you have lost. Our joy and happiness multiply your torments; your torments augment our happiness."[56] Notice the text's change of the "we" of Lazarus and Abraham in Luke 16 to the "we" and "our" of the preacher and his audience. As could Lazarus and Abraham, so too the preacher and his audience could see that the damned are tormented, and that, even if they wish to help, the nature of the afterlife is such that they cannot. Indeed, that Jerome and his audience have escaped torments

Table 5a. Jerome's Dialogue, *Homily* 86, ll. 110–24

	(1) Citation of biblical text	(2) Jer. *to* rich man	(3) Jer. *as* rich man	(4) Jer. to audience
1	"Send Lazarus to dip the tip of his finger in water."			
2	"Send Lazarus."			
3		You are mistaken, miserable man; Abraham cannot send, but he can receive.		
4	"To dip the tip of his finger in water."			
5		Recall your lifetime, rich man; you did not condescend to see Lazarus and now you are longing for the tip of his finger.		
6	"Send Lazarus."			
7		You should have done that for him while he lived.		
8	"To dip the tip of his finger in water."			
9				See the conscience of the sinner; he does not dare ask for the whole finger.
10	"Cool my tongue, for I am tormented in this flame."			
11			Cool my tongue, for it has uttered many a proud word.	
12				Where there is sin, there is also the penalty for sin.
13	"To cool my tongue, for I am tormented in this flame."			
14				How evil the tongue can be, James has told us in his letter: "The tongue also is a little member, but it boasts mightily." The more it has sinned, the more it is tortured.
15		You long for water, who formerly were so fastidious at the mere sight of smeary and spattered dishes.		

Table 5b. Jerome's Dialogue, *Homily* 86, ll. 110–14, a contemporary version

	(1) Citation of biblical text	(2) Jer. *to* rich man	(3) Jer. *as* rich man	(4) Jer. to audience
1	"Send Lazarus to dip the tip of his finger in water."			
2	"Send Lazarus."			
3			Send Lazarus? Like pearls before swine, that would be like sending Mother Theresa to help *you-name-it-self-destructing-celebrity* improve his or her image!	
4	"To dip the tip of his finger in water."			
5			You want relief from pain? You should have shared your wealth with your family members when they got in over their heads on a home mortgage loan. You should have supported the local food bank when it made an appeal for contributions. You should have been more just with the salaries you paid to your workers.	

is all the more reason for joy! To Jerome, since his own experience in the afterlife and that of his audience will be that of Lazarus and Abraham, there is no reason not to anticipate what that will be like by imagining himself and them in Lazarus's place in the story.[57]

There is something troubling about the feeling of satisfaction the homily conjures up in reference to the suffering of the rich man. "Our joy and happiness multiply your torments; your torments augment our happiness."[58] This goes back to the earlier discussion about justice; how often it is that we find ourselves joyful at the punishment of a person at the hand of whom we have been victimized. For example, not only is it the case that we desire a criminal to be in jail, but we also want him or her to suffer while in jail. We do not want him or her to have access to television, libraries, exercise gyms, continuing education, and so on. We want the person who harmed us to feel the pain of knowing that we are enjoying freedom while he or she has lost it. We want him or her to suffer not only physically (e.g., confinement in jail), but also emotionally or even spiritually. This is the dark side of vengeance to which few will admit, but this homily does not hide it as a fact in the audience's soul. In fact, the homily celebrates it. Exposing the problem is helpful, but the homily nowhere suggests what Christian social thought should rather do in our context, which is to explain the danger such vengeance and bitterness poses to our own souls.

Returning to the chasm metaphor, the homily continues to use it in a play with the biblical text. For many churches in our context, the chasm metaphor is a prooftext for the existence of a literal eternal hell. Once in hell, there is no possibility of redemption, so the best course of action is to align oneself with God in the present life. This homily plays with the metaphor in much the same way. Consider, for example, that whereas in Luke 16 the rich man arguably is portrayed as penitent, even if to no avail, Jerome portrays him as opportunistic. Jerome wrote, "Torments, not the disposition of your soul, force you to repent."[59] This is a very interesting point, since it reveals that, to Jerome, this chasm is more than just an unbridgeable divide. It is also a way both of *marking* and *blurring* the boundary lines separating this life and the next. On the one hand, the chasm reminds one that death is the time limit for repentance, but, on the other hand, the dispositions of one's soul continue from this life to the next. The reason one cannot be reformed in the afterlife is because one cannot be repentant for any of the right reasons. Torments cloud the soul in the afterlife much as greed or pride clouded it in the life on earth.

Fifth, the homily invites us to play with another metaphor in the biblical text. In Luke 16:21, the parable says of Lazarus that he desired only the crumbs that fell from the rich man's table. To Lazarus, the crumbs were certainly food, and it would seem natural to interpret the reference to the crumbs as food as an instruction to one's audience that it is important not to deny food to the poor. Indeed, this comports well with Matthew 25:35. Yet, our homily turns the "crumbs" into a metaphor, first, for superfluous wealth. Superfluous wealth, like crumbs, is wasted resources. Such excess was not consumed in the proper way (i.e., to meet the needs of others), so it has been wasted. By the same token, since it has been wasted, superfluous wealth is like crumbs in that both are destined for the rubbish heap. At death, the goods, land, or houses acquired with superfluous wealth will be taken away from us. They will flee from us just as quickly as we go from them. They may even end up in the hands of those we wish had not received them. The homily also turns the crumbs into a metaphor for the *damna,* that part of the rich man's resources that have already been determined to be a loss. One thinks here of bread in a supermarket that is nearing its expiration date. Since it is no longer saleable, it is a loss, and the store wants to replace it on the shelf with fresh, saleable bread. The supermarket could throw the bread away, but it would be preferable to give it away to a needy person. It is the same to the supermarket whether the bread is placed in the rubbish heap or given to a needy person, but it would mean life to the person who had no bread. Wasted resources, expired or worn-out goods ready for the rubbish heap, and goods we hold onto not wanting to believe they are destined for an eternal rubbish heap are but three illustrations of how "crumbs" may be used profitably for rethinking superfluous wealth in Christian social thought today.

Sixth, *Homily* 86 reflects an otherness in distinguishing between the righteous and the unrighteous poor. Poverty for the sake of Christ (i.e., being a monk) is the type of poverty that makes you "blessed" (ll. 306–13). It is largely impractical in our context to define righteousness in terms of monastic voluntary poverty. Yet, the social ethic at work here is a concern to give up what one possesses in order to follow Christ wherever he may lead one to go. Thus, the homily encourages the reader to consider there is a missional aspect to the idea of poverty. Being known in one's social setting as one who voluntarily lives on less invites evangelistic opportunities. Take, for example, the decision on the part of a person not to own a television. Such a person will not have to advertise this fact, for it will be immediately obvious once this person is engaged in conversations at work with others about what had appeared on the television or what happened in a televised sports event the night before. Or consider the individual who insists on bicycling to work or to school in a context where motorized transportation is normative. Again, the evangelistic opportunity to speak about sacrifice for the sake of Christ and for Christ's creation will present itself naturally in conversations with others. As the homily suggests, our aim is to love those like Lazarus, to love poverty. It is a short leap from that to loving Christ, who, as we noted above, ultimately takes the place of Lazarus and poverty. When Christ is the object of our love, then a love for evangelical poverty grows more naturally within us.

There are further aspects of the homily that estrange it from our experience. The homily castigates the memories of two persons, Mani and Marcion. Time has so successfully expunged their memories, precious few would have any idea who these individuals once were, to say nothing of understanding why they might not have liked the Old Testament. The homily also castigates Jews for not having listened to their "brother," Jesus, when he rose from the dead. The text implies the Jews were stubborn much as the rich man's "brothers" would also be stubborn even if Lazarus could rise from the dead to appear to them. This stereotyping of Jews, not unlike the propensity to excoriate perceived heretics, in patristic texts is one area in which Christian social thought has an opportunity to build a happy memory. The patristic authors made mistakes; in this case, justice is best served when the mistakes are acknowledged, this part of the tradition is repudiated and then set aside in favor of its more productive elements. In a way, patristic social thought finds a seat at the table of Christian social thought when these happy memories are created.

To conclude, the distanciation model reveals several ways in which *Homily* 86 helps readers construct new meaning from the biblical text. For one thing, the homily exploits the reader's discomfort with the finality of eternal judgment while equally exploiting the satisfaction we feel at watching unjust people get punished. The reader is left wondering how to balance cultivating compassion and forgiveness in this life with leaving to God whatever will be in the afterlife. Another point is that the homily plays with the biblical text in several interesting ways. It strings together texts from the Hebrew Bible and the New Testament in unexpected ways. It embellishes the dialogue of the characters in the story. It encourages new ways of thinking about the chasm and the crumbs-from-the-table metaphors. It also blurs the lines between Lazarus, poverty, and the person and work of Jesus. The homily argues that to love people like Lazarus is to love poverty, to love poverty is to love Jesus, and to love Jesus is to love living out an evangelical form of poverty. In the end, the reader can become rather overwhelmed at the sensory overload in this homily. So many aspects of the biblical text are moved, twisted, and reshaped into new ideas that one senses the possibilities for creating new meaning out of this biblical text are limitless.

CHAPTER SUMMARY

In this chapter we have explored the potential contributions of a distanciation hermeneutical model. A reading both of Gadamer's *Truth and Method*, secondarily, and Ricoeur's works, primarily, was the basis of our understanding of what it means to distance ourselves from the author of a text and to learn how to "play" with a text to create new meaning. With respect to our project of reading early Christian socioethical texts, three things have become clear. First, the early Christian texts are a guide to writing ourselves into the biblical narratives. Second, the early Christian texts confront prejudices, prejudgments, and presuppositions we have about what biblical texts mean. At the same time, they also try to form new prejudices, so not only do we become conscious of the distance between ourselves and the authors of the text with this model, but we also appreciate the distance between ourselves and the text. For example, Ricoeur's idea of allowing forgiveness to fashion happy memories encourages us to appreciate the distance between patristic texts that incorporate attacks on the Jews or heretics and ourselves who seek understanding of members of other religions or other denominations. The patristic texts invite us to play with the biblical narratives at the same time that they seek to play with us and we want to play with them. Third, and finally, the need to apply the new meanings we create to as concrete a situation as possible suggests each early Christian text may be read fruitfully many times over the course of one's life. Every new socio-ethical problem today raises new questions for us to pose to the patristic text and to the biblical text through the patristic text.

Chapter 5

A "NORMATIVITY OF THE FUTURE" MODEL

In the introduction, this study tipped its hat toward the model that is the focus of this chapter, so it would not be inappropriate to remind the reader here that this study argues that this model holds significant potential for reading patristic socioethical texts in light of the contemporary concerns of Christian social thought. By comparison to the other models in this study, the normativity of the future model (hereafter, NOF) is quite new. It appeared first in a paper prepared for a 1996 conference at the university in Tilburg, The Netherlands. Since then, its proponents, Reimund Bieringer and Mary Elsbernd, have published together and separately a number of works in which this model is articulated, expanded, and applied to an ever wider collection of texts. Most recently, and particularly important for our study, Bieringer applied the model to Theodoret of Cyrus's *Discourse on Providence* 6, a socioethical text from the fifth century that wrestled with the problem of God's sovereignty in the face of human poverty and suffering. This chapter begins with a review of the corpus of publications from Bieringer and Elsbernd in which the NOF model is constructed and applied to various texts. Then, expanding upon Bieringer's work with Theodoret's text, this chapter applies the NOF model to our two case study texts, Asterius of Amasea's *Homily* 1 and Jerome's *Homily* 86.

SURVEY OF THE NORMATIVITY OF THE FUTURE MODEL

Bieringer and Elsbernd chronicled the genesis and key developments of their model in an introduction to a new book they have edited and to which they have contributed several articles.[1] In the introduction Bieringer recalls the article he wrote for the 1996 conference, which was later published in *ET Bulletin*,[2] which started him thinking in the NOF direction. However, he steps back to acknowledge the influence of previous scholarship. Importantly, Sandra Schneiders's work on dialogue and normativity in biblical interpretation, which is connected to her work on feminist readings of the Bible, alerted him to the intrinsically oppressive aspect of the biblical text.[3] Bieringer also notes his debt to Gadamer and Ricoeur, to whom Schneiders too was indebted. Bieringer acknowledges that Ricoeur's emphasis on the "world of the text" as the locus of interpretation was particularly helpful.[4] Eventually, this led to his consideration of the possibility that a future-oriented hermeneutic could solve the problem of interpreting oppressive biblical texts. This idea, combined with the notion of dialogical dimensions in theological discourse, about which he had written in a paper for a 1995 conference, eventually led to the first, joint publication of Bieringer and Elsbernd.[5] Their 2002 book, *When Love Is Not Enough: A Theo-Ethic of Justice*, asked what would be the Christian vision for social justice in the present if the eschatological future that God will bring defined its vision.[6] Since that time, several further articles have appeared in which Bieringer and Elsbernd, either separately or together, have explored the contribution of NOF to Catholic social teaching,[7] to anti-Judaism in the Gospel of John,[8] to religious education of children and students,[9] and, as noted above, to the text of Theodoret of Cyrus.[10]

Having reviewed the history of publications by Bieringer and Elsbernd on the NOF model, it remains to articulate the details of the model. First and foremost, NOF is dialogical. In Bieringer's 1995 paper (pub. 2002), he situated NOF in the authority rubric articulated by Schneiders.[11] There are absolute/unilateral and relative/dialogical authorities, with a further segmentation of the dialogical type into evidential and disclosive authorities. Evidential authorities are those that a person discovers to be self-evident, say, in a text. Disclosive authorities appeal to a person to accept their authority by disclosing something attractive about them. According to Schneiders, one example of this would be the claim of a suffering human being to compassion. The suffering person is the authority that, by disclosing the reality of his or her suffering, appeals to those who are witnesses of the suffering to accept the suffering person and to offer compassion. This is how God works within the biblical text, according to Schneiders, appealing to our inner desire to want to love God by revealing something attractive about itself. In agreement with Schneiders, NOF argues disclosive authorities are the only ones truly capable of drawing people into a genuine commitment or faith. Yet, Bieringer's article then does something quite interesting. Just because Schneiders and others *want* God and the biblical texts to operate as disclosive authorities, that does not mean they actually *do* operate in this way. Taking sample passages from the Gospel of John as a case study in teasing out an answer to this problem, Bieringer concludes that some texts in the gospel do seem to be disclosive (e.g., Jn 1:38, 42, 50, and 2:1–11, among others).[12] Yet, other texts are decidedly absolute/unilateral (e.g., Jn 3:19–21, 8:24).[13] All Bieringer needed was one example to the contrary of Schneiders's position, but he found two in just the first half of one biblical text. The Bible is not disclosive, after all. However, rather than this being an argument against a preference for disclosive/dialogical authority in the NOF model, it actually became a proof for another element of the NOF model.

Actually, before turning to this issue, it is important to back up and highlight a presupposition of the NOF model that bears on its reading of texts, particularly the biblical text. Taking seriously post-Enlightenment critiques of the Bible as a product of human, rather than divine, labor, NOF does not presume the authors or communities of authors behind biblical texts operated under the inspiration of God's spirit. Rather, the biblical stories are accounts of human dialogue with God. One need not look any further than the Hebrew Bible's accounts of Abraham and of Moses to see that, from the beginning, God has sought dialogue partners among the human members of creation. The Bible's stories are accounts of dialogue, and they invite readers today to have a similar dialogue with God.

Returning now to the problem raised above, the fact that some biblical texts evidence an absolute/unilateral authority, particularly with respect to matters of who is or is not among the elect of God, could very easily be a reason to dismiss the Bible as a relic of the past best left in the past. Yet, the NOF model proposes instead that such passages be treated as opportunities to project a better future. This aspect of the NOF model is similar in some ways to Ricoeur's notion of making a "happy memory" from oppressive texts that was discussed in the previous chapter. Since Ricoeur published his work in 2000, it is surprising not to find within it a citation of Bieringer's 1997 article. Likely, Ricoeur's and the NOF's ideas in this regard developed independently along different trajectories. In any case, again drawing upon the work of Schneiders and her argument that the biblical text is inherently oppressive, the NOF model proposes identifying absolute/unilateral texts as "lines of evil." John's condemnation of those who do not believe in Jesus as morally evil (Jn 3:19–21, 8:24) reflects not the divine word of God revealed in a text whose author was inspired by the Spirit to write it. On the contrary, and as discussed above, it reflects the views of the early Christian community who wrote it, likely during a time of feeling both "beleaguered" and fearful.[14] Thus, it may be said thus far that NOF prefers the dialogical model for disclosing authority, particularly in how biblical texts are read in communities today. Where the biblical text discloses itself absolutely/unilaterally, then NOF invites the reader to see this as evidence of the sinfulness of the human author.

Having said that, NOF does not give up on the prospect of using an inherently oppressive text, including those that too frequently employ absolute/unilateral authority, for the benefit of understanding not only the word of God but also a Christian ethic for life in the present. On the contrary, such texts equally possess "transformative potential." The biblical texts, like other texts, are symbols with the potential for a surplus of meaning.[15] Early on, Bieringer wrote only of their ability to propose "an alternative world."[16] Eventually, though, the NOF model argued the alternative world is, in fact, "God's dream of an inclusive future" or "God's dream of all-inclusive love."[17] Finally, it was expanded to the following: "In determining what in a text is sin-filled and what is grace-filled we propose the following criterion: inclusivity that makes possible a future for all. When we say "all," we refer to human and non-human creatures, past, present and future generations, without discrimination according to gender, race, class, health status, sexual orientation, ethnicity, religion etc."[18] To NOF, no part of the biblical text is unfruitful. The grace-filled and the sin-filled elements both are capable of bringing the future crashing into our experience of the present, transforming our vision of what the present ought to be.

The capacity of every part of the biblical text to accomplish this within an NOF framework has given rise to the consideration of how NOF might transform the educational contexts of our day. This is especially prescient, since most students have a visceral reaction even to being asked to read the biblical text, to say nothing of being asked to engage critically its arguments.[19] Previous religious education models stressed a monological approach, "in which an omniscient teacher has the task of imparting the pre-given knowledge (mostly reduced to content) to passively receptive students."[20] The dialogical nature of the NOF model, according to two articles of which Bieringer was a coauthor, is well suited to the ways in which postmodern students approach texts, particularly "classical" ones. If a student is willing to entertain the notion that the Bible is a "classic" text among the world's literary tradition, much as Shakespeare's plays would be seen to be, then the student has created for himself a "fictional contract" with the Bible.[21] What this means is that the student has opened him- or herself to a dialogue about the meaning of various biblical stories, about the future and the eschatological hope different stories project, and about truth claims in the stories, all without submitting to a priori truth claims. The benefits for the instructor and for a religious education class environment are immediately obvious. Whatever hostility may exist between the Bible and students yields to an engagement between, or rather a fusion of, the horizons of the biblical texts and the students' own lives.

If it were not by this point already clear what might be the application of the NOF model to patristic socioethical texts like our case study texts, Bieringer's analysis of Theodoret of Cyrus's text is instructive.[22] Theodoret's sixth *Discourse on Providence* argued that wealth and poverty both are useful for life in this world, and Theodoret directed this argument toward those (presumably poor members of his audience) who were complaining about economic inequality. Theodoret responded to three supposed objections of this latter contingent: (1) sinners are wealthy, but the virtuous are poor; (2) riches are unequally distributed; and (3) most of the wealthy are immoral.[23] Since it is not our aim here to rehearse the content of Theodoret's text, it suffices to say that Theodoret's replies to these objections are less than satisfactory. Under the NOF microscope, several problematic aspects of Theodoret's replies are exposed. First, he "downplays the seriousness of the problem of poverty that his opponents address."[24] Not only does extreme poverty complicate the acquisition of virtue for the poor, according to Bieringer, but it also is the result of injustice on the part of the wealthy. Theodoret wrote what he did from the assumptions that God is responsible for the inequality and that it is a help to salvation for the poor. He legitimated this support for inequality with Paul's body-members metaphor (1 Cor 12:12–30), which by all accounts was rather an attempt on Paul's part to promote equality. To Theodoret, inequality actually sustains human life in that it creates a differentiation in the labor market. If everyone were rich, the argument runs, no one would want to do the more menial tasks necessary for a healthy society.[25] All of these ideas of Theodoret are "sin-filled elements" in his text. Yet, NOF does not consider the text hopelessly irrelevant, for, indeed, every text has the potential for projecting a future world. In this text's case, one such projection is its assumption of "a world in which everyone is well."[26] Another projection is that everyone is equal from the perspective of God's original design with creation. It is remarkable Theodoret can hold to this ontological equality at the same time as he legitimates socioeconomic inequality. Finally, Theodoret projects a world in which God desires health, happiness, and blessings for the poor. He had argued that God directly cares for the poor while leaving the rich to care for themselves with their financial resources. Bieringer concludes his comments on Theodoret's text with these words that will deserve repeating at the end of our analysis of Asterius's and Jerome's homilies, "[I]n dialoguing with the ancient text of Theodoret, we respect the irreducible otherness which we encounter in it. . . . At the same time in the dialogue we go beyond reconstructing the past by engaging the future dimension of the text."[27]

Before concluding this review of the NOF model, it is worth noting that NOF has yet to ground its claim—biblically, philosophically, ideologically, or otherwise—that the future is an inclusive one in which God's love for all is revealed. Much rides on this particular future within the NOF model. It is the one and only control placed on dialogue with texts.[28] Yet, this "future" sounds a lot like what one hears in twenty-first century discussions about Western political, economic, and ecological utopias. Is this "future" really bound to our present myopia? Or are there biblical texts that suggest God has an inclusive future for all? Is this future a function of natural law? Since NOF is still a relatively new model with a promising future (*sic*), it behooves its advocates to lay some further groundwork for its claim that God intends this particular future over possible others.

At this point, the study turns to an application of the NOF model to our two case study texts. In doing so, it will aim at exploring the lines of sin and grace in the texts. It will propose ways in which God writes straight with these crooked, patristic lines.[29] It suggests the ways in which these texts project a future that is helpful to the construction of Christian social thought in our day, a future in which the grace of God is embraced as present in every part of the creation.

APPLICATION OF THE MODEL TO ASTERIUS OF AMASEA'S *HOMILY* 1

The NOF model reveals four features of the world of Asterius's homily that project an inclusive future. The first of these is that the homily universally condemns the experience of and the suffering associated with poverty. In §4, Asterius decried those Christian rich persons who weave pictures of biblical scenes into their garments. Rather than drawing pictures of the story of Jesus healing the blind man, Asterius wrote, "Comfort the living and the one deprived of seeing with deeds of kindness."[30] Likewise, rather than painting pictures of Jesus feeding the large crowds, "feed the hungry."[31] There is no joy for those who suffer and are poor simply because they have been the subject of Jesus' concern. So, too, Asterius critiqued the rich for their love of adornment while the poor are "pitiably naked" (ἐλεεινῶς ἐκδυομένων).[32] The rich man's problem, in fact, was that he had no pity (ἐλεεινὸν, §6.2) for he who was pitiable. This is a genuine problem for the rich man. The word ἐλεεινός in the New Testament, at Revelation 3:17, is said of a rich person who falsely presumes upon his wealth. The problem is so bad, in fact, the verse concludes the rich man is πτωχὸς!

Later in the homily, when Asterius exposits the rich man's failure to give to Lazarus even the crumbs from the table, he is indignant that the dogs are fed better than Lazarus. Poor humans deserve better treatment than the animals. This is not to deny a place to the animals at the table, however, for, as will be explained below, the animals are given an equally prominent future in Asterius's homily. Still, by comparison to how the animals are treated, the poor are to be treated even better. Indeed, the experience of Lazarus was so evil, that were it not for a hope for a better future for people like Lazarus, Asterius wrote, "I should have cried aloud with indignation—that we who are created equal live on such unequal terms with men of the same race."[33] Thus, nothing about the experience of poverty is laudable. The inclusive future is a world in which God seeks to draw the poor, the suffering, and the oppressed to his side. Knowledge of this future heightens the sense of the injustice created by socioeconomic disparities in the present.

A second, inclusive future aspect of this homily is its belief in the underlying equality of all persons. This is particularly prominent in §7, but, arguably, it underlies the critique of the rich man's expensive tastes in clothing, food, and home décor of §§2–5. In §7, where Asterius spoke of the dogs being fed better than Lazarus, he wrote, "You did not consider your brother, who is of the same race, worthy of [the table crumbs]?"[34] It is a rhetorical question, of course. A few sentences earlier, Asterius signaled an even closer term of endearment by saying that Lazarus and the rich man were "relatives" (συγγενῶν).[35] Unfortunately, the rich man had treated Lazarus "as if he were a stone" (παρῄει δὲ ὡς λίθον), rather than treating him as a fellow human. Poor people and rich people are ὁμόφυλον, even συγγενῶν; that is how God sees the world.

This inclusive future among the human race extends also, interestingly enough, to the animal kingdom. (It would be interesting, in fact, if somebody would do a study on animals in Asterius's homilies, as they appear rather frequently). Indeed, the NOF model says that the inclusive future is for every part of creation.[36] In §2, Asterius expressed frustration with rich people who kill shellfish for their blood to make clothing dyes and who misuse the lives of Persian worms to create silk fabrics.[37] These creatures were not made for this purpose; rather, God provided natural, renewable resources for clothing, such as sheep's wool and flax. In the same way, in §6, Asterius wrote of the animals who are more "human" than the rich man insofar as they demonstrate solidarity with the suffering among their kind. "At least, when a hog is slaughtered, the rest of the drove feel some painful sensation and grunt miserably over the freshly spilled blood; and the cattle that stand about when the bull is killed indicate their distress by passionate lowing. Flocks of cranes also when one of their mates is caught in the nets, flutter about him and fill the air with a sort of grieving clamor, seeking to release their mate and fellow."[38] The earlier comparison between how the dogs are fed versus the denial of crumbs to Lazarus is equally important here. The dogs are loved, fed, housed, cared for, and so on. Indeed, the dogs become the symbol of how we are to treat every part of creation. The text's inclusive future reveals God's love for everything that he has created.

Third, there is something striking between the NOF model's idea of an inclusive future and this homily's teaching about the future. It is a problem, in fact, that we will encounter again in our examination of Jerome's homily. Both of our homilies examine a parable in which *the future* is precisely the motivator for action in the present. The problem, from the NOF perspective, is that the future of the parable is not very inclusive. Rather, the way in which it includes the unrighteous rich sits uncomfortably with the idea of God's eternal love for everyone extending into the eschatological age. Asterius's homily, like Jerome's, does not flinch at the dark end to which the unrighteous rich man's life is headed. In fact, Asterius celebrates it. In §5, Asterius says that at death, when the soul separates from the body, it is then that the unrighteous rich man's soul recollects its sins, but by then "repentance is futile" (μάταιος ἡ μετάγνωσις).[39] Likewise, in §12, when discussing the consequences of the chasm metaphor in the biblical text, Asterius wrote, "[N]either any confession of the justice of the judgment lightens the punishment, nor does pity for the one in torment lessen the penalty ordained."[40] The burden to get things straightened out in this life, while one can, is clear. There will be a future for the unrighteous rich person, but it will not be a pleasant one, and it will be a future shared only with other unrighteous people. The righteous will have a decidedly better future, one in which the love of God is expressed in terms of care and favor. Perhaps Asterius would also say the painful future to be expected of the rich man also is a consequence of the love of God, the love of God for justice. That may be one way of identifying the love of God expressed in separate-but-equal futures for the righteous and unrighteous.

Yet, it does not seem that the NOF model would have us construe the text this way. This idea of an eternal hell where repentance is no longer possible is a mark of sin in the text. Going further, the NOF model would suggest that not only has Asterius expressed his human sinfulness in this charge, but so too has Luke, upon whom Asterius has relied in expositing this parable. Luke has betrayed his human sinfulness by pretending this chasm metaphor and its associated consequences came from the mouth of Jesus. Luke had expressed elsewhere in his Gospel the love of God for all. In Luke 2:29–32, we read of the expectation that Jesus will be the savior both for the Gentiles and the Jews. Luke 3:4–6 recalls a prophecy of Isaiah that all the earth and every person will experience the salvation of God. In Luke 5:30–31, Jesus addresses the Pharisees, saying that he has come specifically to save the unrighteous and not the righteous. This is actually a critique of the hypocrisy of the Pharisees, but the fact that Jesus' concern was with the unrighteous, the sinners, is a contrast to Luke 16 where Jesus is quick to condemn the now-penitent rich man to a life of eternal separation from himself. No doubt we could cite other texts from Luke's Gospel, but the point is clear enough: from an NOF perspective, Luke has betrayed his human sinfulness in the parable of Luke 16, and this crooked line extends well into the late fourth or early fifth century with Asterius's homily.

At the same time, however, there is evidence even in Asterius's homily that he, too, sought to balance the difficulties the parable presented. In §9, Asterius explained that the bosom of Abraham actually is the bosom of Christ, and that it is Christ who makes himself a place of rest for the righteous (δικαίων).[41] In the next sentence, however, Asterius said that Christ is the savior of "all of us" (πάντων ἡμῶν) with no explicit limitation of ἡμῶν to the δικαίων.[42] Asterius is addressing his Christian audience, but, even if his audience included some non-Christian hearers, their presence would not preclude him from speaking in this presumptive way. Might it not be the case that Asterius saw the salvation of Christ in universal terms, even though, at the same time, he was willing to accept that some will continue to resist Christ's will? It should not be ruled out, for Asterius concluded his homily with these words, "Is the hand of the Lord not strong to save, or is his ear heavy that it cannot hear? But our sins stand between us and God."[43] It is we, sinners, who hold at bay the salvation of the Lord. God's will is for all to be saved. Asterius pleads with his audience to enjoy the favor of the Lord's salvation now, not to spurn God's advances.

Thus, even though we have encountered this crooked line extending from Luke's to Asterius's respective pens, we have nevertheless also encountered in each writer's text a vision for the great love of God for every member of his creation. We have seen the desire of God to draw everyone into a saving relationship with himself. This discloses for Christian social thought an inclusive future where the love of God will be made known to everyone. It invades the present with a call to foster that love for our ὁμόφυλον, our συγγενῶν. It demands proper use of the environment, including sustainable approaches to agriculture and animal husbandry. Even the crooked lines of this and Luke's text are capable of being made straight by God in the human experience of justice in our present.

APPLICATION OF THE MODEL TO JEROME'S *HOMILY* 86

We now apply the NOF model to Jerome's homily. In some ways, the issues are similar, since Jerome exposited the same biblical text as did Asterius. Yet, Jerome's homily is markedly different in rhetoric, concept, and even content. Thus, although there are some points of contact and overlap with what I said above in reference to Asterius's homily, Jerome's homily presents new challenges for applying the NOF model. I will now explore several ideas in Jerome's homily that project an inclusive future.

To begin with, Jerome thinks of poverty in decidedly positive terms. This comports well with his predominantly monastic audience, as we discussed in the previous chapter. Lazarus is not to be pitied, but to be followed. He is the one who receives eternal rewards; those who voluntarily accept poverty will receive eternal rewards. It was Lazarus, not the rich man, who was deemed worthy of a name in the biblical text,[44] which Jerome said was from "the kindness of the Lord."[45] It is Lazarus, not the rich man, who is carried along by angels.[46] It is he who receives succor at Abraham's bosom.[47] Jerome wrote, "If ever we are sick, if we are beggars, if we are wasting away in sickness, if we are perishing from the cold, if there is no hospitality for us, let us be glad and rejoice; let us receive evil things in our lifetime."[48] It is to be counted a joy if one suffers any of the types of things Lazarus experienced.

It seems, then, Jerome is entirely oblivious to the distinction between Lazarus's poverty and voluntary poverty; he is keen only on the shared experiences of Lazarus and his monks that poverty brings.

However, at the end of the homily, Jerome dabbles in a brief moment of sophistication. He wrote, "Poverty, too, has its martyrdom; need well borne is martyrdom—but need suffered for the sake of Christ and not from necessity. How many beggars there are who long to be rich men and, therefore, commit crime! Poverty of itself does not render one blessed, but poverty for the sake of Christ."[49] Here Jerome distinguishes between what he thinks are the righteous and the unrighteous poor. The righteous poor are those who voluntarily accept poverty for the sake of Christ; the unrighteous poor are those who are poor from necessity but want to become rich. Yet, what about people like Lazarus, who were poor from necessity but did *not* evidence envy of the rich? Jerome nowhere comments on this. He was so keen to connect the life of Lazarus to the life of an ascetic that he forgot about Lazarus entirely.

This is surprising, for Jerome repeatedly joined the biblical text in its criticism of the rich man. When the rich man asks Abraham for pity, Jerome responded that Abraham can give no pity. In one scene where Jerome acts out the rich man's part, he had the rich man recalling the story of the prodigal son, "Even though I am in the grip of torments, nevertheless, I call upon my father. Just as that son who squandered all his possessions calls his father, even so I call you father, despite my punishments."[50] Here, the rich man has accepted his eternal lot. We read later that Jerome and his audience find joy in the rich man's torments, much as the rich man's torments increase at the knowledge of these saints' happiness.[51] Yet, and as we noted in the third chapter, the justification for the pain and suffering of the rich man, according to Jerome, was his pride.[52] The rich man did not steal. He did not commit adultery. He was not envious. Presumably, like the rich young ruler who encountered Jesus (cf. Mk 10:17–22), the rich man in this parable would say, "I have kept all these since my youth" (Mk 10:20). However, unlike the story in Mark's Gospel, Jerome does not say to the rich man that he should have sold all of his possessions and given them to the poor. The rich man needed only to have dispensed with his pride.

In applying the NOF model to this aspect of Jerome's text, there is an aspect of human sin finding its way through the otherwise admirable call to voluntary poverty. The neglect of Lazarus, the neglect of the conditions that led Lazarus to the state he was in, the rich man's neglect of Lazarus's needs, and the rich man's only sin being pride—these are the ways in which Jerome's text conceals an inclusive future for the marginalized and for the poor who are such out of necessity. Yet, such crooked lines may be straightened. The underlying dimension to Jerome's text is that the lives of people like Lazarus are special to God, even if Jerome has mistakenly assigned that type of life only to ascetics. Also, that God deigns to call even the wealthy into a relationship with himself is equally admirable—again, though, in spite of Jerome's feeling that this call ends at the point of death. There are at least two other aspects of Jerome's text that project an inclusive future, and these begin from a more positive perspective than what I have noted thus far. They give the reader a sense that Jerome has eclipsed himself in his defense of the joy of poverty.

The first of these two is Jerome's belief in the inherent equality between people like Lazarus and the rich man on the basis of their common humanity. He expressed this view in two places. One is at lines 29–30. There, Jerome proposes that one symptom of the rich man's problem of pride is his lack of compassion for people who are suffering. "Most wretched of men, you see a member of your own body lying there outside at your gate, and have you no compassion?"[53] Lazarus is *partem corporis tui*. Jerome does not wish for his audience to become like the rich man. He urges them, "Give in alms to your own member what you waste,"[54] the "waste" being a reference to a rich person's superfluous wealth. Here, again, the needy person is identified as *membro tuo*. The other passage is at lines 150–56. In this text Jerome has begun his allegory of the five brothers.[55] The problem the five brothers (i.e., the rich man's five senses) have is that they, like the rich man to whom they are attached, do not love poverty. The rich man loved what his senses loved, which was wealth. Thus, neither the rich man nor his senses could love someone like Lazarus. More to the point, neither the rich man nor his senses could love poverty. "Since they were the brothers you loved, you could not love your brother, Lazarus. Naturally, you could not love him as brother, because you loved them. Those brothers have no love for poverty."⁵⁶ Importantly, Jerome has turned Lazarus into one of the rich man's brothers. He is now a kin of the rich man. Lazarus has become *partem corporis tui* and *membro tuo*. The inclusive future disclosed in this idea is that our experience of human fellowship is tied to our openness to seeing the other as part of ourselves. Indeed, to be human at all is to appreciate the diversity of the members of our body.

The second aspect of Jerome's text that projects a positive, inclusive future is his regular affirmation that God wants all to be saved. Whereas I more or less teased this aspect out of Asterius's homily, Jerome was rather more explicit. The first instance of this idea is at lines 109–10. After denouncing the prospect of the rich man receiving pity from Abraham, Jerome allowed that God may offer it. He wrote, "The Creator pities His creature; one Physician came to restore the dead, for the others could not."⁵⁷ Not only may God pity, but God already has pitied. Jerome refers to Jesus when he says the Physician came to restore the dead. Medical language for Jesus followed naturally from the language for salvation itself (χρίστος, i.e., an ointment for a wound; = *salve*).⁵⁸ The Father sending the Son to heal the wounds of the postlapsarian world is evidence of God's pity upon us. The homily nowhere suggests we should see this pity in anything less than a universal light, particularly due to the fact he addresses it to the rich man suffering in Hades.

A second instance of this love of God for everyone is Jerome's discussion of the place of Moses and the prophets in the economy of salvation. At lines 161–78, Jerome exposits the interchange between the rich man and Abraham over whether or not to send Lazarus to "save" the rich man's five brothers. Abraham's reply is that Lazarus will not be sent, for, besides, the rich man's brothers have Moses and the prophets to teach them. Within this discourse, at lines 165–69, Jerome wrote, "Why do you ask me to send Lazarus? They have Lazarus in Moses and the prophets. Moses was Lazarus; he was a poor man; he was naked. He esteemed the poverty of Christ as greater riches than the treasures of Pharaoh."⁵⁹ Recall earlier that we said Jerome fused the identity of Lazarus with that of the ascetic in his audience. Here, Jerome fused the identity of Lazarus with Moses and the prophets. *Moyses Lazarus fuit.*

Before going any further, it is important at this point to turn to the related discussion about Moses and the prophets a few paragraphs later in the homily, at lines 215–31. There, Jerome digressed into a critique of Mani and Marcion for their misdeed of separating the God of the Hebrew Bible from the God of the New Testament, preferring the former to the latter. One reason Jerome gives for justly condemning Mani and Marcion is that it was possible for Hebrew Bible characters to know Jesus, the Christ of the New Testament.[60] Jerome recalled John 5:46, in which Jesus acknowledged that Moses wrote about him in the Torah.[61] Thus, as far as Jerome was concerned, Mani and Marcion were wrong because they did not acknowledge that it was possible for people who had never met or known Jesus to nevertheless have known him in some other way. Abraham, Moses, and the prophets were but some examples of this knowing.

Now, tying these two passages on Moses and the prophets together, it seems that Jerome understood Jesus to have been present in the lives of any person who was like Lazarus. Abraham, Moses, and the prophets were like Lazarus; therefore it was possible for them to have known Jesus. Indeed, Jesus confirmed that these individuals knew him without having any idea about the incarnation. From an NOF perspective, Jerome's text discloses a world in which it is possible to have a saving knowledge of Jesus without being acquainted with the particular details of the incarnation of Jesus. What is required is to be like Lazarus. There is a mystical connection to living like Lazarus and having the knowledge of Jesus rooted within one's soul.

However, there is still one additional piece of evidence from Jerome's text that takes us further in this direction. In the concluding paragraphs of the homily, particularly at lines 269–301, we discover that Jerome set the bar of salvation at a surprisingly low height. While discoursing on the timing of the particular events of the parable, Jerome concluded that they must be happening at the moment Jesus was speaking, or, at the very latest, prior to the death of Jesus. This was because the thief who died with Jesus on the cross was supposed to enter with Jesus into paradise that very day (cf. Lk 22:43),[62] and once Jesus enters paradise, then the gates of Hades will be opened and everyone in it will come out to be judged.[63] Having secured the timing of the events in relation to the salvation of the thief being crucified alongside Jesus, the stage is now set for Jerome to argue that, if the thief can be saved, everyone can be saved. Consider how little information about Jesus the thief had. Jerome wrote,

> The thief was the first to enter with Christ; his great faith merited the greatest of rewards. His faith in the kingdom was not attendant upon seeing Christ; he did not see Him in His radiant glory nor behold Him looking down from heaven; he did not see the angels administering to Him. Certainly, to put it plainly, he did not see Christ walking about in freedom, but on a gibbet, drinking vinegar, crowned with thorns; he saw Him fixed to the cross and heard Him beseeching help: "My God, my God, why have you forsaken me?" Under such circumstances, he believed, O fickle, fallen state of man![64]

Jerome then adds that Peter and John had abandoned Jesus after promising to stay by his side.[65] The bar of achieving salvation is so remarkably low that even a thief with the least amount of information about Jesus was capable of expressing faith and entering paradise. Peter and John, with comparatively far greater knowledge, do not reveal so steady a temperament, although they, too, surely entered paradise.

Thus, we have three pieces of evidence from Jerome's homily that suggest to us in more or less unequivocal terms not only that God *wants* all to be saved, but that God has lowered the bar to salvation so low that there is little excuse for anyone not to be saved. God took pity on the human race and deigned to enter into it himself by taking on human flesh. Yet, even before the incarnation, it was possible to have saving knowledge of Jesus by choosing to live like Lazarus. Finally, even without any more basic knowledge than a fear of God and a belief that Jesus died not for any sins he committed, which was the only confession of faith we get from the thief on the cross (Lk 22:40–41), it is possible to be saved. Taken together, these elements of the text disclose an inclusive future in which the knowledge and love of God is made known to all for it is a consequence of

God, rather than humans, having pity and so taking the initiative. Thus, all are welcome at the table of the Lord. The evangelistic consequences of this future in the present are obvious, and equally important are its socioethical consequences. Following in God's footsteps, Christian social action in the present ought to direct its efforts to lowering the bar for access to justice and to upending assumptions about who is and who is not worthy (cf. the thief vs. Peter and John) to be the beneficiary of God's love.

In sum, Jerome's text has disclosed several elements of an inclusive future. The text's praise for the joys of poverty betrayed its author's sinfulness, but these crooked lines are capable of being made straight when the underlying assumptions of the equal worth to God of people like Lazarus and even the sinners like the rich man are drawn out. Jerome, like Asterius, did not waver in his insistence that the human nature everyone shares is the basis of this inherent equality before God. Finally, God does not distinguish between persons in his pity for the human members of his creation and in his desire to draw all persons to himself.

CHAPTER SUMMARY

This chapter introduced the NOF model, which has been developed since the mid-1990s by Reimund Bieringer and Mary Elsbernd. Like the distanciation model of the previous chapter, this model identifies the world of the text as the locus of interpretation. The problem, however, is that the world of the text often projects a world we would not wish to inhabit. Taking a cue from the work of Sandra Schneiders, the world of the text—the biblical text, at least—is deemed inherently oppressive. Thus, the NOF model asks what of the world of an ancient text, be it biblical or patristic, discloses an inclusive future. It is an inclusive future that becomes normative for the present; an inclusive future unsettles and shapes meaning in the present.

At a practical level, this is accomplished by identifying and analyzing the lines of sin and grace in ancient texts. It is accomplished by proposing how God may write straight with whatever lines are found in the text that sin has made crooked. Asterius's homily disclosed a future in which the love of God will be made manifest to all, and one in which every part of creation is treated as a sharer with us in this divine love. Jerome's homily, too, confirmed the equality of all people before God. Jerome also emphasized the great lengths to which God has gone and to which he will continue to go in drawing all persons into a saving knowledge of himself.

At this point, we turn to a consideration of our final, hermeneutical model. The "new intellectual history" model also has its roots in the post-Romantic hermeneutics of Gadamer and Ricoeur, as we have seen also in the NOF model. By the same token, the model draws heavily upon the poststructuralist literary theories of Derrida, Foucault, Barthes, and others. So, the next chapter takes us in yet another new direction with respect to how best to appropriate patristic socioethical texts for the benefit of Christian social thought in our day.

Chapter 6

A "NEW INTELLECTUAL HISTORY" MODEL

In the preceding chapters, we have completed a review of three hermeneutical models. Each model has emphasized something different: authorial intent, distanciation, and the future that a text projects. In this chapter we turn to our fourth and final model. This model has been variously described as postmodern, literary, poststructural, and deconstructionist, among others, but the title "new intellectual history" is given to it by Elizabeth Clark, whose ideas will be the focus of this chapter. (What, precisely, is "new" about this model will be explained below.) As Clark herself traced in her 2004 book, *History, Theory, Text,* her approach to texts is heavily influenced by the work of theorists whose work often passes under other names, including the work of Jacques Derrida, Michel Foucault, Roland Barthes, Michel de Certeau, and Dominick LaCapra. Certainly, we could easily have devoted our attention here to the work of any one of these writers. However, Clark is a historian of Christianity in late antiquity, so Clark's publications are a treasure trove of examples of how to apply this new intellectual history model to early Christian texts.

Indeed, Clark has so many publications—no fewer than eighty articles and books, an equally large quantity of book reviews, and likely a countless list of conference papers—that one can agree with a comment once made by David Hunter that reading Clark's book, *History, Theory, Text*, which is a summation of her entire scholarly enterprise, is an exercise in catechesis.[1] The weight of her many years of interacting with literary theorists is on display in this book. It is appropriate that the analysis of the intellectual history model that follows begins with this book. Then, we turn to a selection of Clark's publications, especially her more recent ones, in which she highlights different applications of the model to patristic texts. Following that, I apply the intellectual history model to my two case study texts. By comparison to the other three models, the invitation of this model to play with the texts expands our horizons quite dramatically.

SURVEY OF THE INTELLECTUAL HISTORY MODEL

As has already been indicated, we enter into an understanding of the new intellectual history model of Elizabeth Clark with the publication in which she both situates the model on the hermeneutical map and even proposes some applications of it to particular research projects with early Christian texts.[2] *History, Theory, Text* begins with a critique of the history of *doing* history. Too many historians and readers of ancient texts stubbornly refuse to acknowledge that they are biased readers and interpreters of texts, and of the material of historical scholarship, more broadly. The "noble dream" of objectivity should have been shelved long ago.[3] Then, from its second through fifth chapters, Clark surveys key developments during the twentieth century in the fields of philosophy of history, hermeneutics, and, importantly, literary theory. Then, in the sixth chapter, Clark introduces the "new intellectual history" model, which, she explains, in its reincarnation within her own work, has moved beyond the model's earlier proponents, Arthur Lovejoy and R. G. Collingwood, whose support for intellectual history were still too "idealist."[4] In the seventh chapter, Clark explains how the work of later, twentieth-century literary theorists and philosophers has moved intellectual history toward deconstruction. Finally, in the eighth chapter, Clark highlights some examples of how the new intellectual history model may fruitfully be applied to early Christian texts.

Since the book is a direct challenge to the ways academics, particularly academics in history-oriented disciplines, have been conducting their business for decades, it is not surprising that her book provoked a host of reviews, some positive, others less so. In one case, a journal, *Church History,* on whose editorial board Clark has long been a member, included a response from Clark to a special issue that included several reviews of her book.[5] On balance, the reviews in this collection were supportive of her project of bringing studies of early Christian texts into dialogue with poststructuralist literary theories. However, one reviewer, Mark Vessey,[6] a professor of English literature with interests also in the texts of late antiquity, pointed out that poststructuralist literary studies already since the early 1990s has moved beyond the new intellectual history approach Clark advocates to "culture (or transculture) studies." So Clark admirably helps historians catch up to what had been the hot topic nearly two decades ago. By the same token, and here I rephrase Vessey's point, Clark has walked historians to the well of literary theory studies such that when they begin to drink from it on their own they will discover there the new interest in culture studies. Another reviewer, Kim Haines-Eitzen,[7] pointed out that Clark's book is but one of a handful of texts appearing at this time with more or less the same agenda. She cited LaCapra's *History in Transit* (2004), Terry Eagleton's *After Theory* (2003), and a 2003 lecture at Cornell University by Joan Wallach Scott entitled "Against Eclecticism." She also critiqued Clark for disregarding material aspects of a culture (to which I will return in a moment), such as monuments, relics, and even the forms and formats of the highly rhetorical, intellectual texts that Clark prefers.[8] This critique is similarly expressed in the review of Richard Lim, who felt that this more narrow approach to the historian's task actually makes them less of a historian and more of a specialist in "postmodern textual reading."[9]

Before this, too, becomes a review of *History, Theory, Text*, or a review of the reviews, we must turn instead to what Clark explains in the book are the particular contours of the new intellectual history model. Clark defines new intellectual history this way: "[It] explores the material embeddedness of ideas and their relation to power; it acknowledges the historian's present situation and interests. It appeals to climates of opinion, literary movements, ideologies and their diffusion, and to an anthropologically infused notion of culture."[10] Intellectual history is concerned with texts, that is, written "high" texts. That is because, in the main, high texts are what late antiquity has left for us; reading such texts is the gift historians of late antiquity may give to the wider academy and the wider public today.[11] So, it is not concerned with reading the more-or-less pedestrian texts of late antiquity, but with what some critics of the model say are only the texts of the elite. It is not even concerned with reading cultures as texts, which seems almost to relegate to a second tier of research the social history approach she brought to her own studies of early Christianity during the 1970s and 1980s.[12] This is why, in fact, Clark disagrees with Geertz's anthropological approach within poststructuralist literary theory, for he supplants written texts with "speech" at the starting point of his analysis.[13] In reaction to this, Clark agrees with the work of Dominick LaCapra in that texts are to be read as literary productions before they are mined for social data.[14] On this score, readers of texts are obliged to pay attention to language, rhetoric, gaps, absences, and to how differences are created by the text.[15] Thus, when in the last chapter of the book Clark "applies" the new intellectual history model to some examples of early Christian texts, although it is rather more a case of encouraging research to be done or citing it in the finished work of others, it is not surprising to see that she divides this piece into four parts: (1) authors, contexts, metaphors, and aporias; (2) ideology critique; (3) social-theological logic of texts; and (4) postcolonial theory.[16]

Under (1) she proposes analyses of texts where authorship is uncertain but where "author-function" empowered the text. She also raises questions about why collections of documents, such as the Nag Hammadi documents, were preserved. She asks how language about God the Father eternally begetting the Son in New Testament jargon came to be seen as asexual begetting in early Christian discourse. Under (2) Clark gives several examples, but one is pertinent to this study. She suggests there are competing ideologies operating behind the acceptance or the rejection of rich people into the Christian communities by Clement of Alexandria and the anonymous Pelagian author of *On Riches,* respectively.[17] It is these ideologies that determine their reading of Mark 10, rather than Mark 10 determining their ideologies. As for (3), Clark explains that texts arise through particular social-theological dimensions. In the case of Gregory of Nyssa's *De vita Macrina,* one discovers a Macrina who sounds much more like Gregory. Social and theological reasons dictated this style of writing, Clark suggests, but this does not mean one can say we come only to know Gregory here. Rather, we come to know a Christianity that Gregory believed was open equally to women such as his sister, despite the fact her own ideas get dissolved into something of his own. Finally, for (4) Clark cites the work of her former student, Andrew Jacobs, who applied postcolonial theory to a reading of texts and material culture that expose how the traditional Jewish homeland of Judaea came to be taken over by Christians as their "holy land."[18]

To sum up what has been said thus far, Clark's appeal for a "new intellectual history" model asks of readers of premodern texts to expose the many ways in which these texts distort, diffuse, or otherwise conceal agendas. This is done in part by identifying gaps, aporias, ideologies, and rhetorical constructions. In the next publication by Clark that we will consider, additional items may be placed on this list: intertextuality, textual implosion, and changing contexts. Such were the tools premodern texts used to distort, diffuse, and conceal their agendas.

As has already been noted, Clark is conscious of the shift since the early 1990s in her own application of the new intellectual history approach to early Christian texts. Her 1999 book, *Reading Renunciation: Asceticism and Scripture in Early Christianity,* is probably the best evidence of her thorough application of the model.[19] In this book Clark explores how early Christian writers (she focuses on Origen,

Jerome, Chrysostom, and Augustine) manipulated the exegesis of biblical texts in order to justify renunciation and the ascetic life. For example, they make texts such as Ephesians 5:22–33 sound like God treats marriage as a condescension to the problem of human sin. Manipulating the meaning of biblical texts came so easily to the writers because they held to a decidedly premodern view of the Bible, that it is a text inspired by God. The meaning of Ephesians 5:22–33 *must* be consistent with texts such as 1 Corinthians 7:32–35, despite the two "seeming" to represent different points of view. Not only that, the Christian writers dissociated the Hebrew Bible from its Jewish context, believing instead it was to be read together with the New Testament. This, too, encouraged play and manipulation of texts across the two testaments.

Now, in terms of what form that play took, Clark focuses mostly on these writers' use of intertextuality, which is the creation of new meaning for one text by tying it together with other texts.[20] Clark writes, "A prime function of intertextuality in ascetic exegesis . . . is to press a mildly ascetic text in a more ascetic direction by the citation of other verses that are taken to counsel repudiation of 'the world.'"[21] One of the literally dozens of examples Clark gives is Gregory of Nyssa's argument that Genesis 1:27b, on sexual differentiation, is a departure from the prototype, Christ, for in Christ, according to Galatians 3:28, there is no male or female. Consequently, sexual differentiation must be a consequence of sin, according to Gregory, since also, according to Luke 20:35–36, it will not be present in the eschatological era either. Thus, writes Clark, Genesis 1:27b gets "outflanked" by Galatians 3:28 and Luke 20:35–36.[22] Nonascetic passages are pressed into ascetic service by intertextuality. Clark also analyzed these writers' use of other techniques, such as "talking back,"[23] textual implosion,[24] changing context,[25] changing audience,[26] changing sex/gender-bending,[27] hierarchy of voice,[28] and "difference in times."[29] These sorts of textual plays would be less troublesome had they been applied consistently, but that was not the case. The ascetic ideology had to be proven with biblical texts by whatever means possible. *Reading Renunciation* provides our project with a host of tools with which to analyze early Christian texts for the agenda(s) they might otherwise have wished to keep in the background.

Remaining with the problem of asceticism and its agendas in texts, we turn finally to a more recent article by Clark, "The Celibate Bridegroom and His Virginal Brides: Metaphor and the Marriage of Jesus in Early Christian Ascetic Exegesis."[30] As the title suggests, Clark here adds yet another tool to the new intellectual history model's toolbox, and that is texts' use of metaphor. One perhaps instinctively thinks of Ricoeur's *The Rule of Metaphor* as Clark's inspiration.[31] However, in her review of the history of literary theories about metaphor, Clark dismisses Ricoeur's ideas and those of many others in favor of "interanimation" theory. This is a theory first put forward by I. A. Richards and, later, Janet Soskice.[32] This theory says metaphor is "'cognitively unique' (that is, that it offers a concept that cannot be expressed in another way), gives 'two ideas for one,' and takes into account intention, context and reception."[33] In other words, interanimation theory looks at how metaphors concretize a subject in one part of a text without diminishing the possibility that it can "animate" additional subjects elsewhere in the same text or in different texts. The liveliest metaphors are those that foster expansion into ever larger "associative networks."

In this study, Clark explores just how lively is the metaphor "celibate bridegroom" from the perspective of interanimation theory. In the first place, at the textual level, the metaphor "withdraws as well as supplements." The adjective "celibate" withdraws the sexual element from "bridegroom" and supplements it with "newly intimate relations with the divine."[34] Clark briefly reviews some early Christian interpretations of Song of Songs, Psalm 45, and Ephesians 5, all of which play with the image of Christ as the bridegroom of his "lovers," which depending on the author are either ascetics, virgins, or all believers. Clark, however, is concerned with the asceticism aspect of the metaphor, so the focus shifts to those who employ the metaphor in those contexts. In early Christian texts ascetical marriage to the celibate bridegroom in this life better accommodated the context of the postapostolic era since it was clear Jesus was not returning as imminently as suggested in 1 Corinthians 7:26–31. Second, the metaphor took on an extratextual life in that it contributed to early Christian debates about the equal worthiness of celibacy and marriage. This new associative network called for Christian exegetes not to alienate their married and widowed brethren, which was actually the largest demographic in the community. Thus, Augustine wrote not of virginity of the body but of the virginity of faithfulness.[35] In another, extratextual associative network, the metaphor surpassed its gender limitation by including males among those capable of marrying this celibate bridegroom. Extending to yet another extratextual associative network, the metaphor retrieved some of its physical lover/marriage notion when early Christians taught that, in the eschaton, our physical bodies will be raised up to join with Christ in heaven. There, believers will be inseparably married to Jesus in a bodily, physical way.[36] Clark concludes the article by saying that, in the hands of pro-asceticism writers, the metaphor easily promoted the ideals of the ascetical life; yet, that it was pressed into the service of so many additional associations strained credulity. Try though the authors did, the metaphor became more of a problem than probably it was worth once it left the realm of traditional asceticism.[37]

Although Clark's bibliography offers many further examples of the new intellectual history model, what we have reviewed above already is an able guide in our task of reading our two case study texts. Somewhat surprising, to this author at least, the new intellectual history model seems not altogether different from the authorial intent model. Whereas that earlier model concerned itself with authorial intent, this model, while not concerned with the author, per se, is nevertheless interested in intent. Better, it is interested in a text's *agendas,* which the text aims to conceal. This is not quite Roland Barthes's "death of the author,"[38] for this model assumes texts consciously or unconsciously conceal their author's real agendas, and Clark seems to agree with Michel de Certeau that "historical analysis, unlike literature, cannot be separated from the situation of its production."[39] This is why it is necessary to deconstruct texts and, subsequently, to expose hidden agendas, which is accomplished with a variety of literary analysis tools, including identifying gaps, aporias, rhetoric, intertextuality, changing contexts, metaphors, and more. In the end, deconstruction of patristic socioethical texts invites Christian social thought to consider its own agendas and the ways in which those agendas control the production of its texts.

APPLICATION OF THE MODEL TO ASTERIUS OF AMASEA'S *HOMILY* 1

Knowing so little about the context in which Asterius wrote, the audience to whom he preached, or even the chronology of this or any of his sermons, we are quite a bit in the dark about what Asterius's agendas *might* have been. Any scrap of evidence would help confirm or deny whatever conclusions the new intellectual history model invites us to draw. Thus, with some healthy skepticism of our own, in this section we argue that Asterius's text indeed conceals an agenda. *Homily* 1 reveals a heavy-handed Asterius who sought to strengthen the grip of his spiritual power over his congregants. There are several elements of Asterius's text that point us in this direction.

First, Asterius played the role of law-giver when it comes to deciding what is the right type of life to lead. At §2 we read of the obligation of each person to lead a "well-ordered" (εὐπολίτευτον) or a "balanced" (μέτρον) and "frugal life" (ζωὴν ἀπερίεργον).[40] The "legal" reasons behind this are both a humoristic, medical understanding of health as a function of balance in the human body and a theological anthropology of the soul. It is important to recall at this point that the parable of the rich man and Lazarus follows Jesus' comment to the Pharisees that it is not possible both to love God and to love wealth (Lk 16:13), and Luke had added his own comment that the Pharisees were lovers of wealth (Lk 16:14). Thus, it is unsurprising that we read this line in Asterius's text, "Luxury, then, is a thing at war with the virtuous life, but reveals dissolution and laziness."[41] The disconnect between luxury and virtue suggests Stoicism is not far in the background.[42] Indeed, Asterius believed a poor man will be happy if he bears his burdens with a "philosophic mind."[43] The point is the body and the soul are to be a unity. The soul of each person bears the *imago Dei;* consequently, a "balanced" human is characterized by equilibrium between the soul and the body.[44] The soul yearns for spiritual truth and the eschatological life, so too the body ought to reflect that yearning in its balanced approach to displays of wealth. Thus, Asterius has laid down the law that his congregants are to follow.

Second, Asterius exchanged his legislative hat for a prosecutorial one. The text pressed charges against those who broke the law of balanced existence. Exhibit A is the money rich people spend on clothing. This is not the normal behavior of people until they come into wealth. Asterius wrote that they "were changing normal behavior to foolish ways of thinking and to senseless desires."[45] One wonders if this homily was written after a particularly profitable harvest or a successful year of trade with other communities along the Black Sea. Suddenly, people who before were balanced in their outward appearance now start spending their newfound wealth in lavish ways. What this suggests, in fact, and perhaps was at the root of Asterius's concern, was that the soul of these people never yearned for spiritual truths in the first place. It is only that the economy has improved such that people are able to let their body's activities catch up to where their souls had always been. The people are now "balanced," all right, but that balanced existence is orientated toward earthly rather than spiritual things.

This would explain why Asterius urged his Christian audience not to weave pictures of Jesus' love for the poor and suffering upon their robes, but to love those who are poor and suffering in the world about them. Moreover, he tells them not to put pictures of Christ on their robes, but to put his image upon their souls.[46] Christ may never have been on their souls in the first place!

Exhibit B is along the same lines. The rich have spent lavishly on their homes. They have taken too many trips to home decorating stores. "For [the rich person] anxiously decorates everything and even the inanimate things."[47] Asterius engages in some playful, sarcastic rhetoric. Pretending to be an architectural consultant to a rich person, he wrote that such a person "needs first a costly home . . . warm, comfortable in winter . . . open toward the north in summer."[48] Then, playing the part of an interior design consultant, he suggested they buy expensive things to decorate couches, beds, and doors, and to buy exotic birds and wine.[49] Such rhetoric invites laughter and bemusement at the misdeeds of "those rich people," but it seems the rhetoric underscores the concern of Asterius to control when and where his congregants spent their newfound wealth.

Exhibit C for the prosecution is the rich person's neglect of the poor. The previous paragraph included this quote from Asterius's text: "For [the rich person] anxiously decorates everything and even the inanimate things." But the sentence actually continues with these words, "[but he decorates] pitifully the naked poor."[50] The rich have spent their resources upon themselves, and they have devoted little to nothing to the poor. Most of Asterius's critique is centered on the rich man in the biblical text who neglected Lazarus. The neglect of Lazarus revealed the rich man's "hard-heartedness" (σκληρότητα), his lack of pity.[51] Asterius wondered at "how unnatural that man, endowed with reason and blessed with culture, who has also been taught goodness by the example of God, should take so little thought of his kinsman in pain and misfortune!"[52] Since, at this point, Asterius turned his attention to expositing the biblical text, and he remained focused on the text for several paragraphs, one might suspect Asterius had lost sight of strengthening his spiritual grip on his own community. Yet, in the last paragraph, Asterius returned to his audience to warn them not to be that rich man, not to forsake living a balanced life. Indeed, the wise person, according to Asterius, is the one who "practices sympathy and philanthropy as the condition of the coming life [i.e., eschatological life]."[53] The parable is medicine (humoristic and otherwise) to those now living like the rich man with the intention to heal them and bring them back to a balanced life.

Having seen the evidence, we discover, third, Asterius played the role of the jury in weighing the violations of law and finding the perpetrators guilty. At §3 he concludes that the wealthy were "misusing life by not using it."[54] This comes during Asterius's criticism of the pictures woven into the fabric of clothing. The parable in Luke had only mentioned the rich man's "purple" and "fine linen," so Asterius has extended those two words into quite an elaborate set of problems. By §3 he needed to ground his extended critique with a new Scripture text. In what is likely an allusion to the discussion of immoderate clothing at 1 Timothy 2:9–10, Asterius says that Paul joins him in condemning the wealthy. Then, Asterius adds that "the divinely inspired voices" (θεοπνεύστοις φωναῖς)[55] also critique this behavior. So, it is not just Paul who stands with Asterius against the wealthy, but so does God who presumably was responsible for Paul having written what he did in the first place. The stakes have been raised, for surely this jury will see the truth clearly. Moreover, by having included himself among the company of Paul and of God, Asterius has sought to raise his own stature before his audience.

It is at §8 the guilty verdict finally comes. Asterius had just concluded his review of the suffering of Lazarus. He ended it by saying the *imago Dei* that the wealthy had repudiated was none other than Lazarus. What the wealthy should have embraced, they spurned. Thus, Asterius wrote, "Now if the story of Lazarus had ended at this point, and the nature of things were such that *our life* was truly represented by the inequality of his career with that of the rich man, I should have cried aloud with indignation, that we who are created equal live on such unequal terms with men of the same race"[56] (italics mine). It seems that the inequality of the biblical parable sadly reflected the inequality of life in Asterius's community. He is indignant at the violation of justice, at the mistreatment of the poor. The unbalanced wealthy are responsible for injustice. Interestingly, the biblical text nowhere distinguishes between balanced (or, righteous) and unbalanced (or, unrighteous) wealthy people. This distinction coincided with the increase in the number of wealthy people within the Christian communities in the mid-third century.[57] Asterius is merely repeating what has been standard ideology for nearly two centuries. Still, Asterius wanted a biblical parallel, and he found one in the story of Job in the Hebrew Bible. Job was wealthy *and* virtuous. "For who is more wealthy than the godly Job? But still, in great wealth the man was not separated from righteousness."[58] So Asterius asks Job 1:1–5 to critique Luke 16:19–21. Likewise, he created a distinction between the righteous and the unrighteous poor through an intertextual reading of Matthew 26:25, Matthew 27:3, et al., with Luke 16:22. "Who was poorer than [Judas] Isacariot? Yet the poverty did not lead to salvation."[59] Thus, although the biblical text condemns the "rich man," it could not possibly be the case for Asterius that all rich people are to be condemned. The stories of Job and Judas help with that.

This divide-and-conquer strategy is Asterius's power play. He reserved to himself the right to name, to classify, and to categorize people. By preaching it, he instructs his audience to do the same. The resultant stereotypes can be devastating for those who would fall under the category "unrighteous poor," for it becomes all too easy at that point to chalk up their poverty as a consequence of personal faults and failure. Even admiration for the righteous poor yields to admiration for the wealth *and* virtue of the righteous rich. All the while, Asterius retains the moral high ground for having seen the world so "clearly" in the first place. It seems Asterius's moral clarity has, in fact, laid the foundation for a new brand of righteous *in*justice, where Christians find a moral excuse for not attending to the needs of the poor.

Asterius betrayed the depth of the problem in his own attempt at enforcing socioeconomic class discrimination against the poor. Asterius was explicit in telling the poor they are not to want more than they presently have. "It is clear that the Scripture accounts that poor man happy who bears his hardships with a philosophic mind, and shows himself nobly steadfast in the face of his circumstances in life, and does not wickedly do any evil deed to gain for himself the enjoyment of luxury."[60] Asterius then tied the beatitude of Jesus, "Blessed are the poor in spirit" (Mt 5:3), to the financially righteous poor in his own population matrix. It is unimportant that the beatitude says "poor *in spirit*," not "poor *in money*."[61] We have seen this argument throughout now. Asterius has argued for a balanced life—not only in terms of how one uses wealth, but also in terms of an equilibrium between the soul and the body. The intertextual reading of Matthew 5:3 and Luke 16:22 serves Asterius's purpose in articulating that the need for a balanced life applies equally to the poor as it does to the rich. The attitude of the poor toward money, the manner in which the poor acquire money, and the decisions of the poor in regards to how they spend their money each are indicative of the spiritual mindset and balance of the poor. Thankfully, the poor have Asterius who, presumably, knows their needs better than they themselves. Asterius happily extends his authority in offering himself as their financial counselor.

In sum, application of the new intellectual history model to this homily reveals an author with an agenda for controlling the lives of its readers, particularly the financial lives of its readers. Asterius presumes to know best what is and is not the right use of wealth. Such matters are not to be left to personal conviction stemming from the indwelling presence of the Holy Spirit. Not only this, Asterius overlays his own socioeconomic class discrimination scheme upon the existing, traditional social class problems of the Greco-Roman culture. This empowers him to decide just what members of each class division are obliged to do, what they are obliged to give, and how they are obliged to relate toward one another. Recall that in chapter one, a distinction was made between CST and Catholic social thought, the latter including the broader world of activists concerned not only to carry on the work of social justice, but also concerned to keep the harbingers of CST honest. In the hands of the new intellectual history model, Asterius's homily is a perfect example of why CST must continue to keep the holders of power accountable to the real needs of people in the world.

APPLICATION OF THE MODEL TO JEROME'S *HOMILY* 86

Earlier models raised the suspicion that Jerome's homily was at least equally interested in the ascetic experience as he was in the rich/poor dynamic of the biblical text he was expositing, if not more so. The application of the new intellectual history model to Jerome's text, however, reveals the ascetic agenda was the *only* agenda with which Jerome was concerned. In Jerome's hands, the biblical story was not a contrast between rich and poor people; it was a contrast between unrighteous poor and righteous poor people, the latter of whom were those who had chosen the ascetic life. Already discussed under our previous models is the explicit claim at the end of the homily that Jerome saw the face of Lazarus in the face of those who choose voluntary poverty. Yet, since it comes at the end, it is not entirely clear that was his point throughout. When this statement of Jerome's is taken up as the lens through which the rest of the homily is read, then the ascetical agenda of the entire homily reveals itself in several ways.

The first indication that Jerome's only concern was asceticism is the charge that the rich man's problem was pride. "The rich man, in purple splendor, is not accused of being avaricious, nor of carrying off the property of another, nor of committing adultery, nor, in fact, of any wrongdoing; the evil alone of which he is guilty is pride."[62] The rich man's pride problem is raised again several paragraphs later when Jerome is expositing the rich man's request in Hades for Lazarus to come and cool his tongue with some water. Jerome wondered why the rich man's tongue, rather than other body parts, was in agony. No explanation is given in Luke 16, so Jerome goes in search of another biblical text to make his desired point. The warning about the tongue in the New Testament Epistle of James (cf. 3:5), proved apt. "The tongue also is a little member, but it boasts mightily," Jerome quotes from the verse, which helps the rich man's request: "Cool my tongue, for it has uttered many a proud word."[63] Thus, the rich man not only thought prideful thoughts (ll. 24–26), but he also talked prideful talk (ll. 119–24). These problems may equally be said of those who are poor but yearn for the wealth they do not have. They are the type of people who pretend to be wealthier than they are, and who, most tragically, live beyond their means. Thus, pride, not money, had to be the rich man's problem. Pride morphs the "rich man" into the "unrighteous poor man" more easily than does real wealth.

A second indication Jerome's concern was ascetical rather than fiscal is found at lines 58–63. Jerome cited Luke 16:22, about the deaths of Lazarus and the rich man. Jerome began his exposition of this verse with the words, "We have heard what each has suffered on earth; let us consider how they fare in Hades."[64] Nowhere does the biblical text suggest the rich man suffered anything on earth. Likewise, nowhere does this homily refer to problems the rich man suffered. What may be behind this is Jerome's one complaint against the rich man's life on earth, which was his problem of pride. Still, Jerome did not suggest the rich man was conscious that he "suffered" from this while on earth, and he does not mention the pride problem again in this context. However, if you substitute the rich man for an unrighteous poor person, then the context makes better sense. Both unrighteous and righteous poor people suffered poverty while on earth, but now that they are dead, the eternal consequences for their dispositions toward that lack of wealth now are revealed.

Third, Jerome employed an intertextual reading of Jesus' parable of the wise merchant (Mt 13:45–46) with our parable. Jerome closed his homily with reference to this parable.[65] Under other circumstances, it would have provided a perfect opportunity for Jerome to expose the problem of the difficulty of loving Christ that a love for money presents. The rich merchant had many pearls, but he was quick to give up every one of them for the sake of following Christ. It fits the context of Luke 16, too, which was the rejection of the love of wealth in favor of love for God. Now, Jerome followed the script as far as interpreting the merchant as the ideal ascetic, another Lazarus, but then he went an entirely different direction with the pearls. Rather than being indicative of money, they were Moses, Isaiah, Jeremiah, and the other Hebrew prophets. One should be willing to part with these Hebrew testimonies the moment the opportunity to receive Christ presents itself. The ascetic, the lover of Christ, deems them worthless pearls compared to the object of their love.

This anti-Judaism move on Jerome's part coincides, in fact, with what he had said about the place of these Hebrew voices a few paragraphs earlier in the homily. When expositing Luke 16:29, Jerome wrote that Moses and the prophets were rejected as prophetic voices by people like Mani and Marcion.[66] It seems, then, that rejecting Moses and the prophets is as dangerous a heresy (Mani and Marcion) as loving them too much (Judaism). In light of this, Jerome suggests that to be a lover of poverty, which is to say a lover of Christ, is simultaneously to be a despiser of those who do not love Christ correctly (Mani and Marcion) or do not love Christ at all (Judaism). To be an ascetic, then, is to be vigilant both against pride within and the heresies without.

Fourth, Jerome upended any privileging of the faith of apostolic men like Peter and John at the expense of more humble converts such as the thief who died alongside Jesus on a cross.[67] The thief on the cross knew so little about Jesus, maybe nothing more than he had gained during those hours spent with him on the cross, or in what he had heard from people in the days before his death. Of Peter and John, by contrast, Jerome wrote, "The apostles had followed him, and they had run away; . . . O Peter, O John, you who had boldly asserted: 'Even if I should have to die with thee, I will not desert thee!' You make a promise and you do not keep it; behold another who is condemned for homicide fulfills the promise that he had not made! You have been excluded from your place; a thief has shut you out and is the first to enter Paradise with Christ."[68] There is not just one complaint against Peter and John here, but several. They were apostles, but squandered that knowledge. They made promises, but did not keep them. They have lost some supposed (from Jerome's point of view) special privilege of entering heaven first with Christ. Thus, the praise of the thief at the expense of Peter and John reveals a predilection for faith over knowledge. This fits well the ascetical agenda without Jerome having to say so explicitly.

A fifth, and final, aspect of Jerome's text that lends itself to an ascetic over and against a fiscal reading of the parable is his exposition of the five "brothers" of the rich man.[69] As has already been discussed in the third chapter and elsewhere, Jerome interprets this reference to the brothers as an allegory. The brothers are identified as the rich man's five senses. Within the framework of an ascetical reading, this allegorical interpretation is no flight of Jerome's fancy. The rich man's brothers could not be five other rich men who remained "lost" to the truth of their need to spend their superfluous wealth wisely in support of the poor. No, the brothers had to be something that keeps unrighteous poor people from fully loving their poverty, or loving Christ. The body's senses are a natural fit within this rubric. The senses keep an unrighteous poor person constantly in a state of excitement about what he or she could enjoy if only he or she had more resources. The senses enslave him or her while in the world.[70] The senses keep him or her from enjoying the far greater gift of the love of Christ for him or her.[71]

To conclude this section, the new intellectual history model reveals an ascetical agenda that Jerome's text obscures by mentioning only briefly a comparison between Lazarus and his ascetic audience in the final paragraph. Yet, by reframing the "rich man's" problem as pride, by letting slip that the "rich man" suffered from something while on earth, by turning the parable of the wise merchant into a call for correct love of Christ, by praising the thief over against Peter and John, and by an embrace of this allegorical reading of the five brothers, the substitution of "unrighteous poor" for "rich man" is no great leap. What the new intellectual history model suggests to us, then, among other things, is that Jerome's homily is actually not about social ethics at all! It is about assuming a life of voluntary poverty. The rich versus poor language in the homily is nothing more than a cover for upholding a love for the demands of voluntary poverty. This is not to suggest the new intellectual history model is unhelpful. Quite to the contrary, were it not for an awareness of Jerome's attempt to paint his asceticism in such decorative, biblical colors, the modern reader might assume it holds great value to the task of constructing Christian social ethics in our day. Sifting the wheat from the chaff in the construction of a dialogue between patristic and CST is an invaluable starting point.

CHAPTER SUMMARY

The new intellectual history model has taken us on what has proven to be a journey with many surprising twists and turns. The model grew out of the "old" history of ideas approaches whose idealism and positivism had run their course decades ago. Clark's revision of that idealism in light of poststructuralist literary theories has sought to return early Christian texts to a place of prominence among ancient texts that deserve careful consideration in our present day, not least because they continue to influence how Christians think about the faith. Clark's aim in all of this is to have a more three-dimensional reading of the texts, to expose the agendas the texts attempt to obscure.

With respect to Asterius's text, the model pulled back a veil of pastoral concern for the poor to reveal a power-hungry preacher quick to impose new social hierarchies on his congregation and his community. This lent itself to a warning for Christian social thought activists today not to let their own agendas be taken over or controlled by a power-hungry elite. The text is an occasion to celebrate the unofficial work of social activists in many spheres of life. Jerome's text was a different matter. Here, the new intellectual history model uncovered a preacher entirely unconcerned, in fact, with social thought. Rather, he was concerned only with the survival of his own ascetic community and with drawing more converts to his ascetic cause. The model has helped save Christian social thought the valuable time it might otherwise have spent, for example, dwelling upon particular problems related to a rich person's pride and his or her use of superfluous wealth.

With the conclusion of this chapter, I have reached the end of my analysis of four hermeneutical models that offer the potential for a fruitful exchange between the worlds of patristic and Christian social thought. In the next chapter, the conclusion, I not only summarize what has been accomplished with this study, but I also propose which of these models, or which aspects of several models, will be most beneficial to this exchange.

CONCLUSION

According to Paul Hanson, there are three levels to revolutionary breakthroughs in social thought within a culture: (1) worldview, (2) laws/institutions, and (3) practice (or daily life). In reference to the stories of Israel in the Hebrew Bible, Hanson wrote,

> Israel's breakthrough occurred on the level of worldview; it has some impact on laws and structures. As the narratives of the Book of Judges indicate . . . practice often remained unaffected by the story of gracious deliverance. But we are not searching for Utopia. We are interested in observing and comparing the interplay of worldview, social structures, and behavior in different cultures.[1]

So, too, have we been interested in observing the social ideas of the early Christians, and in observing how they might be constructive dialogue partners with CST today, rather than in finding utopia. At the same time, we have assumed the patristic texts are capable of inspiring the moral imaginations of today's readers. Utopia this side of the eschaton will never exist, but we are responsible for contributing to the formation of a just society.

Having said that, it is hoped that this study opens some new spaces for dialogue between the Christian authors in late antiquity of texts that speak to social ethics and today's scholars in the field of social ethics. More broadly, it is hoped this study fosters a constructive dialogue for Christians today—lay faithful and scholars—who want to understand how their efforts at relieving social injustices connect with the historical contours of Christian teaching on the same issues. Time, in this case, may seem to be the enemy of the good, for with so much to do and so much social action to be done, one wonders when might such a luxury (to put it most charitably) of reading patristic texts be afforded. Even then, one wonders if the patristic texts hold sufficient promise as to make that investment of time worthwhile in comparison with time spent reading the biblical texts or modern documents of social teaching. In this concluding chapter I propose not only that such time is well spent, but that Christian social thought today is held back from a constructive future if it is avoided.

REVIEW OF THE STUDY

Chapter 1 analyzed six problems with how CST has appropriated patristic sources into its formulations. CST is the systematic and doctrinal base upon which the broad world of Catholic social thought is built. CST is a prominent subset of the wider world of Christian social thought. Thus, our examination of patristic sources in CST served as a manageable case study, which I suspect is not altogether far from the experience of other, contemporary Christian expressions of social ethics.[2] At the same time, it is true that only separate, thorough investigations of the socioethical texts within Protestantism, Orthodoxy, and other Christian movements would substantiate or revise this claim.

Having said that, CST's use of patristic sources reflected a general unease with the material. There was both a wide lack of use of patristic socioethical texts and an uncontextualized use of the patristic sources that are included. This suggests the drafters of CST documents were generally uninterested in what patristic sources had to say on questions of social concern. On doctrinal issues, they were welcome contributors, and in half of the instances of patristic source citations within CST documents, it was discovered that they were used to strengthen pastoral and theological ideas. However, the citation of patristic socioethical texts and ideas in CST's explication of its concerns with economic, political, legislative, and judiciary concerns was remarkably rare. This analysis is fairly consistent with what one experiences in reading the academic literature in the field of CST. The hyperdivision of specialization in academic disciplines has left ethicists largely bereft of the historical resources of the Christian tradition. Thus, the operating assumption of this study has been that the CST tradition would be happy to engage the texts of patristic social thought, if only it knew what those texts were and had some analytical tools at hand when it came to knowing how best to incorporate them.

That was why the second part of this chapter began to pull back the veil on just what CST will find when it explores the world of patristic social thought. It explored some caveats about the entire enterprise. Even a cursory engagement with patristic texts reveals a myriad of problems with the authorship, dating, and provenance of many texts. Then, even if these things are known about a text, there may be other challenges in identifying the particular historical context or the particular theological or philosophical questions that drove the creation of the text in the first place. Understandably, such problems would discourage even the most intrepid of social ethics researchers. For these reasons, the remaining chapters of this study sought to bridge this potential divide.

Chapter 2 eased for social ethicists their wading into the world of patristic social thought as much as possible by exploring three significant points of contact between contemporary and patristic social thought. The chapter surveyed patristic social ideas about the common good, private property, and the poor. On each topic, the chapter introduced the Greco-Roman context out of which the patristic ideas grew. It then surveyed the important authors, texts, and ideas among the patristic writers themselves. Thus, it is no longer necessary for social ethicists today to engage patristic social thought in a decontextualized haze. A *more fruitful* use of patristic social thought is possible with a good hermeneutical approach.

With respect to the case study texts that dominate the remainder of my study, chapters one and two alerted readers to those features of patristic social thought that preceded Asterius and Jerome on several questions, including the long debate on detachment versus renunciation of private property, anti-entrepreneurial notions about money, eschatological orientations to articulating justice, and of the different notions of common good held by early Christians compared to that held by modern Christians. When read within their historical contexts, Asterius's and Jerome's texts are rather pedestrian, in fact. Yet, rather than letting this be an excuse for setting all such texts aside, they instead become examples of how to cultivate the moral imagination, which feeds the narrative ethic approach suggested at the conclusion of the first chapter. With this, then, the study turned to a particular examination of how four hermeneutical models would facilitate the cultivation of the moral imagination while reading patristic texts for the benefit of contemporary, CST.

Chapters 3 through 6 explored this dialogue between the ancient and modern worlds. The four hermeneutical models were applied to two case study texts from the world of patristic social thought. Asterius of Amasea's *Homily* 1 and Jerome's *Homily* 86 are both homiletic expositions of Jesus' parable of the rich man and Lazarus in Luke 16. Also significant, both texts likely were preached during the early years of the fifth century, which reduces further any inclination to justify their distinguishing elements on the basis of the time during which they were written. Indeed, these two texts have a remarkable number of differences, and it is precisely this feature of the texts of patristic social thought—that even when they have much in common, they can still be so different in style and arguments—that makes them so productive for creating new meaning in light of Christian social thought today.

Chapter 3 introduced and applied to the case study texts the "authorial intent" model. This model constructs, as best as possible, the life situation of the author and the common background of the author and audience. Armed with this information, the model then studies the text itself with the expectation the contextual information will help to reveal the author's particular intention in writing what he or she did in the first place. Applied to Asterius's *Homily* 1, it was revealed that Asterius's intent was the promotion of a "measured" approach to wealth. This applied not only to one's own wealth, but also to one's attitude about the wealth (or poverty) of others and to the use of resources from the earth. Applied to Jerome's *Homily* 86, the model reveals Jerome's intent to encourage an eschatological orientation in his audience's attitude toward wealth. The overwhelming majority of the homily, in fact, was concerned with the torments of the rich man in Hades for having neglected the needs of the poor while on earth.

Chapter 4 focused on the "distanciation" model, which begins with the text itself, not the author of the text. The world of the text, not the world of the author, is the locus of interpretation. The model was constructed largely from the ideas of Paul Ricoeur, though in many ways he continued a shift away from an author-centered hermeneutic that we find in earlier authors, namely Hans-Georg Gadamer. Working from the homiletic genre, the distanciation model was concerned to identify in what ways our case study texts aid their readers in writing themselves back into the biblical narrative, in becoming more imaginative readers of the biblical text, and in constructing new meaning from the biblical narrative as a result. When applied to Asterius's homily, the distanciation model revealed that the homily created from the biblical story new stories that more nearly approximated current events. Each new story exposed prejudices, arrogance, and pride within the reader. The stories evoked compassion for the oppressed and the marginalized. Application of the distanciation model to Jerome's homily revealed similarly playful ways of reading the biblical text. The homily exploited the reader's discomfort with the finality of judgment in the eschaton, it played with intertextual readings of passages from the Hebrew Bible and the New Testament, it spun the biblical reference to table crumbs into a multireferential metaphor, and it did similar things with the chasm metaphor. Most interesting of all, Jerome's entire homily was a reworking of the biblical narrative into a play, where not just the words but also the thoughts of the biblical characters were put on display. Thus, the distanciation model invites contemporary readers to reimagine entirely the biblical story, to see none of its elements as fixed in time or space, and to write the story into any of a myriad of socio-ethical concerns.

Chapter 5 introduced us to the "normativity of the future" (NOF) model. Like the distanciation model, this model too identifies the locus of interpretation as the world of the text. However, where this model differs from the distanciation model is that it emphasizes the future that the world of the text discloses. More specifically, this model seeks to identify how a text projects an *inclusive* future, a future in which the love of God for all of the creation is expressed and valued. Texts may disclose this inclusive future both in its grace-filled aspects, where the love of God is more or less explicit, and in its sin-filled aspects, where understanding of God's universal love is buried under expressions of sinfulness (e.g., stereotypes and prejudices) to which the author held. In the latter case, the aim is to expose the sins of the text, which are the sins of its author, and then to identify what aspect of God's universal love lies buried beneath them. Application of the NOF model to Asterius's homily revealed several grace-filled aspects, including a deep concern for the welfare of every part of creation. The critique of the wealthy is centered around their misuse or abuse of the world God had created. Jerome's homily, too, incorporated grace-filled aspects that disclosed an inclusive future. Jerome consistently throughout the text spoke of God's love for and pursuit of every person for his or her salvation. Both Jerome and Asterius accepted without question the equality of every person before God on the basis of a shared, common humanity. Even so, each text also has sin-filled aspects. Both authors denied an inclusive future to the "unrighteous rich." The biblical text they exposit in their respective homilies itself is problematic in this regard, and so what we may have here is evidence of the biblical author's human sinfulness beginning a "crooked line of sin" that is carried further in our patristic writers. Yet, the very fact that there is a concern for restorative justice after the misdeeds of the unrighteous rich lends itself to God writing straight with this crooked line.

Chapter 6, finally, introduced the "new intellectual history" model. This model takes the post-Romantic notion of distanciation to a further level with the application of poststructuralist literary theories to ancient texts. At a practical level, this means texts not only have the capacity to create new meaning once separated from their authors, but they have also the capacity to expose relations of power and networks of control that the author attempted to conceal and that may continue to exist if left unchecked by later readers within that author's "community." Some of the literary tools at the disposal of a reader to uncover the problematic aspects of ancient texts are intertextual readings, textual gaps, aporias, applications of metaphors, rhetorical devices, and the like. When applied to Asterius's homily, the new intellectual history model revealed a text that demands subjection of its readers' financial decision making to the authority of local church leaders. As if socioeconomic class distinctions in late antiquity were not harmful enough, this text creates its own class divisions and then directs the behavior of members of each division. The autocracy of the text serves as a warning to the potential for corruption when the construction of social teaching and doctrine is centered in the hands of a few. When applied to Jerome's text, the model actually revealed that we are not dealing with a socioethical text at all, but rather a text promoting the cause of asceticism. The homily masked its pitting the unrighteous poor against the righteous poor under the garb of the rich man and Lazarus in the biblical story. Yet, rather than being deemed a failure, the model has demonstrated there is a benefit in knowing when a text is not particularly helpful, measured perhaps by the further time and effort saved by not working a text such as this into modern CST discourse.

Looking back over the four models, it is noteworthy that several of the socioethical concerns of our case study texts were teased out by more than one model. The concern with protection and right use of the environment was identified in Asterius's text by the authorial intent model and the NOF model. All four models picked up on the problem of injustice when the poor are marginalized. Three models teased out the implications of and responsibilities to dispense with superfluous wealth as a major problem for rich persons. Thus, the models were certainly unique in their approaches to texts, and they certainly challenged different aspects of the texts, but in more than one instance they converged around central themes of social concern. This suggests to us the reader of patristic texts will not go too far afield no matter which model he or she chooses to apply. By the same token, there may be some good reasons for being more selective among the models, which is the subject to which I now turn and with which I conclude this study.

SOME SPACES FOR DIALOGUE BETWEEN PATRISTIC AND CHRISTIAN SOCIAL THOUGHT

Having surveyed the preceding chapters of this study, it remains to draw some conclusions about which model, or which aspects of several models, holds the greatest promise for constructing a dialogue between patristic socioethical texts and CST. To begin with, the most important starting point for any dialogue is the recognition that Christians today do not look to the writings of the Fathers as the final authorities for faith, life, or doctrine. Pride of place in this regard goes to the biblical text. That is true as much for Christians in the West as it is for Christians in the East. The Fathers' writings are important, but they are not infallible guides. Thus, whatever model or models we incorporate, it or they must direct CST back to the biblical texts. Furthermore, we proposed at the conclusion to chapter one that a narrative ethics approach to incorporating patristic sources would fit well the pastoral objectives of Catholic social teaching (and, presumably, other social documents in the broader, Christian traditions).

For this reason, we may already rule out the authorial intent model as unhelpful. As historically interesting as the particular intent, ideologies, or machinations of any patristic writer may seem to be, such things are entirely unhelpful to the work of CST today. The authorial intent model only leads us into making particular social pronouncements or elucidating particular social concerns that were of interest to the patristic writer himself. The reader of these texts is not directed back to the biblical text in any meaningful way, which limits the opportunity for a reader to imagine the historical narrative of the biblical text in any constructive way. Moreover, the time-bound nature of those concerns, together with the fact some of those concerns may be troubling in and of themselves (e.g., repression of the rights of the poor) would just as quickly turn away the CST community today as it would enrich their understanding. While we were able to create connections between Asterius's and Jerome's own concerns with contemporary issues, those connections are speculative and, thus, contingent. It seems best to direct the energies of Christian social thought elsewhere in regards to its appropriation of patristic social thought toward its own ends. Besides, as was noted above, more than one model was capable of teasing out some of the same socioethical ideas of our case study texts.

Perhaps for this reason also the fourth of our hermeneutical models, the new intellectual history model, seems less attractive. It was as equally concerned with intent, or agendas, as the first model; however, its concern to expose hidden agendas has some continuing appeal. Christian social thought will be served poorly by embracing uncritically any tradition or history, including its own. Yet, this was not our only model that encouraged a critical appropriation of the patristic tradition for the benefit of Christians today. The distanciation model begins with a "prejudice against prejudice," and the NOF model works with the sin-filled aspects of texts to construct an inclusive future. Thus, since we do not get back to the biblical text in any meaningful way with the "new intellectual history" model, and since its beneficial aspects of critical appropriation of ancient texts has been similarly embraced by other models, it seems best to direct our dialogical efforts elsewhere.

This leads us to another important aspect of any future, fruitful dialogue, and that is the postmodern context in which we live. Our cultures have moved beyond metanarratives to stories. This is why I have sought to strengthen CST's use of patristic sources within a narrative approach to ethics. Moreover, I noted in the first chapter that, even if the stories and social ideas to emerge from the Christian tradition initially have limited appeal, their incorporation into the work of activists on behalf of justice may lead to the assumption of the universal "rightness" of the ideas in future generations. Thus, the CST tradition is as much missional as any other Christian community or tradition.

Keeping this in mind, the distanciation model holds great promise. It's explicit aim is to help the reader of patristic texts see those texts as guides to how best to write oneself back into the biblical narrative, how best to relive that narrative, and how to create from that narrative new meaning. The model encourages play with the metaphors, with the dialogue, and with the intertextual readings from the Bible itself. This play shapes the moral imagination of the reader, which is precisely what will move the reader to action. One wonders, for example, how many readers of Luke 16 today have heard from their parish pulpits that it is concerned with just use of the environment, or, how many readers have heard from their parish pulpits the story retold as a dramatic play. I suspect very few, but this is precisely what Asterius and Jerome, respectively, have done. The distanciation model directs our attention not to Asterius and Jerome or the particular "issues" they faced in the late fourth or early fifth century, but with two texts that give us new ways of interpreting, new ways of imagining, this parable of the rich man and Lazarus. With countless biblical texts, the distanciation model invites CST today to open the texts of the patristic writers to discover what other new and interesting ways of reading the biblical texts are in store.

This leads us to consider one final aspect of a dialogue between patristic text and CST. This is the concern to join Christ in proclaiming the arrival of the kingdom of God on earth. Thus, while reading the patristic texts and discovering within them new ways of reading the biblical texts is good, the consequent forming of the moral imagination may not always necessarily be directed toward the promotion of the kingdom of God. This is where the NOF model distinguishes itself from the distanciation model. The NOF model is nothing, in fact, if not a guide for how Christians today may incorporate biblical and patristic texts into their framework for thinking about the call to justice, the call to proclaim the kingdom of God, in this world.

It is for this reason that this study concludes that the NOF model holds the greatest promise for forming a dialogue between the worlds of patristic and Christian social thought. It provides all the benefits of the distanciation model and adds to those a guide for reading biblical and patristic texts that is commensurate with the concerns of justice and equality. The NOF model appreciates the difficulties of reading biblical and patristic texts that are prejudicial, defamatory, and oppressive. Its analytical tools that distinguish such sin-filled aspects from a text's grace-filled aspects cut across a spectrum of academic disciplines, which provides multiple entry points for scholars wishing to engage patristic texts. The very fact that this model embraces texts with difficulties makes it an agent of hope for a CST tradition that may, at times, see itself besieged by an increasingly secularized and polarized world.

AN ILLUSTRATION OF THIS STUDY'S IMPACT ON A CST DOCUMENT

Before concluding this study, the reader would be right to demand at least one example of how this study may be applied to a particular document of CST. Indeed, the study has taken sufficient pains to draw connections between two patristic texts and CST today via four hermeneutical models. It is only fitting now to connect the preferred hermeneutical model—NOF—to the use of a patristic source citation in a recent CST document. For this purpose, I propose two passages from an encyclical of Pope Benedict XVI, *Caritas in veritate*. Remarkably, considering the fact Benedict's previous social encyclical, *Deus caritas est*, was near bursting at the seams with patristic source citations, *Caritas in veritate* has only one patristic source citation.[3] Even then, the encyclical's discussion of the import of the citation is buried in a footnote. Also remarkable, it is not only patristic citations that suffer from a lack of inclusion in this text, but so does Thomas Aquinas (he is mentioned in only one footnote) and all other medieval sources. One is hard-pressed even to find more than a couple dozen biblical citations! This CST document seems rather ahistorical, in fact. Thus, *Caritas in veritate* is ripe with opportunity for exploring where it could have been more appreciative or inclusive of the patristic tradition.

I propose two examples. One is from chapter two of "Human Development in Our Time," at paragraph 21. The paragraph begins:

> 21. Paul VI had an *articulated vision of development*. He understood the term to indicate the goal of rescuing peoples, first and foremost, from hunger, deprivation, endemic diseases and illiteracy. From the economic point of view, this meant their active participation, on equal terms, in the international economic process; from the social point of view, it meant their evolution into educated societies marked by solidarity; from the political point of view, it meant the consolidation of democratic regimes capable of ensuring freedom and peace. After so many years, as we observe with concern the developments and perspectives of the succession of crises that afflict the world today, *we ask to what extent Paul VI's expectations have been fulfilled* by the model of development adopted in recent decades. We recognize, therefore, that the Church had good reason to be concerned about the capacity of a purely technological society to set realistic goals and to make good use of the instruments at its disposal. <u>Profit is useful if it serves as a means towards an end that provides a sense both of how to produce it and how to make good use of it. Once profit becomes the exclusive goal, if it is produced by improper means and without the common good as its ultimate end, it risks destroying wealth and creating poverty</u>. . . . [underlining mine]

The underlined portion of the quote is particularly poignant, and so it is here that I propose connecting this delightful social ethic with a patristic source citation that itself draws the Christian audience of the encyclical back into the gospel story. I would have written the following in place of the underlined text:

> We acknowledge that Jesus has rightly directed societies to concern themselves first and foremost with protecting the dignity of every

human person. Indeed, the Gospel writer Luke argued there are eternal ramifications for doing so or failing to do so. Jesus had said in the parable that the rich man had five brothers whom he wished to save from future torment for having neglected poor people like Lazarus. Thus, for having preserved this parable of Jesus, the Gospel reminds us that God wishes for all to turn from their propensity toward injustice and to be saved. In fact, St. Jerome, who in the early fifth century expounded upon this text in one of his homilies to his largely monastic audience in Bethlehem, taught that every one of us has these same "five brothers"—our five senses. When we repudiate the demand of these senses for the hoarding of wealth and private goods, we then can direct the profits of our world's business and technological enterprises toward the common good, particularly the good of the poor and the least educated who suffer most from current models of development. According to Jerome, an appreciation for human dignity is a function of our willingness to shed not only the pride in our wealth, but also, indeed, the very wealth we possess that is superfluous to our needs.

This alternative reconnects the reader with the biblical text, which moves us toward a narrative approach to ethics. It expands the reader's imagination in suggesting that the biblical text's reference to the rich man's "five brothers" is actually a critique of our propensity toward pride when we aim to please our senses with hoarded wealth and goods (a concern to which the distanciation model alerts us). Finally, it emphasizes the will of God for all to work toward justice by participation in a community that defers to the inherent equality of all persons (a concern to which the NOF model alerts us).

The second example is also in chapter two, this time at paragraph 22. It begins:

22. Today the picture of development has *many overlapping layers.* The actors and the causes in both underdevelopment and development are manifold, the faults and the merits are differentiated. This fact should prompt us to liberate ourselves from ideologies, which often oversimplify reality in artificial ways, and it should lead us to

examine objectively the full human dimension of the problems. As John Paul II has already observed, the demarcation line between rich and poor countries is no longer as clear as it was at the time of *Populorum Progressio*. *The world's wealth is growing in absolute terms, but inequalities are on the increase.* In rich countries, new sectors of society are succumbing to poverty and new forms of poverty are emerging. <u>In poorer areas some groups enjoy a sort of "superdevelopment" of a wasteful and consumerist kind which forms an unacceptable contrast with the ongoing situations of dehumanizing deprivation. "The scandal of glaring inequalities" continues. Corruption and illegality are unfortunately evident in the conduct of the economic and political class in rich countries, both old and new, as well as in poor ones.</u> Among those who sometimes fail to respect the human rights of workers are large multinational companies as well as local producers. . . . [underlining mine]

Once again, the underlined portion of the encyclical's text is a delightful socioethical critique. Here too, though, I would argue the encyclical lost an opportunity to pack an even greater punch by failing to incorporate rich aspects of the biblical and patristic tradition. An alternative for the underlined portion above may read:

To the neglect of the poor, some groups enjoy a sort of "superdevelopment" of a wasteful and consumerist kind. We continue the repudiation of this superdevelopment articulated both in the Gospels and in early Christian literature. Jesus told a parable of a rich man who had neglected the needs of a poor man named Lazarus (Lk 16:18–31). A fourth-century homily on this text by Asterius of Amasea explored the complexities of our world even further. While affirming the right of people to own private property, he nevertheless denounced the unjust use and ownership of that property. What is more, in expanding upon Jesus' critique of the rich man for his love of "purple and fine linen," Asterius added that rich people contribute to the destruction of the environment by their conspicuous consumption habits. They destroy fish and animal life to create and to decorate garments beyond what is needful. They build larger houses—and own more than one house—than are needful, and they spend their money on sumptuous parties rather than diverting their resources to meeting the needs of the poor. Although we may not agree entirely with his pessimism about the eternal destiny of such wealthy people, we nevertheless continue his critique of the lack of environmental and social conscience among wealthy persons.

Like the first example, this alternative too reconnects the reader with the biblical text, which moves us toward a narrative approach to ethics. It expands the reader's imagination about what the biblical text's critique of the rich man's love for "purple and fine linen" might actually mean in real life (a concern to which the distanciation model alerts us). Finally, it emphasizes the continuity without shying away from discontinuity between CST and the Christian tradition (a concern to which the NOF model alerts us).

After crafting these examples of a better use of early Christian texts within contemporary pastoral documents on social ethics, and with some prompting by an early reader of this manuscript, I had the occasion to share them with a bishop and two others who have served extensively on drafting committees for pastoral letters from the U.S. Conference of Catholic Bishops. Their view was rather dim. One acknowledged he preferred short quotes from patristic authors inserted without attribution into such documents. This best preserved, in his view, the "natural flow" of a pastoral letter. The others were more appreciative of the wider context such additions to the letters provided. Their concern was not with the length of added material but with the arguably more difficult problem of knowing that material in the first place. I was told that the documents are drawn up first and only then sent over to experts in particular fields of knowledge to add illustrative and ornamental quotes and footnotes. This was stated as especially true of patristic and medieval citations in pastoral letters. It is simply a fact that the material I propose to be added is simply not known by members of drafting committees or requested of those experts to whom the documents are sent. Now, whether or not the views of these individuals is true all the time or represents the opinions of even a majority of those who draft pastoral letters, I cannot say. What I can attest is that they illustrate the very problem I have sought to correct in this book.

My study has attempted to offer a release valve for the pressure to draw Catholic social thought more tightly into its rich heritage of social ethics within the biblical and patristic tradition. Indeed, this pressure exists not just for Catholics but for Christian social thought in the broadest sense. The students I teach are eager to learn that the faith they live out today in socially responsible ways is not a mere product of the political ideologies of the nineteenth or later centuries. Rather, it is rooted in the texts of Scripture and in the appropriation of those texts by later Christians. There is no doubt that wading into that world has its share of difficulties and potential pitfalls. Yet the hermeneutical models examined here ease that burden tremendously. A new world of social ethics awaits. *Nunc dimittis*.

Appendix 1

ASTERIUS OF AMASEA'S *HOMILY* 1

SOURCES

Asterius of Amasea. *Homilies I–XIV. Text, Introduction and Notes*, pp. 7–15. Edited by Cornelius Datema. Leiden: E. J. Brill, 1970.

ET: Anderson, Galusha, and Edgar J. Goodspeed, eds. *Ancient Sermons for Modern Times*, pp. 17–44. New York: Pilgrim Press, 1904. Text updated with numeration corresponding to Datema's text and some grammatical and spelling changes. In the public domain.

TEXT

1. Our God and Saviour does not lead men to hate wickedness and love virtue by negative precepts alone, but also by examples he makes clear the lessons of good conduct, bringing us both by deeds and words to the apprehension of a good and godly life. As he has often told us by the mouths of both prophets and evangelists, nay, even by his own voice also, that he turns away from the overbearing and haughty man of wealth, and loves a kindly disposition, and poverty when united to righteousness; so also in this parable, in

order to confirm his teaching, he brings effective examples to attest the word, and in the narrative of the rich man and the beggar [πένητα] points out the lavish enjoyment of the one, the straitened life of the other, and the end to which each finally came, in order that we, having discerned the truth from the practices of others, may justly judge our own lives.

2. "There was a rich man who was clothed in purple and fine linen" (Lk 16:19). By two brief words (i.e., "purple" and "fine linen" [πορφύραν and βύσσον]) the Scripture ridicules and satirizes the prodigal and unmeasured wastefulness of those who are wickedly rich. For purple is an expensive and superfluous color, and fine linen is not necessary. It is the nature and delight of those that choose a well-ordered and frugal life to measure the use of necessary things by the need of them; and to avoid the rubbish of empty vainglory and deceptive amusement as the mother of wickedness. And that we may see more clearly the meaning and force of this teaching, let us note the original use of clothing; to what extent it is to be employed when kept within rational limits.

What, then, says the law of the Just One? God created sheep with well-fleeced skins, abounding in wool. Take them, shear it off, and give it to a skilful weaver, and fashion for yourself tunic and mantle, that you may escape both the distress of winter, and the harm of the sun's burning rays. But if you need for greater comfort lighter clothing in the time of summer, God has given the use of flax, and it is very easy for you to get from it a becoming covering, that at once clothes and refreshes you by its lightness. And while enjoying these garments, give thanks to the Creator that he has not only made us, but has also provided for us comfort and security in living. But if, rejecting the sheep and the wool, the needful provision of the Creator of all things, and departing from rational custom through vain devices and capricious desires, you seek out fine linen, and gather the threads of the Persian worms and weave the spider's airy web; and going to the dyer, pay large prices in order that he may fish the shell-fish out of the sea and stain the garment with the blood of the creature. This is the act of a man surfeited, who misuses his substance, having no place to pour out the superfluity of his wealth. For this in the Gospel such a man is scourged, being portrayed as stupid and womanish, adorning himself with the embellishments of wretched girls.

3. Others again, according to common report are lovers of like vanity; but having cherished wickedness to a greater degree, they have not restricted their foolish invention even to the things already mentioned; but having found some idle and extravagant style of weaving, which by the twining of

the warp and the woof, produces the effect of a picture, and imprints upon their robes the forms of all creatures, they artfully produce, both for themselves and for their wives and children, clothing beflowered and wrought with ten thousand objects. Thenceforth they become self-confident. They no longer engage in serious business; from the vastness of their wealth they misuse life, by not using it; they act contrary to Paul and contend against the divinely inspired voices, not by words, but by deeds. For what he by word forbade, these men by their deeds support and confirm. When, therefore, they dress themselves and appear in public, they look like pictured walls in the eyes of those that meet them. And perhaps even the children surround them, smiling to one another and pointing out with the finger the picture on the garment; and walk along after them, following them for a long time. On these garments are lions and leopards; bears and bulls and dogs; woods and rocks and hunters; and all attempts to imitate nature by painting. For it was necessary, as it seems, to adorn not only their houses, but finally also their tunics and their mantles.

4. But such rich men and women as are more pious, have gathered up the gospel history and turned it over to the weavers; I mean Christ himself with all the disciples, and each of the miracles, as recorded in the Gospel. You may see the wedding of Galilee, and the water-pots; the paralytic carrying his bed on his shoulders; the blind man being healed with the clay; the woman with the bloody issue, taking hold of the border of the garment; the sinful woman falling at the feet of Jesus; Lazarus returning to life from the grave. In doing this they consider that they are acting piously and are clad in garments pleasing to God. But if they take my advice let them sell those clothes and honor the living image of God. Do not picture Christ on your garments. It is enough that he once suffered the humiliation of dwelling in a human body which of his own accord he assumed for our sakes. So, not upon your robes but upon your soul carry about his image.

Do not portray the paralytic on your garments, but seek out him that lies sick. Do not tell continually the story of the woman with the bloody issue, but have pity on the straitened widow. Do not contemplate the sinful woman kneeling before the Lord, but, with contrition for your own faults, shed copious tears. Do not sketch Lazarus rising from the dead, but see to it that you attain to the resurrection of the just. Do not carry the blind man about on your clothing, but by your good deeds comfort the living, who has been deprived of sight. Do not paint to life the baskets of fragments that remained, but feed the hungry [πεινῶντας]. Do not carry upon your mantles the water-pots which were filled in Cana of Galilee, but give the thirsty drink. Thus we have profited by the magnificent raiment of the rich man.

What follows must not, however, be overlooked; for there is added to the purple and fine linen, that he fared sumptuously every day. For of course both the adorning of one's self with useless magnificence, and serving the belly and the palate luxuriously, belong to the same disposition.

5. Luxuriousness, then, is a thing hostile to virtuous life, but characteristic of idleness and inconsiderate wastefulness, of unmeasured enjoyment and slavish habit. And though at first blush it may seem a simple matter, it proves upon careful investigation to include manifold, great and many-headed evils. Luxuriousness would be impossible without great wealth; but to heap up riches without sin is also impossible; unless indeed it happens to some one rarely, as to Job, both to be abundantly rich, and at the same time to live in exact accord with justice. The man who will give himself to luxury, then, needs first a costly home, adorned like a bride, with gems and marbles and gold, and well adapted to the changes of the seasons of the year. For a dwelling is required that is warm, comfortable in winter, and turned toward the brightness of the south; but open toward the north in the summer, that it may be fanned by northern breezes, light and cool. Besides this, expensive stuffs are demanded to cover the seats, the couches, the beds, the doors. For the rich carefully adorn all things, even things inanimate, while the poor are pitiably naked. Moreover, enumerate the gold and silver vessels, the costly birds from Phasis, wines from Phoenicia, which the vines of Tyre produce in abundance and at a high price, for the rich; and all the rest of the wasteful equipment which only those who use it can name with particularity.

Now luxury, steadily increasing in elaborateness, even mingles Indian spices with the food; and the apothecaries furnish supplies to the cooks rather than to the physicians. Then consider the multitude that serve the table—the table-setters, the cupbearers, the stewardesses and the musicians that go before them, women musicians, dancing girls, flute-players, jesters, flatterers, parasites—the rabble that follows vanity. That these things may be gained, how many poor are robbed! how many orphans maltreated! how many widows weep! how many, dreadfully tortured, are driven to suicide!

Like one who has tasted some Lethean stream, the self-indulgent soul absolutely forgets what it itself is, and the body to which it has been joined, and that some day it shall be released from this union, and again at some future time inhabit the reconstructed body. But when the appointed time shall come, and the inexorable command separates the soul from the body, then also shall come the recollection of things done in the past life, and vain repentance, too late! For repentance helps when the penitent has power of amendment, but the possibility of reform being taken away, grief is useless and repentance vain.

6. "There was a certain beggar [πτωχὸς] named Lazarus" (Lk 16:20). The narrative describes him not simply as poor, destitute of money, and of the necessaries of life, but also as afflicted with a painful disease, emaciated in body, houseless, homeless, incurable, cast down at the rich man's gate. And very carefully the narrative finally works up the circumstances of the beggar [πτωχοῦ] to signalize the hard-heartedness of him who had no pity; for the man that has no feeling of pity or sympathy for hunger or disease is an unreasoning wild beast in human form, deliberately and wickedly deceiving men; nay more, he is less sympathetic than the very beasts themselves; since, at least, when a hog is slaughtered, the rest of the drove feel some painful sensation and grunt miserably over the freshly spilled blood; and the cattle that stand about when the bull is killed indicate their distress by passionate lowing. Flocks of cranes also when one of their mates is caught in the nets, flutter about him and fill the air with a sort of grieving clamor, seeking to release their mate and fellow. And how unnatural that man, endowed with reason and blessed with culture, who has also been taught goodness by the example of God, should take so little thought of his kinsman in pain and misfortune!

7. So the suffering but grateful pauper [πένης] lay without feet, or else certainly he would have fled from the accursed and haughty man, and sought another place instead of the inhospitable gate, which was closed against the poor [πένησιν]; he lay without hands, having not even a palm to stretch forth for alms; his very organs of speech were so impaired that his voice was hoarse and harsh; in fact, he was quite mutilated in all his members, the wreck of a foul disease, a pitiable illustration of human infirmity. Yet not even such a list of misfortunes moved the haughty man to attention, but he passed the beggar as if he were a stone, deliberately filling up the measure of his sin; for, if accused, he could not utter this common and specious excuse, "I did not know: I was not aware: I did not notice the beggar howling." For the beggar lay before his gate, a spectacle as he went in and out to make the condemnation of the proud man inevitable. He was even denied the crumbs from the table; and while the rich man was bursting with fullness, he was wasting away with want. Therefore it would have been fair and right to have made the Canaanitish Phoenician woman the teacher of the misanthropic man of wealth, saying those things that are written: "Haughty wretch, even the dogs eat of the crumbs which fall from their masters' table, and did you not think your brother, one who belongs to the same race, worthy of that bounty?" But the dogs were carefully fed, the watch-dogs by themselves and the hunting-dogs by themselves, and they were deemed worthy of a roof, and

beds and attendants were carefully allotted to them; but the image of God was cast on the earth uncared for and trampled on, that image which the great Builder and Maker of all fashioned with his own hand, if one regards Moses as having given credible testimony to the genesis of man.

8. Now if the story of Lazarus had ended at this point, and the nature of things were such that our life was truly represented by the inequality of his career with that of the rich man, I should have cried aloud with indignation, that we who are created equal live on such unequal terms with men of the same race. But since that which remains is good to hear, poor man [πένης], who groan over the past, do take courage from the sequel, when you learn the blessed enjoyment of your fellow in poverty [συμπτώχου]. For you will find that the just Judge renders exact judgment, so that the man who has lived a life of ease groans, and he who has had hardship finds luxury, each receiving his due reward.

9. And it came to pass that the beggar [πτωχὸν] died and was carried away by the angels into Abraham's bosom. Do you see who they were who ministered to the poor and just man, and who took him to heaven? For angels were his bodyguard, looking upon him gently and mildly, and betokening by their manner the attendance and relief that awaited him. And he was taken and placed in the bosom of the patriarch, a statement which affords ground for doubt to those who like to question minutely the deep things of the Scriptures, for if every just man, when he dies, should be taken to the same place, the bosom would be a great one and expanded to an endless extent, if it were intended to accommodate the whole multitude of the saints. But if this is absolutely impossible - for the bosom can scarcely embrace one man and hardly two infants,—the thought presents itself to us that the material [αἰσθητοῦ] bosom is the symbol of a spiritual truth [νοητήν]; for what is it that is meant? Abraham, he says, receives those who have lived an upright life. Then tell us, wonderful Luke—for I will address you as though visibly present—why, when there were many just men, even older than Abraham, did you withhold this distinction from his predecessors, passing in silence over Enoch, Noah and many others who were like these in their manner of life? But perhaps I understand you, and my judgment does not go wide of the mark. For Abraham was a minister of Christ, and, beyond other men, received the things of the revelation of Christ, and the mystery of the Trinity was adequately bodied forth in the tent of this old man when he entertained the three angels as wayfaring men. In short, after many mystical enigmas, he became the friend of God, who in after time put on flesh and, through the medium of this human veil, openly associated with men. On this account,

Christ says that Abraham's bosom is a sort of fair haven, and sheltered resting-place for the just. For we all have our salvation and expectation of the life to come, in Christ, who, in his human descent, sprang from the flesh of Abraham. And I think the honor in the case of this old man has reference to the Saviour, who is the judge and rewarder of virtue, and who calls the just with a gracious voice, saying: "Come, ye blessed of my Father, inherit the kingdom prepared for you."

10. "And it came to pass that the beggar died" (Lk 16:22). Two sides of the beggar's [πτωχὸν] life are indicated: on the one hand is shown his poverty, and on the other his modesty and the humility of his character. Let not, therefore, the man who is without substance, in want of money, and clothed in pitiable garb appropriate to himself the praise of virtue, nor think that want will secure for him salvation. For not he who is poor [πενόμενος] from necessity is commended, but he is held up to admiration who of his own accord moderates his desires. For the poverty of those who are in extreme want [ἁπλῶς], and have at the same time an unmanageable or incorrigible disposition, leads to many evil deeds of daring. Whenever I have come near a ruler's judgment-seat, I have seen that all housebreakers and kidnappers, thieves and robbers, and even murderers, were poor men, unknown, houseless and hearthless. So that from this it is clear that the Scripture accounts that poor man [πτωχὸν] happy who bears his hardships with a philosophic mind, and shows himself nobly steadfast in the face of his circumstances in life, and does not wickedly do any evil deed to gain for himself the enjoyment of luxury. Such a man the Lord describes even more clearly in the first of the beatitudes, where he says: "Blessed are the poor in spirit." So, not every poor person [πτωχός] is righteous, but only one who is like Lazarus; nor is every rich man to be despaired of, but only one who has the disposition of him that neglected Lazarus; and in real life we easily find witnesses of this truth. For who is richer than was the godly Job? Nevertheless his great prosperity did not divorce him from righteousness nor, to speak briefly, did it estrange him from virtue. Who is poorer [πενέστερον] than was Iscariot? His poverty [ἐνδείας] did not secure salvation for him; but while associating with the eleven poor men who loved wisdom, and with the Lord himself, who for our sakes voluntarily became poor [πτωχεύσαντι], he was carried away by the wickedness of his covetous disposition and finally was guilty even of the betrayal.

11. It is also worthwhile to examine intelligently how each of these men when dead was carried forth. The poor man [πτωχός] when he fell asleep had angels as his guards and attendants, who carried him, full of joyful ex-

pectation, to the place of rest; and the rich man, Christ says, died and was buried. It is not possible in any respect to improve the declaration of the Scriptures, since a single sentence adequately indicates the unhonored decease of the rich man. For the sinner when he dies is indeed buried, being earthy in body, and worldly in soul. He debases the spiritual within him to the material by yielding to the enticements of the flesh, leaving behind no good memorial of his life, but, dying the death of beasts, is wrapped in unhonored forgetfulness. For the grave holds the body, and Hades the soul,—two gloomy prisons dividing between them the punishment of the wicked. And who would not blame the wretched man for his thoughtlessness? Since when he was on earth he prided himself, held his head high, exulted over all who lived about him and were of the same race, deeming those whom he chanced to meet hardly better than ants and worms, and vainly boasting of his short-lived glory. But when he dies, and like a scourged slave is deprived of those usurped possessions of which in his folly he thought himself master, he is as deeply humiliated as he was previously highly exalted, and, uttering complaints like a lamenting old woman, calls loudly and vainly on the patriarch, saying, "Father Abraham, have mercy on me, and send Lazarus, that he may dip the tip of his finger in water, and cool my tongue; for I am tormented in this flame." He seeks mercy, which he had not given when he had the power of benefiting another, and demands that Lazarus shall come down into the fire to him to help him. He prays that he may suck the finger of the leper slightly moistened in water. Such is the thoughtlessness of those who love the body. This is the end of those who love wealth and pleasure.

12. It therefore becomes the wise man who is provident of the future, to consider the parable as a sort of medicine, preventive of sickness; and to flee the experience of like evil, preferring the sympathetic and philanthropic disposition as the condition of the life to come. For the Scripture has presented the admonition to us dramatically in the persons of particular characters in order to impress upon us by a concrete and vivid example the law of good conduct, so that we may never think lightly of the precepts of the Scripture as terrifying in word only, without inflicting the threatened punishment. I know that most men, snared by such fancies, take the liberty of sinning. But the Scripture before us teaches quite the contrary, that neither any confession of the justice of the judgment lightens the punishment, nor does pity for the one in torment lessen the penalty ordained; if indeed it is necessary that the Scripture attest the word of the patriarch. For after the manifold supplications of the rich man, and after hearing countless piteous appeals, Abraham was neither moved by the laments of the suppliant, nor did he remove

from his pain the one who was bitterly scourged; but with austere mind he confirmed the final judgment, saying that God had allotted to each according to his desert. And he said to the rich man, "Since in life you lived in luxury through the calamities of others, what you are suffering is imposed upon you as the penalty of your sin. But to him who once had hardships, and was trampled on and endured in bitterness life in the flesh, there is allotted here a sweet and joyful existence. And besides," he says, "There is also a great gulf" which prevents them from intercourse with one another, and separates those who are being punished from those who are being honored, that they may live apart from each other, not mixing the rewards of good and evil deeds. And I suppose the parable to be a material representation of a spiritual truth. For let us not imagine that there is in reality a ditch dug by angels, like the trenches on the outer borders of military camps, but Luke by the similitude of a gulf has represented for us the separation of those who have lived virtuously and those who have lived otherwise. And this thought Isaiah also stamps for us with his approval, speaking somewhat thus: Is the hand of the Lord not strong to save, or is his ear heavy that it cannot hear? But our sins stand between us and God.

Appendix 2

Jerome's *Homily* 86

SOURCES

Jerome. *S. Hieronymi presbyteri opera. Pars II: Opera homiletica,* pp. 507–16. Edited by Germain Morin. CCSL 78. Turnhout: Brepols.

ET: *The Homilies of Saint Jerome,* vol. 2, pp. 200–211. Translated by Marie Liguori Ewald. FOTC 57. Washington, D.C.: Catholic University of America Press, 1966. Text updated with minor punctuation and spelling changes. The text is reprinted here with the permission of Catholic University of America Press.

Numbers in square brackets correspond to the line numbers in the CCSL edition.

TEXT

"There was a certain rich man." When the Lord had declared: "No servant can serve two masters; you cannot serve God and mammon," and the greedy Pharisees had rebuked Him, He set before them an example, or rather, a truth, in the form of an example and parable. Strictly speaking, it is not really a parable when the names of the characters are given. A parable poses an example, but suppresses identification. Where Abraham is mentioned by name, and Lazarus, the prophets, and Moses, there Lazarus is genuine; if Abraham is a true person, so also is Lazarus. We have read who Abraham was; we have not read of Lazarus, but He who made Lazarus, also made Abraham. If he speaks of Abraham as a real person, then we understand Lazarus, also, as a living reality, for fiction is not congruous with the actual.

[13] "There was a certain rich man." Just think of the kindness of the Lord! Lazarus, the beggar, is called by his name because he was a saint, but the man who is rich and proud is not deemed worthy of a name. "There was a certain rich man." I say, "certain," because he has passed like a shadow. "There was a certain rich man who used to clothe himself in purple and fine linen." Ashes, dust, and earth, he covered up with purple and silk. "Who used to clothe himself in purple and fine linen, and who feasted every day in splendid fashion." As his garments, so his food; and with us, likewise; as our food, so our garments.

[22] "There was a certain poor man, named Lazarus." The meaning of Lazarus' name is βοηθούμενος, one who has been helped; he is not a helper, but one who has been helped. He was a poor man and, in his poverty, the Lord came to his assistance. "Who lay at his gate, covered with sores." The rich man, in purple splendor, is not accused of being avaricious, nor of carrying off the property of another, nor of committing adultery, nor, in fact, of any wrongdoing; the evil alone of which he is guilty is pride. Most wretched of men, you see a member of your own body lying there outside at your gate, and have you no compassion? If the precepts of God mean nothing to you, at least take pity on your own plight, and be in fear lest you become such as he. Why do you save what is superfluous to your pleasures? Give in alms to your own member what you waste. I am not telling you to throw away your wealth. What you throw out, the crumbs from your table, offer as alms.

[35] "Who lay at his gate." He was lying at the gate in order to draw attention to the cruelty paid to his body and to prevent the rich man from saying, I did not notice him; he was in a corner; I could not see him; no one announced him to me. He lay at the gate; you saw him every time you went out and every time you came in. When your throngs of servants and clients were attending you, he lay there full of ulcers. If your eyes disdained to look upon putrid flesh, did not your ears, at least, hear his plea? "Who lay at his gate, covered with sores." He did not have just one sore, his whole body was sores, so that the magnitude of his suffering might arouse your utmost compassion. "Who lay at his gate, covered with sores, and longing to be filled with the crumbs that fell from the rich man's table." There is some relief to sickness if one has resources, but if you add poverty to extreme weakness the infirmity is doubled. Sickness is always fastidious and cannot take anything indelicate; it is nauseated by it. How much real suffering that causes! In the

midst of so many wounds, he does not, however, think of the pain of his afflictions, but of the pangs of hunger. "Longing to be filled with the crumbs that fell from the rich man's table." In a certain way, he is saying to the rich man: The crumbs from your table are enough for me; what you brush off the table, give in alms; draw profit from your losses. "Even the dogs would come and lick his sores." What no man deigned to bathe and touch, gentle beasts lick.

[58] "It came to pass that the poor man died and was borne away by the angels into Abraham's bosom; but the rich man also died and was buried; and in hell lifting up his eyes. . . ." We have heard what each has suffered on earth; let us consider how they fare in the nether world. The temporal has passed and is over; what follows is for all eternity. Both are dead; the one is met by angels, the other with torments; the one is borne away on the shoulders of angels, the other goes to his punishment; the one, Abraham receives into his bosom of happiness; the other, hell devours. Lazarus "was borne away by the angels." Great sufferings are suddenly exchanged for delights. He is carried by angels and borne away without even the effort of walking. He is carried after his great trials because he was exhausted. "Was borne away by the angels." One angel was not enough to carry the pauper, but many came to form a chorus of jubilation. "Was borne away by angels." Every angel rejoices to touch so precious a burden. With pleasure, they bear such burdens in order to conduct men into the kingdom of heaven. He was escorted and carried into the bosom of Abraham, not to the side of Abraham, but into the bosom of Abraham, that Abraham might caress him, revivify him; that he might hold him in his bosom and, like a tender and compassionate father, warm him back to life again.

[78] "The rich man also died and was buried," earth has returned to its earth. "In hell lifting up his eyes." Note the import and appropriateness of each word. "In hell lifting up his eyes." Lazarus was above; he was below; he lifted up his eyes to behold Lazarus, not to despise him. "Lifting up his eyes, being in torments." His whole being was in anguish; his eyes alone were free, free to gaze upon the happiness of the other man. He was allowed the liberty of his eyes to be tortured the more because he does not enjoy what the other has. The riches of others are torments to those who are in poverty. "Lifting up his eyes, being in torments." The one many angels carry away; the other is held fixed in never-ending torments. Being in torments: the Gospel did not say in torment, but in torments, for such are the rewards of covetous wealth. He saw Abraham afar off; he looked up at him only to increase his torture. "Lazarus in his bosom." Abraham's bosom was the poor man's Paradise.

"Abraham afar off and Lazarus in his bosom." Someone may say to me: Is Paradise in the nether world? I say this, that Abraham's bosom is true Paradise, but I also grant that the bosom of a holy man is Paradise.

[97] "He cried out and said," (excruciating pain increases the volume of the voice) "Father Abraham have pity on me." "Father Abraham." Even though I am in the grip of torments, nevertheless, I call upon my father. Just as that son who squandered all his possessions calls his father, even so I call you father, despite my punishments. By nature, I call you father, even though I have lost you as father through sin. Have pity on me. "In the nether world who gives you thanks?" Vain is your repentance in a place where there is no room for repentance. Torments, not the disposition of your soul, force you to repent. "Have pity on me." A saint, indeed, is Abraham, holy and blessed, and all of us are in haste to enter his bosom, but I am not so sure that it is possible for anyone in hell or in heaven to feel pity. The Creator pities His creature; one Physician came to restore the dead, for the others could not.

[110] "Send Lazarus to dip the tip of his finger in water." "Send Lazarus." You are mistaken, miserable man; Abraham cannot send, but he can receive. "To dip the tip of his finger in water." Recall your lifetime, rich man; you did not condescend to see Lazarus and now you are longing for the tip of his finger. "Send Lazarus." You should have done that for him while he lived. "To dip the tip of his finger in water." See the conscience of the sinner; he does not dare ask for the whole finger. "Cool my tongue, for I am tormented in this flame." Cool my tongue, for it has uttered many a proud word. Where there is sin, there is also the penalty for sin. "To cool my tongue, for I am tormented in this flame." How evil the tongue can be, James has told us in his Letter: "The tongue also is a little member, but it boasts mightily." The more it has sinned, the more it is tortured. You long for water, who formerly were so fastidious at the mere sight of smeary and spattered dishes.

[125] "Abraham said to him, 'Son, remember that thou in thy lifetime hast received good things.'" Be sure you know what he means: good things to you; but they are not good. You have received what you thought were good, but you cannot have been a lord upon earth and reign here too. It is not possible to have wealth both on earth and in hell. "Lazarus in like manner evil things." If ever we are sick, if we are beggars, if we are wasting away in sickness, if we are perishing from the cold, if there is no hospitality for us, let us be glad and rejoice; let us receive evil things in our lifetime. When the crushing weight of infirmity and sickness bears down upon us, let us think of Lazarus. "Besides all that, between us and you a great gulf is fixed." It

cannot be bridged, removed, or levelled. We can see it, but cannot cross it. We see what we have escaped; you see what you have lost; our joy and happiness multiply your torments; your torments augment our happiness.

[139] "He said, 'Then, father, I beseech thee.'" The miserable creature does not cease to call him father. "Then, father, I beseech thee." You should have called him father in former times, for he was your true father. Did you acknowledge your father, you who despised your brother? "To send him to my father's house." Notice the perversity; not even in pain does he speak truth. You see what he says: "Then, father, I beseech thee." Your father, then, is Abraham; how can you say, therefore, send him to my father's house? You have not forgotten your father; you have not forgotten that he who was your father has destroyed you. Because he was your father, you have five brothers. You have five brothers: sight, smell, taste, hearing, touch. These are the brothers to whom formerly you were enslaved; they were your brothers. Since they were the brothers you loved, you could not love your brother, Lazarus. Naturally, you could not love him as brother, because you loved them. Those brothers have no love for poverty. Your sight, your sense of smell, your taste, your sense of touch, was your brother. These brothers of yours loved wealth; they had no eye for poverty. "I have five brothers, that he may testify to them." They are the brothers who sent you into these torments; they cannot be saved unless they die. "Lest they too come into this place of torments." Why do you want to save those brothers who have no love for poverty? It must needs be that brothers dwell with their brother.

[161] "Abraham said to him, 'They have Moses and the Prophets, let them hearken to them.'" Why do you ask that Lazarus go? "They have Moses and the Prophets." Besides, Moses and the prophets went about in goatskins, wandering in their caves and in holes in the ground; they were poor men just like Lazarus, and they suffered calamities and endured hunger. Why do you ask me to send Lazarus? They have Lazarus in Moses and the prophets. Moses was Lazarus; he was a poor man; he was naked. He esteemed the poverty of Christ greater riches than the treasures of Pharaoh. They also have the prophets. They have Jeremiah who is thrown into a cistern of mud and who fed upon the bread of tribulation. They have all the prophets; let them hearken to them. Every day Moses and the prophets are preaching against your five brothers; let them teach them; let them instruct them. Let them summon the eye; and what do they say to it? Do not look upon the carnal, but discern the spiritual. "What we have seen with our eyes," says the apostle, "what we have heard, what our hands have handled: of the Word of God." He instructs the ear, too, the sense of smell, of taste. All the prophets and all the saints teach these brothers.

[179] "He answered, 'No, father Abraham, but if someone from the dead goes to them, they will repent.'" Here, a dogma is being revealed without our realizing it. One thing is said, another is foreshadowed. He knows that these brothers of his cannot be saved unless someone rises from the dead. The Jews, indeed, hearken only to Moses and the prophets, and no one has come back to them from the dead, therefore, our Savior has such brothers. "If someone from the dead goes to them, they will repent." "If someone from the dead goes." I do not know who will go, for I who am fixed in punishment do not deserve to know Him who will rise from the dead. This I do know, however. Whoever rises from the dead and teaches can save these brothers. He has saved ears, for He says: "He who has ears to hear, let him hear"; and eyes, for He says: "The lamp of the body is your eye." In His name, the apostle says: "We are the fragrance of Christ"; and the psalmist: "Taste and see how good the Lord is." He saves, also, the sense of touch, for, in a way, John is speaking of all these brothers when he says: "What we have seen, what we have heard, what our hands have handled." To these brothers, the Resurrection of the Lord brought salvation.

[198] These brothers were in us, also, before our Lord rose from the dead. My eyes used to look upon evil; they led me in pursuit of a prostitute. I simply could not look at a beautiful woman without her beauty setting me aflame. Formerly, my ear was a snare, for I used to delight in popular songs and to listen gladly to shameful tales. Perfumes were my pleasure, not, indeed, good fragrance, but evil, for they were destroying my soul. Neither land nor sea was able to satisfy my palate. With every kind of delicacy, my slaves catered to me as an epicure. My sense of touch held me captive; I was seduced in the embrace of women. Do you see how these brothers, before the Resurrection of Christ, were leading me into death? He died and I lived; He died and these brothers rose from the dead; rather, they died in order that they might live; they died in the flesh that they might live in the Spirit. Now, my eye looks upon Christ; my ear hears only Him; my taste relishes Him alone; my sense of smell detects Him; my touch embraces Him.

[215] "He said to him, 'If they do not hearken to Moses and the Prophets.'" Mark how our Lord instructs the soul by His own word and by recalling Scripture. When we had said, moreover, that these brothers could not be saved unless someone rose from the dead, we had, by no means, given place to Marcion and to Mani, who tear down the Old Testament. They maintain that the soul cannot be saved except through, and only through, the Gospel; they do away completely with the Old Testament. Abraham, on the other hand, does not do away with Him who is going to rise from the dead, for he

does not say, let them hearken to Moses and the prophets; why do you wait for Him who is going to rise from the dead? If he had said that, he would have destroyed the Gospel. What does he say? "If they do not hearken to Moses and the Prophets, they will not believe even if someone rises from the dead." "If you believed Moses you would believe me also, for he wrote of me." See now what Abraham means? few do well, indeed, to wait for Him who will rise from the dead, but Moses and the prophets proclaim that He is the One who is going to rise from the dead. It is Christ, in fact, who speaks in them; if you hearken to them, you will hearken, also, to Him.

[232] There is so much more to be said. The psalm that has been read, the one-hundred-third, is mystical, especially so where it says: "With Leviathan, which you formed to make sport of it"; and: "The highest of them is the home of the stork." The whole psalm is replete with mystical meaning, and but a day, not an hour, is scarcely long enough to do it justice. Since, however, it is already Lent, we shall, if the Lord grants an opportunity, attempt at another time to unveil the mysteries hidden in it. For the present, let it suffice to hear about Lazarus, or rather, to hear that he was the rich man. May the torments of the rich man be a restraint upon us and the example of the poor man an incentive to us. The Christian soul, the soul of the monk, the soul of him who naked follows the naked Christ, when it looks with envy upon a rich man, or when it itself revels in wealth and display, may it call to mind Dives; may it ponder well his voice as he cries out and begs for the touch of Lazarus' finger.

[247] While we are still thinking about Lazarus, let us consider something we had all but forgotten to mention, for someone may, by this question introduce a false doctrine: Is this scene presented to us as taking place before the last judgment or after? One answer might be, after the judgment because the one is suffering punishment and the other is enjoying consolation. What, then, is the meaning of: "They have Moses and the Prophets"? On the other hand, if Christ Himself is the one speaking and He is teaching before the Resurrection which, according to our interpretations is in expectations then, the scene is taking place before the Resurrection, and, reasonably, is before the last judgment. I shall give an example to bring out the truth. Imagine that a man has been caught in the act of robbery and is sent to a very dark prison; he has been put into prison and is in torments while actually waiting for sentence. He, surely, is subject to some kind of punishment, and comes to realize what he is going to suffer in the future. Even though he has not yet received final condemnation, and the day of the trial, or judgment, has not yet come; nevertheless, from the imprisonments from the darkness,

filth, hunger, creaking of chains, groaning of the fettered, weeping of those who are with him, he understands fully what kind of penalty will be his. If the prelude to punishment is so painful, what will the punishment itself be like? If he has not yet come to trial, and his penalty is not yet meted out, yet he longs for cool water, what will he suffer after judgment!

[269] It must also be taken into account that Abraham was in the nether world. Christ had not yet risen from the dead to lead him into Paradise, for, before Christ died, no one had ascended into heaven, not even the thief. That flaming, flashing sword was keeping Paradise safe; no one could open the gates which Christ had closed. The thief was the first to enter with Christ; his great faith merited the greatest of rewards. His faith in the kingdom was not attendant upon seeing Christ; he did not see Him in His radiant glory nor behold Him looking down from heaven; he did not see the angels administering to Him. Certainly, to put it plainly, he did not see Christ walking about in freedom, but on a gibbet, drinking vinegar, crowned with thorns; he saw Him fixed to the cross and heard Him beseeching help: "My God, my God, why have you forsaken me?" Under such circumstances, he believed, O fickle, fallen state of man! The apostles had followed Him, and they had run away; this criminal on the cross acknowledged the Lord. O Peter, O John, you who had boldly asserted: "Even if I should have to die with thee, I will not desert thee!" You make a promise and you do not keep it; behold another who is condemned for homicide fulfills the promise that he had not made! You have been excluded from your place; a thief has shut you out and is the first to enter Paradise with Christ.

[289] We have digressed on the thief, but we have not forgotten the theme of our discussion, for when speaking of Paradise, we had said that no one would go there before the coming of Christ. Let us return, therefore, to that proposition. The thief's crown must not lead us astray; let it rather incite us to win the crown. Abraham was not yet in Paradise because Christ had not yet entered with the thief. Christ came, and He suffered, and many bodies of the saints arose from their graves and were seen in the holy city. The cross of Christ is the key to Paradise, the cross of Christ opened it. Has He not said to you: "The kingdom of heaven has been enduring violent assault, and the violent have been seizing it by force"? Does not the One on the cross cause the violence? There is nothing between; the cross and, at once, Paradise. The greatest of pains produces the greatest of rewards.

[302] So much for what we have been saying. Let us pray the Lord that we may imitate the thief and this Lazarus, the beggar; if there is persecution, the thief; if peace, Lazarus. If we become martyrs, straightway we are in

Paradise; if we endure the pains of poverty, instantly we are in Abraham's bosom. Blood has its own abode and so has peace. Poverty, too, has its martyrdom; need well borne is martyrdom—but need suffered for the sake of Christ and not from necessity. How many beggars there are who long to be rich men and, therefore, commit crime! Poverty of itself does not render one blessed, but poverty for the sake of Christ. Faith does not fear hunger. The lover of Christ has no fear of hunger; he who has Christ, with Him possesses all riches. A certain merchant, a very wise man, sold all his material possessions, all his pearls? and purchased for himself a single pearl, the most precious of all. He, certainly, had pearls, and they were very beautiful and precious pearls. He had Moses, Isaiah, Jeremiah, the holy prophets, but, in comparison to Christ he deemed these pearls as dung, wherefore the apostle says: "But the things that were gain to me, I count them as dung that I may gain Christ," that I may buy the one pearl. Similarly, one of the prophets says: "Stand beside the roads, ask the pathway." It is as if he were saying, sell the pearls and, with the pearls, purchase the one pearl. The prophet did not say, abandon the ways, but stand on the ways, and ask and seek the Way, Christ. To whom be glory forever and ever. Amen.

Notes

INTRODUCTION

1. Brian J. Matz, *Patristic Sources and Catholic Social Teaching: A Forgotten Dimension. A Textual, Historical, and Rhetorical Analysis of Patristic Source Citations in the Church's Social Documents*, ANL 59 (Leuven: Peeters Press, 2008).

2. Johan Leemans, Brian J. Matz, and Johan Verstraeten, eds., *Reading Patristic Texts on Social Ethics: Issues and Challenges for Twenty-First-Century Christian Social Thought*, CUA Studies in Early Christianity (Washington, D.C.: Catholic University of America Press, 2011).

3. This is probably true for many of Gregory Nazianzen's homilies; cf. Čelica Milovanović, "Sailing to *Sophistopolis:* Gregory of Nazianzus and Greek Declamation," *Journal of Early Christian Studies* 13 (2005): 187–232.

CHAPTER 1

1. This phrase, "Catholic social teaching," refers to a set of documents that have emerged out of the Vatican and certain regional bishops' conferences since the late nineteenth century, and is not to be confused with "Catholic social thought." This latter phrase refers to the official texts *plus* the unofficial activities that take place in parishes, lay institutes, and Catholic worker movements, among other places. These unofficial activities not only engage in the work of alleviating injustice and caring for the marginalized, they also exhort the hierarchy to rethink continually its commitment to those concerns.

For a listing of documents that comprise CST, the reader is invited to consider David J. O'Brien and Thomas A. Shannon, *Catholic Social Thought: The*

Documentary Heritage (Maryknoll, N.Y.: Orbis Books, 1992); and Kenneth Himes, ed., *Modern Catholic Social Teaching: Commentaries and Interpretations* (Washington, D.C.: Georgetown University Press, 2005). Of course, it is the case social teaching existed prior to the late nineteenth century, and the interested reader of these earlier sources is directed to the oft-cited book, Michael Schuck, *That They Be One: The Social Teaching of the Papal Encyclicals, 1740–1989* (Washington, D.C.: Georgetown University Press, 1991). This present study has limited itself to the so-called modern CST documents for the simple reason that they comprise a body of literature that is a particular focus of study for many scholars of CST. There is no reason why a study such as this could not also be carried out for the premodern CST documents.

2. I am aware of two earlier articles that evaluate the role of patristic sources in CST, both of which are concerned only with *Rerum Novarum* and appear consecutively in a volume devoted to a study of that CST document: Jean-Marie Salamito, "*Rerum novarum,* une encyclique néo-scolastique? La question sociale ou le déclin de la communauté," in *Rerum Novarum: Écriture, contenu et reception d'une encyclique: Actes du colloque international organize par l'École française de Rome et le Greco n 2 du CNRS (Rome, 18–20 avril 1991)* (Rome: École française de Rome, 1997), 187–206, and Françoise Monfrin, "Pauvreté et richesse: Le lexique latin de l'encyclique: Inspiration classique ou inspiration patristique?" in *Rerum Novarum: Écriture, contenu et reception d'une encyclique,* 133–86.

Salamito, cf. esp. 196, concluded that patristic ideas were more influential than any particular patristic text or author. He argued the drafters were hardly aware of particular patristic texts relying instead, most likely, on a qualitatively poor sourcebook. Monfrin's article is not, strictly speaking, an examination of the patristic sources, but it evaluates the linguistic choices made by the drafters of this CST document. Monfrin concluded that the document's drafters were favorably disposed to classical Latin and that they took it upon themselves to reword quotations of biblical and historical sources to fit their particular disposition. My own study has confirmed Salamito's and Monfrin's findings.

3. For a list of the authors and texts from this period, see Maurits Geerard, ed., *Clavis Patrum Graecorum,* Corpus Christianorum, 5 vols. (Turnhout: Brepols, 1974, 1979, 1980, 1983, 1987, respectively), together with the supplement by Geerard et al., eds., *Clavis Patrum Graecorum Supplementum* (Turnhout: Brepols, 1998); and Eligius Dekkers, ed., *Clavis Patrum Latinorum,* 3rd ed., CCSL (Turnhout: Brepols, 1995).

4. For some surveys of patristic theology, see Lewis Ayres, *Nicaea and Its Legacy: An Approach to Fourth-Century Trinitarian Theology* (Oxford:

Oxford University Press, 2004); John Behr, *The Way to Nicaea,* Formation of Christian Theology 1 (Crestwood, N.Y.: St. Vladimir's Press, 2001); Angelo Di Berardino and Basil Studer, eds., *History of Theology,* vol. 1, *The Patristic Period,* trans. Matthew J. O'Connell (Collegeville, Minn.: Liturgical Press, 1997); and J. N. D. Kelly, *Early Christian Doctrines,* 5th rev. ed. (London: Black, 1985).

5. John Paul II, *Centesimus Annus* (1991), 11. English translation (hereafter ET): O'Brien and Shannon, *Catholic Social Thought: The Documentary Heritage,* 447.

6. For the full monograph, see Matz, *Patristic Sources and Catholic Social Teaching.*

7. See above n. 2.

8. The excluded items are numbered 4, 7, 21, 22, 23, 24, 25, 30, 38, 50, 54, 55, 66, 73, 74, 75, 76, 77, 86, 88, 89, 95, 103, and 106. *Didache* and *Shepherd of Hermas* are early texts and had a significant influence in both the Greek- and Latin-speaking worlds. Similarly, Irenaeus of Lyon wrote in Greek, yet his influence extended both to Latin and Greek Fathers. Emperor Julian the Apostate is excluded for he was not a Christian source.

9. Historical notations may also be found at source numbers 8 and 93.

10. The footnote directing the reader to these patristic sources appears at the end of the last sentence at *GS* 44, which reads, "Indeed, the Church admits that she has greatly profited and still profits from the antagonism of those who oppose or persecute her" (Immo Ecclesia, ex ipsa oppositione eorum qui ei adversantur vel eam persequuntur, se multum profecisse et proficere posse fatetur). See *Acta Apostolicae Sedis,* vol. 58, 1065; ET: O'Brien and Shannon, *Catholic Social Thought: The Documentary Heritage,* 194.

11. Justin Martyr's *Dialogue with Trypho* 110. The critical edition is Justin Martyr, *Dialogus cum Tryphone,* PTS 47, ed. Miroslav Marcovich (Berlin: Walter de Gruyter, 1997), 259. ET: Thomas B. Falls, *Justin Martyr: The First Apology; The Second Apology; Dialogue with Trypho; Exhortation to the Greeks; Discourse to the Greeks; The Monarchy or the Rule of God,* FOTC 6 (Washington, D.C.: Catholic University of America Press, 1977), 318.

Tertullian's *Apology* 50.13. The critical editions are Tertullian, *Opera, Pars I: Opera Catholica, Adversus Marcionem,* ed. Eligius Dekkers, Janus G. P. Borleffs, and R. Willems, CCSL 1 (Turnhout: Brepols, 1954), 171; *Apologeticum,* ed. Heinrich Hoppe, CSEL 69 (Vienna: Tempsky, 1939), 120. ET: Emily Joseph Daly, *Tertullian. Apologetical Works,* FOTC 10 (Washington, D.C.: Catholic University of America Press, 1950), 125.

12. Wendy Mayer, "The Audience(s) for Patristic Social Teaching: A Case Study," in *Reading Patristic Texts on Social Ethics,* ed. Leemans, Matz, and Verstraeten, 85–99.

13. Gregory Nazianzen, *Discours 6–12,* ed. Marie-Ange Calvet-Sebasti, SC 405 (Paris: Éditions du Cerf, 1995), 120–78. ET: Martha Vinson, *Saint Gregory of Nazianzus: Select Orations,* FOTC 107 (Washington, D.C.: Catholic University of America Press, 2004).

14. The dispute arose because Gregory the Elder had apparently signed a document emerging from one of the neo-Arian councils. The statement to which Gregory the Elder gave his affirmation was likely that emerging from a council held in Antioch in October 363 at which the word ὁμοιούσιος was preferred to ὁμοούσιος. See introduction in Calvet-Sebasti, ed., *Discours 6–12,* SC 405, 29–30. Cf. also Vinson, *Select Orations,* 3, n. 2.

15. Gregory, *Or.* 6.20. See also 6.22 (ed. Calvet-Sebasti, *Discours 6–12,* SC 405, 174–76; ET: Vinson, *Select Orations,* FOTC 107, 19–20), where Gregory argued that it is because of a common baptismal confession that the striving parties ought to seek reconciliation and peace. "Let us all abide in one spirit, . . . guarding the truth that we have received from our fathers, reverencing Father and Son and Holy Spirit, in which names we have been baptized, in which we believe" (ἀλλὰ πάντες μένωμεν <<ἐν ἑνὶ πνεύματι,...>> ... φυλάσσοντες τὴν καλὴν παρακαταθήκην ἣν παρὰ τῶν Πατέρων εἰλήφαμεν, προσκυνοῦντες Πατέρα καὶ Υἱὸν καὶ ἅγιον Πνεῦμα, ἐν Υἱῷ τὸν Πατέρα, ἐν Πνεύματι τὸν Υἱὸν γινώσκοντες, εἰς ἃ βεβαπτίσμεθα, εἰς ἃ πεπιστεύκαμεν).

The orthodox baptismal confession is that of belief in a triune Godhead, as Gregory affirmed also in *Oration* 33.17 (ed. Claudio Moreschini, *Discours 32–37,* SC 318 [Paris: Éditions du Cerf, 1985], 196); ET: my own: "Into what were you baptized? In the Father? Good, albeit Jewish still. In the Son? Good, it is not still Jewish, but not yet perfect. In the Holy Spirit? Very good, this is perfect" (Εἰς τί ἐβαπτίσθης; εἰς Πατέρα; Καλῶς, πλήν, Ἰουδαϊκὸν ἔτι. Εἰς Υἱόν; Καλῶς, οὐκέτι μὲν Ἰουδαϊκόν, οὔπω δὲ τέλειον. Εἰς τὸ ἅγιον Πνεῦμα; Ὑπέρευγε, τοῦτο τέλειον).

16. This is the argument of Peter Brown, *Poverty and Leadership in the Later Roman Empire* (Hanover, N.H.: University Press of New England, 2002).

17. For Justin Martyr, cf. *Apology* I.67 in PG 6.429; Justin Martyr, *Apologies: Introduction, texte critique, traduction, commentaire et index,* ed. André Wartelle, Études Augustiniennes, Série antiquité 117 (Paris: Études Augustiniennes, 1987), 190–92; *Apologie pour les Chrétiens,* ed. Charles Munier, Paradosis: Études de littérature et de théologie anciennes (Fribourg, Switzerland:

Éditions Universitaires, 1995), 122; *Apologiae pro Christianis,* ed. Miroslav Marcovich, PTS 38 (Berlin: Walter de Gruyter, 1994), 129–30. ET: Leslie William Barnard, *Justin Martyr: The First and Second Apologies,* ACW 56 (Mahwah, N.J.: Paulist Press, 1997), 71–72.

For Tertullian, cf. *Apology* 39 in PL 1.470; Tertullian, *Opera, Pars I: Opera Catholica, Adversus Marcionem,* ed. Eligius Dekkers, Janus G. P. Borleffs, and R. Willems, CCSL 1 (Turnhout: Brepols, 1954), 150–53; *Apologeticum,* ed. Heinrich Hoppe, CSEL 69 (Vienna: Tempsky, 1939), 91–95; ET: Emily Joseph Daly, *Tertullian: Apologetical Works,* FOTC 10 (Washington, D.C.: Catholic University of America Press, 1950), 98–102.

For Minucius Felix, cf. PL 3.260–63 and 335–38; Minucius Felix, *Octavius,* ed. Michael Pellegrino, Corpus Scriptorum Latinorum Paravianum (Turin: G. B. Paravia, 1972), 11–13, 47–48; Rudolph Arbesmann, trans., *Minucius Felix. Octavius,* FOTC 10 (Washington, D.C.: Catholic University of America Press, 1950), 335–38 and 387–89; G. W. Clarke, trans., *The Octavius of Marcus Minucius Felix,* ACW 39 (New York: Newman Press, 1974), 82–85 and 109–11.

The parallels between Tertullian's *Apology* and Minucius Felix's *Octavius* are striking, such that most scholars have concluded that one is dependent on the other, or that both are dependent on a third source. A helpful summary of this debate since the early nineteenth century is available in Michael E. Hardwick, *Josephus as an Historical Source in Patristic Literature through Eusebius,* Brown Judaic Studies 128 (Atlanta: Scholars Press, 1989), 21–22. Examination of the interdependency is also in Clarke, *The Octavius of Marcus Minucius Felix,* 9–10 (supports priority of Tertullian).

18. E.g., *Codex Theodosianus* 16.2.6 (Theodore Mommsen, ed., *Theodosiani libri xvi cum constitutionibus sirmondianis* [Bern: Apud Weidmannos, 1905], 836–37; ET: Clyde Pharr, *The Theodosian Code and Novels and the Sirmondian Constitutions,* The Corpus of Roman Law, vol. 1 [Princeton, N.J.: Princeton University Press, 1952], 441).

19. Cf. Valerie Karras, "Overcoming Greed: An Eastern Christian Perspective," *Buddhist-Christian Studies* 24 (2004): 47–53; and Robert Slesinsky, "The Doctrine of Virtue in St. Gregory of Nyssa's 'The Life of Moses,'" in *Prayer and Spirituality in the Early Church,* vol. 1, ed. Pauline Allen, Raymond Canning, and Lawrence Cross (Everton Park, Australia: Centre for Early Christian Studies, 1998), 341–52.

20. Seneca, *De vita beata* xxii.4. See Marcia L. Colish, *The Stoic Tradition from Antiquity to the Early Middle Ages* (Leiden: E. J. Brill, 1990).

21. E.g., Irenaeus, *Adversus haereses* III.21.9. John Lawson, *The Biblical Theology of Saint Irenaeus* (London: Epworth Press, 1948), 140; Eric Osborn, *Irenaeus of Lyons* (Cambridge: Cambridge University Press, 2001), 103.

22. See, e.g., Gregory of Nyssa, *De opificio hominis* 17.2; this is also reminiscent of another early Christian teaching on the *apokatastasis*. It is a commonplace in the literature to acknowledge that Gregory of Nyssa held to a universal salvation as did Origen, although he expressed this view somewhat differently. See Michael J. Tori, "Apokatastasis in Gregory of Nyssa: From Origen to Orthodoxy," *Patristic and Byzantine Review* 15 (1996–1997): 87–100; Alden A. Mosshammer, "Historical Time and the Apokatastasis according to Gregory of Nyssa," *Studia Patristica* 27 (1993): 70–93; Celia Rabinowitz, "Personal and Cosmic Salvation in Origen," *Vigiliae Christianae* 38 (1984): 319–29; David Kelly, "Apokatastasis in the Early Church," *Patristic and Byzantine Review* 9 (1990): 71–74. An examination of apokatastasis ideas beyond the fourth century can be found in Brian Daley, "Apokatastasis and 'Honorable Silence' in the Eschatology of Maximus the Confessor," in *Maximus Confessor* (Fribourg: Editions Universitaires, 1982), 309–39.

23. See the discussion below on private property in early Christian teaching.

24. See the discussion of our two case study texts in the next chapter of this study, as well as the discussion later in this chapter on the poor.

25. This theme of great reversal of fortunes in Jesus' parables has been studied by Joachim Jeremias, in *The Parables of Jesus*, trans. S. H. Hooke (New York: Charles Scribner's Sons, 1963; based on 6th German edition of 1962); Norman Perrin, *The New Testament, An Introduction: Proclamation and Parénesis, Myth and History* (New York: Harcourt Brace Jovanovich, 1974). Helen Rhee has studied this concept in second- and third-century Christian texts in "Wealth, Poverty, and Eschatology: Pre-Constantine, Christian Social Thought and the Hope for the World to Come," in *Reading Patristic Texts on Social Ethics*, ed. Leemans, Matz, and Verstraeten, 64–84.

26. See above n. 7; Tertullian, in *Apology* 39 (ed. Dekkers, Borleffs, and Willems, *Opera Catholica*, CCSL 1, 151; ET in Daly, *Apologetical Works*, FOTC 10, 99), wrote, "The money therefrom is spent not for banquets or drinking parties or good-for-nothing eating houses, but for feeding the needy, in burying them, in the support of boys and girls destitute of means and deprived of their parents, in the care of the aged, and in the relief of the shipwrecked."

27. Basil, *Hom.* 6.5 (ed. Y. Courtonne, *Homélies sur la richesse*, Collection d'études anciennes [Paris: Firm-Didot, 1935], 26; ET: H. Janis, "Homily on the Words of St. Luke's Gospel: 'I will pull down my barns and build larger ones' and on Avarice," *Orthodox Life* 42 [1992]: 13); John Chrysostom, *Homilies on Matthew, Hom.* 77.5 (PG 58.700).

28. Asterius of Amasea, *Hom.* 2.7.3 (Asterius of Amasea, *Homilies I–XIV. Text, Introduction and Notes,* ed. Cornelius Datema [Leiden: E. J. Brill, 1970], 21). Cf. also Basil of Caesarea, *Homily* 21.8 ("On Detachment from Worldly Goods").

29. For an examination of this issue in John Chrysostom's works, see Blake Leyerle, "John Chrysostom on Almsgiving and the Use of Money," *Harvard Theological Review* 87 (1994): 29–47.

30. The collection of patristic texts in Oliver O'Donovan and Joan O'Donovan, *From Irenaeus to Grotius: A Sourcebook in Christian Political Thought, 100–1625* (Grand Rapids, Mich.: Eerdmans, 1999), reveals a world concerned with healthy church-state relations and not with political theory as such. Still, an intriguing study is William Banner, "Origen and the Tradition of Natural Law Concepts," in *Dumbarton Oaks Papers,* vol. 8 (Washington, D.C.: Dumbarton Oaks, 1954), 49–82.

31. Gregory Nazianzen, *Or.* 43.63 (PG 36.580).

32. Eusebius of Caesarea, *De vita Constantini* (Paul Dräger, ed., *De vita Constantini,* Bibliotheca classicorum 1 [Oberhaid: Utopica, 2007]; ET: Averil Cameron and Stuart Hill, eds., *Eusebius. Life of Constantine,* Clarendon Ancient History [Oxford: Clarendon Press, 1999]).

33. E.g., Julian the Apostate. Cf. Gregory Nazianzen, *Ors.* 3 and 4 (Jean Bernardi, ed., *Grégoire de Nazianz. Discours 1–3.* SC 247 [Paris: Éditions du Cerf, 1978]).

34. Augustine, *City of God,* Book II (Bernardus Dombart and Alphonsus Kalb, eds., *De civitate Dei, Libri I–X,* CCSL 47 [Turnhout: Brepols, 1955], 34–65; ET: R. W. Dyson, *Augustine: The City of God against the Pagans,* Cambridge Texts in the History of Political Thought [Cambridge: Cambridge University Press, 1998], 51–93).

35. On *paideia* in late antiquity, cf. Donald L. Clark, *Rhetoric in Greco-Roman Education* (New York: Columbia University Press, 1957); Henri-Irénée Marrou, *A History of Education in Antiquity,* trans. George Lamb, 3rd ed. (New York: The New American Library, for Mentor Books, 1964). Marrou explains the content and format of grammar studies at the primary school level on 142–49; with respect to mathematical, literary, and scientific studies at the secondary school level, see 160–85; finally, with respect to rhetorical studies at levels beyond secondary schools, see 194–205. On early Christian appropriation of Greco-Roman *paideia,* especially in the Cappadocian Fathers, see Robert C. Gregg, *Consolation Philosophy: Greek and Christian* Paideia *in Basil and the Two Gregories,* Patristic Monograph Series 3 (Philadelphia: Philadelphia Patristic Foundation, 1975); Frederick Norris, "The Theologian and Technical

Rhetoric: Gregory of Nazianzus and Hermogenes of Tarsus," in *Nova et Vetera: Patristic Studies in Honor of Thomas Patrick Halton*, ed. John Petruccione (Washington, D.C.: Catholic University of America Press, 1998).

36. For a more full articulation of this vision, see Johan Verstraeten, "Re-Thinking Catholic Social Thought as Tradition," in *Catholic Social Thought: Twilight or Renaissance?*, ed. J. S. Boswell, F. P. McHugh, and J. Verstraeten, BETL 157 (Leuven: Peeters Press, 2000), 59–77.

37. Cf. Charles Curran, *Catholic Social Teaching, 1891–Present: A Historical, Theological, and Ethical Analysis* (Washington, D.C.: Georgetown University Press, 2002). Curran points out that, beginning with Vatican II, CST has shifted from a "natural law" approach to an *attempt at* an integrated theological approach. However, he does not believe they have succeeded, in part because of the twofold audience of church and "people of goodwill" to whom the documents are addressed. In fact, the only one addressed to a church audience only (*Evangelii nuntiandi*) is, in Curran's opinion, the most theologically integrated.

38. Johan Verstraeten, "Catholic Social Thought as Discernment," *Logos* 8 (2005): 94–111, here 103.

CHAPTER 2

1. These topics, together with usury, are those included in Brian Matz, Johan Leemans, and Johan Verstraeten, eds., *Compendium of Early Christian Social Thought: Translations from the Greek and Latin Fathers* (under review at an academic press).

2. The Catechism of the Catholic Church defines the common good as "the sum total of social conditions which allow people, either as groups or as individuals, to reach their fulfillment more fully and more easily." The Catechism notes that the common good involves three essential elements: respect for the person, the social well-being and development of the group, and peace, which is the stability of a just order (Catechism of the Catholic Church, nn. 1907–9). For common good teaching in Catholic social thought, which aims at even greater specificity than what is found in official documents such as the Catechism, cf. David Hollenbach, *The Common Good and Christian Ethics*, New Studies in Christian Ethics (Cambridge: Cambridge University Press, 2002).

3. An adequate warning of the need to make distinctions between Aquinas and the Fathers on this matter of the common good may be found in Jean

Porter, "The Common Good in Thomas Aquinas," in *In Search of the Common Good*, ed. Dennis P. McCann and Patrick D. Miller (New York: T. & T. Clark, 2005), 94–120. Porter documents several differences between Augustine and the thirteenth-century context out of which Aquinas emerged and exposes some reasons for why Aquinas writes of the common good in natural law terms as opposed to the theological terms used by Augustine.

4. Susan Holman, "Out of the Fitting Room: Rethinking Patristic Social Texts on 'The Common Good,'" in *Reading Patristic Texts on Social Ethics*, ed. Leemans, Matz, and Verstraeten, both correctly identifies κοινωφελής as the preferred term for "common good" in the Greek Fathers and traces out the implications of its meaning in Basil's *Homily* 6, primarily, and, to a lesser extent, in some texts by Chrysostom and later Byzantine writers. Holman explains that the Greek Fathers used "common good" language in two of the three realms discussed above—that of the Christian community and of the economy. Holman also highlights the significance of early Christian eschatology within "common good" discourse. The Fathers accepted that ultimate justice would be restored in the eschaton, and that as a consequence of the judgment of God against our and the culture's sins. Finally, and within the framework of the volume in which the article is published, Holman connects the Greek Fathers' understanding of the common good to contemporary understandings of the common good in Catholic social thought. For having done so, Holman is able, in the conclusion, to offer a first-ever definition of what is the common good in Greek patristic thought.

5. Aristotle, *Politics* 1297a and 1280b (ET: Aristotle, *A Treatise on Government, or The Politics of Aristotle*, trans. William Ellis [London: J. M Dent and Sons, 1912], 78 and 83, respectively).

6. Cicero, *De officiis* III.28 (M. T. Griffin and E. M. Atkins, trans., *Cicero. On Duties*, Cambridge Texts in the History of Political Thought [Cambridge: Cambridge University Press, 1991], 110).

7. Cf. also Cicero, *De finibus* III.62–63 and other Stoic texts as cited in Julia Annas, "Aristotelian Political Theory in the Hellenistic Period," in *Justice and Generosity: Studies in Hellenistic Social and Political Philosophy. Proceedings of the Sixth Symposium Hellenisticum*, ed. André Laks and Malcolm Schofield (Cambridge: Cambridge University Press, 1995), 74–94, here 77–79.

8. Cf., e.g., John Chrysostom, *Two Homilies on Those Who Hate Riches*, Hom. II.4; *Homilies on John*, Hom. XV.3; *Homilies on 1 Timothy*, Hom. XII.4.

9. Annas, "Aristotelian Political Theory in the Hellenistic Period," 82–92.

10. Theodoret of Cyrus, *Comm. on Romans* 12.4–5 (PG 82.188).

11. Gregory of Nyssa(?), *De vita s. Ephraem* (PG 46.841).

12. Origen, *Contra Celsum* VII.59–60 (Miroslav Marcovich, ed., *Origen. Contra Celsum libri VIII*, Supplements to Vigiliae Christianae 54 [Leiden: E. J. Brill, 2001], 509–51; ET: Henry Chadwick, *Origen. Contra Celsum* [Cambridge: Cambridge University Press, 1965], 444–46).

13. Gregory of Nyssa, "De virginitate," in *GNO* 8, part 1, ed. J. P. Cavarnos (Leiden: E. J. Brill, 1952), 253–55.

14. Ps.-Chrysostom, *In parabolam de filio prodigo* 1 (PG 59.515).

15. Basil of Caesarea, *Ep.* 265, cited in Holman, "Out of the Fitting Room," 109.

16. John Chrysostom, *Homilies on Matthew* 78.3 (7.775A; PG 58.714; ET: NPNF I.10, 472). Cited in Holman, "Out of the Fitting Room," 110.

17. Basil, *Hom.* 6.5, trans. Martin Francis Toal, *The Sunday Sermons of the Great Fathers,* 4 vols. (Chicago: Henry Regnery, 1957–1963), 3:329, slightly revised.

18. Cf. John Chrysostom, *Homilies on Matthew, Hom.* 77.5, in which he urges everyone to share what they have, and then focuses principally on why the wealthy must distribute their goods. Chrysostom writes, "You [i.e., the wealthy] have been entrusted with the goods of the poor, irrespective of whether you acquired the goods by honest labor or by an inheritance from your father." Chrysostom understood that, rather than distributing goods directly to the poor, God makes wealthy people the middle men in the economy. Cf. also Chrysostom, *Peccata fratrum non evulganda* 1 (PG 51.355), who, after wondering why the rich and poor do not share equally in the "common good" (κοινον ὠφελεια), suggested it was possible that some poor people are not themselves virtuous, and so have not deserved an equal share of the economic good of a community.

19. Chrysostom, *Homilies on 1 Corinthians* 10.4 (PG 61.86–88).

20. Chrysostom, *Homilies on John* 15.3 (PG 59.100). Cf. Wendy Mayer, "Poverty and Society in the World of John Chrysostom," in *Social and Political Archaeology in Late Antiquity,* Late Antique Archaeology 3, ed. L. Lavan, W. Bowden, A. Gutteridge, and C. Machado (Leiden: E. J. Brill 2006), 465–84; W. Mayer and Pauline Allen, *John Chrysostom,* The Early Church Fathers (London: Routledge, 2000), esp. 47–52. Interested scholars are invited to review W. Mayer's comprehensive bibliography on her website, http://www.cecs.acu.edu.au/chrysostombibliography.htm. In a related part of her website, Mayer provides a search tool for identifying passages in Chrysostom's corpus on matters of social ethics.

21. Cf. Sheldon Wolin, *Politics and Vision: Continuity and Innovation in Western Political Thought* (Princeton, N.J.: Princeton University Press, 1960; rev. ed. 2006), 86–126. Since the common good is intimately linked with political philosophy, Wolin's survey of the transition the Christian community made from an apolitical to a decidedly parallel, political institution is instructive. Wolin identifies the proliferation of heterodox groups in the third and fourth centuries as one indicator of the struggles within the community against this transition. Wolin points both to the legitimation of bishops and apostolic succession and to securing of a shared orthodox theology as key steps to securing a common identity for people dispersed across a wide geographic, cultural, and linguistic landscape. To Wolin, what was perceived by Christians to be the common good of their own community could not help but also be seen by those same Christians to be a common good for all communities.

22. Gregory Nazianzen, *Oration* 4.75 (PG 35.600). ET: C. W. King, *Julian the Emperor Containing Gregory Nazianzen's Two Invectives and Libanius' Monody* (London: George Bell and Sons, 1888), 44, with a change only of King's "peculators" to "embezzlers."

23. Salvian of Marseille, *De Gubernatore Dei* V (ed. Georges Lagarrigue, *Oeuvres II: Du gouvernement de Dieu*, SC 220 [Paris: Éditions du Cerf, 1975], 310–58; ET: *The Writings of Salvian the Presbyter*, FOTC 3, trans. Jeremiah F. O'Sullivan [Washington, D.C.: Catholic University of America Press, 1947], 127–50).

24. Robert A. Markus, "De civitate dei: Pride and the Common Good," in *Collectanea Augustiniana: Augustine: "Second Founder of the Faith,"* ed. Joseph C. Schnaubelt and Frederick Van Fleteren (Frankfurt: Peter Lang, 1990), 245–59, explores the connection between pride and the common good in Augustine's *City of God*. He argues that, although Augustine situated the common good in terms of the heavenly city, it was entirely possible, from Augustine's perspective, for the same to exist in the earthly city were it not for human pride.

Raymond Canning, in "St. Augustine's Vocabulary of the Common Good and the Place of Love for Neighbour," *Studia Patristica* 33 (1997): 48–54, outlines a three-part framework for studying the common good in Augustine's texts (changes in Augustine's ideas over time; distinctions between what is private and what is common; and the identification of the common good with God himself), which as yet remains to be further developed.

25. See esp. Markus, "De civitate dei: Pride and the Common Good," esp. 253–54.

26. Basil of Caesarea, *Homily* 12.2 (also known as *Homilia in principium Proverbiorum;* PG 31.389).

27. Irenaeus, *Against Heresies* V.24 (ANF 1, 552).
28. Clement, *Stromateis* I.27 (ANF 2, 339).
29. John Chrysostom, *Homilies on the Acts of the Apostles* 5.4 (PG 60.55).
30. Aristophanes, *Ecclesiazousae*, in *The Comedies of Aristophanes*, vol. 10 (Warminster: Aris and Phillips, 1998), esp. ll. 590–710. Aristophanes' play is set within the time of war in which the poor of Athens experienced continually degrading conditions. Praxagora, a woman, dresses up as a man to participate in a city council debate. She convinces the other council members that they delegate to women the task of managing a common stock of civic resources in order to alleviate suffering of all, including the poor.
31. Cf. Plato, *Republic*, in *Plato: Complete Works*, trans. G. M. A. Grube, trans. rev. by C. D. C. Reeve (Indianapolis, Ind.: Hackett Publishing, 1997), books III and V. On the comparison between Plato's Guardians and Aristophanes' women, cf. Alan Sommerstein, ed. and trans., *Ecclesiazousae*, 13–18. Sommerstein dismisses as unlikely two other arguments put forward for this comparison, either that Plato surmised his ideas before Aristophanes wrote or that both Plato and Aristophanes relied on an earlier, common source. Both of these arguments are based on silence in the historical record and, what is worse, they seem to Sommerstein to be an attempt to protect Plato from being thought of as influenced by a comedic play.
32. Plato, *Republic*, 971–1223. In his *Republic* Plato exposited a vision for justice and for its preservation in the context of a Greek *polis*.
33. Plato, *Republic*, book III, argued Guardians must be housed and cared for at the expense of the city (416c–417b). This was to protect the integrity of the Guardians, insofar as this arrangement preserved as the source of the Guardians' happiness the good of the city rather than the acquisition of property, land, or power for personal gain. In book IV, a challenger to this argument puts forward the claim that Guardians will be disposed toward unhappiness in this arrangement since they can enjoy none of the goods that a city offers its citizens (419). Plato, through the voice of Socrates, rejoins that the goal is the good of the *polis*, not the good of individual members of the *polis*.
34. Plato suggests both wealth and poverty can corrupt a person, for a wealthy craftsperson will no longer want to work at his craft, and a poor craftsperson will not have the resources to do so. The same is true for farmers and for Guardians. Wealth and poverty equally distract a person from the work to be done.
35. Aristophanes, *Wealth*, in *The Comedies of Aristophanes*, vol. 11, ed. and trans. Alan H. Sommerstein (Warminster: Aris and Phillips, 2001).
36. Importantly, Aristophanes distinguishes between people who are poor (πτωχοι) and people who are destitute (πενης). The Church Fathers also

seemed to accept some social stratification as a necessary part of a functioning society. E.g., John Chrysostom, *De Anna hom.* 5 (PG 54.673) argued similarly to Aristophanes that, without poverty, there would be no artisans, laborers, or workers (i.e., productivity), and society would collapse. Cf. Susan Holman, *The Hungry Are Dying: Beggars and Bishops in Roman Cappadocia*, Oxford Studies in Historical Theology (Oxford: Oxford University Press, 2001), 32; Mary Sheather, "Pronouncements of the Cappadocians on Issues of Poverty and Wealth," in *Prayer and Spirituality in the Early Church*, vol. 1, ed. Pauline Allen, Raymond Canning, and Lawrence Cross (Everton Park, Australia: Centre for Early Christian Studies, 1998), 375–92, here 376.

37. Xenophon, *The Education of Cyrus*, Agora Editions, trans. Wayne Amber (Ithaca, N.Y.: Cornell University Press, 2001), here 32–33. Xenophon's *Education of Cyrus* is important to social ethicists for a variety of reasons, not the least of which is its significant contribution to Machiavelli's understanding of the common good. Indeed, Xenophon's text is the only classical source to which Machiavelli referred in *The Prince*, and it was the classical text most frequently cited in his *Discourses*. Cf. Christopher Nadon, "From Republic to Empire: Political Revolution and the Common Good in Xenophon's *Education of Cyrus*," American Political Science Review 90 (1996): 361–74; see esp. 373–74 on comparisons to Machiavelli.

38. Aristotle, *Politics*, trans. Carnes Lord (Chicago: University of Chicago Press, 1984), here 2.1263a–b.I, on pp. 60–62. One must read all of books I and II to appreciate the argument at stake, for in them is a long discussion of how it is inappropriate to look to the man successful either in business or in overseeing slaves or in managing a household for the care and administration of a city. The three realms of business, slave management, and household management do share things in common with civic rule, but none fully prepare a person or persons for the just rule of free citizens. On that note, *Politics* is a training manual for just such an aspiring civic ruler or rulers, and one of the first questions tackled is that of how to administer property.

39. To be clear, Aristotle distinguishes between the *care* of possessions and the *use* of them. Care of possessions ought to be private, but the use of possessions ought to be common. This distinction between care and use preserves a sense of dignity for each property owner insofar as both pleasure is derived from calling something one's own and greed is restrained. What is more, Aristotle asserts that the distinction between care and use instills two important virtues: moderation and liberality. With respect to the former, this distinction preserves an awareness that some goods are not properly shareable (e.g., wives,

women); for the latter, it recognizes that sharing is only possible when goods are held privately (2.1263b).

40. Cicero, *De officiis,* LCL, ed. and trans. Walter Miller (Cambridge, Mass.: Harvard University Press, 1913), here I.7, p. 21. Cicero writes, "There is, however, no such thing as private ownership established by nature, but property becomes private either through long occupancy (as in the case of those who long ago settled in unoccupied territory) or through conquest (as in the case of those who took it in war) or by due process of law, bargain, or purchase, or by allotment. . . . Therefore, inasmuch as in each case some of those things which by nature had been common property became the property of individuals, each one should retain possession of that which has fallen to his lot; and if anyone appropriates to himself anything beyond that, he will be violating the laws of human society."

41. Even so, Cicero, *De officiis* III.5, argued one should not take the goods of one's neighbor even if it means bringing upon oneself pain, poverty, or even death! The taking of the goods of another is itself a violation of nature, an injustice. Cicero argues, "[H]e is mistaken in thinking that any ills affecting either his person or his property are more serious than those affecting his soul."

42. Menander, *The Bad-Tempered Man (Dyskolos),* trans. Stanley Ireland (Warminster, U.K.: Aris & Phillips,1995).

43. Menander, *The Bad-Tempered Man,* 85. Sostratos, a character in Menander's play, asks his father for his blessing for Sostratos's planned wedding. Sostratos's father hesitates, for the family of the woman his son wants to marry is poor and he is afraid of becoming responsible for the care of a poorer family. Sostratos counters (cf. ll. 797–812) with two points that convert his father, and the wedding is able to proceed. The first point was that the money or property of a hoarder may very well end up in the hands of those thought to be undeserving by a hoarder at the hoarder's death. The second point was that it is okay to have wealth so long as it is shared liberally with those who have needs.

44. Seneca, *De vita beata,* in *Seneca: Moral Essays,* vol. 2, ed. and trans. John W. Basore, LCL (Cambridge, Mass.: Harvard University Press, 1965). As the tutor of the young Nero, Seneca's political and financial fortunes swung like a pendulum largely in sync with those of Nero's mother and, then, Nero himself. Seneca's position gave him ample opportunities not only to acquire substantial wealth but also to write, and much of his corpus is devoted to ethics and the promotion of a life of philosophy. For an appreciation of Seneca's views about private property and, more generally, wealth, one could turn either to his *Ep.* 20 or *Ep.* 90 or to one of his other ethical treatises, *De brevitate vitae.* The writing of *De vita beata* may date to 58, following the exile of Sullius, who

had criticized Seneca for the seeming contradiction of his life: on the one hand, great wealth and, on the other hand, claims to Stoic *indifferentia*. This would also coincide with the time during which Nero's own decisions were growing increasingly ethically questionable. Cf. Paul Veyne, *Seneca: The Life of a Stoic*, trans. David Sullivan (New York and London: Routledge, 2003), esp. 20–22, 191.

45. Here one may also look to Seneca's exposée on the pitiable life of the wealthy and politically powerful found in his *De brevitate vitae*. No sooner do they acquire wealth or power, they are looking to give it away because of the burdens such things bring upon them.

46. Seneca, *De vita beata* xxiii.3 (ed. and trans. Basore, *Seneca: Moral Essays*, 2:158): Sapiens nullum denarium intra limen suum admittet male intrantem.

47. *Epistle of Barnabas* 19.8a (ed. Bart Ehrman, *The Apostolic Fathers*, LCL [Cambridge, Mass.: Harvard University Press, 2003], 2:78; translation mine): Κοινωνήσεις ἐν πᾶσιν τῷ πλησίον σου καὶ οὐκ ἐρεῖς ἴδια εἶναι· εἰ γὰρ ἐν τῷ ἀφθάρτῳ κοινωνοί ἐστε, πόσῳ μᾶλλον ἐν τοῖς φθαρτοῖς. Even so, it is possible the author of the epistle harbored some allowance for private property. At §10, the author reads Leviticus 17:11 and Deuteronomy 14:8 in a spiritual way: "don't eat the pig" means "don't cling to those who act like pigs." This is in support of the larger point by the author that labor, rather than thievery, is the way to acquire food. May we read into this the author's appreciation for the acquisition of some private property following the application of personal labor? I suspect so, but this is by no means conclusive.

48. Cf. *Didache* 13 (ed. Bart Ehrman, *The Apostolic Fathers*, LCL [Cambridge, Mass.: Harvard University Press, 2003], 1:438) at which place the author asks that the first fruits of one's food, money, clothing, and everything else(!) be given to support the teaching ministry of a local prophet or pastor. In the absence of such a person, then the first fruits are to be given to the poor. Presumably, what remains beyond the first fruits belongs to each person. So, the command in §4.8 to claim nothing is one's own may suggest a life of detachment from goods; offering the first fruits of one's goods to a prophet or to a poor person would serve as a regular reminder of this call to detachment. In this case, early readers of *Didache* would accept that its theological instruction cannot be separated from the practices of daily life.

49. Irenaeus of Lyon, *Adversus haereses* IV.30.1–2 (ed. Adelin Rousseau, *Contre les hérésies, Livre 4*, SC 100 [Paris: Éditions du Cerf, 1965], 770–79; ed. Norbert Brox, *Adversus haereses*, Fontes Christiani 8, part 4 [Freiburg: Herder Press, 1997], 236–41; ET: Alexander Roberts and James Donaldson, "Against

Heresies," in *The Apostolic Fathers with Justin Martyr and Irenaeus*, ANF 1 [Edinburgh: T. & T. Clark, 1867], 502–3). Hermas, *Shepherd*, Parables/Similitudes 1 and 2 (ed. Ehrman, *The Apostolic Fathers*, LCL, 2:304–14; ET: Ehrman, LCL, 2:305–15).

John A. McGuckin, in "The Vine and the Elm Tree: The Patristic Interpretation of Jesus' Teaching on Wealth," in *The Church and Wealth: Papers Read at the 1986 Summer Meeting and the 1987 Winter Meeting of the Ecclesiastical History Society*, ed. W. J. Shiels and Diana Wood (Oxford: Basil Blackwell, 1987), 1–14, suggests that this tension over renunciation versus detachment may be due not simply to shifting cultural forces in late antiquity but perhaps even more to a tension in how the *logia* of Jesus were brought together into the canonical gospels themselves. McGuckin argues, contra those who think passages like Mark 10:21 are apocalyptic teaching, that Jesus is concerned with the prophetic/missionary role his disciples must assume. By the time the *logia* of Jesus are incorporated into the canonical gospels the community had settled into an early pattern of doing church, and thus *logia* such as Mark 10:21 were recalled in order to encourage *some* in the church to pursue a lifestyle of living lightly and traveling broadly for the sake of missions. Cf. also Howard Clark Kee, "Rich and Poor in the New Testament and Early Christianity," in *Through the Eye of a Needle: Judeo-Christian Roots of Social Welfare*, ed. Emly A. Hanawalt and Carter Lindberg (Kirksville, Mo.: Thomas Jefferson University Press, 1994), 29–42.

For a different perspective on the question, one may turn to G. E. M. de Ste. Croix, "Early Christian Attitudes to Property and Slavery," in *Church, Society and Politics: Papers Read at the Thirteenth Summer Meeting and the Fourteenth Winter Meeting of the Ecclesiastical History Society*, ed. Derek Baker, Studies in Church History 12 (Oxford: Basil Blackwell, 1975), 1–38. He argued that the Church Fathers were interested more in man-to-man or man-to-God relationships and not in the men-to-men relationship (the latter of which would have concerned conflicts of class, social status, economic condition, political rights, etc.). This meant the Fathers were able to talk about the dangers of riches and property without demanding that Christians renounce all riches and property. So long as a person's use of his or her riches honored God and other people, the economic and social class realities could remain in place—they were no hindrance to personal relationships with God.

50. Inherited wealth would be a particular evil in such a scheme, for not only did it require no labor from the beneficiary, but also its own origins likely are stained with injustice. The only way to redeem for God's glory such tainted goods would be to put them at the disposal of the poor. Cf. Irenaeus, *A.H.*

IV.30.3. He compared the offering up to God of inherited property to the redeeming use of building the Temple with goods the Israelites took from the Egyptians. Two centuries later, Epiphanius, in his *Panarion* 61.3–4 (PG 41.1040; ET: Frank Williams, *The Panarion of Epiphanius of Salamis, Books II and III*, Nag Hammadi and Manichaean Studies 36 [Leiden: E. J. Brill, 1994], 116), argued that the true Church does not despise those who have inherited wealth if such individuals use that wealth to meet the needs both of their family and of others. Chrysostom would agree, for he wrote in *Homilies on Matthew* 77.5 that goods possessed either by inheritance or by honest labor all belong to the poor.

51. Hermas, *Shepherd*, Similitudes 2, suggested the rich aid the poor by their wealth in exchange for the poor aiding the rich by their prayer. This argument will surface many times in later centuries. Cf., e.g., Theodoret of Cyrus, *On Providence* 6.31, who says that the rich have been blessed by God with money and the poor have been blessed by God with skills in trades and crafts. In such a situation it is the rich, he argues, who are compelled to come begging at the door of the poor person. I find this to be an interesting point, and perhaps what Theodoret says was true regarding the mobility of goods in the economic context of Cyrus in the early fifth century. However, our modern economic context no longer limits the choices of to which poor the rich are obliged to beg. The global marketplace allows the rich regularly to move from one poor person to another until they find a satisfactorily low enough price for the crafts they desire. The poor are not in an advantageous position in such a market.

On Hermas, see Carolyn Osiek, *Rich and Poor in the* Shepherd of Hermas: *An Exegetical-Social Investigation*, The Catholic Biblical Quarterly Monograph Series 15 (Washington, D.C.: Catholic Biblical Association of America, 1983).

52. Clement of Alexandria, *Quis dives salvetur* 4–5 (ed. Otto Stählin, Ludwig Früchtel, and Ursula Treu, *Stromata: Buch VII und VIII; Excerpta ex Theodoto; Eclogae propheticae; Quis dives salvetur; Fragmente*, GCS 17 [Berlin: Akademie Verlag, 1970], 162–63; ET: G. W. Butterworth, *Clement of Alexandria. The Exhortation to the Greeks, The Rich Man's Salvation, and the Fragment of an Address Entitled To the Newly Baptized*, LCL [Cambridge, Mass.: Harvard University Press, 1919' repr. 1982], 279–83). Clement made a similar point in another of his works, *Stromata* 4.13. There, he affirmed that goods and possessions are not, in themselves, bad lest they be not a creation of God.

53. Clement, *Quis dives salvetur* 13 (ed. Stählin, Früchtel, and Treu, *Quis dives salvetur*, GCS 17, 167–68. ET: Butterworth, *Clement of Alexandria*, LCL,

295–97). Cf. also Clement, *Paedogogus* 2.3, 2.12, 3.7, and *Stromata* 6.12. In these passages he argued we ought to acquire only such objects as are useful for completing more than one task. Clement even identifies the types of "superfluities" he has in mind, including makeup, jewelry, silver dishware, and other such decorous goods. True adornment is the pursuit of Christ and spiritual life rather than the wearing of jewelry.

54. Cf. last paragraph of n. 49 above. Not surprisingly, the Marxist question dominated studies of early Christian texts on this question of wealth and private property during the nineteenth and early twentieth centuries. The secondary literature affirming the voluntary nature of early Christian poverty and wealth sharing includes, among many others, Etienne Chastel, *Études historiques sur l'influence de la charité durant les premiers siècles chrétiens, et considérations sur son rôle dans les sociétés modernes* (Paris: Capelle, 1853); ET: Chastel, *The Charity of the Primitive Churches: Historical Studies upon the Influence of Christian Charity during the First Centuries of Our Era, with Some Considerations Touching Its Bearings upon Modern Society*, trans. George-Auguste Matile (Philadelphia: J. B. Lippincott, 1857); Edmond Le Blant, "La richesse et las christianisme a l'age des persecutions," *Revue archéologique* (Series 2) 39 (1880): 220–30; Gerhard Uhlhorn, *Die christliche Liebestätigkeit in der alten Kirche* (Stuttgart: Gundert, 1882); Shailer Matthews, *The Social Teachings of Jesus: An Essay in Christian Sociology* (New York: Macmillan, 1897); F. X. Funk, "Über Reichtum und Handel im christlichen Altertum," *Historisch-politische Blätter* 130 (1902): 888–99; Ephrem Baumgartner, "Der Kommunismus im Urchristentum," *Zeitschrift für katholische Theologie* 33 (1909): 625–45; Stanislas Giet, "La doctrine de l'appropriation des biens chez quelques-uns des Pères," *Recherches de science religieuse* 35 (1948): 55–91.

Those who find in the early Christian literature a less voluntary and more controlled system of property redistribution include W. Haller, "Die Eigentum im Glauben und Leben der nachapostolischen Kirche," *Theologische Studien und Kritiken* 64 (1891): 478–563; Lujo Brentano, "Die wirtschaftlichen Lehren des christlichen Altertums," in *Sitzungsberichte der philosophische-philologischen und der historischen Klasse der kgl. Akademie der Wissenschaften* (Munich, 1902), 141–93; Karl Kautszy, *Der Ursprung des Christentums, eine historische Untersuchung* (Stuttgart: J. H. W. Dietz Nachf., 1908), of which there were many subsequent editions; Gérard Walter, *Les origines du communisme, judaiques, chrétiennes, grecques, latines* (Paris: Bibliothéque historique, 1931).

Perhaps less interested in lamenting the lack of a vibrant, Christian socialism by the third century and more interested in explaining how it came to pass is the article by Wolf-Dieter von Hauschild, "Christentum und Eigentum:

Zum Problem eines altkirchlichen 'Sozialismus,'" *Zeitschrift für Evangelische Ethik* 16 (1972): 34–49. He argues that, while Jesus' teachings and the second-century Christians had laid the groundwork for a socialist trajectory, the views of Clement of Alexandria were so quickly accepted and disseminated that the earlier momentum was derailed. The teachings of Basil and John Chrysostom served to cement Clement's view for the late fourth and into the fifth centuries.

See L. William Countryman, *The Rich Christian in the Church of the Early Empire: Contradictions and Accommodations,* Texts and Studies in Religion 7 (New York: Edwin Mellen Press, 1980), 1–18. For an earlier summary of the debate, cf. Franz Meffert, *Der "Kommunismus" Jesu und der Kirchenväter* (München-Gladbach: Volksvereinverlag, 1922). Countryman rather capably summarized this body of literature up to the mid-1970s insisting, at the end, that contemporary political questions are ultimately unhelpful when approaching early Christian texts. His own study began by accepting as fact that the Fathers were asking different questions than those asked by nineteenth- and twentieth-century Westerners. To avoid the importation of contemporary questions into what are admittedly fragmentary pieces of data from the ancient world, Countryman suggested limiting the scope of any inquiry to the few Christian texts both which can be reliably dated and whose authorship is in little doubt. For his part, he focused on Clement of Alexandria's *Quis dives salvetur?* and related texts from Clement that shed light on his understanding of private property.

On the further influence of Clement within the Christian tradition, see Sophie Lunn-Rockliffe, "A Pragmatic Approach to Poverty and Riches: Ambrosiaster's Quaestio CXXIV," in *Poverty in the Roman World,* ed. M. Atkins and R. Osborne (Cambridge: Cambridge University Press, 2006). Lunn-Rockliffe points to the influences of the Gospel of Luke, Clement of Alexandria, and the Roman legal system on Ambrosiaster's encouragement toward a just use of wealth, particularly directed toward those with excessive levels of wealth. Cf. also her more recent book, *Ambrosiaster's Political Theology,* Oxford Early Christian Studies (Oxford: Oxford University Press, 2007).

55. Hauschild, in "Christentum und Eigentum," argues that while Jesus' teachings and the second-century Christians had laid the groundwork for a socialist, or protocommunist, trajectory, the views of Clement of Alexandria were so quickly accepted and disseminated that the earlier momentum was derailed. The teachings of Basil and John Chrysostom served to cement Clement's view for the late fourth and into the fifth centuries.

56. Rainer Kampling, "'Have We Not Then Made a Heaven of Earth?': Rich and Poor in the Early Church," *Concilium* 22 (1986): 51–62, here 58–59.

57. Epiphanius, *Panarion* 80.4 (PG 42.761, 764; ET: Williams, *The Panarion of Epiphanius,* 631–32). A sign that Clement's arguments held sway well into the late fourth century, Epiphanius at *Panarion* 60.1 (Her. 64) suggested that, were it not for the serpent's infusion of envy into human desires (cf. Gen 3), humans would be able to keep their material desires in check in accordance with their need. Furthermore, Epiphanius, at *Panarion* 61.3–4, argued that the acquisition of property through labor or other honest means is appropriate insofar as such behavior makes possible fulfilling the command of Christ to feed and care for the needy.

58. The Pelagian tract is entitled *On Wealth* (ed. Andreas Kessler, *Reichtumskritik und Pelagianismus: Die pelagianische Diatribe de divitiis; Situierung, Lesetext, Übersetzung, Kommentar,* Paradosis 43 [Freiburg: Universitätsverlag, 1999]; ET: B. R. Rees, ed., *The Letters of Pelagius and His Followers* [Suffolk, U.K.: Boydell Press, 1991], 171–211). However, Richard Newhauser, in *The Early History of Greed: The Sin of Avarice in Early Medieval Thought and Literature* (Cambridge: Cambridge University Press, 2000), 89–90, suggests that the text is not so much about renunciation as about sufficiency of property, that readers since Augustine have been too influenced by his exaggerated reaction in his correspondence with Hilary of Syracuse. Perhaps Newhauser is right and the critique of avarice masks an acceptance of owning sufficient property, but one would be hardpressed to find in this Pelagian treatise a particular passage that supports this view. The author yields no ground to those who would support some ownership of private property.

The renunciation view was not only that of some divisive Christians, but may already be found in Philo. In one of the collected essays by Valentin Nikiprowetzky, included in his *Études Philoniennes,* Patrimoines Judaisme (Paris: Éditions du Cerf, 1996), 243–91, it is argued that Philo was like the Essenes insofar as he believed riches were useless and were very often the fruit of injustice. Philo believed the scriptural ideal is poverty and opulence is an affront to one's claims of love for men and love for the Torah.

59. Birger Pearson and Tim Vivian, eds., *Two Coptic Homilies Attributed to Saint Peter of Alexandria: On Riches, On the Epiphany* (Rome: C.I.M., 1993). On the original "core homily" and its author, Peter, see 26–31. See also Tim Vivian, *St. Peter of Alexandria: Bishop and Martyr,* Studies in Antiquity and Christianity (Philadelphia: Fortress Press, 1988).

60. Lactantius, *Divine Institutes* III.23, although the context for the quote begins at 21 (PL 6.421–25). ET: Lactantius, *Divine Institutes,* trans. Anthony Bowen, with introduction and notes by Peter Garnsey, Translated Texts for Historians 40 (Liverpool: Liverpool University Press, 2003), 211.

61. Gregory of Nazianzus, *Oration* 14.25. This argument is found in other Greek Fathers, including Clement of Alexandria, *Quis dives salvetur* 15; Asterius of Amasea, *The Unjust Steward;* Chrysostom, *Homilies on John* 19.3; and Basil of Caesarea, *Hom.* 8.2 and 4, especially the former on account of the fact that Basil suggests that God has brought drought on the land in order to punish the people for their hoarding of goods.

62. Gregory Nazianzen, *Oration* 14.29. Cf. John Chrysostom, *Homilies on I Corinthians* 10.3–4.

63. Asterius of Amasea, *Hom.* 2 (*The Unjust Steward*).

64. Asterius, *Hom.* 2.

65. Blake Leyerle, "John Chrysostom on Almsgiving and the Use of Money," surveys Chrysostom's homilies with respect to his teaching about the correct use of wealth by those otherwise prone to lavish displays of it in the marketplace. Chrysostom exposes the vainglory of it all and argues that via almsgiving the wealthy can both put their wealth to proper use and receive from God, alone whose view of the wealthy counts, honor in heaven. Leyerle argues further that this same notion puts clergy on notice, especially those who oversee the distribution of the church's wealth to the poor. They are in a position of social honor, and so a vain cleric casts a shadow over the whole enterprise of the church as social benefactor. This is where Peter Brown's book, *Poverty and Leadership in the Later Roman Empire* (Hanover, N.H.: University Press of New England, 2002), 45–73, is helpful, for he teases out even further than Leyerle the social implications of this new euergetism for not only the church as an institution but also for the bishops.

66. John Chrysostom, *Homilies on Matthew* 77.4; *On the Statues* II.6: he discusses the idea that present and future rewards await those who cultivate such virtue. Cf. also Chrysostom, *Homilies on 1 Corinthians* 10.4, at which place this paradox is offered: property is really God's but can be considered our own once we do with it what God intended, which is to share it with the needy. In addition, consider Gregory Nazianzen, *Or.* 14.19, at which place it is said that distribution of one's property to the poor is sanctifying insofar as it allows us to demonstrate distrust of the present world and trust in the future world.

67. Chrysostom, *Homilies on Matthew* 77.4. Gregory Nazianzen, in *Or.* 14.28, laments that people have a greater compassion for their animals than they do for those of similar constitution, their fellow humans.

68. Chrysostom, *Homilies on Matthew* 77.6.

69. Chrysostom, *Homilies on 2 Corinthians* 19.3–4.

70. Chrysostom, *Homilies on 1 Corinthians* 10.4.

71. Chrysostom, *Homilies on John* 69.3.

72. Chrysostom, *Homilies on John* 77.4–5. He also suggests that almsgiving is of little use to the one otherwise given over to the acquisition of luxuries.

73. Rabbula, "Commands and Admonitions of Mar Rabbula, Bishop of Edessa to the Priests and the 'Benai Qeiama,'" in *Syriac and Arabic Documents Regarding Legislation Relative to Syrian Asceticism*, ed. and trans. Arthur Vööbus (Stockholm: Etse, 1960), 36–50. I found interesting a prohibition against priests taking by force during festivals the goods of the wealthy for the purpose of distributing those goods to the poor. Cf. Canon 8, p. 38.

74. Cf. James Goehring, "Monasticisim in Byzantine Egypt: Continuity and Memory," in *Egypt in the Byzantine World, 300–700*, ed. Roger S. Bagnall (Cambridge: Cambridge University Press, 2007), 390–407. Goehring relies on archaeological and epigraphic evidence rather than only evidence from the writings of the monks themselves for his claims.

75. The notion that the poor are actually rich before God strikes many who work with the poor as particularly disingenuous. Cf. William Robert Domeris, *Touching the Heart of God: The Social Construction of Poverty among Biblical Peasants*, Library of Hebrew Bible/Old Testament Studies 466 (Edinburgh: T. & T. Clark, 2007), here 10.

76. Cf. Santiago Guijarro, "The Family in First-Century Galilee," in *Constructing Early Christian Families: Family as Social Reality and Metaphor*, ed. Halvor Moxnes (London: Routledge, 1997). Guijarro explores how the scarcity of goods created unstable family structures in the first through the third centuries. As well, Evelyne Patlagean published in 1977 a groundbreaking study of economic poverty in Byzantium between the fourth and seventh centuries; see Evelyne Patlagean, *Pauvreté économique et pauvreté sociale á Byzance 4e–7e siècles*, Civilisations et Sociétés 48 (Paris: Mouton, 1977). Cf. also by Patlagean, "The Poor," in *The Byzantines*, ed. Guglielmo Cavallo (Chicago: University of Chicago Press, 1997), 15–42, although only the first few pages overlap with the period of the Fathers considered here. Patlagean made careful distinctions both between types of poverty and the impact of poverty on different communities of persons both within cities and rural areas. Patlagean laid the groundwork for a host of further studies of the interchange between Christian teaching about social ethics and the real-life impact on social policies and mentalities.

Notably, cf. Peter Brown, *Poverty and Leadership in the Later Roman Empire*, 14–16. There he explains that we should no longer think of late antique societies as being comprised of "the poor" and "the rich," but that there was a broad middle class—likely 80 percent or more of the total population—that forever lived in "shallow poverty," meaning that any one bad economic year could thrust even skilled craftspeople or farmers into destitution. My own research suggests that we can not only speak about "shallow poverty" but also "shallow wealth," for during the good economic years, those same groups of people were prone to take advantage of the destitute. Cf. Gregory of Nyssa's homily *Against the Usurers* (*Contra Usurarios,* in *GNO* 9, ed. Ernest Gebhardt [Leiden: E. J. Brill, 1967], 195–207; ET: Casimir McCambley, "Against Those Who Practice Usury by Gregory of Nyssa," *Greek Orthodox Theological Review* 36 [1991]: 287–302), in which he does not address himself only to "the rich" so much but to all who take advantage of the needy during times of want. It seems that "shallow wealth" could be a spiritual problem as much as shallow poverty was a social and economic problem.

Other studies deserving some consideration here include Roger Bagnall, "Monk and Property: Rhetoric, Law, and Patronage in the *Apophthegmata Patrum* and the Papyri," *Greek, Roman, and Byzantine Studies* 42 (2001): 7–24; Andrew T. Crislip, *From Monastery to Hospital: Christian Monasticism and the Transformation of Health Care in Late Antiquity* (Ann Arbor: University of Michigan Press, 2005); Richard Finn, *Almsgiving in the Later Roman Empire: Christian Promotion and Practice, 313–450,* Oxford Classical Monographs (Oxford: Oxford University Press, 2006); Holman, *The Hungry Are Dying*.

A modern economist would argue the Fathers did not appreciate the value of entrepreneurship, which is what could develop out of excess land and possessions among the wealthy, in addition to the gainful employment such entrepreneurship would provide. Barry Gordon suggests that the empire was not set up to accommodate such entrepreneurship and thus it did not enter the Fathers' minds. See B. Gordon, "The Problem of Scarcity and the Christian Fathers: John Chrysostom and Some Contemporaries," *Studia Patristica* 22 (1989): 108–20; Gordon, *The Economic Problem in Biblical and Patristic Thought*, Supplements to Vigiliae Christianae, Texts and Studies of Early Christian Life and Language 9 (Leiden: E. J. Brill, 1989).

Finally, to complicate matters a bit further, recent work by Steven Friesen has suggested there were at least three such levels of "poor" in the second century, along a spectrum of seven socioeconomic classes. See Steven J. Friesen, "Injustice or God's Will? Early Christian Explanations of Poverty," in *Wealth and Poverty in Early Church and Society,* ed. Susan Holman, Holy Cross Studies in Patristic Theology and History (Grand Rapids, Mich.: Baker Academic, 2008), 17–36. Assuming those classifications held for later centuries, it is imperative that readers of early Christian texts that refer to "the poor" judge between the type(s) of poor people of whom the texts are speaking. This should be read together with Christel Freu's work, *Les figures du pauvre dans les sources Ita-*

liennes de l'antiquité tardive, Études d'archéologie et d'histoire ancienne (Paris: De Boccard, 2007), on the different words used of the poor at least in the Western part of the empire.

77. Holman, *The Hungry Are Dying*. Fernando Rivas Rebaque, *Defensor pauperum. Los pobres en Basilio de Cesarea: Homilias VI, VII, VIII y XIVB,* Biblioteca de Auctores Cristianos 657 (Madrid: Biblioteca de Autores Cristianos, 2005), stokes the discussion a bit further by arguing "the poor" are not actually the objects of particular sympathy in fourth-century Christian texts. The travails of the poor are certainly diagnosed, but the ultimate aim of each lesson was not to raise the status of the poor, but instead to move the sympathies of the wealthy.

Cf. also Finn, *Almsgiving in the Later Roman Empire*. The book may be divided roughly between the first half, which is concerned both about the different types of alms and the different ways in which they were distributed, and the second half, which is concerned about the meaning of alms both to the poor and to the givers of alms insofar as almsgiving constructed identities for the poor.

78. Patlagean, *Pauvreté économique et pauvreté soicale à Byzance,* documents a substantial rise in the overall population of the empire beginning in the fourth century that was matched by an increasing percentage of poor persons within that population. The social structures—be they financially or class-defined—were either unable or unwilling to respond sufficiently to the growing needs of the burgeoning underclass, thus creating for the first time a noticeable constituency of "the poor." Patlagean's work is really the point of departure insofar as later scholars have had to wrestle with her claim that "the poor" became an object of interest in late antiquity starting in the fourth century.

Cf. also Giuliano Volpe, *San Giusto: Le ville, le ecclesiae* (Bari: Edipuglia, 1998), esp. 234–36. Volpe's book documents the results of long-term poverty by comparing the physical condition of bodies between peasant and leisured classes.

79. Cf. studies on early Christian friendship for, as noted above, the classical world expressed the common good in terms of a society of friends. See Donald Burt, "Friendship and Subordination in Earthly Societies," in *Christianity and Society: The Social World of Early Christianity,* ed. Everett Ferguson (New York: Garland, 1999), 315–55; David Konstan, "Problems in the History of Christian Friendship," in *Christianity and Society,* ed. Ferguson, 357–83; and Carolinne White, *Christian Friendship in the Fourth Century* (Cambridge: Cambridge University Press, 1992). White, e.g., argues that Christians, although

accepting biblical claims of equality and in founding friendship on a unity of faith, co-opted and furthered earlier Greek ideas about friendship with respect to its mutual obligations and concern with loyalty. The Fathers' ideas about how "common" is to be the "common good" depended, in part, on whether or not they were writing from the biblical or the classical perspective.

80. Hesiod, *Works and Days* (David Tandy and Walter Neale, eds., *Hesiod's Works and Days: A Translation and Commentary for the Social Sciences* [Berkeley and Los Angeles: University of California Press, 1996]), ll. 286–341.

81. Seneca, *Moral Essays,* LCL, trans. John W. Basore (London: W. Heinemann, 1928–1935), 1:39–41.

82. Plotinus, *Ennead* 1.8.5 (A. H. Armstrong, ed., *Enneads,* vol. 1, *Porphyry on the Life of Plotinus, Ennead 1,* LCL [Cambridge, Mass.: Harvard University Press, 1969], 291).

83. Lucian, "The Dream" 9, in *Selected Dialogues,* trans. and ed. Desmond Costa (Oxford: Oxford University Press, 2005), 7–12, here 9.

84. Elisabeth Herrmann, in *Ecclesia in Re Publica: Die Entwicklung der Kirche von pseudostaatlicher zu staatlich inkorporierter Existenz,* Europaisches Forum, vol. 2 (Frankfurt: Peter Lang, 1980), 205–348, chronicles the state's growing acceptance of bishops as official protectors of the poor.

85. Emperor Julian (the Apostate), *Letters* 22 and 83.

86. Michael Sherwin, "Friends at the Table of the Lord: Friendship with God and the Transformation of Patronage in the Thought of John Chrysostom," *New Blackfriars* 85 (2004): 387–98.

87. John Chrysostom, *Homilies on Matthew* 66.3 (PG 58.630). Cited in Brown, *Poverty and Leadership in the Later Roman Empire,* 14.

88. There is an article critical of Chrysostom's concern for the poor in his homilies as really being a cover for his concern for the middle-class landowners who are being squeezed economically from a variety of sides. Chrysostom himself hailed from this class. Thus, the author suggests that Chrysostom is rather more concerned about this middle 80 percent than the lowest 10 percent of society. See G. L. Kurbatov, "Klassavoja suscnost ucenija Ioanna Zlatausta," *Ezegodnik muzeja istorii i religii i ateiznoz* 2 (1958): 80–106; ET by Andrius Valevicius, "The Nature of Class in the Teaching of John Chrysostom," available through the website of the Center for Early Christian Studies, Australian Catholic University, at http://www.cecs.acu.edu.au/chrysostomresearch.

89. Finn, *Almsgiving in the Later Roman Empire,* 18–26.

90. Friesen, "Injustice or God's Will?," 20–21. This income scale is based on archaeological and textual evidence among the remains of the larger Roman cities. Also see Tim Parkin, *Demography and Roman Society* (Baltimore: Johns Hopkins University Press, 1992).

91. Asterius of Amasea, *Homily* 3, "Against Covetousness," 6 (Asterius of Amasea, *Homilies I–XIV: Text, Introduction and Notes,* ed. Cornelius Datema [Leiden: E. J. Brill, 1970], 31; ET: Galusha Anderson and Edgar Goodspeed, eds., *Ancient Sermons for Modern Times* [New York: Pilgrim Press, 1904], 100).

92. Asterius of Amasea, *Homily* 3, "Against Covetousness," 6.

93. See discussion in n. 76 above of recent work by Steven Friesen that there were at least three such levels of "poor" in the second century. Perhaps those classifications held for the third, fourth, and fifth centuries.

94. Brown, *Poverty and Leadership in the Later Roman Empire,* 33–44. Brown provides a fresh evaluation of Basil's own actions in light of a possible redating of the construction of the *Basileias* (from 368 to 370) on 41–42. Basil defends his *Basileias* and its benefit to the state in his *Ep.* 94 (ed. Yves Courtonne, *Saint Basile: Lettres,* 3 vols. [Paris: Belles Lettres, 1957–1966], 1:204–7).

95. Cf. Gregory Nazianzen, *Oration* 44.63. See also Brian Daley, "Building a New City: The Cappadocian Fathers and the Rhetoric of Philanthropy," *Journal of Early Christian Studies* 7 (1999): 431–61.

96. Cf. Gilbert Dagron, "Les moines et la ville. Le monachisme à Constantinople jusqu'au concile de Chalcédone," *Travaux et Mémoires* 4 (1970): 229–76, esp. 246–53, a study of Eustathius's program of poor relief in Constantinople during his years as bishop there, 337–341. See also Nina Garsoian, "Nersês le Grand, Basile de Césarée et Eustathe de Sébaste," *Revue des études arméniennes* 17 (1983): 145–69, a study of poverty relief programs in Armenia also during the early fourth century. In addition, an article by Konstantina Mentzou-Meimari, "Eparkhiaka evagé idrymata mekhri tou telous tés eikonomakhias," *Byzantina* 11 (1982): 243–308, provides a list of institutions for poor relief in and around Constantinople during late antiquity.

97. Palladius, *Lausiac History* (Cuthbert Butler, ed., *The Lausiac History of Palladius: The Greek Text Edited with Introduction and Notes,* Texts and Studies: Contributions to Biblical and Patristic Literature 6, no. 2 [Cambridge: Cambridge University Press, 1904]; ET: Robert T. Meyer, *Palladius: The Lausiac History,* ACW 34 [New York: Paulist Press, 1964]). Palladius had lived in various parts of the eastern half of the empire during the late fourth and early fifth centuries. His travels included time in Egypt, and during such times he encountered some of the monks whose stories he relates. Other stories probably came to him through his spiritual mentor, Evagrius, and still others likely came to him through written records and oral accounts.

98. Palladius, *Lausiac History* 40.2. ET: Meyer, *Palladius,* ACW 34, 116–17.

99. Palladius, *Lausiac History* 40.3. ET: Meyer, *Palladius,* ACW 34, 117.

100. Cf. Ambrose of Milan, *On the Work of Ministry* II.28.140–43, PL 16:139–41; the critical edition is Ambrose, *De officiis*, CCSL 15, ed. Maurice Testard (Turnhout: Brepols, 2000), 148–49. ET: Ivor J. Davidson, *Ambrose. De officiis, Volume I: Introduction, Text, and Translation*, Oxford Early Christian Studies (Oxford: Oxford University Press, 2001), 347–49.

101. Finn, *Almsgiving in the Later Roman Empire*, 31, cites an unpublished dissertation on the language for the poor in homilies by Greek and Latin Fathers, and how such language reveals a growing prominence of the poor in that period. See also Holman, *The Hungry Are Dying*. My own study of the homilies has made me aware of the constancy of the Matthew 25 image throughout the second through fifth centuries. There is no appreciable increase in its penetration into the homilies at one point or another.

102. Cyril, *Homilies on Luke*, Hom. 111. Cf. R. Payne Smith, trans., *A Commentary upon the Gospel according to S. Luke by S. Cyril, Patriarch of Alexandria*, 2 vols. (Oxford: Oxford University Press, 1859), 2:525. Cyril's exposition of Luke 16, Jesus' parable of Lazarus and the rich man, gives us some glimpse into his understanding of the common good. He began the exposition with a vision for the type of society that Christ had called his followers to effect. Cyril writes, "For He [i.e., Christ] would have us be lovers one of another, and ready to communicate: prompt to give, and merciful, and careful of showing love to the poor, and manfully persisting in the diligent discharge of this duty." The common good, then, is a society in which each of its members accepts as a duty love for the poorest and weakest members. In fact, at several places in his exposition he urged his hearers to "make friends with the poor."

103. Cf. Bradley Nassif, "The Starving Body of Christ," *Christian History and Biography Online*, no. 94 (March 11, 2007). Nassif draws on homilies from John Chrysostom to demonstrate a connection between a theology of the Incarnation and a theology of loving the poor.

CHAPTER 3

1. Manfred Frank, ed., *Hermeneutik und Kritik: Mit einem Anhang sprachphilosophischer Texte Schleiermachers*, Suhrkamp Taschenbucher Wissenschaft 211 (Frankfurt: Suhrkamp, 1977). There exists no English translation of the complete work. However, a nearly complete translation is Friedrich Schleiermacher, *Hermeneutics and Criticism and Other Writings*, trans. Andrew Bowie, Cambridge Texts in the History of Philosophy (Cambridge: Cambridge University Press, 1995), 5–224.

The only material excised by Bowie, according to his introduction, was those portions where Schleiermacher engages in lengthy treatment of particular New Testament texts. In doing so, he follows the lead of Frank's edition; however, Bowie has included a translation of some of the material Frank omitted. He does this, he said, in order to make the work accessible to New Testament scholars in addition to scholars in the fields of philosophy and hermeneutics. Excerpts from Schleiermacher's *Hermeneutik und Kritik* and excerpts from some of his other, shorter texts on the subject were translated in Friedrich Schleiermacher, *Hermeneutics: The Handwritten Manuscripts*, trans. James Duke and Jack Forstman (Missoula, Mont.: Scholars Press, 1977).

2. Schleiermacher, *Hermeneutik und Kritik*, Introduction §1 (ed. Frank, *Hermeneutik und Kritik*, 75; ET: Bowie, *Hermeneutics and Criticism*, 5): die Kunst, die Rede eines andern richtig zu verstehen.

3. Schleiermacher, *Hermeneutik und Kritik*, Introduction §5 (ed. Frank, *Hermeneutik und Kritik*, 77; ET: Bowie, *Hermeneutics and Criticism*, 8): Tatsache im Denkenden.

4. Cf. Schleiermacher, *Hermeneutik und Kritik*, Introduction §§19–20 (ed. Frank, *Hermeneutik und Kritik*, 94–95; ET: Bowie, *Hermeneutics and Criticism*, 24).

5. Cf. Schleiermacher, *Hermeneutik und Kritik*, Introduction §21, Part 1 §1.7 (ed. Frank, *Hermeneutik und Kritik*, 95–96, 104–6, respectively; ET: Bowie, *Hermeneutics and Criticism*, 24, 34, respectively).

6. Schleiermacher, *Hermeneutik und Kritik*, Part 1 §1 (ed. Frank, *Hermeneutik und Kritik*, 101; ET: Bowie, *Hermeneutics and Criticism*, 30): Alles, was noch einer näheren Bestimmung bedarf in einer gegebenen Rede, darf nur aus dem dem Verfasser und seinem ursprünglichen Publikum gemeinsamen Sprachgebiet bestimmt werden.

7. Schleiermacher, *Hermeneutik und Kritik*, Part 1 §1.5 (ed. Frank, *Hermeneutik und Kritik*, 104; ET: Bowie, *Hermeneutics and Criticism*, 33).

8. Schleiermacher, *Hermeneutik und Kritik*, Part 1 §1.8–9 (ed. Frank, *Hermeneutik und Kritik*, 106–7; ET: Bowie, *Hermeneutics and Criticism*, 35).

9. Schleiermacher, *Hermeneutik und Kritik*, Part 1 §3 (ed. Frank, *Hermeneutik und Kritik*, 116; ET: Bowie, *Hermeneutics and Criticism*, 44): Der Sinn eines jeden Wortes an einer gegebenen Stelle muß bestimmt werden nach seinem Zusammensein mit denen, die es umgeben.

10. Schleiermacher, *Hermeneutik und Kritik*, Part 1 §§4, 6, 7 and Part 1 Conclusion (ed. Frank, *Hermeneutik und Kritik*, 117–19, 120–21, and 151, respectively; ET: Bowie, *Hermeneutics and Criticism*, 45–49 and 75, respectively).

11. For a prehistory to this notion of a "hermeneutic circle," see Baruch Spinoza, *Tractatus theologico-politicus*, ed. Fokke Akkerman, Épiméthée: Essais philosophiques, Oeuvres B. Spinoza 3 (Paris: PUF, 1999; orig. pub. 1670); Friedrich Ast, *Grundlinien der Grammatik, Hermeneutik und Kritik* (Landshut: Jos. Thomann, 1808).

12. Schleiermacher, *Hermeneutik und Kritik*, Part 2 §1 (ed. Frank, *Hermeneutik und Kritik*, 167; ET: Bowie, *Hermeneutics and Criticism*, 90): die Einheit des Werkes, das Thema, wird hier angesehen als das den Schreibenden bewegende Prinzip, und die Grundzüge der Komposition als seine in jener Bewegung sich offenbarende eigentümliche Natur. Cf. also Part 2 in "On the Technical Task" (ed. Frank, *Hermeneutik und Kritik*, 209–12; ET: Bowie, *Hermeneutics and Criticism*, 132–35).

13. Schleiermacher, *Hermeneutik und Kritik*, Part 2 §5 (ed. Frank, *Hermeneutik und Kritik*, 169; ET: Bowie, *Hermeneutics and Criticism*, 92).

14. Schleiermacher, *Hermeneutik und Kritik*, Part 2 (ed. Frank, *Hermeneutik und Kritik*, 209 and 223; ET: Bowie, *Hermeneutics and Criticism*, 131 and 143). Schleiermacher proposes that secondary thoughts are those that have the feeling of being inserted into the text, like marginalia. The interpreter who has come to know an author well through an acquaintance with that author's entire corpus will have the sense of which thoughts in a text contribute to its unity and which are mere asides.

15. Schleiermacher, *Hermeneutik und Kritik*, Part 1 Conclusion (ed. Frank, *Hermeneutik und Kritik*, 133–35; ET: Bowie, *Hermeneutics and Criticism*, 60–62).

16. Cf. Schleiermacher, *Hermeneutik und Kritik*, Introduction §18 (ed. Frank, *Hermeneutik und Kritik*, 94; ET: Bowie, *Hermeneutics and Criticism*, 23).

17. Belatedly, the study of economics today, with its increasing attention to human behavior, has come to the conclusion that humans do not always act "rationally" or in their supposed best financial interest. Behavioral economics is a subdiscipline of the field now on the rise.

18. Wilhelm Dilthey, "Das Verstehen anderer Personen und ihrer Lebensäusserungen," in *Der Aufbau der geschichtlichen Welt in den Geisteswissenschaften, Gesammelte Schriften*, vol. 7, ed. Bernard Groethuysen (Leipzig: Teubner, 1927), 208; ET: H. A. Hodges, *Wilhelm Dilthey: An Introduction* (London: Routledge and Kegan Paul, 1944), 118. Text is in §3: Das Kind wächst heran in einer Ordnung und Sitte der Familie. . . . Ehe es sprechen lernt, ist es schon ganz eingetaucht in das Medium von Gemeinsamkeiten.

19. Dilthey, "Das Verstehen anderer Personen und ihrer Lebensäusserungen," 5 (ed. Groethuysen, in *Der Aufbau der geschichtlichen Welt in den Gei-

steswissenschaften, Gesammelte Schriften, vol. 7, 214; ET: Hodges, *Wilhelm Dilthey,* 122): Das Verstehen ist an sich eine dem Wirkungsverlauf selber inverse Operation. Ein vollkommenes Mitleben ist daran gebunden, daß das Verständnis in der Linie des Geschehens selber fortgeht. Es rückt, beständig fortschreitend, mit dem Lebensverlauf selber vorwärts. So erweitert sich der Vorgang des Sichhineinversetzens, der Transposition.

20. Wilhelm Dilthey, "Die Entstehung der Hermeneutik (1900)," in *Die geistige Welt: Einleitung in die Philosophie des Lebens, Gesammelte Schriften,* vol. 5, ed. Georg Misch (Leipzig: Teubner, 1924), 317–38, here 331; ET: H. P. Rickman, *W. Dilthey: Selected Writings* [Cambridge: Cambridge University Press, 1976], 260): Verstehen wird nur Sprachdenkmalen gegenüber zu einer Auslegung, welche Allgemeingültigkeit erreicht . . . sie soll gegenüber dem beständigen Einbruch romantischer Willkür und skeptischer Subjektivität in das Gebiet der Geschichte die Allgemeingültigkeit der Interpretation theoretisch begründen, auf welcher alle Sicherheit der Geschichte beruht.

21. Cf. Dilthey, "Die Entstehung der Hermeneutik (1900)," in *Die geistige Welt: Einleitung in die Philosophie des Lebens, Gesammelte Schriften,* vol. 5, ed. Misch, 317; ET: Rickman, *W. Dilthey,* 247.

22. As cited in chapter 2 notes, the critical edition of the sixteen homilies is Asterius of Amasea, *Homilies I–XIV. Text, Introduction and Notes,* ed. Cornelius Datema (Leiden: E. J. Brill, 1970); the only published English translation of five of Asterius's homilies, including *Hom.* 1, which is our concern here, is that of Galusha Anderson and Edgar J. Goodspeed, eds., *Ancient Sermons for Modern Times* (New York: Pilgrim Press, 1904).

For some examination of the history of homilies that at one time or another passed under Asterius's name, see Datema's introduction and cf. Johan Leemans, Wendy Mayer, Pauline Allen, et al., eds., *Let Us Die That We May Live: Greek Homilies on Christian Martyrs from Asia Minor, Palestine, and Syria, c. 350–c. 450 AD* (London: Routledge, 2003), 162–66.

Two studies that mine Asterius's homilies for data are of interest. One is on his biblical exegesis. See Maria Veronese, "L'esegesi di Asterio di Amasea," in *Origene e l'alessandrinismo cappadoce (III–IV secolo). Atti del V Convegno del Gruppo Italiano di ricerca su "Origene e la tradizione alessandrina" (Bari, 20–22 settembre 2000),* ed. Mario Girardi and Marcello Marin (Bari: Edipuglia, 2002), 299–331. Although Veronese only rarely discusses our homily, she discusses Asterius's treatment of the parable's reality on pp. 318–19. The other study is Vincent Vasey, "The Social Ideas of Asterius of Amasea," *Augustinianum* 26 (1986): 413–36. Vasey, like Veronese, also attempts a synthesis of Asterius's texts, though his concern is the social thought of the first four homilies, with limited attention paid to the others.

23. For a sense of the culture, the education, and the politics of Asterius's day, with extensive reference to the Christian leaders in Cappadocia, see the three-volume set on Cappadocia in the fourth century by Raymond Van Dam, *Kingdom of Snow: Roman Rule and Greek Culture in Cappadocia* (Philadelphia: University of Pennsylvania Press, 2002); *On Becoming Christian: The Conversion of Roman Cappadocia* (Philadelphia: University of Pennsylvania Press, 2003); and *Families and Friends in Late Roman Cappadocia* (Philadelphia: University of Pennsylvania Press, 2003).

24. Cf. Peter Brown, *Poverty and Leadership in the Later Roman Empire*, 26–44, esp. 26–32.

25. Asterius, *Hom.* 1.2 (ed. Datema, *Homilies I–XIV*, 7; ET: mine, here and elsewhere, unless otherwise noted): Ἄνθρωπός τις ἦν πλούσιος καὶ ἐνδιδύσκετο πορφύραν καὶ βύσσον. By comparison to the NT text (ed. Aland et al.) Asterius leaves out only the postpositve δέ, which is understandable since Asterius treats this parable as a story separable from what preceded in Luke.

26. Asterius, *Hom.* 1.2.1 (ed. Datema, *Homilies I–XIV*, 7): Τῶν δὲ τὴν εὐπολίτευτον ζωὴν αἱρουμένων καὶ ἀπερίεργον οἰκεῖον καὶ φίλον τὸ τῇ τῶν ἀναγκαίων τὴν χρῆσιν μετρεῖν.

27. Asterius, *Hom.* 1.4.2 (ed. Datema, *Homilies I–XIV*, 9): Μὴ γράφε τὸν Χριστόν ... ἐπὶ δὲ τῆς ψυχῆς σου βαστάζων νοητῶς τὸν ἀσώματον Λόγον περίφερε.

28. Asterius, *Hom.* 1.4.4 (ed. Datema, *Homilies I–XIV*, 9): [Ἐπὶ ταῦτα] ἡμᾶς ὠφέλησε τὸ ὑπερήφανον ἔνδυμα τοῦ πλουσίου.

29. Regarding the background to Asterius's understanding of *ametria*, see the essays in John T. Fitzgerald, ed., *Passions and Moral Progress in Greco-Roman Thought* (London: Routledge, 2007).

30. Asterius, *Hom.* 1.5 (ed. C. Datema, *Homilies I–XIV*, 10): πόσοι πένητες ἀδικοῦνται! πόσοι δὲ ὀρφανοὶ κονδυλίζονται!

31. Basil of Caesarea, *Commentary on Isaiah* 1.33; Gregory of Nyssa, *Life of Macrina* 6; Theophilus of Alexandria, *Festal Letters* 19.15; John Chrysostom, *Homilies on Genesis* 25.22–23; Theodoret of Cyrus, *Discourse* 6.9, 11, 36–37 ("On Providence").

32. Asterius, *Hom.* 1.6.1 (ed. Datema, *Homilies I–XIV*, 10): Καὶ λίαν ἐπιμελῶς τῇ διηγήσει τὰς συμφορὰς ἐπὶ τέλει ἐκτραγῳδεῖ τοῦ πτωχοῦ, ἵνα τὴν τοῦ μὴ ἐλεοῦντος στηλιτεύσῃ σκληρότητα.

33. Asterius, *Hom.* 1.8.2 (ed. Datema, *Homilies I–XIV*, 12): Ἐπειδὴ δὲ καλὰ τὰ λειπόμενα πρὸς ἀκρόασιν, ἐν τοῖς παρελθοῦσι στενάξας, ὁ πένης, ἐν τοῖς ἀκολούθοις εὐθύμησον....

34. Cf. Gregory Nazianzen, *Or.* 14.1 (PG 35.857), where he calls his audience both συμπένητες and πτωχοί. The inconsistent use of the terms continues in at least 14.4 and 14.10–11, and presumably elsewhere, but I have not looked further in this rather long homily.

35. Asterius, *Hom.* 1.9.1 (ed. C. Datema, *Homilies I–XIV,* 12): Ἐγένετο δὲ ἀποθανεῖν τὸν πτωχὸν καὶ ἀπενεχθῆναι ὑπὸ τῶν ἀγγέλων εἰς τὸν κόλπον Ἀβραάμ.

36. Asterius, *Hom.* 1.9.2 (ed. C. Datema, *Homilies I–XIV,* 12): θεωρία τις ἡμᾶς ἐκδέχεται τῇ εἰκόνι τοῦ αἰσθητοῦ κόλπου πρὸς νοητὴν τινα πραγματείαν ξειραγωγοῦσα.

37. The exegetical methods of the Church Fathers have been the focus of much study. A standard reference for this field is Charles Kannengiesser, *Handbook of Patristic Exegesis: The Bible in Ancient Christianity,* 2 vols., The Bible in Ancient Christianity 1, 2 (Leiden: E. J. Brill, 2004), esp. 1:206–58. Also helpful are Jaroslav Broz, "From Allegory to the Four Senses of Scripture: Hermeneutics of the Church Fathers and of the Christian Middle Ages," in *Philosophical Hermeneutics and Biblical Exegesis,* WUNT 153, ed. Petr Pokorny and Jan Roskovec (Tübingen: Mohr Siebeck, 2002), 301–9; and Frances M. Young, *Biblical Exegesis and the Formation of Christian Culture* (Cambridge: Cambridge University Press, 1997). Young underscores the difficulty readers of early Christian exegesis will have in teasing out distinctions between typology and allegory in their attempts to define spiritual exegesis. Finally, the legacy of patristic exegesis into the medieval period with its four senses of Scripture is traced in Henri de Lubac, *Medieval Exegesis,* 2 vols., trans. Mark Sebanc and E. M. Macieroweski (Grand Rapids, Mich.: Eerdmans, 1998–2000).

38. Samuel Taylor Coleridge, *The Collected Works of Samuel Taylor Coleridge, VII: Biographia literaria, or, Biographical Sketches of My Literary Life and Opinions,* Bollingen Series 75, trans. James Engell and Walter J. Bate (London: Routledge and Kegan Paul, 1983, orig. pub. 1817), ch. 14.

39. Asterius, *Hom.* 1.9.5 (ed. C. Datema, *Homilies I–XIV,* 13): κριτὴν ὄντα καὶ μισθαποδότην τῆς ἀρετῆς καὶ τῇ θεραπευτικῇ φωνῇ προσκαλούμενον τοὺς δικαίους καὶ λέγοντα.

40. Asterius, *Hom.* 1.10.3 (ed. C. Datema, *Homilies I–XIV,* 13): Οὔτε οὖν πᾶς πτωχὸς δίκαιος, ἀλλ' ἐκεῖνος οἷος ὁ Λάζαρος.

41. Asterius, *Hom.* 1.10.3 (ed. C. Datema, *Homilies I–XIV,* 13): οὔτε πᾶς πλούσιος ἀπεγνωσμένος, ἀλλ' ὁ μετὰ τοιαύτης ζῶν προαιρέσεως, οἵαν εἶχεν ὁ τοῦ Λαζάρου σύγχρονος.

42. One thinks here of Gregory Nazianzen, *Oration* 14, or John Chrysostom, *Sermons on Genesis* 5.

43. Asterius, *Hom.* 1.1 (ed. C. Datema, *Homilies I–XIV*, 7; ET: Anderson and Goodspeed, 17): ἀποστρέφεσθαι μὲν τὸν ὑπερήφανον καὶ ὑψαύχενα πλοῦτον, ἀγαπᾶν δὲ γνώμην φιλάνθρωπον καὶ τὴν μετὰ δικαιοσύνης πενίαν.

44. Cf. Robin Attfield, "Christianity," in *A Companion to Environmental Philosophy*, ed. D. Jameson (Oxford: Blackwell, 2001), 96–110; R. J. Berry, "Creation and the Environment," *Science and Christian Belief* 7 (1995): 21–43; Roderick Nash, *The Rights of Nature: A History of Environmental Ethics* (Madison: University of Wisconsin Press, 1989); and Clare Palmer, "Stewardship: A Case Study in Environmental Ethics," in *The Earth Beneath: A Critical Guide to Green Theology*, ed. Ian Ball, Margaret Goodall, Clare Palmer, and John Reader (London: SPCK, 1992), 67–86.

Susan P. Bratton, in "The Original Desert Solitaire: Early Christian Monasticism and Wilderness," *Environmental Ethics* 10 (1988): 31–53, brings early Christian texts into dialogue with contemporary environmental ethics. Somewhat different, but nevertheless important, for understanding early Christian ideas of nature and the role of the environment is Jaroslav Pelikan, *Christianity and Classical Culture: The Metamorphosis of Natural Theology in the Christian Encounter with Hellenism* (New Haven, Conn.: Yale University Press, 1993), 256–62. Pelikan relies upon Cappadocian texts in situating the natural world, with all about it that is good, within a framework of knowledge of the Light of God.

45. Andres Duany, Elizabeth Plater-Zyberk, and Robert Alminana, *New Civic Art: Elements of Town Planning* (New York: Rizzoli, 2003); Peter Katz, *The New Urbanism: Toward an Architecture of Community* (New York: McGraw-Hill, 2004); particularly interesting is R. J. Chaskin, M. L. Joseph, and H. S. Webber, "The Theoretical Basis for Addressing Poverty through Mixed-Income Development," *Urban Affairs Review* 42 (2007): 369–409.

46. Cf., e.g., Mark E. Graham, *Sustainable Agriculture: A Christian Ethic of Gratitude* (Portland, Ore.: Wipf and Stock, 2005, 2009); Church of Scotland, *Justice and Markets*, Report of the Church and Society Council (May 2009), 18–19; and numerous weblogs promoting the "buy local" and "slow food" movements within the Christian community.

47. Rutba House, ed., *School(s) for Conversion: 12 Marks of a New Monasticism*, New Monastic Library: Resources for Radical Discipleship (Portland, Ore.: Wipf and Stock, 2005); C. Christopher Smith, ed., *Introductory Bibliography of the New Monasticism: Resources for a New Monasticism*, vol. 1 (Indianapolis: Doulos Christou Press, 2007); Jonathan Wilson-Hartgrove, *New Monasticism: What It Has to Say to Today's Church* (Grand Rapids, Mich.: Brazos Press, 2008).

48. It is the third-century Clement of Alexandria to whom we look for the first significant Christian exposition of what constitutes sufficient wealth. Cf. Stählin, Früchtel, and Treu, eds., *Clemens Alexandrinus,* vol. 3, GCS 17 (Berlin: Akademie-Verlag, 1970), 159–91; J. Armitage Robinson, ed., *Clement of Alexandria: Quis dives salvetur,* Texts and Studies: Contributions to Biblical and Patristic Literature 5, no. 2 (Cambridge: Cambridge University Press, 1897), 1–15; repr. with ET (Portland, Ore.: Wipf and Stock, 2004).

49. Clement, *Paedagogus* II.3, had encouraged his followers to purchase goods for their use that had more than one purpose. For example, he would not have been a proponent of having chinaware in one's house reserved for special occasions in addition to everyday dishware. One set of dishes is sufficient; acquiring more would be a needless expense and a waste of financial resources better intended for the poor. Clement also identified a number of extravagances, including possessing more than a handful of pieces of jewelry, makeup, decorative clothing, glass bowls, etc.

50. Asterius, *Hom.* 1.2 (ed. C. Datema, *Homilies I–XIV,* 7): Τῶν δὲ τὴν εὐπολίτευτον ζωὴν αἱρουμένων καὶ ἀπερίεργον οἰκεῖον καὶ φίλον τὸ τῇ χρείᾳ τῶν ἀναγκαίων τὴν χρῆσιν μετρεῖν.

51. Asterius, *Hom.* 1.3 (ed. C. Datema, *Homilies I–XIV,* 8): παραχρώμενοι τῷ βίῳ.

52. Asterius, *Hom.* 1.5 (ed. C. Datema, *Homilies I–XIV,* 10): πόσοι πένητες ἀδικοῦνται! πόσοι δὲ ὀρφανοὶ κονδυλίζονται!

53. Asterius, *Hom.* 1.10 (ed. C. Datema, *Homilies I–XIV,* 13; ET: Anderson and Goodspeed, 38): Ἐπεὶ τοῖς ἀπορουμένοις ἁπλῶς, ἔχουσι δὲ τὸν τρόπον ἀπαιδαγώγητον ἢ ἀκατόρθωτον, ἐφόδιον γίνεται πολλῶν καὶ πονηρῶν τολμημάτων ἢ πρὸς ἀνάγκην ἀκτημοσύνη.

54. Cf. Donal Dorr, *Option for the Poor: A Hundred Years of Vatican Social Teaching* (Dublin: Gill and Macmillan, 1983; rev. ed. 1992) 191–92, 210–11, 222–23, 320–21.

55. Richard Falk, "Reviving the 1990s Trend toward Transnational Justice: Innovations and Institutions," *Journal of Human Development and Capabilities* 3 (2002): 167–90; H. Richard Friman, ed., *Challenges and Paths to Global Justice* (New York: Palgrave MacMillan, 2007); Naomi Roht-Arriaza, *The Pinochet Effect: Transnational Justice in the Age of Human Rights* (Philadelphia: University of Pennsylvania Press, 2005).

56. Wendy Mayer, "The Audience(s) for Patristic Social Teaching" in *Reading Patristic Texts on Social Ethics,* ed. Leemans, Matz, and Verstraeten, 85–99.

57. Germain Morin, ed., *S. Hieronymi presbyteri opera. Pars II: Opera homiletica*, CCSL 78 (Turnhout: Brepols, 1958), 507–16. ET: Marie Liguori Ewald, *The Homilies of Saint Jerome*, vol. 2, FOTC 57 (Washington, D.C.: Catholic University of America Press, 1966), 200–211.

58. On the relationship between Jerome and Paula, see Jerome's *Ep.* 45. Importantly for this study, it should be noted that simply because one has chosen an ascetic life, that does not necessarily mean the person has chosen to live an austere life. Paula was famously wealthy and donated generously throughout her life, suggesting that she did not suddenly divest herself of all wealth. See R. Teja and M. Marcos, "Modelos de ascetismo femenino aristocrático en la época de Juan Crisóstomo: Constantinopla y Palestina," in *Giovanni Crisostomo: Oriente e Occidente tra IV e V secolo, XXXIII Incontro di Studiosi dell'Antichità Cristiana, Augustinianum 6–8 maggio 2004, Roma*, Studia Ephemeridis Augustinianum 93 (Rome: Institutum Patristicum Augustinianum, 2005), 619–25, who compare the institutions established by Olympias and Paula and argue that Paula's, in particular, was modeled on the wealthy senatorial household, with different ascetic expectations imposed on the servants she brought with her versus herself and other women of the same elite social rank. See also Bronwen Neil, "*On True Humility:* An Anonymous Letter on Poverty and the Female Ascetic," in *Prayer and Spirituality in the Early Church*, vol. 4, *The Spiritual Life*, ed. Wendy Mayer, Pauline Allen, and Lawrence Cross (Strathfield: St Paul's Publications, 2006), 233–46; Geoffrey Dunn, "The Elements of Ascetical Widowhood: Augustine's *de Bono Viduitatis* and *Epistula* 130," in *Prayer and Spirituality in the Early Church*, vol. 4, ed. Mayer, Allen, and Cross, 247–56.

Studies on the wealth of monasteries, and the use of that wealth ostensibly for the benefit of the poor, include James Goehring, "Monasticisim in Byzantine Egypt: Continuity and Memory," in *Egypt in the Byzantine World, 300–700*, ed. Roger S. Bagnall (Cambridge: Cambridge University Press, 2007), 390–407; Ewa Wipszycka, "Diaconia," in *The Coptic Encylopedia*, vol. 3, ed. Azis S. Atiya (New York: Macmillan, 1991), 895–67; and Adam Serfass, "Wine for Widows: Papyrological Evidence for Christian Charity in Late Antique Egypt," in *Wealth and Poverty in Early Church and Society*, ed. Susan R. Holman (Grand Rapids, Mich.: Baker Academic; Boston, Mass.: Holy Cross Orthodox Press, 2008).

59. On Jerome's life and his preaching in Bethlehem, see esp. Ewald, *The Homilies of Saint Jerome*, xvii–xxi; Andrew Cain, *The Letters of Jerome: Asceticism, Biblical Exegesis and the Construction of Christian Authority in Late Antiquity* (Oxford: Oxford University Press, 2009); J. N. D. Kelly, *Jerome: His Life, Writings and Controversies* (London: Duckworth, 1975), see 116–40, esp.

134–38; Germain Morin, "Les monuments de la prédication de S. Jérôme," in *Études, Textes, Découvertes: Contributions à la littérature et à l'histoire des douze premiers siècles,* Anecdota Maredsolana, Seconde Série 1 (Abbaye de Maredsous: Duculot-Roulin, 1913); and A. Olivar, *La predicación cristianan antiqua* (Barcelona: Herder, 1991), 415–20, 611, 898, 915, 932.

Other secondary literature on Jerome's life does not discuss his preaching, but is still valuable as a context for Jerome's life in Bethlehem and his travels during the later decades of his life, particularly the Origenist and Pelagian controversies in which he was embroiled. See Georg Grützmacher, *Hieronymus: Eine biographische Studie zur alten Kirchengeschichte,* 3 vols., Studien zur Geschichte der Theologie und der Kirche (Leipzig: Dieterich, 1901–1908), and cf. vol. 3 for Jerome's life post-400; Ferdinand Cavallera, *Saint Jérôme: Sa vie et son oeuvre,* vols. 1–2, Spicilegium sacrum Lovaniense, Études et documents (Louvain: Spicilegium sacrum Lovaniense, 1922), cf. 1:123–29; Stefan Rebenich, *Jerome,* The Early Church Fathers (London: Routledge, 2002), 41–59; and Rebenich, *Hieronymus und sein Kreis: Prosopographische und sozialgeschichtliche Untersuchungen,* Historia—Einzelschriften (Stuttgart: Franz Steiner Verlag, 1992).

60. Cf. Kelly, *Jerome,* 135–36.

61. Kelly, *Jerome,* 131–33, where he cites Palladius's *Lausiac History* 41, which reported that fifty nuns were a part of Paula's convent, and where he cites Epiphanius, who reported "a multitude of dedicated brothers" in the monastery. If that "multitude" is understood to indicate a community of at least the size of the convent, then at least one hundred monks and nuns were in the area of Bethlehem at the time in question.

62. Jerome, *Hom.* 86, ll. 232–39 (ed. Morin, *Opera homiletica,* CCSL 78, 514).

63. Steven M. Oberhelman, *Rhetoric and Homiletics in Fourth-Century Christian Literature,* American Classical Studies 26 (Atlanta: Scholars Press, 1991), 86; Ewald, *The Homilies of Saint Jerome,* xix. For a discussion of the art of and training for speaking ex tempore in Greco-Roman *paideia,* see Jürgen Hammerstaedt and Peri Terbuyken, "Improvisation," *Reallexicon für Antike Christentum* 17 (1996): 1202–84.

64. The homily's paragraphs are not numbered in either the critical edition or the English translation. The line numbers used here correspond to the scheme used in the edition.

65. Jerome, *Hom.* 86.6–12 (ed. Morin, CCSL 78, 507; ET: Ewald, FOTC 57, 200): Parabolae illae sunt, ubi exemplum ponitur, et tacentur nomina. Ubi autem dicitur Abraham et Lazarus et prophetae et Moyses, hic verus Lazarus. . . . Neque enim . . . mendacium potest congruere veritati.

66. Jerome, *Hom.* 86.29–30 (ed. Morin, CCSL 78, 508; ET: Ewald, FOTC 57, 201): Infelicissime hominem, partem corporis tui vides iacere ante ianuam, et non misereris?

67. Jerome, *Hom.* 86.41, 43–44, 47–49 (ed. Morin, CCSL 78, 508; ET: Ewald, FOTC 57, 201): ille iacebat in ulceribus. . . Non habebat unum ulcus: totum corpus ulcera erant. . . Aegrogatio habet aliquod solacium, si opes habet: sin autem ad infirmitates magnitudinem et paupertas, duplex infirmitas.

68. Jerome, *Hom.* 86.35–37 (ed. Morin, CCSL 78, 508; ET: Ewald, FOTC 57, 201): Ideo iacebat ad ianuam, crudelitatem dum in suo corpore demonstraret: ideo iacebat ad ianuam, ne dives diceret, Non vidi. When used with the subjunctive, *dum* expresses "a desired end, or refers to an indefinite future" (Lewis and Short, *A Latin Dictionary,* s.v. "dum," I.B.1., p. 618).

69. Jerome, *Hom.* 86.72–74 (ed. Morin, CCSL 78, 509; ET: Ewald, FOTC 57, 202): Gaudet unusquisque angelorum tantum onus tangere: libentertalibus oneribus praegrauantur, ut adducant homines ad regna caelorum.

70. Jerome's bibilical text included the phrase καὶ ἐν τῷ ᾅδῃ ("and into Hades") following καὶ ἐτάφη ("and was buried"), which is a reading found in a number of mss. of the Alexandrian text type, of most of the translations into Eastern languages, and of several Fathers (incl. Marcion, Cyril, Tertullian, and Augustine). Other manuscripts, including importantly the first corrector of Codex Sinaiticus, repeated ἐτάφη as the start of this phrase, stressing that the man's burial was in Hades. This addition turns the fragment into a complete sentence, but the textual criticism canon *lectio brevior* suggests it was probably not original.

71. Jerome, *Hom.* 86.86–87 (ed. Morin, CCSL 78, 509; ET: Ewald, FOTC 57, 203): Aliorum divitiae, eorum qui in paupertate sunt, tormenta sunt.

72. Jerome, *Hom.* 86.94 (ed. Morin, CCSL 78, 510; ET: mine): Dicat mihi aliquis: In inferno est paradisus? I have switched from the otherwise good translation of Ewald here to my own, because for some inexplicable reason Ewald inconsistently translates *inferno* (sometimes as Hades, other times as Hell, and still other times, such as here, as netherworld). It seems better, in my view, to maintain consistency, especially since the exact place of the parable's action was of particular concern to Jerome here and at the end of the homily.

73. The reader interested in varying types of exegesis is directed to Craig Evans et al., eds., *Early Jewish and Christian Exegesis: Studies in Memory of William Hugh Brownlee* (Atlanta, Ga.: Scholars Press, 1987); Kannengiesser, *Handbook of Patristic Exegesis,* vol. 2; and Frances Young, *Exegesis and Theology in Early Christianity* (London: Ashgate, 2012).

74. Jerome, *Hom.* 86.124 (ed. Morin, CCSL 78, 511; ET: Ewald, FOTC 57, 204): Aquam desideras, qui delibutos cibos ante fastidiebas.

75. Jerome, *Hom.* 86.126–28 (ed. Morin, CCSL 78, 511; ET: Ewald, FOTC 57, 204): Vide quid dicat, bona tua: ceterum bona non sunt. Quae putabas bona, recepisti: non potes et in terra regnasse, et hic regnare.

76. Jerome, *Hom.* 86.129–32 (ed. Morin, CCSL 78, 511; ET: Ewald, FOTC 57, 204): Si quando aegrotamus, si pauperes sumus, si aegrotatione conficimur, si frigore, si hospitium non habemus: laetemur gaudeamus.

77. A helpful background study on Jerome's propensity toward a "spiritual sense" of Scripture, although it nowhere mentions our homily or discusses Jerome's treatment of Luke 16, is Dennis Brown, *Vir trilinguis: A Study in the Biblical Exegesis of Saint Jerome* (Kampen: Kok Pharos, 1992), 139–65.

78. Jerome, *Hom.* 86.155–56 (ed. Morin, CCSL 78, 511; ET: Ewald, FOTC 57, 205): Hi fratres tui amabant divitias, non poterant videre paupertatem.

79. Jerome, *Hom.* 86.157–58 (ed. Morin, CCSL 78, 511; ET: Ewald, FOTC 57, 205): illi fratres saluari non possunt, nisi moriantur.

80. Jerome, *Hom.* 86.180–81 (ed. Morin, CCSL 78, 512; ET: Ewald, FOTC 57, 206): Dum nescimus, hic dogma monstratur: aliud quidem dicitur, sed significatur aliud.

81. Jerome, *Hom.* 86.198–99 (ed. Morin, CCSL 78, 513; ET: Ewald, FOTC 57, 207): Denique isti fratres et in nobis erant antequam nobis Xristus resurgeret.

82. One wonders also if there is a connection between these comments and the charges of impropriety leveled against him when he was in Rome several years earlier, which were apparently the cause of his departure from there. Cf. Jerome *Ep.* 45.

83. Jerome, *Hom.* 86.239–40 (ed. Morin, CCSL 78, 514; ET: Ewald, FOTC 57, 208): Nunc sufficit nobis audire de Lazaro, immo Lazarum fuisse divitem.

84. Jerome, *Hom.* 86.240–41 (ed. Morin, CCSL 78, 514; ET: Ewald, FOTC 57, 208): Et divitis nos tormenta deterreant, et pauperis exempla provocent.

85. Jerome, *Hom.* 86.241–46 (ed. Morin, CCSL 78, 514; ET: Ewald, FOTC 57, 208, with one change, translating *divitem,* in bold, as "rich man" not "Dives" as did Ewald): Anima Xristiana, anima monachi, anima eius qui nudus nudum Xristum sequitur, quando aliquem divitem viderit . . . illum divitem cogitat: consideret vocem et clamorem divitis, et Lazari digitum postulantem.

86. Jerome, *Hom.* 86.271–74 (ed. Morin, CCSL 78, 515; ET: Ewald, FOTC 57, 209): Antequam Xristus moreretur, nemo in paradisum conscenderat nisi latro. Romphaea illa flamma et vertigo illa claudebat paradisum: non poterat aliquis intrare in paradisum, quem Xristus clauserat.

87. Jerome, *Hom.* 86.262–64 (ed. Morin, CCSL 78, 514–15; ET: Ewald, FOTC 57, 209): de tenebris, de squalore, de fame, de stridoribus catenarum, de gemitu compeditorum, de lacrimus eorum qui cum eo sunt.

88. Cf., e.g., Clement of Alexandria, discussed in the previous chapter, who seems to have been influential in shifting the attitude among Christian leaders in late antiquity toward rich Christians.

89. Jerome, *Hom.* 86.32–35 (ed. Morin, CCSL 78, 508; Ewald, FOTC 57, 201): Quid servas in deliciis tuis quod superfluum est? Quod iactas, tribue in elemosinam membro tuo. Non dico ut auferas divitiis tuis: quod foras iactas, micas mensae tuae praebe in elemosinam membro tuo.

90. Jerome, *Hom.* 86.29–30 (ed. Morin, CCSL 78, 508; Ewald, FOTC 57, 201): Infelicissime hominum, partem corporis tui vides iacere ante ianuam, et non misereris?

91. This last remark may be an allusion to Luke 18:30, in which Jesus teaches that what we give up to follow the will of God, God will repay many times over (πολλαπλασίονα). This text and others like it are used by other Fathers to suggest that, in God's economy, it is safe to give alms to the poor since God will be their guarantor and be ready to repay you with heavenly rewards for having taken care of the poor. Cf., e.g., Origen, *On Psalm 36, Hom.* 3.11; John Chrysostom, *Homilies on Genesis* 41.3–5; Commodianus, *Explanation of the Psalms, On Psalm 14/15;* Ps.-Basil, *On Beneficence.*

92. Jerome, *Hom.* 86.129–33 (ed. Morin, CCSL 78, 511; Ewald, FOTC 57, 204–5): Si quando aegrotamus, si pauperes sumus, si aegrotatione conficimur, si frigore, si hospitium non habemus: laetemur, gaudeamus, accipiamus mala in vita nostra. Quando nos infirmitatis et aegrotationis magnitudo premit, Lazarum cogitemus.

93. Cf., e.g., Dorr, *Option for the Poor,* 191–92, 210–11, 222–23, 320–21.

94. See above, chapter 2, n. 7.

CHAPTER 4

1. For studies of structuralism, see John Sturrock, *Structuralism,* 2d ed. (Oxford: Blackwell, 2003); and Peter Barry, "Structuralism," in Peter Barry, *Beginning Theory: An Introduction to Literary and Cultural Theory* (Manchester: Manchester University Press, 2002), 39–60. A bibliography of structuralism has been compiled by W. Diederich, A. Ibarra, and T. Mormann in two articles: (1) "Bibliography of Structuralism," *Erkenntnis* 30 (1989): 387–407, and (2) "Bibliography of Structuralism II (1989–1994 and Additions)," *Erkenntnis* 41 (1994): 403–18.

2. Hans-Georg Gadamer, *Wahrheit und Methode: Grundzüge einer philosophischen Hermeneutik* (Tübingen: Mohr Siebeck, 1960; repr. 1986, 1990). ET: *Truth and Method,* trans. Joel Weinsheimer and Donald Marshall (New York: Crossroad, 1989). Citations in notes below refer to ET. Cf. also Joel Weinsheimer, *Gadamer's Hermeneutics: A Reading of "Truth and Method"* (New Haven, Conn.: Yale University Press, 1985).

3. Gadamer, *Truth and Method,* see esp. 181–206, though discussion of these and other writers may be found throughout the book.

4. Gadamer, *Truth and Method,* 119–20.

5. Gadamer, *Truth and Method,* 335–41.

6. Gadamer, *Truth and Method,* 336.

7. Gadamer, *Truth and Method,* 269–71.

8. Gadamer, *Truth and Method,* 270.

9. Gadamer, *Truth and Method,* 270: Erst solche Anerkennung der wesenhaften Vorurteilshaftigkeit alles Verstehens schärft das hermeneutische Problem zu siener wirklichen Spitze zu (Gadamer, *Wahrheit und Methode,* 274).

10. Gadamer, *Truth and Method,* 355–66.

11. Gadamer, *Truth and Method,* 362.

12. Consider, e.g., Gregory Nazianzen, *Oration* 32.33 (ed. Claudio Moreschini, *Discours 32–37,* SC 318 [Paris: Éditions du Cerf, 1985], 152–54; ET: Martha Vinson, *Saint Gregory of Nazianzus: Select Orations,* FOTC 107 [Washington, D.C.: Catholic University of America Press, 2004], 215), who suggests the salvation journey is not unlike climbing a mountain. There are many paths up the mountain, but all lead to the summit. Donald Winslow, in *The Dynamics of Salvation: A Study of Gregory of Nazianzus* (Philadelphia: Philadelphia Patristic Foundation, 1979), 139–41, suggests this meant Gregory believed people from different faiths could still reach God. However, this was not Gregory's point at all. Rather, the image of the mountain paths was tied to different spiritual disciplines that could be cultivated in the life of a Christian person. All the spiritual disciplines were good and worthy of aiding a Christian in his or her salvation journey up the mountain.

13. Gadamer, *Truth and Method,* 330–34.

14. Gadamer, *Truth and Method,* 331.

15. Paul Ricoeur, "The Hermeneutical Function of Distanciation," *Philosophy Today* 17 (1973): 129–41, here 134–37. For a comparison between Ricoeur's notion of genre to that of Hirsch, Todorov, and Gadamer, see Mary Gerhart, "Generic Studies: Their Renewed Importance in Religious and Literary Interpretation," *Journal of the American Academy of Religion* 45 (1977): 309–25.

16. Paul Ricoeur, *Conflict of Interpretations: Essays in Hermeneutics*, Northwestern University Studies in Phenomenology and Existential Philosophy (Evanston, Ill.: Northwestern University Press, 1996), 22, 169–72. Cf. Andrew Cutrufello, *Continental Philosophy: A Contemporary Introduction* (London: Routledge, 2005), 259–60.

17. Paul Ricoeur, François Azouvi, and Marc B. De Launay, *Critique and Conviction: Conversations with François Azouvi and Marc de Launay*, trans. Kathleen Blamey (New York: Columbia University Press, 1998). David E. Klemm, *The Hermeneutical Theory of Paul Ricoeur: A Constructive Analysis* (Lewisburg, Pa.: Bucknell University Press, 1983), explains there are two axes on which one may map out human values. One axis goes from the general to the particular. The other axis goes from origin (*arche*) to possibility (*telos*).

18. Paul Ricoeur, "The Canon between the Text and the Community," in *Philosophical Hermeneutics and Biblical Exegesis,* ed. Petr Pokorný and Jan Rosovec, WUNT (Tübingen: Mohr Siebeck, 2002), 7–6; cf. Gilbert Vincent, *La religion de Ricoeur*, La religion des philosophes (Paris: Les Éditions de l'Atelier, 2008), 38–41.

19. Paul Ricoeur, *Mémoire, l'histoire, l'oubli*, L'ordre philosophique (Paris: Seuil, 2000); ET: *Memory, History, Forgetting*, trans. Kathleen Blamey and David Pellauer (Chicago and London: University of Chicago Press, 2004).

20. Ricoeur, *Memory, History, Forgetting*, 27–28.

21. Ricoeur, *Memory, History, Forgetting*, 48–55.

22. Further discussion of Ricoeur's understanding of the imagination's role in filling in textual gaps, including the time separating ancient texts from our own, may be found in Richard Kearney, *On Paul Ricoeur: The Owl of Minerva*, Transcending Boundaries in Philosophy and Theology (Aldershot: Ashgate, 2004), 35–58; and Jeanne Evans, *Paul Ricoeur's Hermeneutics of the Imagination*, American University Studies, Series VII: Theology and Religion 143 (New York: Peter Lang, 1995), esp. 151–74.

23. Ricoeur, *Memory, History, Forgetting*, 53–55.

24. Ricoeur, *Memory, History, Forgetting*, 440, defines forgetting as "the *unperceived* character of the perseverance of memories, their removal from the vigilance of consciousness" (italics in the original text).

25. Ricoeur, *Memory, History, Forgetting*, 56–57, but see all of part 1, chapter 2, where Ricoeur evaluates the contributions of Bergson and Freud to the notion of recollection of memories.

26. Ricoeur, *Memory, History, Forgetting*, 88–89.

27. Ricoeur, *Memory, History, Forgetting*, 494–500; Paul Ricoeur, "The Difficulty to Forgive" (and the postscript "Discussion after 'The Difficulty to

Forgive'"), in *Memory, Narrativity, Self and the Challenge to Think God: The Reception within Theology of the Recent Work of Paul Ricoeur*, ed. Maureen Junker-Kenny and Peter Kenny, Religion—Geschichte—Gesellschaft: Fundamentaltheologische Studien 17 (Munster: LIT Verlag, 2004), 6–18.

28. Cf. Kearney, *On Paul Ricoeur*, 104–8.

29. The three volumes are Paul Ricoeur, *Conflict of Interpretations: Essays in Hermeneutics*, Northwestern University Studies in Phenomenology and Existential Philosophy (Evanston, Ill.: Northwestern University Press, 1996); *From Text to Action: Essays in Hermeneutics II*, trans. Kathleen Blamey and John B. Thompson (Evanston, Ill.: Northwestern University Press, 1991); *Time and Narrative*, 3 vols., trans. Kathleen Blamey (Chicago: University of Chicago Press, 1984, 1985, and 1988). In the second of these three volumes, in fact, in the essay "On Interpretation," 19–20, Ricoeur both acknowledges his debt to Gadamer and then outlines the important refinements he has made to Gadamer's ideas. Cf. also his "Le statut de la *Vorstellung* dans la philosophie hégélienne de la religion (1985)," in *Lectures 3 aux frontières de la philosophie* (Paris: Seuil, 1994), 41–62.

There are, of course, countless books and articles on Ricoeur's hermeneutical ideas. The interested reader is directed to Theo de Boer, "Paul Ricoeur: Thinking the Bible," in *God in France: Eight Contemporary French Thinkers on God*, ed. Peter Jonkers and Ruud Welten, Studies in Philosophical Theology (Leuven: Peeters, 2005), 43–67; Christophe Brabant, "The Truth Narrated: Ricoeur on Religious Experience," in *Divinising Experience: Essays in the History of Religious Experience from Origen to Ricoeur*, ed. Lieven Boeve and Laurence P. Hemming, Studies in Philosophical Theology (Leuven: Peeters, 2004), 246–69. In Paul Ricoeur's *Essays on Biblical Interpretation*, ed. Lewis S. Mudge (Philadelphia: Fortress Press, 1980), 44–45, Ricoeur, in responding to Mudge's review of his works to that point, agreed that the main problem is identifying the "critical moment" where application of methods and theories has revealed sufficient enough truth that it is then possible to move on to appropriation.

30. Ricoeur, *From Text to Action*, 84

31. Ricoeur, *From Text to Action*, 76. Cf. Paul Ricoeur, *Interpretation Theory: Discourse and the Surplus of Meaning* (Forth Worth: Texas Christian University Press, 1976), 44: "Interpretation, philosophically understood, is nothing else than an attempt to make estrangement and distanciation productive."

32. More to the point, Ricoeur, in "Le problème du fondement de la morale," *Sapienza* 28 (1975): 313–37, here 335–36, taught a "hermeneutics of alienation" in which the first, simplistic reading might have us see ourselves in the

text, but a second reading helps us push back a bit from that and see the "otherness" in the text.

33. Ricoeur, *From Text to Action*, 95.

34. On the need to return to a text over time, see Ricoeur, "Metaphor and the Central Problem of Hermeneutics," in *Hermeneutics and the Human Sciences: Essays on Language, Action and Interpretation*, ed. and trans. John B. Thompson (Cambridge: Cambridge University Press, 1981), 165–80, here 171.

35. Paul Ricoeur, *Interpretation Theory: Discourse and the Surplus of Meaning* (Fort Worth: Texas Christian University Press, 1976), 71–88; "The Model of the Text: Meaningful Action Considered as a Text," in *Hermeneutics and the Human Sciences*, 197–245; *The Rule of Metaphor: Multi-disciplinary Studies of the Creation of Meaning in Language*, trans. Robert Czerny with Kathleen McLaughlin and John Costello (Toronto: University of Toronto Press, 1977 (trans. of *La Métaphore vive*, L'ordre philosophique [Paris: Seuil, 1975]). Cf. Dan R. Stiver, *Theology after Ricoeur: New Directions in Hermeneutical Theology* (Louisville, London, Leiden: Westminster John Knox Press, 2001), esp. 56–78.

36. Ricoeur, *Time and Narrative*, vol. 1, ch. 3. On the correlation between Ricoeur's hermeneutic and mimetic circles, see Francois Xavier-Amherdt, *L'herméneutique philosophique de Paul Ricoeur et son importance pour l'exégèse biblique* (Paris: Éditions du Cerf, 2004). Mimesis$_1$ concerns the preunderstandings readers have about texts, particularly related to linguistic structures and the notion that texts have a *point*. Mimesis$_2$ concerns the configurative work both that authors engage in to construct texts and that readers engage in to make sense of the texts for their own lives. Mimesis$_3$ concerns the fruit of a reader's work to refigure texts, which is to say that readers give texts meaning in their own lives.

This is akin to what is known as reader-response criticism. See, among other works, Jane B. Tompkins, ed., *Reader-Response Criticism: From Formalism to Post-Structuralism* (Baltimore: Johns Hopkins University Press, 1980); Louise M. Rosenblatt, *The Reader, the Text, the Poem* (Carbondale: Southern Illinois University Press, 1978); and Joyce Many and Carole Cox, eds., *Reader Stance and Literary Understanding: Exploring the Theories, Research, and Practice* (Norwood, N.J.: Ablex, 1992).

37. Christophe Potworowski, "Origen's Hermeneutics in Light of Paul Ricoeur," in *Origeniana Quinta: Papers of the 5th International Origen Congress, Boston College, 14–18 August 1989*, ed. Robert J. Daly, BETL 105 (Leuven: Peeters Press, 1992), 161–66, argues that Origen's rejection of the literal sense of texts where the literal sense is meaningless is akin to Ricoeur's notion

that interpretation is a work of the productive imagination. Furthermore, Origen's rejection of the literary or historical sense of a text as its control on interpretation foreshadows Ricoeur's idea that appropriation of a text into contemporary experience is a necessary stage in the act of interpretation.

38. Paul Ricoeur, "Le projet d'une morale sociale," *Le Christianisme social* 74 (1966): 285–95; later republished with other, similarly styled articles in Paul Ricoeur, *Political and Social Essays,* ed. David Stewart and Joseph Bien (Athens: Ohio University Press), cf. 160–75.

39. Paul Ricoeur, "Le projet d'une morale sociale" (The Project of a Social Ethic), trans. David Stewart, in Ricoeur, *Political and Social Essays,* 164–65. Italics are in the original text.

40. Asterius, *Homily* 1.9.3 (ed. C. Datema, *Homilies I–XIV,* 12; ET: mine): Εἶπε τοίνυν, ὦ θεσπέσιε Λουκᾶ – ὡς πρὸς παρόντα γάρ σε καὶ ὁρώμενον διαλέξομαι – . . . .

41. Asterius, *Homily* 1.3.2 (ed. C. Datema, *Homilies I–XIV,* 8).

42. Asterius, *Homily* 1.3.1 (ed. C. Datema, *Homilies I–XIV,* 8; ET: mine): παίζοντες λοιπόν, οὐ σπουδάζοντες.

43. Asterius, *Homily* 1.7.2 (ed. C. Datema, *Homilies I–XIV,* 11; ET: mine): παρῄει δὲ ὡς λίθον.

44. Asterius, *Homily* 1.10.2 (ed. C. Datema, *Homilies I–XIV,* 13; ET: mine): Καὶ πάντας ἐγὼ τοὺς τοιχωρύχους καὶ ἀνδραποδιστάς, ἔτι μὴν λωποδύτας καὶ κλέπτας καὶ τοὺς ἀνδροφόνους αὐτούς, εἴ ποτε παρέβαλον ἀρχοντικῷ κριτηρίῳ, πένητας ἐθεασάμην, ἀγνώστους, ἀοίκους, ἀνεστίους.

45. Asterius, *Homily* 1.11.2 (ed. C. Datema, *Homilies I–XIV,* 14; ET: mine): τὸ φυσικὸν ἐκείνης ἀξίωμα τῇ συμπαθείᾳ τῆς σαρκὸς πρὸς τὴν ὕλην καταγαγών.

46. Asterius, *Homily* 1.11.2 (ed. C. Datema, *Homilies I–XIV,* 14; ET: mine): οὐδὲν χρηστὸν τῆς ἑαυτοῦ ζωῆς καταλιμπάνων ὑπόμνημα.

47. Asterius, *Homily* 1.11.2 (ed. C. Datema, *Homilies I–XIV,* 14; ET: mine): λήθῃ δὲ ἀτίμῳ καλυπτόμενος καὶ τὸν τῶν βοσκημάτων θάνατον τελευτῶν.

48. Asterius, *Homily* 1.11.3 (ed. C. Datema, *Homilies I–XIV,* 14; ET: mine): ὡς μαστιγίας δοῦλος ἀφῃρέθη τῶν ἀλλοτρίων. I have difficulty with ἀφῃρέθη for two reasons. The context demands that it be a third-person singular verb, but the form here is closer to a second-person plural. Also, it seems to be a rare form of φέρω, built upon that verb's first principal part, but the orthography does not indicate well either if the voice is active or passive or if the mood is indicative or subjunctive.

49. Asterius, *Homily* 1.11.3 (ed. C. Datema, *Homilies I–XIV,* 14; ET: Anderson and Goodspeed): ὑπερηφανίας . . . γραὸς θρηνούσης ὀδυρμοὺς προβαλλόμενος μακρά.

50. Asterius, *Homily* 1.11.4 (ed. C. Datema, *Homilies I–XIV,* 14; ET: Anderson and Goodspeed): ζητῶν ἔλεον, ὃν οὐκ ἔδωκεν ἡνίκα τοῦ εὐεργετεῖν πρόχειρον εἶχεν τὴν ἐξουσίαν. . . . Τοιαῦται τῶν φιλοσωμάτων αἱ α–βουλίαι, τοῦτο τῶν φιλοπλούτων καὶ φιληδόνων τὸ τέλος.

51. Asterius, *Homily* 1.12.2 (ed. C. Datema, *Homilies I–XIV,* 15; ET: Anderson and Goodspeed): ὡς ου–δὲ συγγνώμη τις τῆς ἐκεῖ κρίσεως ἐπελαφρύνει τὴν κόλασιν, οὐδ' ἐλαττοῖ τὴν ὡρισμένην τιμωρίαν φιλανθρωπία.

52. D. Schichor and D. K. Sechrest, *Three Strikes and You're Out: Vengeance as Public Policy* (Thousand Oaks, Calif.: Sage Publications, 1996); Tom R. Tyler and Robert J. Boeckmann, "Three Strikes and You Are Out, but Why? The Psychology of Public Support for Punishing Rule Breakers," *Law and Society Review* 31 (1997): 237–65; Gary LaFree, "Review Essay: Too Much Democracy or Too Much Crime? Lessons from California's Three-Strikes Law," *Law and Social Inquiry* 27 (2002): 875–902; Juan Ramirez and William Crano, "Deterrence and Incapacitation: An Interrupted Time-Series Analysis of California's Three-Strikes Law," *Journal of Applied Social Psychology* 33 (2006): 110–44.

53. Jerome, *Hom.* 86.161–78 (ed. Morin, CCSL 78, 511–12).

54. Ricoeur, *Time and Narrative,* 1:64–70.

55. Jerome, *Hom.* 86.110–24 (ed. Morin, CCSL 78, 510–11; trans. Ewald, FOTC 57, 204): *Mitte Lazarum, ut intinguat extremum digiti sui in aquam.* Mitte Lazarum. Erras, miser. Abraham mittere non potest, sed suscipere potest. Ut intinguat extremum digiti sui in aquam. Recordare, dives, vitae tuae: Lazarum videre non dignabaris, et nunc digitum eius desideras. Mitte Lazarum. Hoc tu ei debueras facere, dum adviveret. Ut intinguat extremum digiti sui in aquam. Vide conscientiam peccatoris: non totum audet poscere digitum. *Ut refrigeret linguam, quia crucior in hac flamma.* Ut refrigeret linguam meam: multa enim superba locuta est. Ubi peccatrum, ibi et poena. Ut refrigeret linguam meam, quia crucior in hac flamma. Quanta mala lingua habet, Iacobus in epistula sua loquitur: "Modicum quidem membrum est, sed magna exaltat." Qua plurimum peccavit, amplius torquetur. Aquam desideras, qui delibutos cibos ante fastidiebas.

56. Jerome, *Hom.* 86.133–38 (ed. Morin, CCSL 78, 511; trans. Ewald, FOTC 57, 205): *Et in his omnibus inter nos et vos chaos magnum firmatum est.* Dissolui non potest, non potest agitari et concuti. Videre possumus, transire

non possumus: et nos videmus quid fugerimus, et vos videtis quid perdideritis: et nostra gaudia cumulant vestra tormenta, et vestra tormenta cumulant nostra gaudia.

57. Yet, if we push this pastoral move by Jerome too far, we end up exposing a contradiction in his thought. Recall earlier that Jerome had insisted these events were taking place at the time Jesus was speaking and that, according to a footnote above, this was so because Jerome believed Jesus' crucifixion and resurrection would lead to the opening of the doors from the netherworld into heaven. Since that event in Jesus' life has since happened, there should no longer be a netherworld to which Jerome and his fellow believers will descend. They should pass immediately to the day of judgment and then enter heaven. Jerome has now been caught up fully in the web of his own constrained exegesis.

58. Jerome, *Hom.* 86.137–38 (ed. Morin, CCSL 78, 511; trans. Ewald, FOTC 57, 205): nostra gaudia cumulant vestra tormenta, et vestra tormenta cumulant nostra gaudia.

59. Jerome, *Hom.* 86.104–5 (ed. Morin, CCSL 78, 510; trans. Ewald, FOTC 57, 203): Tormenta te cogunt agere paenitentiam, non mentis affectus.

CHAPTER 5

1. Reimund Bieringer and Mary Elsbernd, with Susan M. Garthwaite et al., *Normativity of the Future: Reading Biblical and Other Authoritative Texts in an Eschatological Perspective*, ANL 61 (Leuven: Peeters Press, 2009). I wish to thank Reimund for kindly sharing with me a prepress copy of the book for my use in preparing this book.

2. Reimund Bieringer, "The Normativity of the Future: The Authority of the Bible for Theology," in *ET Bulletin. Zeitschrift für Theologie in Europa* 8 (1997): 52–67.

3. Sandra M. Schneiders, *The Revelatory Text: Interpreting the New Testament as Sacred Scripture* (San Francisco: Harper, 1991); also frequently cited in Bieringer and Elsbernd's works is Schneiders, "Feminist Ideology Criticism and Biblical Hermeneutics," *Biblical Theology Bulletin* 19 (1989): 3–10.

4. Bieringer and Elsbernd, "Introduction: The 'Normativity of the Future' Approach: Its Roots, Development, Current State and Challenges," in *Normativity of the Future*, 5.

5. The 1995 conference paper was eventually published as Reimund Bieringer, "Biblical Revelation and Exegetical Interpretation according to *Dei*

Verbum 12," in *Vatican II and Its Legacy,* ed. Mattijs Lamberigts and Leo Kenis, BETL 166 (Leuven: Peeters Press, 2002), 25–58.

6. Mary Elsbernd and Reimund Bieringer, *When Love Is Not Enough: A Theo-Ethic of Justice* (Collegeville, Minn.: Liturgical Press, 2002).

7. Mary Elsbernd and Reimund Bieringer, "Interpreting the Signs of the Times in the Light of the Gospel: Vision and Normativity of the Future," in *Scrutinizing the Signs of the Times in Light of the Gospel,* ed. Johan Verstraeten, BETL 208 (Leuven, Paris, Dudley, Mass.: Peeters Press, 2007), 41–97.

8. Reimund Bieringer, Didier Pollefeyt, and Frederique Vandecasteele-Vanneuville, "Wrestling with Johannine Anti-Judaism: A Hermeneutical Framework for the Analysis of the Current Debate," in *Anti-Judaism and the Fourth Gospel,* ed. Reimund Bieringer, Didier Pollefeyt, and Frederique Vandecasteele-Vanneuville (Louisville, Ky.: Westminster John Knox, 2001), 3–37.

9. Didier Pollefeyt and Reimund Bieringer, "The Role of the Bible in Religious Education Reconsidered: Risks and Challenges in Teaching the Bible," *International Journal of Practical Theology* 9 (2005): 117–39; Reimund Bieringer, "'Come, and You Will See' (John 1:39): Dialogical Authority and Normativity of the Future in the Fourth Gospel and in Religious Education," in *Hermeneutics and Religious Education,* ed. Herman Lombaerts and Didier Pollefeyt, BETL 180 (Leuven, Paris, Dudley, Mass.: Peeters Press, 2005), 179–201. This article is really about much more than religious education; it is equally a shorter catechism on the history of biblical interpretation and a critique of the viability of John's claims that Jesus is the *via, veritas et vita*.

10. Reimund Bieringer, "Texts That Create a Future: The Function of Ancient Texts for Theology Today," in Bieringer and Elsbernd, with Garthwaite et al., *Normativity of the Future,* 91–116; also in in *Reading Patristic Texts on Social Ethics,* ed. Leemans, Matz, and Johan Verstraeten, 3–29. Subsequently cited from *Normativity of the Future.*

11. Schneiders, *The Revelatory Text,* 55–59, cited in Bieringer, "'Come and You Will See' (John 1:39)," at 179, n 1.

12. Bieringer, "'Come and You Will See' (John 1:39)," 181–82.

13. Bieringer, "'Come and You Will See' (John 1:39)," 183–85.

14. Bieringer, "'Come and You Will See' (John 1:39)," 197.

15. Bieringer, "The Normativity of the Future: The Authority of the Bible for Theology," 63, with an acknowledged debt to Ricoeur, *From Text to Action,* 148.

16. Bieringer, "The Normativity of the Future: The Authority of the Bible for Theology," 67.

17. Bieringer, "'Come and You Will See' (John 1:39)," 197; Bieringer, Pollefeyt, and Vandecasteele-Vanneuville, "Wrestling with Johannine Anti-Judaism," 36; Pollefeyt and Bieringer, "The Role of the Bible in Religious Education Reconsidered,"139.

18. Elsbernd and Bieringer, "Interpreting the Signs of the Times in the Light of the Gospel," 60.

19. Pollefeyt and Bieringer, "The Role of the Bible in Religious Education Reconsidered," 117–18.

20. Bieringer, "'Come, and You Will See' (John 1:39)," 199.

21. Pollefeyt and Bieringer, "The Role of the Bible in Religious Education Reconsidered," 132.

22. Bieringer, "Texts That Create a Future," 110–16.

23. PG 83.643–65; ET: Thomas Halton, *Theodoret of Cyrus. On Divine Providence*, ACW 49 (New York: Newman Press, 1988), 73–87. See also G. N. Gotsis and G. A. Merianos, "Wealth and Poverty in Theodoret of Cyrrhus' 'On Providence,'" *Journal of Eastern Christian Studies* 59 (2007): 11–48. Readers interested in further details about Theodoret of Cyrus are directed to Adam Schor, *Theodoret's People: Social Networks and Religious Conflict in Late Roman Syria* (Berkeley and Los Angeles: University of California Press, 2011); Theresa Urbainczyk, *Theodoret of Cyrrhus: The Bishop and the Holy Man* (Ann Arbor: University of Michigan Press, 2002); and István Pásztori-Kupán, *Theodoret of Cyrus*, The Early Church Fathers (London and New York: Routledge, 2006).

24. Bieringer, "Texts That Create a Future," 112.

25. By Theodoret's time, this may have become something of a stock rhetorical image, for it appears in the writings of several Church Fathers. Cf., e.g., Chrysostom, *Homilies on 1 Corinthians, Hom*. 10.4.

26. Reimund Bieringer, "Texts That Create a Future," 114.

27. Reimund Bieringer, "Texts That Create a Future," 115–16.

28. Elsbernd and Bieringer, "Interpreting the Signs of the Times in the Light of the Gospel," 60.

29. This image of God writing straight with crooked lines is one found in two NOF publications, including Bieringer, Pollefeyt, and Vandecasteele-Vanneuville, "Wrestling with Johannine Anti-Judaism," 35; Elsbernd and Bieringer, "Interpreting the Signs of the Times in the Light of the Gospel," 59.

30. Asterius, *Hom*. 1.4.3 (ed. Datema, *Homilies I–XIV*, 9; ET: mine): τὸν ζῶντα καὶ τῶ ὄψεων αφηρημένον ταῖς εὐποιίαις παραμυθοῦ.

31. Asterius, *Hom*. 1.4.3 (ed. Datema, *Homilies I–XIV*, 9; ET: mine): τρέφε τοὺς πεινῶντας.

32. Asterius, *Hom.* 1.4.2 (ed. Datema, *Homilies I–XIV*, 9).

33. Asterius, *Hom.* 1.8.1 (ed. Datema, *Homilies I–XIV*, 12; ET: Anderson and Goodspeed): μεγάλας ἂν ἀφῆκα σχετλιάζων φωνάς, ἐφ' οἷς οἱ κτισθέντες ὁμοτίμως οὕτως ἀνίσως μετὰ τῶν ὁμοφύλων διάγομεν.

34. Asterius, *Hom.* 1.7.3 (ed. Datema, *Homilies I–XIV*, 11; ET: mine): σὺ δὲ τὸν ἀδελφόν σου, τὸν ὁμόφυλον, ταύτης τῆς δωρεᾶς οὐκ ἠξίωσας.

35. Asterius, *Hom.* 1.6.3 (ed. Datema, *Homilies I–XIV*, 11).

36. Mary Elsbernd and Reimund Bieringer, "Interpreting the Signs of the Times in the Light of the Gospel," 60.

37. Asterius, *Hom.* 1.2.4 (ed. Datema, *Homilies I–XIV*, 8).

38. Asterius, *Hom.* 1.6.2 (ed. Datema, *Homilies I–XIV*, 11; ET: Anderson and Goodspeed): εἴ γε χοίρου μὲν σφαζομένου ἕλκονται πρός τινα λυπηρὰν αἴσθησιν οἱ χοῖροι καὶ τῷ νεορρύτῳ αἵματι ἀνιαρὰ ἐπιτρύζουσι. περιίστανται δὲ τοῦ ταύρου τὸν φόνον οἱ βόες ἐμπαθεῖ μυκηθμῷ τὴν ἄλγιδα σημαίνοντες. Ἀγέλαι δὲ γεράνων, μιᾶς τῶν συννόμων περιπεσούσης θηράτροις, περιίπτανται τὴν κρατουμένην καί τινος ὀδυρτικῆς κλαγγῆς τὸν ἀέρα πληροῦσιν, τὴν ὁμόφυλον ζητοῦσαι καὶ σύννομον.

39. Asterius, *Hom.* 1.5.5 (ed. Datema, *Homilies I–XIV*, 10).

40. Asterius, *Hom.* 1.12.2 (ed. Datema, *Homilies I–XIV*, 15; ET: Anderson and Goodspeed): οὐδὲ συγγνώμη τις τῆς ἐκεῖ κρίσεως ἐπελαφρύνει τὴν κόλασιν, οὐδ' ἐλαττοῖ τὴν ὡρισμένην τιμωρίαν φιλανθρωπία.

41. Asterius, *Hom.* 1.9.4 (ed. Datema, *Homilies I–XIV*, 13).

42. Asterius, *Hom.* 1.9.5 (ed. Datema, *Homilies I–XIV*, 13): Ἐν Χριστῷ γὰρ πάντων ἡμῶν ἡ σωτηρία καὶ ἡ ἐλπὶς καὶ ἡ ἀπεκδοχὴ τοῦ μέλλοντος αἰῶνος.

43. Asterius, *Hom.* 1.12.5 (ed. Datema, *Homilies I–XIV*, 15): Μὴ οὐκ ἰσχύει ἡ χεὶρ Κυρίου τοῦ σῶσαι ἢ ἐβάρυνε τὸ οὖς αὐτοῦ τοῦ μὴ ἀκοῦσαι; Ἀλλὰ τὰ ἁμαρτήματα ὑμῶν διιστῶσιν ἀνὰ μέσον ὑμῶν καὶ ἀνὰ μέσον τοῦ Θεοῦ.

44. Jerome, *Hom.* 86.13–15 (ed. Morin, CCSL 78, 506).

45. Jerome, *Hom.* 86.13 (ed. Morin, CCSL 78, 507; ET: Ewald, FOTC 57, 200): misericordiam Dei.

46. Jerome, *Hom.* 86.58–74 (ed. Morin, CCSL 78, 508–9).

47. Jerome, *Hom.* 86.74–77 (ed. Morin, CCSL 78, 509).

48. Jerome, *Hom.* 86.129–32 (ed. Morin, CCSL 78, 511; ET: Ewald, FOTC 57, 204): Si quando aegrotamus, si pauperes sumus, si aegrotatione conficimur, si frigore, si hospitium non habemus: laetemur gaudeamus. Mala in nostra aetate accipiamus.

49. Jerome, *Hom.* 86.307–12 (ed. Morin, CCSL 78, 516; ET: Ewald, FOTC 57, 211): Habet et paupertas martyrium suum, et egestas bene tolerata facit martyrium: sed egestas propter Xristum, non propter necessitatem. Ce-

terum quanti pauperes sunt, et divites esse desiderant, et scelera faciunt. Non ergo paupertas simplex beatum facit, sed paupertas propter Xristum.

50. Jerome, *Hom.* 86.99–101 (ed. Morin, CCSL 78, 510; ET: Ewald, FOTC 57, 203): Licet me tormenta possideant, tamen patrem voco. Quomodo ille filius, qui perdiderat universam substantiam, patrem vocat: sic et ego licet in poenis sim, te patrem voco.

51. Jerome, *Hom.* 86.137–38 (ed. Morin, CCSL 78, 511).

52. Jerome, *Hom.* 86.25–30 (ed. Morin, CCSL 78, 507–8).

53. Jerome, *Hom.* 86.29–30 (ed. Morin, CCSL 78, 508; ET: Ewald, FOTC 57, 201): Infelicissime hominum, partem corporis tui vides iacere ante ianuam, et non misereris?

54. Jerome, *Hom.* 86.32–33 (ed. Morin, CCSL 78, 508; ET: Ewald, FOTC 57, 201): Quod iactas, tribue in elemosinam membro tuo.

55. Cf. above, ch. 3, section on *Hom.* 86.139–231.

56. Jerome, *Hom.* 86.151–53 (ed. Morin, CCSL 78, 511; ET: Ewald, FOTC 57, 205): Recte non amasti Lazarum fratrem, quia illos amabas fratres. Illi fratres non amant paupertatem.

57. Jerome, *Hom.* 86.109–10 (ed. Morin, CCSL 78, 510; ET: Ewald, FOTC 57, 204): Creator creaturae miseretur suae: unus venit medicus, qui sanaret mortuos: nam alii sanare non potuerunt.

58. Henrey Liddell et al., *Greek-English Lexicon,* s.v., χρίστος.

59. Jerome, *Hom.* 86.109–10 (ed. Morin, CCSL 78, 510; ET: Ewald, FOTC 57, 204): Quid quaeris, ut mittam Lazarum? Habent ibi Moysen Lazarum, habent ibi prophetas Lazaros. Et Moyses Lazarus fuit, pauper fuit, nudus fuit: meliores divitias esse arbitratus est paupertatem Xristi, quam divitias Pharaonis.

60. Jerome, *Hom.* 86.218–23 (ed. Morin, CCSL 78, 513).

61. Jerome, *Hom.* 86.226–27 (ed. Morin, CCSL 78, 513).

62. Jerome, *Hom.* 86.274–75 (ed. Morin, CCSL 78, 515).

63. Jerome, *Hom.* 86.252–55 (ed. Morin, CCSL 78, 514).

64. Jerome, *Hom.* 86.274–83 (ed. Morin, CCSL 78, 515; ET: Ewald, FOTC 57, 209–10): Latro primus intravit cum Xristo. Magnitudo enim fidei meruit magnitudinem praemiorum. Non enim credidit in regno videns Xristum, non illum vidit fulgentem, non illum vidit de caelo respicientem, non vidit ei ministrantes angelos. Certe, ut libere dicam, non vidit libere ambulantem, sed vidit eum in cruce, vidit illum bibentem acetum, vidit eum sentibus coranatum, vidit eum confixum ad crucem, vidit eum precantem auxilium: "Deus Deus meus respice in me, quare me dereliquisti?" et sic credidit. O conditio varia, et casus hominum!

65. Jerome, *Hom.* 86.284–85 (ed. Morin, CCSL 78, 515).

CHAPTER 6

1. I refer here to David Hunter's comment made during his presentation on a panel discussing Clark's book at the May 2006 annual meeting of the North American Patristics Society.

2. Elizabeth Clark, *History, Theory, Text: Historians and the Linguistic Turn* (Cambridge, Mass.: Harvard University Press, 2004).

3. Clark here is critical of those who naively believe in Leopold van Ranke's phrase, *wie es eigentlich gewesen*. See Leopold von Ranke, *The Theory and Practice of History*, ed. and intro. Georg G. Iggers and Konrad von Moltke (Indianapolis: Bobbs-Merrill, 1973).

4. Clark, *History, Theory, Text*, 110. In reaction to the critique of some reviewers that "new intellectual history" left out too much culture in favor of texts, Clark entertained the possibility that her model could just as easily be called "new cultural history," but that she preferred to stay with "new intellectual history" because "it resonates with Gareth Stedman Jones's claim that history 'is an entirely intellectual operation which takes place in the present and in the head'" (Gareth Stedman Jones, "From Historical Sociology to Theoretic History," *British Journal of Sociology* 27 [1976]: 195–305, here 296). See Clark, "Response to Comments on *History, Theory, Text*," *Church History* 74 (2005): 834.

5. See the issue of *Church History* 74 (2005): 812–36. Clark's response is on pp. 830–36.

6. Mark Vessey's review is in *Church History* 74 (2005): 826–30.

7. Haines-Eitzen's review is in *Church History* 74 (2005): 816–20.

8. Kim Haines-Eitzen directs the interested reader to Roger Chartier, "Texts, Printing, Readings," in *The New Cultural History*, ed. Lynn Hunt (Berkeley and Los Angeles: University of California Press, 1989), esp. 175.

9. Lim's review is in *Church History* 74 (2005): 820–26, here 825.

10. Clark, *History, Theory, Text*, 110.

11. Clark, *History, Theory, Text*, 7, 158–61.

12. Clark says that social history had "reigned supreme. By the late 1970s, however, a challenge to its dominance began to emerge in the form of a new cultural history" (Clark, *History, Theory, Text*, 106). However, in her reaction to the reviews in *Church History* 74 (2005) (see p. 833), Clark sought to regain ground for her earlier social-history approach. She said social history, along with cultural history, were tools to aid in the overall production of scholarship that begins with intellectual history.

For some illustrations of Clark's own use of social history, see especially *The Origenist Controversy* (Princeton, N.J.: Princeton University Press, 1992). During her research for the book, Clark published several related articles, including "New Perspectives on the Origenist Controversy: Human Embodiment and Ascetic Strategies," *Church History* 59 (1990): 145–62, and "Elite Networks and Heresy Accusations: Towards a Social Description of the Origenist Controversy," *Semeia* (1991): 79–117.

Another major work applying social history, in particular social-network theory, is Clark, *Jerome, Chrysostom, and Friends,* Studies in Women and Religion 1 (Lewiston, N.Y.: Edwin Mellen Press, 1979). Still other works are Clark, "Ascetic Renunciation and Feminine Advancement: A Paradox of Late Ancient Christianity," *Anglican Theological Review* 63 (1981): 240–57; "Claims on the Bones of Saint Stephen: The Partisans of Melania and Eudocia," *Church History* 51 (1982): 141–56; "Piety, Propaganda, and Politics in the Life of Melania the Younger," *Studia patristica* 18, no. 2 (1989): 167–83; and many others.

13. Clark, *History, Theory, Text,* 145–55, here 147. Cf. Clifford Geertz, "Thick Description: Toward an Interpretive Theory of Culture," in *The Interpretation of Cultures: Selected Essays* (London: Fontana, 1993), and *Local Knowledge: Further Essays in Interpretive Anthropology* (New York: Basic Books, 1983; repr. 1993).

14. Clark, *History, Theory, Text,* 159.

15. Clark, *History, Theory, Text,* 113.

16. Clark, *History, Theory, Text,* 170–85.

17. Cf. my own discussion of both texts in chapter 2 of this study, under "Private Property."

18. Andrew Jacobs, *Remains of the Jews: The Holy Land and Christian Empire in Late Antiquity,* Divinations: Rereading Late Ancient Religion (Stanford, Calif.: Stanford University Press, 2004).

19. Elizabeth Clark, *Reading Renunciation: Asceticism and Scripture in Early Christianity* (Princeton, N.J.: Princeton University Press, 1999).

20. For intertextuality, Clark relies here on the work of Julia Kristeva, *Sēmeiōtikē* (Paris: Seuil, 1969), and *Desire in Language: A Semiotic Approach to Literature and Art* (New York: Columbia University Press, 1980); Mikhail Bakhtin, *The Dialogic Imagination: Four Essays,* ed. Michael Holquist, trans. Caryl Emerson and Michael Holquist (Austin: University of Texas Press, 1981).

21. Clark, *Reading Renunciation,* 125.

22. This example is found at Clark, *Reading Renunciation,* 127.

23. Clark, *Reading Renunciation,* 128–32. This is a debate style of writing, in which, say, a pro-asceticism author assumes his opponent will want to

cite one or another biblical text. The pro-asceticism author then corrects his opponent's interpretation by citing a text supporting just the opposite view. The assumption to be held by the reader, then, is that the opponent is mistaken and not the other way around.

24. Clark, *Reading Renunciation*, 132–34. Texts that on the surface seem to have nothing to do with a particular argument implode when they are made to appear as though they fit perfectly into the argument at hand. E.g., 1 Corinthians 8:13, on abstaining from meat if it creates a scandal, is shown to be an argument for separating ascetic men and women because their associations could create a scandal.

25. Clark, *Reading Renunciation*, 134–36. Clark cites John Cassian's interpretation of the purity laws of Leviticus as being instead purity laws for the lives of monks. Nocturnal emissions are a cause for impurity in the Levitical laws; they are a cause for impurity in the lives of monks.

26. Clark, *Reading Renunciation*, 136–38. This is related to changing contexts but is more narrow. Whereas with changing contexts, the early Christian texts simply disregarded the entire literary, social, or historical context of a biblical passage, here they are concerned solely about changing the intended audience. So, for example, one can accept that God spoke to Hosea about security during the night (Hos 2:18), but can say that God equally spoke that to monks in a dormitory who are promised security from impurity during their sleep (from nocturnal emissions; sex-charged dreams; etc.).

27. Clark, *Reading Renunciation*, 138–40. Texts that are about men are applied to women, and vice versa. For example, 1 Corinthians 6:15, on men who frequent prostitutes, in the hands of Basil of Caesarea is a critique of a woman ascetic for having drawn men into harlotry after she admitted to having sexual relations.

28. Clark, *Reading Renunciation*, 141–45. This is where early Christians debate whether or not a text is the opinion of the human author, which is apparently allowed by the Spirit from time to time, or the words of the Spirit itself piercing through the human language. It can also involve a debate between Jesus' authority and Paul's, if words from the mouths of each person seem to be contradictory. Once a hierarchy is defined, pressing the texts into conformity with one another begins.

29. Clark, *Reading Renunciation*, 145–52. The differences between Hebrew Bible mores and New Testament ones are attributed to God's toleration of lax behavior and standards to Jews who could only handle the "milk" of truth. Christians, capable of handling the "meat" of the New Testament are held to higher standards, including ascetical standards.

30. Elizabeth Clark, "The Celibate Bridegroom and His Virginal Brides: Metaphor and the Marriage of Jesus in Early Christian Ascetic Exegesis," *Church History* 77 (2008): 1–25.

31. Paul Ricoeur, *The Rule of Metaphor: Multi-disciplinary Studies of the Creation of Meaning in Language,* trans. Robert Czerny, Kathleen McLaughlin, and John Costello (Toronto: University of Toronto Press, 1977). In footnote 25 of "The Celibate Bridegroom and His Virginal Brides," Clark rehearses the objections to Ricoeur's phenomenological approach to metaphor in the writings of Dominick LaCapra and Jacques Derrida.

32. Clark, "The Celibate Bridegroom and His Virginal Brides," 5. Cf. I. A. Richards, *The Philosophy of Rhetoric* (New York: Oxford University Press, 1936); and Janet Soskice, *Metaphor and Religious Language* (Oxford: Clarendon Press, 1985), 43–53, for her definition of the theory.

33. Clark, "The Celibate Bridegroom and His Virginal Brides," 5.

34. Clark, "The Celibate Bridegroom and His Virginal Brides," 7–8.

35. Clark, "The Celibate Bridegroom and His Virginal Brides," 16. Clark cites Augustine's *Tractates on John* 13.124.

36. Clark, "The Celibate Bridegroom and His Virginal Brides," 18–22.

37. Clark, "The Celibate Bridegroom and His Virginal Brides," 25.

38. Roland Barthes, "The Death of the Author," in *Image, Music, Text: Essays Selected and Translated by Stephen Heath* (London: Fontana Press, 1977), 142–49.

39. Clark, *History, Theory, Text,* 122.

40. Asterius, *Hom.* 1.2.1 (ed. Datema, *Homilies I–XIV,* 7).

41. Asterius, *Hom.* 1.5.1 (ed. Datema, *Homilies I–XIV,* 9; ET: mine): Τρυφὴ τοίνυν ἐστὶν πρᾶγμα πολέμιον φιλαρέτου ζωῆς, βλακείας δὲ καὶ διαχύσεως δηλούσης.

42. See the section on private property in Christian teaching and its context in this study.

43. Asterius, *Hom.* 1.10.3 (ed. Datema, *Homilies I–XIV,* 13; ET: mine): φιλοσόφῳ ψυχῇ.

44. Asterius, *Hom.* 1.4.2 (ed. Datema, *Homilies I–XIV,* 9).

45. Asterius, *Hom.* 1.2.4 (ed. Datema, *Homilies I–XIV,* 9; ET: mine): ταῖς ματαίαις ἐπινοίαις καὶ ταῖς ἐμπλήκτοις ἐπιθυμίαις ἐκδιατώμενος.

46. Asterius, *Hom.* 1.4.2 (ed. Datema, *Homilies I–XIV,* 9).

47. Asterius, *Hom.* 1.5.2 (ed. Datema, *Homilies I–XIV,* 10; ET: mine): Πάντα γὰρ παρ' ἐκείνοις ἐπιμελῶς ἐνδύεται καὶ τὰ ἄψυχα.

48. Asterius, *Hom.* 1.5.2 (ed. Datema, *Homilies I–XIV,* 10; ET: mine): Δεῖ τοίνυν τῷ τρυφῶντι πρῶτον μὲν οἰκίας πολυτελοῦς, . . . [θερμή,] ἀλεεινὴ μὲν ἡ τοῦ χειμῶνος . . . ἀναπεπταμένη δὲ πρὸς τὴν ἄρκτον θερινή.

49. Asterius, *Hom.* 1.5.2-3 (ed. Datema, *Homilies I–XIV*, 10).
50. Asterius, *Hom.* 1.5.2 (ed. Datema, *Homilies I–XIV*, 10; ET: mine): Πάντα γὰρ παρ' ἐκείνοις ἐπιμελῶς ἐνδύεται καὶ τὰ ἄψυχα, ἐλεεινῶς τῶν πενήτων ἐκδυομένων. This treats the last two words as objective genitives.
51. Asterius, *Hom.* 1.6.1 (ed. Datema, *Homilies I–XIV*, 10).
52. Asterius, *Hom.* 1.3.1 (ed. Datema, *Homilies I–XIV*, 8; ET: Anderson and Goodspeed): Ἄνθρωπον δέ, τὸ λογικὸν ζῷον καὶ ἥμερον καὶ καθ' ὁμοίωσιν Θεοῦτὴν ἀγαθότηατ παιδευόμενον, μικρὸν οὕτω φροντίζειν τῶν συγγενῶν ἐν ταῖς ὀδυνηραῖς τῶν συμφορῶν περιστάσεσιν.
53. Asterius, *Hom.* 1.12.1 (ed. Datema, *Homilies I–XIV*, 14–15; ET: mine): τὸ συμπαθὲς καὶ φιλνθρωπον ὡς αἰτίαν τῆς ζωῆς τῆς μελλούσης ἀσκήσαντα.
54. Asterius, *Hom.* 1.3.1 (ed. Datema, *Homilies I–XIV*, 8; ET: mine): παραχρώμενοι τῷ βίῳ, οὐ χρώμενοι.
55. Asterius, *Hom.* 1.3.1 (ed. Datema, *Homilies I–XIV*, 8).
56. Asterius, *Hom.* 1.8.1 (ed. Datema, *Homilies I–XIV*, 12; ET: Anderson and Goodspeed): Εἰ μὲν οὖν ἐτελεύτησεν μέχρι τούτου τὸ τοῦ Λαζάρου διήγημα καὶ οὕτως εἶχε τῶν πραγμάτων ἡ φύσις, ὡς τῇ ἀνωμαλίᾳ τοῦ βίου τούτου τὴν ζωὴν ἡμῶν περιγράφεσθαι, μεγάλας ἂν ἀφῆκα σχετλιάζων φωνάς, ἐφ' οἷς οἱ κτισθέντες ὁμοτίμως οὕτως ἀνίσως μετὰ τῶν ὁμοφύλων διάγομεν.
57. See chapter 3.
58. Asterius, *Hom.* 1.10.4 (ed. Datema, *Homilies I–XIV*, 13; ET: mine): Τί γὰρ τοῦθείου Ἰὼβ πλουσιώτερον; Ἀλλ' ὅμως ἡ εἰς ἄγαν εὐπορια τὸν ἄνδρα οὔτε τῆς δικαιοσύνης ἠλλοτρίωσεν.
59. Asterius, *Hom.* 1.10.4 (ed. Datema, *Homilies I–XIV*, 13; ET: mine): Τί τοῦ Ἰσακαριώτου πενέστερον; Καὶ οὐδὲν ἀπώνατο τῆς ἐνδείας εἰς σωτηρι αν.
60. Asterius, *Hom.* 1.10.3 (ed. Datema, *Homilies I–XIV*, 13; ET: Anderson and Goodspeed): πρόδηλον εἶναι, ὅτι μακαρίζει νῦν ἡ Γραφὴ τὸν πτωχὸν ἐκεῖνον τὸν φιλοσόφῳ ψυχῇ τοὺς μόχθους βαστάζοντα, καρτεροῦντα δὲ γενναίως πρὸς τὰς περιστάσεις τοῦ βίου καὶ οὐδὲν κακουργοῦντα πονηρόν, ἵνα τῇ σαρκὶ χαρίσηται τῆς τρυφῆς τὴν ἀπόλαυσιν.
61. There is some debate among biblical exegetes as to whom Jesus had in mind when he spoke of the πτωχοί. W. D. Davies and Dale Allison, in *A Critical and Exegetical Commentary on the Gospel according to Saint Matthew*, vol. 1, *Matthew 1–7*, International Critical Commentary (Edinburgh: T. & T. Clark, 1988), 442–44, affirm that, while certainly the economic aspect cannot be far from the text, the sense of humiliation or oppression is primary, for that would certainly be in the minds of Jesus' Jewish audience who are fa-

miliar with Hebrew Bible references to the poor in more judicial contexts. Ulrich Luz, in *Matthew 1–7,* Hermeneia (Minneapolis, Minn.: Fortress Press, 2007), 190–92, generally agrees, although he gives even greater weight to the humility/oppression aspect than he does to the economic aspect.

62. Jerome, *Hom.* 86.25–28 (ed. Morin, CCSL 78, 507–8; ET: Ewald, FOTC 57, 201): Dives iste purpuratus et splendidus non accusator quod avarus fuerit, non quia res alienas tulerit, non quia adulter fuerit, non quia aliquid mali fecerti: sola in illo condemnatur superbia.

63. Jerome, *Hom.* 86.119–20 (ed. Morin, CCSL 78, 510; ET: Ewald, FOTC 57, 204): Ut refrigeret linguam meam: multa enim superba locuta est.

64. Jerome, *Hom.* 86.60–63 (ed. Morin, CCSL 78, 509; ET: Ewald, FOTC 57, 202): Audiviums quid utrique in terra passi sint: videamus quid utrique eorum patiantur apud inferos. Here, again, I correct Ewald's inconsistent rendering of *inferos* to Hades.

65. Jerome, *Hom.* 86.314–27 (ed. Morin, CCSL 78, 516).

66. Jerome, *Hom.* 86.215–31 (ed. Morin, CCSL 78, 513–14).

67. Jerome, *Hom.* 86.269–89 (ed. Morin, CCSL 78, 515).

68. Jerome, *Hom.* 86.283–89 (ed. Morin, CCSL 78, 515; ET: Ewald, FOTC 57, 210): Apostoli secuti fuerant, et fugiunt. . . . O Petre, O Iohannes, qui dixeras: "Et si me necesse est mori, numquam te negabo." Promittis, et non facis: ecce alius damnatus in homicidium, quod non promiserat, facit. Exclusus de loco es tuo, exclusit te latro: ipse primus ingreditur cum Xristo in paradisum.

69. Jerome, *Hom.* 86.139–214 (ed. Morin, CCSL 78, 511–13).

70. Jerome, *Hom.* 86.149–50 (ed. Morin, CCSL 78, 511).

71. Jerome, *Hom.* 86.152–53 (ed. Morin, CCSL 78, 511).

CONCLUSION

1. Paul Hanson, "The Ancient Near Eastern Roots of Social Welfare," in *Through the Eye of a Needle: Judeo-Christian Roots of Social Welfare,* ed. Emily A. Hanawalt and Carter Lindberg (Kirksville, Mo.: Thomas Jefferson University Press, 1994), 7–28, here 20.

2. A cursory examination of the first six (of sixteen) sections of the Russian Orthodox Church's 2000 document, "Bases of the Social Concept of the Russian Orthodox Church," revealed citation of or general reference to only eleven patristic sources (from the perspective of Orthodox communities, the patristic age continues in our day; my reference to patristic sources here is

consistent with that applied to the CST documents in chapter 1 of this study, i.e., second- through seventh-century sources). Half of these citations are to conciliar canons or to Justinian's code. None of the sources are footnoted, which complicates the reader's task in exploring the wider context of their comments further. What is more, most citations are ornamental to the arguments already established in the broader context of the patristic source citations. Although further reading might change this assessment, analysis of these first six sections does not reveal any greater comfort level with patristic, socio-ethical sources in this Russian Orthodox Church document than in CST. In fact, CST seems to be more engaging with patristic texts, by comparison.

As well, I am acquainted with the work Thomas Hughson has been preparing—a publication of American Protestant documents on social ethics during the twentieth century. The paucity of patristic references in the materials he has collected, at least, is beyond alarming. One is hard-pressed to find more than a handful of patristic references, in all.

3. *Caritas in veritate* III.34 cites Augustine, *De libero arbitrio,* II, 3, 8ff. There is, at I.12, also a patristic source citation. The encyclical makes a general reference to the "Church Fathers," but this reference is a historiographical remark and not a support for any particular social idea.

Bibliography

ANCIENT, PATRISTIC, AND OTHER MAJOR PRIMARY SOURCES

Ambrose of Milan. *Ambrosiana scritti varii publicati nel XV centenario della morte di Sant Ambrogio*. Edited by Carolus Schenkl. Milan: L. F. Cogliati, 1897.

———. *De Iacob, de Ioseph, de Patriarchis, de fuga saeculi, de interpretatione Iob et David, de apologia David, apologia David altera, de Helia et ieiunio, de Nabuthae, de Tobia*. Edited by Carolus Schenkl. CSEL 32. Vienna: F. Tempsky, 1897.

———. *De obitu Satyri fratris laudation funebris*. Edited by Paulus B. Albers. Florilegium patristicum 15. Bonn: Sumptibus Petri Hanstein, 1921.

———. *De officiis*. Edited by Maurice Testard. CCSL 15. Turnhout: Brepols, 2000.

———. *De virginitate liber unus*. Edited by Egnatius Cazzaniga. CSLP. Turin: In Aedibus Io. Bapt. Paraviae et Sociorum, 1954.

———. *Opera, Pars prima qua continentur libri: Exameron, De paradiso, De Cain et Abel, De Noe, De Abraham, De Isaac, De bono mortis*. Edited by Carolus Schenkl. CSEL 32, Part 1. Vienna: F. Tempsky, 1897.

———. *Opera, Pars VII: Explanatio symboli, de sacramentis, de mysteriis, de paenitentia, de excessu fratris, de obitu Valentiniani, de obitu Theodosii*. Edited by Otto Faller. CCSL 73. Turnhout: Brepols, 1955.

———. *Opera, Pars X: Epistula et Acta, Tome III: Epistularum liber decimus, Epistulae extra collectionem, Gesta concilii Aquileiensis*. Edited by Michaela Zelzer. CSEL 82. Vienna: F. Tempsky, 1982.

Aristophanes. "Ecclesiazousae." In *The Comedies of Aristophanes*, vol. 10. Edited and translated by Alan Sommerstein. Warminster: Aris and Phillips, 1998.

———. "Ploutos." In *The Comedies of Aristophanes*, vol. 11. Edited and translated by Alan Sommerstein. Warminster: Aris and Phillips, 2001).

Asterius of Amasea. *Homilies I–XIV. Text, Introduction and Notes*. Edited by Cornelius Datema. Leiden: E. J. Brill, 1970.

Athanasius of Alexandria. *Vie d'Antoine*. Edited by Gerhardus J. M. Bartelink. SC 400. Paris: Éditions du Cerf, 1994; revised 2004.

Augustine of Hippo. *Confessionum libri tredecim*. Edited by Pius Knoll. CSEL 33. Vienna: F. Tempsky, 1896.

———. *Confessionum libri XIII*. Edited by Lucas Verheijen. CCSL 27. Turnhout: Brepols, 1990.

———. *De civitate Dei, libri I–X*. Edited by Bernardus Dombart and Alphonsus Kalb. CCSL 47. Turnhout: Brepols, 1955.

———. *De civitate Dei, Pars I: libri I–XII*. Edited by Emanuel Hoffmann. CSEL 40, Part 1. Vienna: F. Tempsky, 1899.

———. *De civitate Dei, libri XI–XXII*. Edited by Bernardus Dombart and Alphonsus Kalb. CCSL 48. Turnhout: Brepols, 1955.

———. *De civitate Dei, libri XXII, vol. 2, Libri XIV–XXII*. Edited by Emanuel Hoffmann. CSEL 40, Part 2. Vienna: F. Tempsky, 1899.

———. *De fide et symbolo, de fide et operibus, de agone christiano, de continentia, de bono coniugali, de sancta virginitate*. Edited by Iosephus Zycha. CSEL 41. Vienna: F. Tempsky, 1900.

———. *De Trinitate libri XV, Libri I–XIII*. Edited by W. J. Mountain and F. Glorie. CCSL 50. Turnhout: Brepols, 1968.

———. *Enarrationes in Psalmos 1–50, Pars 2: Enarrationes in Psalmos 34–50*. Edited by Franco Gori and Iuliana Spaccia. CSEL 103, Part 5. Vienna: Österreichischen Akademie der Wissenschaften, 2005.

———. *Enarrationes in Psalmos I–L*. Edited by D. Eligius Dekkers and Johannes Fraipont. CCSL 38. Turnhout: Brepols, 1956.

———. *Enarrationes in Psalmos 51–100, Pars 5: Enarrationes in Psalmos 141–150*. Edited by Franco Gori and Iuliana Spaccia. CSEL 95, Part 5. Vienna: Österreichische Akademie der Wissenschaften, 2005.

———. *Enarrationes in Psalmos LI–C*. Edited by Eligius Dekkers and Johannes Fraipont. CCSL 39. Turnhout: Brepols, 1956.

———. *Enarrationes in Psalmos 101–150, Pars 5: Enarrationes in Psalmos 141–150*. Edited by Franco Gori and Iuliana Spaccia. CSEL 95, Part 5. Vienna: Österreichische Akademie der Wissenschaften, 2005.

———. *Enarrationes in Psalmos CI–CL*. Edited by Eligius Dekkers and J. Fraipont. CCSL 40. Turnhout: Brepols, 1956.

———. *Epistulae I–LV*. Edited by Klaus D. Daur. CCSL 31. Turnhout: Brepols, 2004.

———. *In Iohannis Evangelium, tractatus CXXIV*. Edited by Radbodus Willems. CCSL 36. Turnhout: Brepols, 1954.

———. *Sancti Augustini sermones post Maurinos reperti. Probatae dumtaxat auctoritatis nunc primum disquisiti, in unum collecti et codicum fide instaurati studio et diligentia*. Edited by Germain Morin. Miscellanea Agostiniana: Testi e studi pubblicati a cura dell'ordine eremitano di S. Agostino nel XV centenario dalla morte del santo dottore, 1. Rome: Tipografia Poliglotta Vaticana, 1930.

———. *Scripta contra Donatistas, Pars II: Contra litteras Petiliani libri tres, Epistula ad Catholicos de secta Donatistarum, Contra Cresconium libri quattuor*. Edited by Michael Petschenig. CSEL 52. Vienna: F. Tempsky, 1909.

———. *Sermones de Vetero Testamento, id est sermones I–L secundum ordinem Vulgatum insertis etiam novem sermonibus post Maurinos repertis*. Edited by Cyril Lambot. CCSL 41. Turnhout: Brepols, 1961.

Basil of Caesarea. *Homélies sur la richesse*. Edited and translated by Yves Courtonne. Collection d'études anciennes. Paris: Firm-Didot, 1935.

———. *Homilien zum Hexaemeron*. Edited by Emmanuel Amand de Mendieta. GCS 2. Berlin: Akademie Verlag, 1997.

Bihlmeyer, Karl. *Die Apostolischen Väter*. Sammlung ausgewählter kirchen- und dogmengeschichtlicher Quellenschriften. Tübingen: J. C. B. Mohr, 1924.

Butler, Cuthbert, ed. *The Lausiac History of Palladius: The Greek Text Edited with Introduction and Notes*. Texts and Studies: Contributions to Biblical and Patristic Literature 6, no. 2. Cambridge: Cambridge University Press, 1904.

Cicero, Marcus Tullius. *De officiis*. Edited and translated by Walter Miller. LCL. Cambridge, Mass.: Harvard University Press, 1913.

Clement of Alexandria. *Stromata: Buch I–VI*. Edited by Otto Stahlin and Ludwig Fruchtel. GCS 52. Berlin: Akademie Verlag, 1985.

———. *Stromata: Buch VII und VIII; Excerpta ex Theodoto; Eclogae propheticae; Quis dives salvetur; Fragmente*. Edited by Otto Stählin, Ludwig Früchtel, and Ursula Treu. GCS 17. Berlin: Akademie Verlag, 1970.

———. *Les Stromates: Stromata I*. Edited by Marcel Caster. SC 30. Paris: Éditions du Cerf, 1951.

Conference of Latin American Bishops. *Puebla and Beyond: Documentation and Commentary*. Edited by John Eagleson and Philip Scharper. Translated by John Drury. Maryknoll, N.Y.: Orbis Books, 1980.

———. *Santo Domingo and Beyond: Documents and Commentaries from the Historic Meeting of the Latin American Bishops' Conference*. Edited by Alfred T. Hennelly. Maryknoll, N.Y.: Orbis Books, 1993.

Cyprian of Carthage. *Ad Quirinum, Ad Fortunatum, De lapsis, De ecclesiae catholicae unitate*. Edited by Maurice Bévenot. CCSL 3, Part 1. Turnhout: Brepols, 1972.

———. *La bienfaisance et les aumônes*. Edited by Michel Poirier. SC 440. Paris: Éditions du Cerf, 1999.

———. *Epistularium*. Edited by G. F. Diercks. CCSL 3B, Part 3. Turnhout: Brepols, 1996.

Eusebius of Caesarea. *De vita Constantini*. Edited by Paul Dräger. Bibliotheca classicorum 1. Oberhaid: Utopica, 2007.

———. *Die Praeparatio Evangelica: Einleitung, die Bücher I bis X*. Edited by Édouard des Places. GCS 43. Vol. 2. Berlin: Akademie Verlag, 1982.

———. *La préparation évangélique, Livre I*. Edited by Jean Sirinelli. SC 206. Paris: Éditions du Cerf, 1974.

Gregory the Great. *Homiliae in evangelia*. Edited by Raymond Étaix. CCSL 141. Turnhout: Brepols, 1999.

———. *Homiliae in evangelia*. Edited and translated by Michael Fiedrowicz. Fontes christiani 28, Part 1. Freiburg: Herder, 1997.

———. *Registre des lettres, Livres I et II*. Edited by Pierre Minard. SC 370. Paris: Éditions du Cerf, 1991.

———. *Registrum epistularum libri I–VII*. Edited by Dag Norberg. CCSL 140. Turnhout: Brepols, 1982.

———. *Registrum epistolarum, tome II: Libri VIII–XIV*. Edited by Paulus Ewald. MGH. Berlin: Weidmann, 1899.

———. *Règle pastorale, Tome I*. Edited by Floribert Rommel. Translated by Charles Morel. SC 381. Paris: Éditions du Cerf, 1992.

———. *Règle pastorale, Tome II*. Edited by Floribert Rommel. Translated by Charles Morel. SC 382. Paris: Éditions du Cerf, 1992.

Gregory Nazianzen. *Discours 1–3*. Sources Chrétiennes, 247. Edited by Jean Bernardi. Paris: Éditions du Cerf, 1978.

———. *Discours 6–12*. Edited by Marie-Ange Calvet-Sebasti. SC 405. Paris: Éditions du Cerf, 1995.

———. *Discours 32–37*. Edited by Claudio Moreschini. Translated by Paul Gallay. SC 318. Paris: Éditions du Cerf, 1985.

———. *Discours 38–41*. Edited by Claudio Moreschini. Translated by Paul Gallay. SC 358. Paris: Éditions du Cerf, 1990.

Gregory of Nyssa. *Contra Usurarios*. Edited by Ernest Gebhardt. In *GNO* 9. Leiden: E. J. Brill, 1967.

———. *De virginitate*. Edited by J. P. Cavarnos. In *GNO* 8, part 1. Leiden: E. J. Brill, 1952.

———. *De vita Moysis*. Edited by Herbertus Musurillo. In *GNO* 7, part 1. Leiden: E. J. Brill, 1964.

Hermas. *Le pasteur*. Edited by Robert Joly. SC 53. Paris: Éditions du Cerf, 1958.

Hünermann, Peter, and Heinrich Denzinger, eds. *Enchiridion symbolorum, definitionem et declarationum de rebus fidei et morum*. 31st ed. Bologna: Dehoniana, 2001.

Irenaeus of Lyon. *Adversus haereses*. Edited by Norbert Brox. Fontes Christiani 8, Part 3. Freiburg: Herder, 1995.

———. *Adversus haereses*. Edited by Norbert Brox. Fontes Christiani 8, Part 5. Freiburg: Herder, 2001.

———. *Contre les hérésies*. Edited by Adelin Rousseau. SC 153. Paris: Éditions du Cerf, 1969.

———. *Contre les hérésies, Livre I*. Edited by Adelin Rousseau and Louis Doutreleau. SC 264. Paris: Éditions du Cerf, 1979.

———. *Contre les hérésies, Livre III*. Edited by Adelin Rousseau and Louis Doutreleau. SC 211. Paris: Éditions du Cerf, 1974.

———. *Epideixis Adversus Haereses*. Edited by Norbert Brox. Fontes Christiani 8, Part 1. Freiburg: Herder, 1993.

Jerome. *S. Hieronymi presbyteri opera. Pars II: Opera homiletica*. Edited by Germain Morin. CCSL 78. Turnhout: Brepols, 1958.

John Cassian. *Collationes XXIII*. Edited by Michael Petschenig. Revised by Gottfried Kreuz. CSEL 13. Vienna: Österreichische Akademie der Wissenschaften, 2004.

John Chrysostom. *Sermons sur la Genèse*. Edited by Laurence Brottier. SC 433. Paris: Éditions du Cerf, 1998.

———. *La virginité*. Edited by Herbert Musurillo. SC 125. Paris: Éditions du Cerf, 1966.

John Paul II. "L'homme et la révolution urbaine: Citadins et ruraux devant l'urbanisation." *La documentation Catholique* 62 (1–15 August, 1965): 1363–66.

Julian the Apostate. *Oeuvres Complètes, tome I, 2e partie: Lettres et fragments*. Edited by Joseph Bidez. Paris: Les belles lettres, 1924.

Justin Martyr. *Apologie pour les Chrétiens*. Edited by Charles Munier. Paradosis: Études de littérature et de théologie anciennes. Fribourg, Switzerland: Éditions Universitaires, 1995.

———. *Apologiae pro Christianis*. Edited by Miroslav Marcovich. PTS 38. Berlin: Walter de Gruyter, 1994.

———. *Dialogus cum Tryphone*. Edited by Miroslav Marcovich. PTS 47. Berlin: Walter de Gruyter, 1997.

———. *Opera quae feruntur omnia, Tomi I, Pars I: Opera Iustini indubitata*. Edited by Johan Karl Theodor von Otto. Corpus Apologeticorum Christianorum saeculi secundi. Jena: Fischer, 1876.

Kessler, Andreas, ed. *Reichtumskritik und Pelagianismus: Die pelagianische Diatribe de divitiis; Situierung, Lesetext, Übersetzung, Kommentar*. Paradosis 43. Freiburg: Universitätsverlag, 1999.

Lactantius. *Institutions divines*. Edited by Pierre Monat. SC 204. Paris: Éditions du Cerf, 1973.

———. *Opera omnia, Pars I: Divinae institutiones et epitome divinarum institutionum*. Edited by Samuel Brandt. CSEL 19. Prague: F. Tempsky, 1890.

Leo I. *Sermons, Tome IV*. Edited by René Dolle. SC 200. Paris: Éditions du Cerf, 1973.

———. *Tractatus septem et nonaginta*. Edited by Antoine Chavasse. CCSL 138 and 138A. Turnhout: Brepols, 1973.

Leo XIII. *L'Enciclica Rerum novarum: Testo autentico e redazioni preparatorie dai documenti originali*. Edited by Giovanni Antonazzi. Rome: Storia e letteratura, 1957.

Minucius Felix. *Octavius*. Edited by Michael Pellegrino. CSLP. Turin: G. B. Paravia, 1972.

Origen. *Contra Celsum libri VIII*. Supplements to Vigiliae Christianae 54. Leiden: E. J. Brill, 2001.

Pseudo-Dionysius Areopagita. *De divinis nominibus*. Edited by Beate Regina Suchla. PTS 33. Berlin: Walter de Gruyter, 1990.

Rabbula of Edessa. "Commands and Admonitions of Mar Rabbula, Bishop of Edessa to the Priests and the 'Benai Qeiama.'" In *Syriac and Arabic Documents Regarding Legislation Relative to Syrian Asceticism*, edited and translated by Arthur Vööbus. Stockholm: Etse, 1960.

Salvian of Marseille. *Oeuvres II: Du gouvernement de Dieu*. Edited by Georges Lagarrigue. SC 220. Paris: Éditions du Cerf, 1975.

Seneca. *Moral Essays*. Vol. 2. Edited and translated by John W. Basore. LCL. Cambridge, Mass.: Harvard University Press, 1965.

Sulpitius Severus. *Vie de Saint Martin, Tome I*. Edited by Jacques Fontaine. SC 133. Paris: Éditions du Cerf, 1967.

Tertullian. *Apologeticum*. Edited by Heinrich Hoppe. CSEL 69. Vienna: F. Tempsky, 1939.

———. *À son épouse*. Edited by Charles Munier. SC 273. Paris: Éditions du Cerf, 1980.

———. *Opera, Pars I: Opera Catholica, Adversus Marcionem*. Edited by Eligius Dekkers, Janus G. P. Borleffs, and R. Willems. CCSL 1. Turnhout: Brepols, 1954.

———. *Opera, Pars II: Opera monastica*. Edited by Aloïs Gerlo. CCSL 2. Turnhout: Brepols, 1954.

———. *Opera, Pars III*. Edited by Aemilii Kroymann. CSEL 47. Vienna: F. Tempsky, 1906.

Theodoret of Cyrus, *Commentary on Romans*. PG 82 (Paris, 1864). Cols. 44–225.

Theodosiani libri xvi cum constitutionibus sirmondianis. Edited by Theodore Mommsen. Bern: Apud Weidmannos, 1905.

TRANSLATIONS OF PRIMARY SOURCES

Abbott, Walter M., ed. *The Documents of Vatican II*. New York: America Press, 1966.

Ambrose of Milan. "Consolation on the Death of Emperor Valentinian." In *Funeral Orations by Saint Gregory Nazianzen and Saint Ambrose*. Translated by Roy J. Deferarri. FOTC 22. Washington, D.C.: Catholic University of America Press, 1968.

———. *De officiis, Volume I: Introduction, Text, and Translation*. Translated by Ivor J. Davidson. Oxford Early Christian Studies. Oxford: Oxford University Press, 2001.

———. *Hexameron, Paradise, and Cain and Abel*. Translated by John J. Savage. FOTC 42. New York: Fathers of the Church, 1961.

———. "In Honor of His Brother Satyrus." In *Funeral Orations by Saint Gregory Nazianzen and Saint Ambrose*. Translated by John J. Sullivan and Martin R. P. McGuire. FOTC 22. Washington, D.C.: Catholic University of America Press, 1953.

———. *Letters*. Translated by Mary Melchior Beyenka. FOTC 26. Washington, D.C.: Catholic University of America Press, 1954.

———. *On Virginity*. Translated by Daniel Callam. Peregrina Translations Series 7. Toronto: Peregrina, 1980.

Anderson, Galusha, and Edgar J. Goodspeed, eds. *Ancient Sermons for Modern Times*. New York: Pilgrim Press, 1904.

Aristotle. *A Treatise on Government, or The Politics of Aristotle*. Translated by William Ellis. London: J. M. Dent and Sons, 1912.

Athanasius of Alexandria. *The Life of Antony and the Letter to Marcellinus*. Translated by Robert C. Gregg. CWS. New York: Paulist Press, 1980.

Augustine of Hippo. "Answer to the Letters of Petilian, Bishop of Cirta." In *The Writings Against the Manichaeans and Against the Donatists*. Translated by J. R. King. NPNF, 1st ser., 4. Edinburgh: T. & T. Clark, 1887.

———. *The City of God against the Pagans*. Translated by R. W. Dyson. Cambridge Texts in the History of Political Thought. Cambridge: Cambridge University Press, 1998.

———. *Confessions*. Translated by Henry Chadwick. Oxford: Oxford University Press, 1991.

———. *De bono coniugali, De sancta virginitate*. Translated by P. G. Walsh. Oxford Early Christian Texts. Oxford: Clarendon Press, 2001.

———. *Expositions of the Psalms (Enarrationes in Psalmos) 33–50*. Translated by Maria Boulding. WSA, Part 2, vol. 16. New York: New City Press, 2000.

———. *Expositions of the Psalms (Enarrationes in Psalmos) 73–98*. Translated by Maria Boulding. WSA, Part 2, vol. 18. New York: New City Press, 2004.

———. *Expositions of the Psalms (Enarrationes in Psalmos) 121–150*. Translated by Maria Boulding. WSA, Part 2, vol. 20. New York: New City Press, 2004.

———. *Letters 1–82*. Translated by Wilfrid Parsons. FOTC 12. Washington, D.C.: Catholic University of America Press, 1951.

———. *Letters 1–99*. Translated by Roland Teske. WSA, Part 2, vol. 1. New York: Newman Press, 2001.

———. *On the Trinity, Books 8–15*. Translated by Stephen McKenna. Cambridge Texts in the History of Philosophy. Cambridge: Cambridge University Press, 2002.

———. *Sermones II (20–50) on the Old Testament*. Translated by Edmund Hill. WSA, Part 3, vol. 2. Brooklyn, N.Y.: New City Press, 1990.

———. *Sermones III (51–94) on the New Testament*. Translated by Edmund Hill. WSA, Part 3, vol. 3. Brooklyn, N.Y.: New City Press, 1991.

———. *Tractates on the Gospel of John, 28–54*. Translated by John W. Rettig. FOTC 88. Washington, D.C.: Catholic University of America Press, 1993.

Basil. *Ascetical Works*. Translated by M. Monica Wagner. FOTC 9. Washington, D.C.: Catholic University of America Press, 1950.

Bastiaensen, Anthony A. R., ed. *Vita di Cipriano, Vita di Ambrogio, Vita di Agostino*. Scritti greci e latini: Vite dei santi, 3. Milan: Fondazione Lorenzo Valla, 1997.

Bravo, R. Sierra, and Florentino Del Valle, eds. *Doctrina social y economica de los padres de la Iglesia: Colección general de documentos y textos.* Madrid: Biblioteca Fomento Social, 1967.

Chadwick, Henry. *Origen. Contra Celsum.* Cambridge: Cambridge University Press, 1965.

Cicero, Marcus Tullius. *On Duties.* Cambridge Texts in the History of Political Thought. Translated by M. T. Griffin and E. M. Atkins. Cambridge: Cambridge University Press, 1991.

Clement of Alexandria. *The Exhortation to the Greeks, The Rich Man's Salvation, and the Fragment of an Address Entitled To the Newly Baptized.* Translated by G. W. Butterworth. LCL. Cambridge, Mass.: Harvard University Press, 1919.

―――. *Stromateis: Books One to Three.* Translated by John Ferguson. FOTC 85. Washington, D.C.: Catholic University of America Press, 1991.

Cyprian of Carthage. *De Lapsis and De Ecclesiae Catholicae Unitate.* Translated by Maurice Bévenot. Oxford Early Christian Texts. Oxford: Clarendon Press, 1971.

―――. *Letters (1–81).* Translated by Rose B. Donna. FOTC 51. Washington, D.C.: Catholic University of America Press, 1964.

―――. *The Letters of St. Cyprian of Carthage: Volume III, Letters 55–66.* Translated by G. W. Clarke. ACW 46. New York: Newman Press, 1986.

―――. *Treatises.* Translated by Roy J. Deferrari. FOTC 36. Washington, D.C.: Catholic University of America Press, 1958.

Dionysius the Areopagite. *The Complete Works.* Translated by Colm Luibheid. CWS. New York: Paulist Press, 1987.

Ehrman, Bart, ed. *The Apostolic Fathers.* Vol. 1, *I Clement, II Clement, Ignatius, Polycarp, Didache.* LCL. Cambridge, Mass.: Harvard University Press, 2003.

―――. *The Apostolic Fathers.* Vol. 2, *Epistle of Barnabas, Papias and Quadratus, Epistle to Diognetus, The Shepherd of Hermas.* LCL. Cambridge, Mass.: Harvard University Press, 2003.

Eusebius of Caesarea. *Eusebii Pamphili Evangelicae praeparationis Libri XV. Ad codices manuscriptos denuo collatos recensuit Anglice nunc primum reddidit notis et indicibus instruxit.* 4 vols. Translated by Edwin H. Gifford. Oxford: Typographeo Academico, 1903.

―――. *Life of Constantine.* Edited by Averil Cameron and Stuart Hill. Clarendon Ancient History. Oxford: Clarendon Press, 1999.

Gregory the Great. "The Book of Pastoral Rule and Selected Epistles." In *Leo the Great; Gregory the Great.* Translated by James Barmby. NPNF, 2d ser., 12. Edinburgh: T. & T. Clark, 1895.

———. *Forty Gospel Homilies*. Translated by David Hurst. Cistercian Studies Series, 123. Kalamazoo, Mich.: Cistercian Publications, 1990.

———. *Pastoral Care*. Translated by Henry Davis. ACW 11. Westminster, Md.: Newman Press, 1950.

Gregory of Nyssa. *The Life of Moses*. Translated by A. J. Malherbe and Everett Ferguson. CWS. New York: Paulist Press, 1978.

Irenaeus of Lyon. "Against Heresies." In *The Apostolic Fathers with Justin Martyr and Irenaeus*. Translated by Alexander Roberts and James Donaldson. ANF 1. Edinburgh: T. & T. Clark, 1867.

———. *Against the Heresies, Book 1*. Translated by Dominic J. Unger and John J. Dillon. ACW 55. Mahwah, N.J.: Paulist Press, 1992.

Janis (Berzins), Hieroschemamonk. "Homily on the Words of St. Luke's Gospel: 'I will pull down my barns and build larger ones' and on Avarice." *Orthodox Life* 42 (1992): 10–17.

Jerome. *The Homilies of Saint Jerome*. Translated by Marie Liguori Ewald. 2 vols. FOTC 48 and FOTC 57. Washington, D.C.: Catholic University of America Press, 1966.

John Cassian. *The Conferences*. Translated by Boniface Ramsey. ACW 57. New York: Newman Press, 1997.

John Chrysostom. "Homilies on the Acts of the Apostles." In *John Chrysostom: Homilies on the Acts of the Apostles and the Epistle to the Romans*. Translated by H. Browne and G. B. Stevens. NPNF, 1st ser., 11. Edinburgh: T. & T. Clark, 1889.

———. "The Homilies on the Epistle of St. Paul to the Romans." In *Saint Chrysostom: Homilies on the Acts of the Apostles and The Epistle to the Romans*. Translated by J. B. Morris and W. H. Simcox. NPNF, 1st ser., 11. Edinburgh: T. & T. Clark, 1877.

———. *Homilies on the Gospel of Saint Matthew*. Translated by George Prevost. NPNF, 1st ser., 10. Grand Rapids, Mich.: William B. Eerdmans, 1991.

———. "Homilies on the Statues, to the People of Antioch." In *John Chrysostom: On the Priesthood; Ascetic Treatises; Select Homilies and Letters; Homilies on the Statues*. Translated by W. R. W. Stephens. NPNF, 1st ser., 9. Edinburgh: T. & T. Clark, 1889.

———. *On Virginity, Against Remarriage*. Translated by Sally Rieger Shore. Studies in Women and Religion, 9. New York: Mellen Press, 1983.

———. "Two Homilies on Eutropius." In *John Chrysostom: On the Priesthood; Ascetic Treatises; Select Homilies and Letters; Homilies on the Statues*. Translated by W. R. W. Stephens. NPNF, 1st ser., 9. Edinburgh: T. & T. Clark, 1889.

Julian the Apostate. *The Works of the Emperor Julian in Three Volumes.* Vol. 3. Translated by William Cave Wright. LCL. Cambridge, Mass.: Harvard University Press, 1923.

Justin Martyr. *The First and Second Apologies.* Translated by Leslie William Barnard. ACW 56. Mahwah, N.J.: Paulist Press, 1997.

———. *The First Apology; The Second Apology; Dialogue with Trypho; Exhortation to the Greeks; Discourse to the Greeks; The Monarchy or the Rule of God.* Translated by Thomas B. Falls. FOTC 6. Washington, D.C.: Catholic University of America Press, 1977.

Kelly, Thomas A. *Sancti Ambrosii Liber de consolatione Valentiniani: A Text with a Translation, Introduction and Commentary.* Patristic Studies 58. Washington, D.C.: Catholic University of America Press, 1940.

King, C. W. *Julian the Emperor, Containing Gregory Nazianzen's Two Invectives and Libanius' Monody.* London: George Bell and Sons, 1888.

Lactantius. *Divine Institutes.* Translated by Anthony Bowen and Peter Garnsey. Translated Texts for Historians, 40. Liverpool: Liverpool University Press, 2003.

Leo the Great. *Sermons.* Translated by Jane P. Freeland and Agnes J. Conway. FOTC 93. Washington, D.C.: Catholic University of America Press, 1996.

Lucian. "The Dream." In *Selected Dialogues.* Translated and edited by Desmond Costa, 7–12. Oxford: Oxford University Press, 2005.

McCambley, Casimir. "Against Those Who Practice Usury by Gregory of Nyssa." *Greek Orthodox Theological Review* 36 (1991): 287–302.

McGuire, Martin R. P. S. *Ambrosii De Nabuthae: A Commentary, with an Introduction and Translation.* Patristic Studies 15. Washington, D.C.: Catholic University of America Press, 1927.

Menander. *The Bad-Tempered Man (Dyskolos).* Translated by Stanley Ireland. Warminster, U.K.: Aris & Phillips, 1995.

Meyer, Robert T. *Palladius: The Lausiac History.* ACW 34. New York: Paulist Press, 1964.

Minucius Felix. *Octavius.* Translated by Rudolph Arbesmann. FOTC 10. Washington, D.C.: Catholic University of America Press, 1950.

———. *The Octavius.* Translated by G. W. Clarke. ACW 39. New York: Newman Press, 1974.

O'Sullivan, Jeremiah F. *The Writings of Salvian the Presbyter.* FOTC 3. Washington, D.C.: Catholic University of America Press, 1947.

Pearson, Birger, and Tim Vivian, eds. *Two Coptic Homilies Attributed to Saint Peter of Alexandria: On Riches, On the Epiphany.* Rome: C.I.M., 1993.

Pharr, Clyde. *The Theodosian Code and Novels and the Sirmondian Constitutions*. The Corpus of Roman Law, vol. 1. Princeton, N.J.: Princeton University Press, 1952]

Plato. *Republic*. In *Plato: Complete Works*. Translated by G. M. A. Grube. Revised by C. D. C. Reeve. Indianapolis: Hackett Publishing, 1997.

Possidius. *The Life of Saint Augustine*. Translated by John E. Rotelle. The Augustinian Series 1. Villanova, Pa.: Augustinian Press, 1988.

Ramsey, Boniface. *Ambrose*. The Early Church Fathers. London and New York: Routledge Press, 1997.

Rees, B. R., ed. *The Letters of Pelagius and His Followers*. Suffolk, U.K.: Boydell Press, 1991.

Smith, R. Payne. *A Commentary upon the Gospel according to S. Luke by S. Cyril, Patriarch of Alexandria*. 2 vols. Oxford: Oxford University Press, 1859.

Sulpitius Severus. "Life of St. Martin." In *The Works of Sulpitius Severus*. Translated by Alexander Roberts. NPNF, 2d ser., 11. Edinburgh: T. & T. Clark, 1894.

———. *Writings*. Translated by Bernard Peebles. FOTC 7. Washington, D.C.: Catholic University of America Press, 1949.

Tandy, David, and Walter Neale, eds. *Hesiod's Works and Days: A Translation and Commentary for the Social Sciences*. Berkeley and Los Angeles: University of California Press, 1996.

Tanner, Norman P., ed. *Decrees of the Ecumenical Councils*. 2 vols. Washington, D.C.: Georgetown University Press, 1990.

Tertullian. *Apologetical Works*. Translated by Emily Joseph Daly. FOTC 10. Washington, D.C.: Catholic University of America Press, 1950.

———. *Treatise on the Resurrection*. Translated by Ernest Evans. London: SPCK, 1960.

———. *Treatises on Marriage and Remarriage: To His Wife, An Exhortation to Chastity, Monogamy*. Translated by William P. Le Saint. ACW 13. Westminster, Md.: Newman Press, 1951.

Theodoret of Cyrus. *On Divine Providence*. Translated by Thomas Halton. ACW 49. New York: Newman Press, 1988.

Toal, Martin Francis. *The Sunday Sermons of the Great Fathers*. 4 vols. Chicago: Henry Regnery, 1957–1963.

Ward, Benedicta. *The Sayings of the Desert Fathers: The Alphabetical Collection*. London: Mowbrays, 1975.

Williams, Frank. *The Panarion of Epiphanius of Salamis, Books II and III*. Nag Hammadi and Manichaean Studies 36. Leiden: E. J. Brill, 1994.

Vinson, Martha. *Saint Gregory of Nazianzus: Select Orations.* FOTC 107. Washington, D.C.: Catholic University of America Press, 2004.
Xenophon. *The Education of Cyrus.* Agora Editions. Translated by Wayne Amber. Ithaca, N.Y.: Cornell University Press, 2001.

OTHER PRIMARY AND SECONDARY LITERATURE

Allen, Pauline, Johan Leemans, Wendy Mayer, et al., eds. *Let Us Die That We May Live: Greek Homilies on Christian Martyrs from Asia Minor, Palestine, and Syria, c. 350–450 AD.* London: Routledge, 2003.
Alminana, Robert, Andres Duany, and Elizabeth Plater-Zyberk. *New Civic Art: Elements of Town Planning.* New York: Rizzolik, 2003.
Annas, Julia. "Aristotelian Political Theory in the Hellenistic Period." In *Justice and Generosity: Studies in Hellenistic Social and Political Philosophy. Proceedings of the Sixth Symposium Hellenisticum,* edited by André Laks and Malcolm Schofield, 74–94. Cambridge: Cambridge University Press, 1995.
Ast, Friedrich. *Grundlinien der Grammatik, Hermeneutik und Kritik.* Landshut: Jos. Thomann, 1808.
Attfield, Robin. "Christianity." In *A Companion to Environmental Philosophy,* edited by D. Jameson, 96–110. Oxford: Blackwell, 2001.
Aubert, Roger. *Catholic Social Teaching: An Historical Perspective.* Milwaukee, Wis.: Marquette University Press, 2003.
Avila, Charles. *Ownership: Early Christian Teaching.* Maryknoll, N.Y.: Orbis Books, 1983.
Avi-Yonah, M. "The Bath of the Lepers at Scythopolis." *Israel Exploration Journal* 13 (1963): 325–26.
Ayres, Lewis. *Nicaea and Its Legacy: An Approach to Fourth-Century Trinitarian Theology.* Oxford: Oxford University Press, 2004.
Bagnall, Roger S. "Monks and Property: Rhetoric, Law, and Patronage in the *Apophthegmata Patrum* and the Papyri." *Greek, Roman, and Byzantine Studies* 42 (2001): 7–24.
Bainton, Roland. *Christian Attitudes towards War and Peace.* New York: Abingdon Press, 1960.
Bakhtin, Mikhail. *The Dialogic Imagination: Four Essays.* Edited by Michael Holquist. Translated by Caryl Emerson and Michael Holquist. Austin: University of Texas Press, 1981.
Banfi, Antonio. *Habent illi iudices suos. Studi sull' esclusivita. Della giurisdizione ecclesiastica e sulle origini del privilegium fori in diritto romano e bizantino.* Milan: Dott. A. Giuffre Editore, 2005.

Banner, William. "Origen and the Tradition of Natural Law Concepts." In *Dumbarton Oaks Papers*, vol. 8, 49–82. Washington, D.C.: Dumbarton Oaks, 1954.

Barrera, Albino. *Modern Catholic Social Documents and Political Economy*. Washington, D.C.: Georgetown University Press, 2001.

Barry, Peter. "Structuralism." In Peter Barry, *Beginning Theory: An Introduction to Literary and Cultural Theory*, 39–60. Manchester: Manchester University Press, 2002.

Barthes, Roland. "The Death of the Author." In Roland Barthes, *Image, Music, Text: Essays Selected and Translated by Stephen Heath*, 142–49. London: Fontana Press, 1977.

Baumgartner, Ephrem. "Der Kommunismus im Urchristentum." *Zeitschrift für katholische Theologie* 33 (1909): 625–45.

Behr, John. *The Way to Nicaea*. Formation of Christian Theology 1. Crestwood, N.Y.: St. Vladimir's Press, 2001.

Berry, R. J. "Creation and the Environment." *Science and Christian Belief* 7 (1995): 21–43.

Bieringer, Reimund. "Biblical Revelation and Exegetical Interpretation according to *Dei Verbum* 12." In *Vatican II and Its Legacy*, edited by Mattijs Lamberigts and Leo Kenis, 25–58. BETL 166. Leuven: Peeters Press, 2002.

———. "'Come, and You Will See' (John 1:39): Dialogical Authority and Normativity of the Future in the Fourth Gospel and in Religious Education." In *Hermeneutics and Religious Education*, edited by Herman Lombaerts and Didier Pollefeyt, 179–201. BETL 180. Leuven, Paris; Dudley, Mass.: Peeters Press, 2005.

———. "The Normativity of the Future: The Authority of the Bible for Theology." *ET Bulletin. Zeitschrift für Theologie in Europa* 8 (1997): 52–67.

———. "Texts That Create a Future: The Function of Ancient Texts for Theology Today." In Reimund Bieringer and Mary Elsbernd, with Susan M. Garthwaite et al., *Normativity of the Future: Reading Biblical and Other Authoritative Texts in an Eschatological Perspective*, 91–116. ANL 61. Leuven: Peeters Press, 2009. Also in *Reading Patristic Texts on Social Ethics: Issues and Challenges for Twenty-First-Century Social Thought*, edited by Johan Leemans, Brian J. Matz, and Johan Verstraete, 3–29. CUA Studies in Early Christianity. Washington, D.C.: Catholic University of America Press, 2011.

Bieringer, Reimund, and Mary Elsbernd, with Susan M. Garthwaite et al. *Normativity of the Future: Reading Biblical and Other Authoritative Texts in an Eschatological Perspective*. ANL 61. Leuven: Peeters Press, 2009.

Bieringer, Reimund, Didier Pollefeyt, and Frederique Vandecasteele-Vanneuville. "Wrestling with Johannine Anti-Judaism: A Hermeneutical Framework for the Analysis of the Current Debate." In *Anti-Judaism and the Fourth Gospel,* edited by Reimund Bieringer, Didier Pollefeyt, and Frederique Vandecasteele-Vanneuville, 3–37. Louisville, Ky.: Westminster John Knox, 2001.

Boersma, Hans. "Irenaeus, Derrida and Hospitality: On the Eschatological Overcoming of Violence." *Modern Theology* 19 (2003): 163–80.

Bolkestein, Hendrik. *Wohltätigkeit und Armenpflege im vorchristlichen Altertum.* Utrecht: A. Oosthoek, 1939.

Bourg, Florence Caffrey. *Where Two or Three Are Gathered: Christian Families as Domestic Churches.* Notre Dame, Ind.: University of Notre Dame Press, 2003.

Brabant, Christophe. "The Truth Narrated: Ricoeur on Religious Experience." In *Divinising Experience: Essays in the History of Religious Experience from Origen to Ricoeur,* edited by Lieven Boeve and Laurence P. Hemming, 246–69. Studies in Philosophical Theology. Leuven: Peeters Press, 2004.

Bratton, Susan P. "The Original Desert Solitaire: Early Christian Monasticism and Wilderness." *Environmental Ethics* 10 (1988): 31–53.

Brentano, Lujo. "Die wirtschaftlichen Lehren des christlichen Altertums." In *Sitzungsberichte der philosophische-philologischen und der historischen Klasse der königliche bayerische Akademie der Wissenschaften,* 141–93. Munich, 1902.

Brink, David O. "Eudaimonism, Love and Friendship, and Political Community." *Social Philosophy and Policy* 16 (1999): 252–89.

Brottier, Laurence. "De l'église hors de l'église au ciel anticipé sur quelques paradoxes Chrysostomiens." *Revue d'histoire et de philosophie religieuses* 76 (1996): 277–92.

Brown, Dennis. *Vir trilinguis: A Study in the Biblical Exegesis of Saint Jerome.* Kampen: Kok Pharos, 1992.

Brown, Peter. *Poverty and Leadership in the Later Roman Empire.* Hanover, N.H.: University Press of New England, 2002.

Broz, Jaroslav. "From Allegory to the Four Senses of Scripture: Hermeneutics of the Church Fathers and of the Christian Middle Ages." In *Philosohpical hermeneutics and Biblical Exegesis,* edited by Petr Pokorny and Jan Roskovec, 301–9. WUNT 153. Tübingen: Mohr Siebeck, 2002.

Burns, Mary A. *Saint John Chrysostom's Homilies on the Statues: A Study of Their Rhetorical Qualities and Form.* Patristic Studies 22. Washington, D.C.: Catholic University of America Press, 1930.

Burns, Stuart K. "Pseudo-Macarius and the Messalians: The Use of Time for the Common Good." In *The Use and Abuse of Time in Christian History: Papers Read at the 1999 Summer Meeting and the 2000 Winter Meeting of the Ecclesiastical History Society*, edited by R. N. Swanson, 1–12. Studies in Church History 37. Suffolk: Boydell Press, 2002.

Burt, Donald. "Friendship and Subordination in Earthly Societies." *Augustinian Studies* 22 (1991): 83–123. Repr. and rev. in *Christianity and Society: The Social World of Early Christianity*, edited by Everett Ferguson, 315–55. New York: Garland, 1999.

Cadoux, C. John. *The Early Christian Attitude toward War*. London: Headley Brothers, 1919.

Cain, Andrew. *The Letters of Jerome: Asceticism, Biblical Exegesis and the Construction of Christian Authority in Late Antiquity*. Oxford: Oxford University Press, 2009.

Carrié, Jean-Michel. "*Nil habens praeter quod ipso die vestiebatur:* Comment définir le seuil de pauvreté à Rome?" In *Consuetudinis amor: Fragments d'histoire romaine (IIe–VIe siècles) offerts à Jean-Pierre Callu*, edited by François Chausson and Étienne Wolff, 71–102. Rome: L'Erma di Bretschneider, 2003.

Cameron, Alan. "A Misidentified Homily of Chrysostom." *Nottingham Mediaeval Studies* 32 (1988): 34–48.

Canning, Raymond. "St. Augustine's Vocabulary of the Common Good and the Place of Love for Neighbour." *Studia Patristica* 33 (1997): 48–54.

Case, Shirley Jackson. *The Social Origins of Christianity*. Chicago: University of Chicago Press, 1923.

———. *The Social Triumph of the Ancient Church*. New York: Harper and Row, 1933.

Cavallera, Ferdinand. *Saint Jérôme: Sa vie et son œuvre*. Vols. 1–2. Spicilegium sacrum Lovaniense, Études et documents. Louvain: Spicilegium sacrum Lovaniense, 1922.

Charles, J. Daryl. "Pacifists, Patriots or Both? Second Thoughts on Early Christian Attitudes toward Soldiering and War." Unpublished paper delivered at the Annual Meeting of the Evangelical Theological Society, Philadelphia, 2005.

Chartier, Roger. "Texts, Printing, Readings." In *The New Cultural History*, edited by Lynn Hunt. Berkeley and Los Angeles: University of California Press, 1989.

Chaskin, R. J., M. L. Joseph, and H. S. Webber. "The Theoretical Basis for Addressing Poverty through Mixed-Income Development." *Urban Affairs Review* 42 (2007): 369–409.

Chastel, Etienne. *Études historiques sur l'influence de la charité durant les premiers siècles chrétiens, et considérations sur son rôle dans les sociétés modernes.* Paris: Capelle, 1853. ET: *The Charity of the Primitive Churches: Historical Studies upon the Influence of Christian Charity during the First Centuries of Our Era, with Some Considerations Touching Its Bearings upon Modern Society.* Translated by George-Auguste Matile. Philadelphia: J. B. Lippincott and Co., 1857.

Christophe, Paul. *L'usage chrétien du droit de propriété dans l'Écriture et la tradition patristique.* Paris: P. Lethielleux, 1964.

Church of Scotland. *Justice and Markets.* Report of the Church and Society Council (May 2009), 18–19.

Clark, Donald L. *Rhetoric in Greco-Roman Education.* New York: Columbia University Press, 1957.

Clark, Elizabeth. "Ascetic Renunciation and Feminine Advancement: A Paradox of Late Ancient Christianity." *Anglican Theological Review* 63 (1981): 240–57.

———. "The Celibate Bridegroom and His Virginal Brides: Metaphor and the Marriage of Jesus in Early Christian Ascetic Exegesis." *Church History* 77 (2008): 1–25.

———. "Claims on the Bones of Saint Stephen: The Partisans of Melania and Eudocia." *Church History* 51 (1982): 141–56.

———. "Elite Networks and Heresy Accusations: Towards a Social Description of the Origenist Controversy." *Semeia* (1991): 79–117.

———. *History, Theory, Text: Historians and the Linguistic Turn.* Cambridge, Mass.: Harvard University Press, 2004.

———. *Jerome, Chrysostom, and Friends.* Studies in Women and Religion, 1. Lewiston, N.Y.: Edwin Mellen Press, 1979.

———. "New Perspectives on the Origenist Controversy: Human Embodiment and Ascetic Strategies." *Church History* 59 (1990): 145–62.

———. *The Origenist Controversy.* Princeton, N.J.: Princeton University Press, 1992.

———. "Piety, Propaganda, and Politics in the Life of Melania the Younger." *Studia patristica* 18, no. 2 (1989): 167–83.

———. *Reading Renunciation: Asceticism and Scripture in Early Christianity.* Princeton, N.J.: Princeton University Press, 1999.

———. "Response to Comments on *History, Theory, Text.*" *Church History* 74 (2005): 834.

Coleridge, Samuel Taylor. *The Collected Works of Samuel Taylor Coleridge, VII: Biographia literaria.* Translated by James Engell and Walter J. Bate. Bollingen Series 75. London: Routledge and Kegan Paul, 1983. Orig. pub. 1817.

Colish, Marcia L. *The Stoic Tradition from Antiquity to the Early Middle Ages.* Leiden: E. J. Brill, 1990.

Corcoran, Gervase. "St. Augustine and the Poor." *Milltown Studies* 12 (1983): 69–76.

Coulie, Bernard. *Les richesses dans l'oeuvre de Saint Grégoire de Nazianze.* Publications de l'Institut Orientaliste de Louvain. Louvain-la-neuve: Université Catholique de Louvain, 1985.

Countryman, Louis William. *The Rich Christian in the Church of the Early Empire: Contradictions and Accommodations.* New York: Edward Mellen Press, 1980.

Crislip, Andrew T. *From Monastery to Hospital: Christian Monasticism and the Transformation of Health Care in Late Antiquity.* Ann Arbor: University of Michigan Press, 2005.

Curran, Charles. *Catholic Social Teaching, 1891–Present: A Historical, Theological, and Ethical Analysis.* Washington, D.C.: Georgetown University Press, 2002.

———, ed. *Change in Official Catholic Moral Teachings.* Readings in Moral Theology. New York: Paulist Press, 2003.

Cutrufello, Andrew. *Continental Philosophy: A Contemporary Introduction.* London: Routledge, 2005.

Dagron, Gilbert. "Les moines et la ville. Le monachisme à Constantinople jusqu'au concile de Chalcédone." *Travaux et Mémoires* 4 (1970): 229–76.

Daley, Brian. "Apokatastasis and 'Honorable Silence' in the Eschatology of Maximus the Confessor." In *Maximus Confessor,* 309–39. Fribourg: Editions Universitaires, 1982.

———. "Building a New City: The Cappadocian Fathers and the Rhetoric of Philanthropy." *Journal of Early Christian Studies* 7 (1999): 431–61.

Davidson, Ivor J. *Ambrose. De officiis, Volume II: Commentary.* Oxford Early Christian Studies. Oxford: Oxford University Press, 2001.

Davies, W. D., and Dale Allison. *A Critical and Exegetical Commentary on the Gospel According to Saint Matthew.* Vol. 1. *Matthew 1–7.* International Critical Commentary. Edinburgh: T. & T. Clark, 1988.

Davis, Leo D. *The First Seven Ecumenical Councils (325–787): Their History and Theology.* Theology and Life 21. Wilmington, Del.: Michael Glazier Press, 1987.

de Boer, Theo. "Paul Ricoeur: Thinking the Bible." In *God in France: Eight Contemporary French Thinkers on God,* edited by Peter Jonkers and Ruud Welten, 43–67. Studies in Philosophical Theology. Leuven: Peeters, 2005.

Deissmann, Adolf. *Das Urchristentum und die unteren Schichten.* 2d ed. Göttingen: Vandenhoeck and Ruprecht, 1908.

Dekkers, Eligius, ed., *Clavis Patrum Latinorum*. 3rd ed. CCSL. Turnhout: Brepols, 1995.
de Lubac, Henri. *Medieval Exegesis*. 2 vols. Translated by Mark Sebanc and E. M. Macieroweski. Grand Rapids, Mich.: Eerdmans, 1998, 2000.
der Hagen, Odulphus Josephus van. *De Clementis Alexandrini sententiis oeconomicis, socialibus, politicis*. Utrecht: Dekker and V. D. Vegt, 1920.
Descoeudres, Georges. "Kirche und Diakonia: Gemeinschaftsräume in den Ermitagen der Qusur el-Izeila." In *Explorations aux Qouçour el-Izeila lors des campagnes 1981, 1982, 1984, 1985, 1986, 1989 et 1990*, Mission Suisse d'archéologie copte de l'université de Genève (EK 8184, tome III), edited by Philippe Bridel et al. Louvain: Peeters Press, 1999.
de Ste. Croix, G. E. M. *The Class Struggle in the Ancient Greek World*. London: Duckworth, 1981.
———. "Early Christian Attitudes to Property and Slavery." In *Church, Society and Politics: Papers Read at the Thirteenth Summer Meeting and the Fourteenth Winter Meeting of the Ecclesiastical History Society*, edited by Derek Baker, 1–38. Studies in Church History 12. Oxford: Basil Blackwell, 1975.
Di Berardino, Angelo, and Basil Studer, eds. *History of Theology*. Vol. 1, *The Patristic Period*. Translated by Matthew J. O'Connell. Collegeville, Minn.: Liturgical Press, 1997.
Diederich, W., A. Ibarra, and T. Mormann. "Bibliography of Structuralism." *Erkenntnis* 30 (1989): 387–407.
———. "Bibliography of Structuralism II (1989–1994 and Additions)." *Erkenntnis* 41 (1994): 403–18.
Dilthey, Wilhelm. "Die Entstehung der Hermeneutik (1900)." In *Die geistige Welt: Einleitung in die Philosophie des Lebens, Gesammelte Schriften*, vol. 5, edited by George Misch, 317–38. Leipzig: Teubner, 1924. ET: In *W. Dilthey: Selected Writings*, translated by H. P. Rickman. Cambridge: Cambridge University Press, 1976.
———. "Das Verstehen anderer Personen und ihrer Lebensäusserungen." In *Der Aufbau der geschichtlichen Welt in den Geisteswissenschaften, Gesammelte Schriften*, vol. 7, edited by Bernard Groethuysen. Leipzig: Teubner, 1927. ET: In *Wilhelm Dilthey: An Introduction*, translated by H. P. Rickman. London: Routledge and Kegan Paul, 1944.
Domeris, William Robert. *Touching the Heart of God: The Social Construction of Poverty among Biblical Peasants*. Library of Hebrew Bible/Old Testament Studies 466. Edinburgh: T. & T. Clark, 2007.
Dorr, Donal. *Option for the Poor: A Hundred Years of Vatican Social Teaching*. Dublin: Gill and Macmillan, 1983; rev. ed. 1992.

Drobner, Hubertus R. *Augustinus von Hippo: Sermones ad populum.* Supplements to Vigiliae Christianae. Leiden: E. J. Brill, 2000.

Duncan-Jones, Richard. *The Economy of the Roman Empire.* Cambridge: Cambridge University Press, 1974.

Dunn, Geoffrey. "The Elements of Ascetical Widowhood: Augustine's *de Bono Viduitatis* and *Epistula* 130." In *Prayer and Spirituality in the Early Church*, vol. 4, *The Spiritual Life,* edited by Wendy Mayer, Pauline Allen, and Lawrence Cross, 247–56. Strathfield: St Paul's Publications, 2006.

Elm, Susanna. *"Virgins of God": The Making of Asceticism in Early Christianity.* Oxford Classical Monographs. Oxford: Clarendon Press, 1996.

Elsbernd, Mary, and Reimund Bieringer. "Interpreting the Signs of the Times in the Light of the Gospel: Vision and Normativity of the Future." In *Scrutinizing the Signs of the Times in Light of the Gospel,* edited by Johan Verstraeten, 41–97. BETL 208. Leuven, Paris; Dudley, Mass.: Peeters Press, 2007.

———. *When Love Is Not Enough: A Theo-Ethic of Justice.* Collegeville, Minn.: Liturgical Press, 2002.

Eschmann, I. Th. "A Thomistic Glossary on the Principle of the Pre-Eminence of the Common Good." *Mediaeval Studies* 5 (1943): 123–66.

Evans, Craig, et al., eds. *Early Jewish and Christian Exegesis: Studies in Memory of William Hugh Brownlee.* Atlanta: Scholars Press, 1987.

Evans, Jeanne. *Paul Ricoeur's Hermeneutics of the Imagination.* American University Studies, Series VII: Theology and Religion 143. New York: Peter Lang, 1995.

Falk, Richard. "Reviving the 1990s Trend toward Transnational Justice: Innovations and Institutions." *Journal of Human Development and Capabilities* 3 (2002): 167–90.

Finn, Richard. *Almsgiving in the Later Roman Empire: Christian Promotion and Practice, 313–450.* Oxford Classical Monographs. Oxford: Oxford University Press, 2006.

Fox, M. M. *The Life and Times of Saint Basil the Great as Revealed in His Works.* Washington, D.C.: Catholic University of America Press, 1939.

Freu, Christel. *Les figures du pauvre dans les sources Italiennes de l'antiquité tardive.* Études d'archéologie et d'histoire ancienne. Paris: De Boccard, 2007.

Friesen, Steven J. "Injustice or God's Will? Early Explanations of Poverty." In *Wealth and Poverty in Early Church and Society,* edited by Susan Holman, 17–36. Holy Cross Studies in Patristic Theology and History. Grand Rapids, Mich.: Baker Academic Press, 2008.

Friman, H. Richard, ed. *Challenges and Paths to Global Justice.* New York: Palgrave MacMillan, 2007.
Funk, Francois-Xavier. "Über Reichtum und Handel im christlichen Altertum." *Historisch-politische Blätter* 130 (1902): 888–99.
Gadamer, Hans-Georg. *Wahrheit und Methode: Grundzüge einer philosophischen Hermeneutik.* Tübingen: Mohr Siebeck, 1960. ET: *Truth and Method.* Translated by Joel Weinsheimer and Donald Marshall. New York: Crossroad, 1989.
Garnsey, Peter. *Famine and Food Supply in the Greco-Roman World: Responses to Risk and Crisis.* Cambridge: Cambridge University Press, 1988.
———. "The Originality and Origins of Anonymus, *De Divitiis*." In *From Rome to Constantinople: Studies in Honour of Averil Cameron,* edited by Hagit Amirav and Bas ter Haar Romeny, 29–45. Late Antique History and Religion 1. Leuven, Paris; Dudley, Mass.: Peeters Press, 2007.
Garsoian, Nina. "Nersês le Grand, Basile de Césarée et Eustathe de Sébaste." *Revue des études arméniennes* 17 (1983): 145–69.
Gatier, P.-L. "Villages du Proche Orient protobyzantine (4ème–7ème s.). Étude régionale." In *The Byzantine and Early Islamic Near East,* vol. 2, *Land Use and Settlement Patterns,* edited by G. R. D. King and Averil Cameron, 17–48. Princeton, N.J.: Darwin Press, 1994.
Geerard, Maurits, ed. *Ab Athanasio ad Chrysostomum.* In *Clavis Patrium Graecorum,* vol. 2. Turnhout: Brepols, 1974.
———. *A Cyrillo Alexandrino ad Iohannem Damascenum.* In *Clavis Patrium Graecorum,* vol 3. Turnhout: Brepols, 1979.
———. *Patres Antenicaeni.* In *Clavis Patrium Graecorum,* vol 1. Turnhout: Brepols, 1983.
Geerard, Maurits, et al., eds. *Clavis Patrum Graecorum Supplementum.* Turnhout: Brepols, 1998.
Geertz, Clifford. *Local Knowledge: Further Essays in Interpretive Anthropology.* New York: Basic Books, 1983, 1993.
———. "Thick Description: Toward an Interpretive Theory of Culture." In *The Interpretation of Cultures: Selected Essays.* London: Fontana, 1993.
Gerhart, Mary. "Generic Studies: Their Renewed Importance in Religious and Literary Interpretation." *Journal of the American Academy of Religion* 45 (1977): 309–25.
Giaquinta, Carmelo J. "La función social de la propiedad según la doctrina de los Santos Padres." In *Socialismo y socialismos en America Latina,* 320–35. Bogota: CELAM, 1977.

Giet, Stanislas. "L'argumentation de quelques passages de St. Jean Chrysostome contre la propriéte." In *La revelation chretienne et le droit: Colloque de philosophie du droit (24 et 25 novembre 1959)*, 51–62. Paris: Librairie Dalloz, 1961.

———. "La doctrine de l'appropriation des biens chez quelques-uns des Pères." *Recherches des science religieuse* 35 (1948): 55–91.

Glare, P. G. W., ed. *Oxford Latin Dictionary*. Oxford: Clarendon Press, 1982.

Goehring, James. "Monasticism in Byzantine Egypt: Continuity and Memory." In *Egypt in the Byzantine World, 300–700*. edited by Roger S. Bagnall, 390–407. Cambridge: Cambridge University Press, 2007.

Gonzales, Justo. *Faith and Wealth: A History of Early Christian Ideals on the Origin, Significance and Use of Money*. San Francisco: Harper and Row, 1990.

Gordon, Barry. *The Economic Problem in Biblical and Patristic Thought*. Supplements to Vigiliae Christianae, Texts and Studies of Early Christian Life and Language 9. Leiden: E. J. Brill, 1989.

———. "The Problem of Scarcity and the Christian Fathers: John Chrysostom and Some Contemporaries." *Studia Patristica* 22 (1989): 108–20.

Gotsis, G. N., and G. A. Merianos. "Wealth and Poverty in Theodoret of Cyrrhus' 'On Providence.'" *Journal of Eastern Christian Studies* 59 (2007): 11–48.

Gould, Graham. "Basil of Caesarea and the Problem of the Wealth of Monasteries." In *The Church and Wealth: Papers Read at the 1986 Summer Meeting and the 1987 Winter Meeting of the Ecclesiastical History Society*, edited by W. J. Shiels and Diana Wood, 15–24. Oxford: Basil Blackwell, 1987.

———. *The Desert Fathers on Monastic Community*. Oxford Early Christian Studies. Oxford: Clarendon Press, 1993.

Graham, Mark E. *Sustainable Agriculture: A Christian Ethic of Gratitude*. Portland, Ore.: Wipf and Stock, 2005; repr. 2009.

Grant, Frederick C. *The Economic Background of the Gospels*. London: Oxford University Press, H. Milford, 1926.

Gregg, Robert C. *Consolation Philosophy: Greek and Christian* Paideia *in Basil and the Two Gregories*. Patristic Monograph Series 3. Philadelphia: Philadelphia Patristic Foundation, 1975.

Gribomont, Jean. "Le monachisme au sein de l'eglise en Syrie et en Cappadoce." *Studia Monastica* 7 (1965): 7–24.

Gruszka, P. "Die Stellungnahme der Kirchenväter Kappadoziens zu der Gier um Gold, Silber und andere Luxuswaren im täglichen Leben der Oberschichten des 4 Jhts." *Klio* 63 (1981): 661–68.

Grützmacher, Georg. *Hieronymus: Eine biographische Studie zur alten Kirchengeschichte*. 3 vols. Studien zur Geschichte der Theologie und der Kirche. Leipzig: Dieterich, 1901–1908.

Guijarro, Santiago. "The Family in First-Century Galilee." In *Constructing Early Christian Families: Family as Social Reality and Metaphor,* edited by Halvor Moxnes, 42–64. London: Routledge, 1997.

Guroian, Vigen. "Family and Christian Virtue: Reflections on the Ecclesial Vision of John Chrysostom." In *Ethics after Christendom: Toward an Ecclesial Christian Ethic,* 133–54. Grand Rapids, Mich.: William B. Eerdmans, 1994.

Haidacher, Sebastian. "Quellen der Chrysostomus-Homilie De perfecta caritate (PG 56, 279–290)." *Zeitschrift für katholische Theologie* 19 (1895): 387–89.

Haller, W. "Die Eigentum im Glauben und Leben der nachapostolischen Kirche." *Theologische Studien und Kritiken* 64 (1891): 478–563.

Halton, Thomas. *Theodoret of Cyrus: On Divine Providence*. ACW 49. New York: Newman Press, 1988.

Hamman, Adalbert Gauthier, ed. *Riches et pauvres dans l'église ancienne*. Lettres Chrétiennes, 6. Paris: Grasset, 1962.

Hammerstaedt, Jürgen, and Peri Terbuyken. "Improvisation." *RAC* 17 (1996): 1202–84.

Hankey, Wayne J. "Mind." In *Augustine through the Ages: An Encyclopedia,* edited by Allan D. Fitzgerald, 563–67. Grand Rapids, Mich.: William B. Eerdmans, 1999.

Hanson, Paul. "The Ancient Near Eastern Roots of Social Welfare." In *Through the Eye of a Needle: Judeo-Christian Roots of Social Welfare,* edited by Emily A. Hanawalt and Carter Lindberg, 7–28. Kirksville, Mo.: Thomas Jefferson University Press, 1994.

Hardwick, Michael E. *Josephus as an Historical Source in Patristic Literature through Eusebius*. Brown Judaic Studies 128. Atlanta: Scholars Press, 1989.

Harmless, William. *Desert Christians: An Introduction to the Literature of Early Monasticism*. New York: Oxford University Press, 2004.

Harnack, Adolf von. *Militia Christi: Die christliche Religion und der Soldatenstand in den ersten drei Jahrhunderten*. Tübingen: Mohr Siebeck, 1905. ET: *Militia Christi: The Christian Religion and the Military in the First Three Centuries*. Translated David McInnis Gracie. Philadelphia: Fortress Press, 1981.

Harvey, Susan Ashbrook. "The Holy and the Poor: Models from Early Syriac Christianity." In *Through the Eye of a Needle: Judeo-Christian Roots of*

Social Welfare, edited by Emily A. Hanawalt and Carter Lindberg, 43–66. Kirksville, Mo.: Thomas Jefferson University Press, 1994.

———. "Praying Bodies, Bodies at Prayer: Ritual Relations in Early Syriac Christianity." In *Prayer and Spirituality in the Early Church*, vol. 4, *The Spiritual Life*, edited by Wendy Mayer, Pauline Allen, and Lawrence Cross, 149–67. Strathfield: St Paul's Publications, 2006.

Hauck, Friedrich. *Die Stellung des Urchristentum zu Arbeit und Geld*. Gütersloh: C. Bertelsmann, 1921.

Hauschild, Wolf-Dieter von. "Christentum und Eigentum: Zum Problem eines altkirchlichen 'Sozialismus.'" *Zeitschrift für Evangelische Ethik* 16 (1972): 34–49.

Helgeland, John. "Christians and the Roman Army A.D. 173–337." *Church History* 43 (1974): 149–63.

———. *Christians and the Roman Army from Marcus Aurelius to Constantine*. Berlin: Walter de Gruyter, 1979.

———. "Time and Space: Christian and Roman." In *Religion (Vorkonstantinisches Christentum: Verhältnis zu römischem Staat und heidnischer Religion [Forts.])*, edited by Wolfgang Haase, 724–834. Aufstieg und Niedergang der römischen Welt, t. 2, 23, Part 2. Berlin: Walter de Gruyter, 1980.

Helgeland, John, Robert J. Daly, and J. Patout Burns. *Christians and the Military: The Early Experience*. Philadelphia: Fortress Press, 1985.

Hengel, Martin. *Eigentum und Reichtum in der frühen Kirche*. Stuttgart: Calwer Verlag, 1973. ET: *Property and Riches in the Early Church*. Translated by John Bowden. Philadelphia: Fortress Press, 1974.

Herrmann, Elisabeth. *Ecclesia in Re Publica: Die Entwicklung der Kirche von pseudostaatlicher zu staatlich inkorporierter Existenz*. Europaisches Forum 2. Frankfurt: Peter Lang, 1980.

Himes, Kenneth, ed. *Modern Catholic Social Teaching: Commentaries and Interpretations*. Washington, D.C.: Georgetown University Press, 2005.

Hirschfeld, Yizhar. "Farms and Villages in Byzantine Palestine." *Dumbarton Oaks Papers* 51 (1997): 33–71.

Hollenbach, David. "Common Good." In *The New Dictionary of Catholic Social Thought*, ed. Judith A. Dwyer, 192–97. Collegeville, Minn.: Liturgical Press, 1994.

———. *The Common Good and Christian Ethics*. New Studies in Christian Ethics. Cambridge: Cambridge University Press, 2002.

Holman, Susan. "Healing the Social Leper in Gregory of Nyssa's and Gregory of Nazianzus's *peri philoptochias*." *Harvard Theological Review* 92, no. 3 (1999): 283–309.

———. *The Hungry Are Dying: Beggars and Bishops in Roman Cappadocia.* Oxford Studies in Historical Theology. Oxford: Oxford University Press, 2001.

———. "The Hungry Body: Famine, Poverty and Basil's *Hom.* 8." *Journal of Early Christian Studies* 7 (1999): 337–63.

———. "Out of the Fitting Room: Rethinking Patristic Social Texts on 'The Common Good.'" In *Reading Patristic Texts on Social Ethics: Issues and Challenges for Twenty-First-Century Christian Social Thought,* edited by Johan Leemans, Brian J. Matz, and John Verstraeten. CUA Studies in Early Christianity. Washington, D.C.: Catholic University of America Press, 2011.

———. "Taxing Nazianzus: Gregory and the Other Julian." *Studia Patristica* 37 (2001): 103–9.

Holmes, Augustine. *A Life Pleasing to God: The Spirituality of the Rules of St. Basil.* Cistercian Studies 189. Kalamazoo, Mich.: Cistercian Press, 2000.

Holtzmann, H. "Die Gütergemeinschaft der Apostelgeschichte". In *Strassburger Abhandlungen zur Philosophie: Eduard Zeller, zu seinem siebenzigsten Geburtstage,* 25–60. Tübingen: Mohr, 1884.

Hornus, Jean-Michel. *Évangile et labarum: Étude sur l'attitude du christianisime primitif devant les problèmes de l'État, de la guerre et de la violence.* Nouvelle série théologique 9. Geneva: Labor et Fides, 1960.

House, Rutba, ed. *School(s) for Conversion: 12 Marks of a New Monasticism.* New Monastic Library: Resources for Radical Discipleship. Portland, Ore.: Wipf and Stock, 2005.

Irwin, T. H. "Aristotle's Defense of Private Property." In *A Companion to Aristotle's "Politics,"* edited by David Keyt and Fred Miller Jr., 200–225. Oxford: Blackwell, 1991.

Jacobs, Andrew. *Remains of the Jews: The Holy Land and Christian Empire in Late Antiquity.* Divinations: Rereading Late Ancient Religion. Stanford, Calif.: Stanford University Press, 2004.

Jeremias, Joachim. *The Parables of Jesus.* Translated by S. H. Hooke. New York: Charles Scribner's Sons, 1963. Based on 6th German edition of 1962.

Johnson, James T. *The Quest for Peace: Three Moral Traditions in Western Cultural History.* Princeton, N.J.: Princeton University Press, 1987.

Jones, Gareth Stedman. "From Historical Sociology to Theoretic History." *British Journal of Sociology* 27 (1976): 195–305.

Junker-Kenny, Maureen, and Peter Kenny, eds. *Memory, Narrativity, Self and the Challenge to Think God: The Reception within Theology of the Recent Work of Paul Ricoeur.* Religion—Geschichte—Gesellschaft: Fundamentaltheologische Studien 17. Münster: LIT Verlag, 2004.

Kaczynski, Bernice M. "Some St. Gall Glosses on Greek Philanthropic Nomenclature." *Speculum* 58 (1983): 1008–17.

Kalsbach, A. "Diakonie." In *Reallexikon für Antike und Christentum, Lieferung 22: Deus internus (Forts.)—Diamant*, edited by Theodor Klauser et al., 909–17. Stuttgart: Anton Hiersemann, 1957.

Kalthoff, Adalbert. *Das Christus-problem: Grundlinien zu einer Sozialtheologie*. 2d ed. Leipzig: E. Diederichs, 1903.

———. *Die Entstehung des Christentums*. Leipzig: E. Diederichs, 1904.

Kampling, Rainer. "'Have We Not Then Made a Heaven of Earth?': Rich and Poor in the Early Church." *Concilium* 22 (1986): 51–62.

Kannengiesser, Charles. *Handbook of Patristic Exegesis: The Bible in Ancient Christianity*. 2 vols. The Bible in Ancient Christianity 1, 2. Leiden: E. J. Brill, 2004.

Karayannopoulos, Ioannes. "Basil's Social Activity." In *Basil of Caesarea: Christian, Humanist, Ascetic: A Sixteen-Hundredth Anniversary Symposium, Part One*, edited by Paul J. Fedwick, 375–91. Toronto: Pontifical Institute of Mediaeval Studies, 1981.

Karras, Valerie. "Overcoming Greed: An Eastern Christian Perspective." *Buddhist-Christian Studies* 24 (2004): 47–53.

Katz, Peter. *The New Urbanism: Toward an Architecture of Community*. New York: McGraw-Hill, 2004.

Katz, Sheri. "Person." In *Augustine through the Ages: An Encyclopedia*, edited by Allan D. Fitzgerald, 647–50. Grand Rapids, Mich.: William B. Eerdmans, 1999.

Kautszy, Karl. *Der Ursprung des Christentums, eine historische Untersuchung*. Stuttgart: J. H. W. Dietz Nachf., 1908.

Kazhdan, Alexander. "Byzantium and Social Welfare." In *Through the Eye of a Needle: Judeo-Christian Roots of Social Welfare*, ed. Emly A. Hanawalt and Carter Lindberg, 67–82. Kirksville, Mo.: Thomas Jefferson University Press, 1994.

Kearney, Richard. *On Paul Ricoeur: The Owl of Minerva*. Transcending Boundaries in Philosophy and Theology. Aldershot: Ashgate, 2004.

Keck, L. "The Poor among the Saints in Jewish Christianity and Qumran." *Zeitschrift für neutestamentliche Wissenschaft* 57 (1966): 54–78.

Kee, Howard Clark. "Rich and Poor in the New Testament and Early Christianity." In *Through the Eye of a Needle: Judeo-Christian Roots of Social Welfare*, ed. Emily A. Hanawalt and Carter Lindberg, 29–42. Kirksville, Mo.: Thomas Jefferson University Press, 1994.

Keller, Adalbert. *Translationes Patristicae Graecae et Latinae: Bibliographie der Übersetzungen altchristlicher Quellen*. 2 vols. Stuttgart: Anton Hiersemann, 1997–2004.

Kelly, David. "Apokatastasis in the Early Church." *Patristic and Byzantine Review* 9 (1990): 71–74.
Kelly, J. N. D. *Early Christian Doctrines*. 5th rev. ed. London: Black, 1985.
———. *Jerome: His Life, Writings and Controversies*. London: Duckworth, 1975.
Kempshall, Mathew S. *The Common Good in Late Medieval Political Thought*. Oxford: Clarendon Press, 1999.
Keys, Mary M. *Aquinas, Aristotle, and the Promise of the Common Good*. Cambridge: Cambridge University Press, 2006.
Kislinger, E. "Kaiser Julian und die (christlichen) Zenodochien." In *Byzantios: Festschrift für Herbert Hunger zum 70. Geburtstag*, ed. W. Hörander et al., 171–84. Vienna: E. Beevar, 1984.
Klemm, David E. *The Hermeneutical Theory of Paul Ricoeur: A Constructive Analysis*. Lewisburg, Pa.: Bucknell University Press, 1983.
Konstan, David. "Patrons and Friends." *Classical Philology* 90 (1995): 328–42.
———. "Problems in the History of Christian Friendship." *Journal of Early Christian Studies* 4 (1996): 87–113. Repr. in *Christianity and Society: The Social World of Early Christianity*, edited by Everett Ferguson, 357–83. New York: Garland, 1999.
Kristeva, Julia. *Desire in Language: A Semiotic Approach to Literature and Art*. New York: Columbia University Press, 1980.
———. *Sēmeiōtikē*. Paris: Seuil, 1969.
Kurbatov, G. L. "Klassavoja suscnost ucenija Ioanna Zlatausta." *Ezegodnik muzeja istorii i religii i ateiznoz* 2 (1958): 80–106. Translated by Andrius Valevicius, "The Nature of Class in the Teaching of John Chrysostom." Center for Early Christian Studies (Australian Catholic University) website, http://www.cecs.acu.edu.au/chrysostomresearch.htm.
LaFree, Gary. "Review Essay: Too Much Democracy or Too Much Crime? Lessons from California's Three-Strikes Law." *Law and Social Inquiry* 27 (2002): 875–902.
Laks, André, and Malcolm Schofield, eds. *Justice and Generosity: Studies in Hellenistic Social and Political Philosophy: Proceedings of the Sixth Symposium Hellenisticum*. Cambridge: Cambridge University Press, 1992.
Lawson, John. *The Biblical Theology of Saint Irenaeus*. London: Epworth Press, 1948.
Le Blant, Edmond. "La richesse et las christianisme a l'age des persécutions." *Revue archéologique* (Series 2) 39 (1880): 220–30.
Leemans, Johan, Brian J. Matz, and Johan Verstraeten, eds. *Compendium of Early Christian Social Thought: Translations from the Greek and Latin Fathers* (under review at an academic press).

———. *Reading Patristic Texts on Social Ethics: Issues and Challenges for Twenty-First-Century Christian Social Thought*. CUA Studies in Early Christianity. Washington, D.C.: Catholic University of America Press, 2011.

Leyerle, Blake. "John Chrysostom on Almsgiving and the Use of Money." *Harvard Theological Review* 87 (1994): 29–47.

Loiselle, André. "The Fathers of the Church and Social Inequalities." In *Attentive to the Cry of the Needy*, 27–40. Ottawa: Canadian Religious Conference, 1973.

Lunn-Rockliffe, Sophie. *Ambrosiaster's Political Theology*. Oxford Early Christian Studies. Oxford: Oxford University Press, 2007.

———. "A Pragmatic Approach to Poverty and Riches: Ambrosiaster's Quaestio CXXIV." In *Poverty in the Roman World*, edited by M. Atkins and R. Osborne. Cambridge: Cambridge University Press, 2006.

Luz, Ulrich. *Matthew 1–7*. Hermeneia. Minneapolis: Fortress Press, 2007.

MacQueen, D. J. "The Origins and Dynamics of Society and the State according to St. Augustine (Part 1)." *Augustinian Studies* 4 (1973): 73–101.

———. "St. Augustine's Concept of Property Ownership." *Revue Augustiniennes* 8 (1972): 187–229.

Mansbridge, Jane. "On the Contested Nature of the Public Good." In *Private Action and the Public Good*, edited by Walter W. Powell and Elisabeth S. Clemens, 3–19. New Haven, Conn.: Yale University Press, 1998.

Many, Joyce, and Carole Cox, eds. *Reader Stance and Literary Understanding: Exploring the Theories, Research, and Practice*. Norwood, N.J.: Ablex, 1992.

Marcos, M., and R. Teja. "Modelos de ascetismo femenino aristocrático en la época de Juan Crisóstomo: Constantinopla y Palestina." In *Giovanni Crisostomo: Oriente e Occidente tra IV e V secolo ; XXXIII Incontro di Studiosi dell'Antichità Cristiana, Augustinianum 6–8 maggio 2004, Roma 93*, 619–25. Studia Ephemeridis Augustinianum 93. Rome: Institutum Patristicum Augustinianum, 2005.

Markus, Robert A. "De civitate dei: Pride and the Common Good." In *Collectanea Augustiniana: Augustine: "Second Founder of the Faith,"* edited by Joseph C. Schnaubelt and Frederick Van Fleteren, 245–59. Frankfurt: Peter Lang, 1990.

———. *Saeculum: History and Society in the Theology of Saint Augustine*. Cambridge: Cambridge University Press, 1970; rev. ed. 1989.

Marrou, Henri-Irénée. *A History of Education in Antiquity*. 3rd ed. Translated by George Lamb. New York: The New American Library, for Mentor Books, 1964.

———. "L'origine orientale des diaconies romaines." *Mélanges d'archéologie et d'histoire* 57 (1940): 95–142.

Maspero, Jean. *Papyrus grecs d'époque byzantine.* Catalogue général des antiquités égyptiennes du Musée du Caire, Papyrus grecs d'époque byzantine. 4 vols. Cairo: IFAO, 1911–1916.

———. "Sur quelques objets coptes du Musée du Caire." *Annales du Service des antiquités d'Egypte* 10 (1910): 173–74.

Matthews, Shailer. *The Social Teachings of Jesus : An Essay in Christian Sociology.* New York: Macmillan, 1897.

Matz, Brian J. *Patristic Sources and Catholic Social Teaching: A Forgotten Dimension. A Textual, Historical, and Rhetorical Analysis of Patristic Source Citations in the Church's Social Documents.* ANL 59. Leuven: Peeters Press, 2008.

Mayer, Wendy. "The Audience(s) for Patristic Social Teaching: A Case Study." In *Reading Patristic Texts on Social Ethics: Issues and Challenges for Twenty-First-Century Christian Social Thought,* edited by Johan Leemans, Brian J. Matz, and Johan Verstraeten, 85–99. CUA Studies in Early Christianity. Washington, D.C.: Catholic University of America Press, 2011.

———. "Poverty and Society in the World of John Chrysostom." In *Social and Political Archaeology in Late Antiquity,* edited by L. Lavan, W. Bowden, A. Gutteridge, and C. Machado. 465–84. Late Antique Archaeology. Leiden: E. J. Brill, 2006.

Mayer, Wendy, and Pauline Allen. *John Chrysostom.* The Early Church Fathers. New York: Routledge Press, 2000.

McCoy, Charles N. R. "The Turning Point in Political Philosophy." *American Political Science Review* 44 (1950): 678–88.

McGuckin, John A. "The Vine and the Elm Tree: The Patristic Interpretation of Jesus' Teaching on Wealth." In *The Church and Wealth: Papers Read at the 1986 Summer Meeting and the 1987 Winter Meeting of the Ecclesiastical History Society,* edited by W. J. Shiels and Diana Wood, 1–14. Oxford: Basil Blackwell, 1987.

McLynn, Neil. "Gregory the Peacemaker: A Study of Oration Six." *Kyoyo-Ronso* 101 (1996): 183–216.

Meeks, Wayne A. *The First Urban Christians.* New Haven, Conn.: Yale University Press, 1983.

Meffert, Franz. *Der "Kommunismus" Jesu und der Kirchenväter.* München-Gladbach: Volksvereinverlag, 1922.

Mentzou-Meimari, Konstantina. "Eparkhiaka evagé idrymata mekhri tou telous tés eikonomakhias." *Byzantina* 11 (1982): 243–308.

Miller, Patrick D., and Dennis P. McCann, eds. *In Search of the Common Good. Theology for the Twenty-First Century.* New York and London: T. & T. Clark, 2005.

Miller, T. S. *The Birth of the Hospital in the Byzantine Empire.* Baltimore: Johns Hopkins University Press, 1985.

Milovanović, Čelica. "Sailing to *Sophistopolis:* Gregory of Nazianzus and Greek Declamation." *Journal of Early Christian Studies* 13 (2005): 187–232.

Monfrin, Françoise. "Pauvreté et richesse: Le lexique latin de l'encyclique: Inspiration classique ou inspiration patristique?" In *Rerum Novarum: Écriture, contenu et reception d'une encyclique: Actes du colloque international organize par l'École française de Rome et le Greco n 2 du CNRS (Rome, 18–20 avril 1991),* 133–86. Rome: École française de Rome, 1997.

Morin, Germain. "Les monuments de la prédication de S. Jérôme." In *Études, Textes, Découvertes: Contributions à la littérature et à l'histoire des douze premiers siècles.* Anecdota Maredsolana, Seconde Série 1. Abbaye de Maredsous: Duculot-Roulin, 1913.

Mosheim, Johan Lorenz. *De vera natura communionis bonorum in ecclesia Hierosolymitana commentatio.* Unpublished dissertation, 1733.

Mosshammer, Alden A. "Historical Time and the Apokatastasis according to Gregory of Nyssa." *Studia Patristica* 27 (1993): 70–93.

Nadon, Christopher. "From Republic to Empire: Political Revolution and the Common Good in Xenophon's *Education of Cyrus.*" *American Political Science Review* 90 (1996): 361–74.

Nash, Roderick. *The Rights of Nature: A History of Environmental Ethics.* Madison: University of Wisconsin Press, 1989.

Nassif, Bradley. "The Starving Body of Christ." *Christian History and Biography Online* 94. March 11, 2007.

Nell-Breuning, Oswald von. *Reorganization of Social Economy: The Social Encyclical Developed and Explained.* Translated by Bernard W. Dempsey. New York: Bruce Publishing Co., 1936.

Neil, Bronwen. "*On True Humility:* An Anonymous Letter on Poverty and the Female Ascetic." In *Prayer and Spirituality in the Early Church,* vol. 4, *The Spiritual Life,* ed. Wendy Mayer, Pauline Allen, and Lawrence Cross, 233–46. Strathfield: St Paul's Publications, 2006.

Neri, Valero. *I Marginali nell'Occidente Tardoantico. Poveri, "infames" e criminali nella nascente società cristiana.* Bari: Edipuglia, 1998.

Newhauser, Richard. *The Early History of Greed: The Sin of Avarice in Early Medieval Thought and Literature.* Cambridge: Cambridge University Press, 2000.

Niederer, Francis J. "Early Medieval Charity." *Church History* 21 (1952): 285–95.
Nikiprowetzky, Valentin. *Études Philoniennes*. Patrimoines Judaisme. Paris: Éditions du Cerf, 1996.
Norris, Frederick. "The Theologian and Technical Rhetoric: Gregory of Nazianzus and Hermogenes of Tarsus." In *Nova et Vetera: Patristic Studies in Honor of Thomas Patrick Halton,* edited by John Petruccione. Washington, D.C.: Catholic University of America Press, 1998.
Nuffelen, Peter van. "Deux fausses lettres de Julien l'Apostat (La lettre aux Juifs, *Ep*. 51 [Wright], et la lettre à Arsacius, *Ep*. 84 [Bidez])." *Vigiliae Christianae* 55 (2002): 131–50.
Oberhelman, Steven M. *Rhetoric and Homiletics in Fourth-Century Christian Literature*. American Classical Studies 26. Atlanta: Scholars Press, 1991.
O'Brien, David J., and Thomas A. Shannon. *Catholic Social Thought: The Documentary Heritage*. Maryknoll, N.Y.: Orbis Books, 1992.
O'Donovan, Oliver. "Augustine's *City of God* XIX and Western Political Thought." *Dionysius* 11 (1987): 89–110.
O'Donovan, Oliver, and Joan O'Donovan. *From Irenaeus to Grotius: A Sourcebook in Christian Political Thought, 100–1625*. Grand Rapids, Mich.: Eerdmans, 1999.
Ogilvie, R. M. *The Library of Lactantius*. Oxford: Clarendon Press, 1978.
Olivar, A. *La predicación cristianan antiqua*. Barcelona: Herder, 1991.
Osborn, Eric. *Irenaeus of Lyons*. Cambridge: Cambridge University Press, 2001.
Osiek, Carolyn. *Rich and Poor in the* Shepherd of Hermas: *An Exegetical-Social Investigation*. The Catholic Biblical Quarterly Monograph Series 15. Washington, D.C.: Catholic Biblical Association of America, 1983.
Owen, Richard. "Analysis: Encyclical Is Work of Two Popes." In *The Times Online* (London: Jan 25, 2006).
Palmer, Clare. "Stewardship: A Case Study in Environmental Ethics." In *The Earth Beneath: A Critical Guide to Green Theology,* edited by Ian Ball, Margaret Goodall, Clare Palmer, and John Reader, 67–86. London: SPCK, 1992.
Pásztori-Kupán, István. *Theodoret of Cyrus*. The Early Church Fathers. London and New York: Routledge, 2006.
Patlagean, Evelyne. *Pauvreté économique et pauvreté sociale á Byzance 4e–7e siècles*. Civilisations et Sociétés, 48. Paris: Mouton, 1977.
———. "The Poor." In *The Byzantines,* ed. Guiglielmo Cavallo, 15–42. Chicago: University of Chicago Press, 1997.

Paul, Christophe. *Les pauvres et la pauvreté des origines au XVe siècle.* Bibliothèque d'Histoire du Christianisme 7. Paris: Desclée, 1985.

Paul, Ludwig. "Welche Reiche wird selig werden?" *ZWT* 44 (1901): 504–44.

Paul VI. "L'homme et la révolution urbaine: Citadins et ruraux devant l'urbanisation." *La documentation Catholique* 62 (1–15 August 1965): 1362–65.

Paverd, Frans van de. *St. John Chrysostom. The Homilies on the Statues: An Introduction.* Orientalia Christiana Analecta, 239. Rome: Pontificium Institutum Studiorum Orientalium, 1991.

Peabody, Francis Greenwood. *Jesus Christ and the Social Question: An Examination of the Teaching of Jesus in Its Relation to Some of the Problems of Modern Social Life.* New York: Grosset and Dunlap, 1900.

Pelikan, Jaroslav. *Christianity and Classical Culture: The Metamorphosis of Natural Theology in the Christian Encounter with Hellenism.* New Haven, Conn.: Yale University Press, 1993.

Périn, Charles. *De la richesse dans les societés chrétiennes.* Paris: Lecoffre, 1868.

Perrin, Norman. *The New Testament, An Introduction: Proclamation and Parénesis, Myth and History.* New York: Harcourt Brace Jovanovich, 1974.

Phillips, Charles Stanley. *The New Commandment: An Inquiry into the Social Precept and Practice of the Ancient Church.* London: SPCK, 1930.

Pinches, Charles. "Friendship and Tragedy: The Fragilities of Goodness." *First Things* 3 (1990): 38–45.

Pollefeyt, Didier, and Reimund Bieringer. "The Role of the Bible in Religious Education Reconsidered: Risks and Challenges in Teaching the Bible." *International Journal of Practical Theology* 9 (2005): 117–39.

Porter, Jean. "The Common Good in Thomas Aquinas." In *In Search of the Common Good,* edited by Dennis P. McCann and Patrick D. Miller, 94–120. New York: T. & T. Clark, 2005.

Potworowski, Christophe. "Origen's Hermeneutics in Light of Paul Ricoeur." In *Origeniana Quinta: Papers of the 5th International Origen Congress, Boston College, 14–18 August 1989.* BETL 105. Leuven: Peeters Press, 1992.

Rabinowitz, Celia. "Personal and Cosmic Salvation in Origen." *Vigiliae Christianae* 38 (1984): 319–29.

Ramirez, Juan, and William Crano. "Deterrence and Incapacitation: An Interrupted Time-Series Analysis of California's Three-Strikes Law." *Journal of Applied Social Psychology* 33 (2006): 110–44.

Ramsey, Boniface. "Almsgiving in the Latin Church: The Late Fourth and Early Fifth Centuries." In *Acts of Piety in the Early Church,* edited by Everett Ferguson, 226–59. Studies in Early Christianity 17. New York: Garland, 1993.

———. *Beginning to Read the Fathers*. London: Darton, Longman and Todd, 1986.
Rebenich, Stefan. *Hieronymus und sein Kreis: Prosopographische und sozialgeschichtliche Untersuchungen,* Historia—Einzelschriften. Stuttgart: Franz Steiner Verlag, 1992.
———. *Jerome*. The Early Church Fathers. London: Routledge, 2002.
Reilly, Gerald F. *Imperium and Sacerdotium according to St. Basil the Great*. Studies in Christian Antiquity 7. Washington, D.C.: Catholic University of America Press, 1945.
Rhee, Helen. "Wealth, Poverty, and Eschatology: Pre-Constantine, Christian Social Thought and the Hope for the World to Come." In *Reading Patristic Texts on Social Ethics: Issues and Challenges for Twenty-First-Century Christian Social Thought,* edited by Johan Leemans, Brian J. Matz, and Johan Verstraeten, 64–84. CUA Studies in Early Christianity. Washington, D.C.: Catholic University of America Press, 2011.
Richards, I. A. *The Philosophy of Rhetoric*. New York: Oxford University Press, 1936.
Ricoeur, Paul. "The Canon between the Text and the Community." In *Philosophical Hermeneutics and Biblical Exegesis,* edited by Petr Pokorný and Jan Rosovec, 7–26. WUNT. Tübingen: Mohr Siebeck, 2002.
———. *Conflict of Interpretations: Essays in Hermeneutics*. Northwestern University Studies in Phenomenology and Existential Philosophy. Evanston, Ill.: Northwestern University Press, 1996.
———. "The Difficulty to Forgive." In *Memory, Narrativity, Self and the Challenge to Think God: The Reception within Theology of the Recent Work of Paul Riceour,* edited by Maureen Junker-Kenny and Peter Kenny, 6–18. Religion—Geschichte—Gesellschaft: Fundamentaltheologische Studien 17. Munster: LIT Verlag, 2004.
———. *Essays on Biblical Interpretation*. Philadelphia: Fortress Press, 1980.
———. *From Text to Action: Essays in Hermeneutics II*. Translated by Kathleen Blamey and John B. Thompson. Evanston, Ill.: Northwestern University Press, 1991.
———. "The Hermeneutical Function of Distanciation." *Philosophy Today* 17 (1973): 129–41.
———. *Interpretation Theory: Discourse and the Surplus of Meaning*. Forth Worth: Texas Christian University Press, 1976.
———. *Mémoire, l'histoire, l'oubli*. L'ordre philosophique. Paris: Seuil, 2000. ET: *Memory, History, Forgetting*. Translated by Kathleen Blamey and David Pellauer. Chicago and London: University of Chicago Press, 2004.

———. "Metaphor and the Central Problem of Hermeneutics." In *Hermeneutics and the Human Sciences: Essays on Language, Action and Interpretation*, edited and translated by John B. Thompson. Cambridge: Cambridge University Press, 1981.

———. *La Métaphore vive*. L'ordre philosophique. Paris: Seuil, 1975. ET: *The Rule of Metaphor: Multi-Disciplinary Studies of the Creation of Meaning in Language*. Toronto: University of Toronto Press, 1977.

———. "The Model of the Text: Meaningful Action Considered as a Text." In *Hermeneutics and the Human Sciences: Essays on Language, Action and Interpretation*, edited and translated by John B. Thompson. Cambridge: Cambridge University Press, 1981.

———. "Le problème du fondement de la morale." *Sapienza* 28 (1975): 313–37.

———. "Le projet d'une morale sociale." *Le Christianisme social* 74 (1966): 285–95.

———. *The Rule of Metaphor: Multi-disciplinary Studies of the Creation of Meaning in Language*. Translated by Robert Czerny with Kathleen McLaughlin and John Costello. Toronto: University of Toronto Press, 1977.

———. "Le statut de la *Vorstellung* dans la philosophie hégélienne de la religion (1985)." In *Lectures 3 aux frontières de la philosophie*, 41–62. Paris: Seuil, 1994.

———. *Time and Narrative*. 3 vols. Translated by Kathleen Blamey. Chicago: University of Chicago Press, 1984, 1985, and 1988.

Ricoeur, Paul, François Azouvi, and Marc B. De Launay. *Critique and Conviction: Conversations with François Azouvi and Marc de Launay*. Translated by Kathleen Blamey. New York: Columbia University Press, 1998.

Riddle, Donald Wayne. *The Martyrs: A Study in Social Control*. Chicago: University of Chicago Press, 1931.

Rivas Rebaque, Fernando. *Defensor pauperum. Los pobres en Basilio de Cesarea: Homilias VI, VII, VIII y XIVB*. Biblioteca de Auctores Cristianos 657. Madrid: Biblioteca de Autores Cristianos, 2005.

Robinson, J. Armitage, ed. *Clement of Alexandria : Quis dives salvetur.* Texts and Studies: Contributions to Biblical and Patristic Literature 5, no. 2. Cambridge; Cambridge University Press, 1897. Repr. with ET: Portland, Ore.: Wipf and Stock, 2004.

Roht-Arriaza, Naomi. *The Pinochet Effect: Transnational Justice in the Age of Human Rights*. Philadelphia: University of Pennsylvania Press, 2005.

Rosenblatt, Louise M. *The Reader, the Text, the Poem*. Carbondale: Southern Illinois University Press, 1978.

Rougé, J. "A propos des mendiants au ive siècle." *Cahiers d'Histoire* 20 (1975): 339–46.

Rousseau, Philip. *Pachomius: The Making of a Community in Fourth-Century Egypt*. The Transformation of the Classical Heritage, 6. Berkeley and Los Angeles: University of California Press, 1985.
Rowland, R. J. "The 'Very Poor' and the Grain-Dole at Rome and Oxyrhynchus." *Zeitschrift für Papyrologie und Epigraphik* 21 (1976): 69–72.
Salamito, Jean-Marie. "*Rerum novarum*, une encyclique néo-scolastique? La question sociale ou le déclin de la communauté." In *Rerum Novarum: Écriture, contenu et reception d'une encyclique: Actes du colloque international organize par l'École française de Rome et le Greco n 2 du CNRS (Rome, 18–20 avril 1991)*, 187–206. Rome: École française de Rome, 1997.
Santa Ana, Julio de. *Good News to the Poor: The Challenge of the Poor in the History of the Church*. Translated from Spanish by Helen Whittle. Geneva: World Council of Churches, 1977.
Schichor, D., and D. K. Sechrest. *Three Strikes and You're Out: Vengeance as Public Policy*. Thousand Oaks, Calif.: Sage, 1996.
Schilling, Otto. *Reichtum und Eigentum in der altkirchlichen Literatur: Ein Beitrag zur sozialen Frage*. Freiburg in Breisgau: Herdersche Verlagshandlung, 1908.
Schleiermacher, Friedrich. *Hermeneutik und Kritik: Mit einem Anhang sprachphilosophischer Texte Schleiermachers*. Edited by Manfred Frank. Frankfurt: Suhrkamp, 1977. ET: In *Hermeneutics and Other Writings,* translated by Andrew Bowie, 5–224. Cambridge Texts in the History of Philosophy. Cambridge: Cambridge University Press, 1995.
Schneiders, Sandra M. "Feminist Ideology Criticism and Biblical Hermeneutics." *Biblical Theology Bulletin* 19 (1989): 3–10.
———. *The Revelatory Text: Interpreting the New Testament as Sacred Scripture*. San Francisco: Harper, 1991.
Schöllgen, Georg. *Die Anfänge der Professionalisierung des Kleurs und das kirchliche Amt in der syrischen Didaskalie*. Jahrbuch für Antike und Christentum. Ergänzungsbände 26. Münster: Aschendorff, 1998.
———. *Ecclesia Sordida? Zur Frage der sozialen Schichtung frühchristlicher Gemeinden am Beispiel Karthagos zur Zeit Tertullians*. Jahrbuch für Antike und Christentum. Ergänzungsbände 12. Münster: Aschendorff, 1984.
Schor, Adam. *Theodoret's People: Social Networks and Religious Conflicts in Late Roman Syria*. Berkeley and Los Angeles: University of California Press, 2011.
Schuck, Michael. *That They Be One: The Social Teaching of the Papal Encyclicals, 1740–1989*. Washington, D.C.: Georgetown University Press, 1991.
Serfass, Adam. "Wine for Widows: Papyrological Evidence for Christian Charity in Late Antique Egypt." In *Wealth and Poverty in Early Church*

and Society, edited by Susan R. Holman. Grand Rapids, Mich.: Baker Acadaemic; Boston: Holy Cross Orthodox Press, 2008.

Sheather, Mary. "Pronouncements of the Cappadocians on Issues of Poverty and Wealth." In *Prayer and Spirituality in the Early Church*, vol. 1, ed. Pauline Allen, Wendy Mayer, and Lawrence Cross, 375–92. Brisbane, Australia: Watson Ferguson & Company, 1998.

Sherwin, Michael. "Friends at the Table of the Lord: Friendship with God and the Transformation of Patronage in the Thought of John Chrysostom." *New Blackfriars* 85 (2004): 387–98.

Shewring, Walter. *Rich and Poor in Christian Tradition: Writings of Many Centuries Chosen, Translated, and Introduced*. London: Burns, Oates and Washbourne, 1948.

Singer, Peter. "Famine, Affluence and Morality." *Philosophy and Public Affairs* 1 (1972): 229–43.

Slesinsky, Robert. "The Doctrine of Virtue in St. Gregory of Nyssa's 'The Life of Moses.'" In *Prayer and Spirituality in the Early Church*, vol. 1, ed. Pauline Allen, Raymond Canning, and Lawrence Cross, 341–52. Brisbane, Australia: Watson Ferguson & Company, 1998.

Smith, C. Christopher, ed. *Introductory Bibliography of the New Monasticism: Resources for a New Monasticism*, vol. 1. Indianapolis: Doulos Christou Press, 2007.

Soskice, Janet. *Metaphor and Religious Language*. Oxford: Clarendon Press, 1985.

Spinoza, Baruch. *Tractatus theologico-politicus*. Edited by Fokke Akkerman. Épiméthée: Essais philosophiques. Oeuvres B. Spinoza 3. Paris: PUF, 1999; orig. pub. 1670.

Sternberg, T. *Orientalium More Secutus. Räume und Institutionen der Caritas des 5 bis 7. Jahrhunderts in Gallien*. Jahrbuch für Antike und Christentum. Ergänzungsbände, 16. Münster: Aschendorff, 1991.

Stiver, Dan R. *Theology after Ricoeur: New Directions in Hermeneutical Theology*. Louisville, London, Leiden: Westminster John Knox Press, 2001.

Strubbe, J. "Armenzorg in de Grieks-Romeinse wereld." *Tijdschrift voor Geschiedenis* 107 (1994): 163–83.

Strzygowski, Josef. *Koptische Kunst*. Catalogue général des antiquités égyptiennes du Musée du Caire. Osnabrück: Zeller, 1904.

Sturrock, John. *Structuralism*. Oxford: Blackwell, 2003.

Swift, Louis J. *The Early Fathers on War and Military Service*. Message of the Fathers of the Church 19. Wilmington, Del.: Michael Glazier Press, 1983.

Tanner, Norman P. *The Councils of the Church: A Short History*. New York: Crossroad, 2002.

Teja, Ramon. *Organización económica y social de Capadocia en el siglo iv. según los padres capadocios.* Acta Salmanticensia: Filosofía y letras 78. Salamanca: Universidad de Salamanca, 1974.

TeSelle, Eugene. "The Civic Vision in Augustine's *City of God.*" *Thought* 62 (1987): 268–80.

Teske, Roland J. "Soul." In *Augustine through the Ages: An Encyclopedia,* edited by Allan D. Fitzgerald, 807–12. Grand Rapids, Mich.: William B. Eerdmans, 1999.

Thiessen, Gerd. "Wanderradikalismus: Literatur-soziologische Aspekte der Überlieferung von Worten Jesu im Urchristentum." *Zeitschrift für Theologie und Kirche* 70 (1973): 245–71.

Thomas, J. P. *Private Religious Foundations in the Byzantine Empire.* Dumbarton Oaks Studies 24. Washington, D.C.: Dumbarton Oaks, 1987.

Tompkins, Jane B., ed. *Reader-Response Criticism: From Formalism to Post-Structuralism.* Baltimore: Johns Hopkins University Press, 1980.

Torchia, N. Joseph. "The *Commune/Proprium* Distinction in St. Augustine's Early Moral Theology." *Studia Patristica* 22 (1989): 356–63.

Tori, Michael J. "Apokatastasis in Gregory of Nyssa: From Origen to Orthodoxy." *Patristic and Byzantine Review* 15 (1996–1997): 87–100.

Troeltsch, Ernst. *Augustin, die christliche Antike und das Mittelalter. Im Anschluss an die Schrift "De civitate Dei."* Historische Bibliotheek 36. Munich: Oldenbourg, 1915.

———. *Die Soziallehren der christlichen Kirchen und Gruppen, Gesammelte Schriften.* Bd. 1. Tübingen: J. C. B. Mohr [Paul Siebeck], 1912. ET: *The Social Teaching of the Christian Churches.* Translated by Olive Wyon. London: George Allen and Unwin, 1931.

Tyler, Tom R., and Robert J. Boeckmann. "Three Strikes and You Are Out, but Why? The Psychology of Public Support for Punishing Rule Breakers." *Law and Society Review* 31 (1997): 237–65.

Uhlhorn, Gerhard. *Die christliche Liebestätigkeit in der alten Kirche.* Stuttgart: Verlag von D. Gundert, 1882. ET: *Christian Charity in the Ancient Church.* Translated by Sophia Taylor. New York: Charles Scribner's Sons, 1883.

Urbainczyk, Theresa. *Theodoret of Cyrrhus: The Bishop and the Holy Man.* Ann Arbor: University of Michigan Press, 2002.

Van Dam, Raymond. *Families and Friends in Late Roman Cappadocia.* Philadelphia: University of Pennsylvania Press, 2003.

———. "Governors of Cappadocia during the Fourth Century." *Medieval Prosopography* 17 (1966): 7–93.

———. *Kingdom of Snow: Roman Rule and Greek Culture in Cappadoci.* Philadelphia: University of Pennsylvania Press, 2002.

———. *On Becoming Christian: The Conversion of Roman Cappadocia.* Philadelphia: University of Pennsylvania Press, 2003.

Van Hooff, Anton J. L. "Caring for the Old: 'Quid pro quo' or 'omnia pro Deo.'" In *Fructus Centesimus: Mélanges offerts à Gerard J. M. Bartelink à l'occasion de son soixante-cinquième anniversaire,* edited by A. A. R. Bastiaensen, A. Hilhorst, and C. H. Kneepkens, 325–32. Instrumenta Patristica 19. Steenbrugge, Belgium: Abbey of St. Peter, 1989.

Vasey, Vincent. *The Social Ideas in the Works of St. Ambrose: A Study on De Nabuthe.* Studia Ephemeridis Augustinianum 17. Rome: Institutum Patristicum Augustinianum, 1982.

———. "The Social Ideas of Asterius of Amasea." *Augustinianum* 26 (1986): 413–36.

Verheijen, Luc M. J. "La charité ne cherche pas ses propres intérêts." In *Nouvelle approche de la Règle de saint Augustin II: Chemin vers la vie heureuse,* 220–89. Leuven: Peeters Press, 1988.

Vermeersch, Arthur. *Quaestiones de Iustitia ad usum hodiernum scholastice disputatae.* 2d ed. Brugge: Sumptibus Beyaert, 1904.

Veronese, Marie. "L'esegesi di Asterio di Amasea." In *Origene e l'alessandrinismo cappadoce (III–IV secolo): Atti del V Convegno del Gruppo Italiano di ricerca su "Origene e la tradizione alessandrina,"* edited by Mario Girardi and Marcello Marin, 299–331. Bari: Edipuglia, 2002.

Verstraeten, Johan. "Catholic Social Thought as Discernment." *Logos* 8 (2005): 94–11.

———. "Re-Thinking Catholic Social Thought as Tradition." In *Catholic Social Thought: Twilight or Renaissance?,* edited by J. S. Boswell, F. P. McHugh, and J. Verstraeten, 59–77. BETL 157. Leuven: Peeters Press, 2000.

Veyne, Paul. *Seneca: The Life of a Stoic.* Translated by David Sullivan. New York and London: Routledge, 2003.

Vincent, Gilbert. *La religion de Ricoeur.* La religion des philosophes. Paris: Les Éditions de l'Atelier, 2008.

Vinne, Michael de. "The Advocacy of Empty Bellies: Episcopal Representation of the Poor in the Late Roman Empire." Unpublished Ph.D. dissertation, Stanford University, 1995.

Vives, Josep. "Es el propriedad un robo: Las ideas sobre la propriedad privada en el christianismo primitivo." In *Fe y justicia,* 173–213. Salamanca: Ediciones Sigueme, 1981.

Vivian, Tim. *St. Peter of Alexandria: Bishop and Martyr.* Studies in Antiquity and Christianity. Philadelphia: Fortress Press, 1988.
Voicu, S. "La volontà e il caso: La tipologia dei primi spuri di Crisostomo." In *Giovanni Crisostomo: Oriente e Occidente tra IV e V secolo.* . . . Studia Ephemeridis Augustinianum 93. Rome: Institut Patristicum Augustinianum, 2005.
Volpe, Giuliano. *San Giusto: Le ville, le ecclesiae.* Bari: Edipuglia, 1998.
von Ranke, Leopold. *The Theory and Practice of History.* Edited by Georg G. Iggers and Konrad von Moltke. Indianapolis: Bobbs-Merrill, 1973.
Vööbus, Arthur. *Syriac and Arabic Documents Regarding Legislation Relative to Syrian Asceticism.* Papers of the Estonian Theological Society in Exile, 11. Stockholm: Etse, 1960.
Wacht, Manfred. "Wahre und falsche Armut: Bemerkungen zu Clemens Alexandrinus, Quis dives salvetur Kap 19." In *Vivarium,* Jahrbuch für Antike und Christentum 11, 338–47. Münster: Aschendorff, 1984.
Wallace-Hadrill, A. "The Social Spread of Roman Luxury: Sampling Pompeii and Herculanum." *Papers of the British School of Rome* 58 (1990): 145–92.
Walter, Gérard. *Les origines du communisme, judaiques, chrétiennes, grecques, latines.* Paris: Bibliothéque historique, 1931.
Weinsheimer, Joel. *Gadamer's Hermeneutics: A Reading of "Truth and Method."* New Haven, Conn.: Yale University Press, 1985.
Wheeler, Sondra Ely. *Wealth as Peril and Obligation: The New Testament on Possessions.* Grand Rapids, Mich.: William B. Eerdmans, 1995.
White, Carolinne. *Christian Friendship in the Fourth Century.* Cambridge: Cambridge University Press, 1992.
Whittaker, C. R., and Peter Garnsey. "Rural Life in the Later Roman Empire." In *Cambridge Ancient History 13: The Late Empire* A.D.*337–425,* edited by Averil Cameron and Peter Garnsey, 277–311. Cambridge: Cambridge University Press, 1998.
Wilder, Amos Niven. *Eschatology and Ethics in the Teaching of Jesus.* New York: Harper and Bros., 1939.
Wilson-Hartgrove, Jonathan. *New Monasticism: What It Has to Say to Today's Church.* Grand Rapids, Mich.: Brazos Press, 2008.
Winslow, Donald. *The Dynamics of Salvation: A Study of Gregory of Nazianzus.* Philadelphia: Philadelphia Patristic Foundation, 1979.
Wipszycka, Ewa. "Diaconia." In *The Coptic Encyclopedia,* ed. Azis S. Atiya, 3.895–67. New York: Macmillan, 1991.
Wolin, Sheldon. *Politics and Vision: Continuity and Innovation in Western Political Thought.* Princeton, N.J.: Princeton University Press, 1960; rev. ed. 2006).

Woolf, Greg. "Food, Poverty and Patronage: The Significance of the Epigraphy of the Alimentary Schemes in Early Imperial Italy." *Papers of the British School of Rome* 58 (1990): 197–228.

Xavier-Amherdt, Francois. *L'herméneutique philosophique de Paul Ricoeur et son importance pour l'exégèse biblique*. Paris: Éditions du Cerf, 2004.

Yoder, John Howard. *The Original Revolution: Essays on Christian Pacifism*. Christian Peace Shelf Series, 3. Scottdale, Pa.: Herald Press, 1971.

———. *The Politics of Jesus*. Grand Rapids, Mich.: William B. Eerdmans, 1994.

Young, Frances M. *Biblical Exegesis and the Formation of Christian Culture*. Cambridge: Cambridge University Press, 1997.

———. *Exegesis and Theology in Early Christianity*. London: Ashgate, 2012.

Index of Scriptural Passages

HEBREW SCRIPTURES

Genesis
  1:27   146
  3   88, 113, 213n.57
  18   72
Leviticus
  17:11   208n.47, 246n.25
Deuteronomy
  14:8   208n.47
Job
  1:1–5   152
Psalms
  18   78
  33:9   86
  45   147
  103   81
Hosea
  2:18   246n.26

NEW TESTAMENT

Matthew
  5:3   153
  6   41
  6:22   86
  11:15   86
  13:45–46 156
  25   25, 30, 56, 87, 220n.101
  25:35   118
  26:25   152
  27:3   152
Mark
  10   145
  10:17–22 134
  10:21   45, 208n.49
Luke
  2:29–32   131
  3:4–6   131
  5:30–31   132
  16   30, 66, 79, 87, 114, 117, 132, 155, 156, 163, 169, 220n.102
  16:13–14 149
  16:18–30 6, 93
  16:19   67, 68
  16:19–21 152
  16:21   118
  16:22   72, 152, 153, 155
  16:29   156
  18:30   232n.91
  20:35–36 146
  22:40–41 138
  22:43   137

John			2 Corinthians	
1:38, 42, 50	124		2:15	86
2:1–11	124		Galatians	
3:19–21	124, 125		3:28	25, 146
8:24	124, 125		Ephesians	
Romans			5	147
12	24		5:22–33	146
12:4–5	37, 38		1 Timothy	
13	40		2:9–10	68, 151
1 Corinthians			James	
6:15	246n.27		3:5	155
7:26–31	147		1 John	
7:32–35	146		1:1	86
8:13	246n.24		Revelation	
12:12	37		3:17	129
12:12–30	127			
16:1–2	26			

Index of Early Christian Sources

The term *varia* after a page or page range indicates that numerous endnotes cite the early Christian source; these are not listed individually.

Ambrose of Milan
  De officiis, 220n.100
Asterius of Amasea
  Against Covetousness, 53–54
  Homilies I–XIV, 223n.22
  Homily 1, 56, 65–79, 93, 106–11,
    128–33, 149–54, 163–65, 224–27
    varia, 237–38 *varia*, 241–42
    varia, 247–48 *varia*
  Homily 2 (The Unjust Steward), 47,
    200n.28, 214n.61, 214nn.63–64
  Homily 3 (Against Covetousness),
    219nn.91–92
Augustine
  City of God, 18, 40, 200n.34
  Confessions I.1, 20
Basil of Caesarea
  Commentary on Isaiah, 224n.31
  Epistle 265, 203n.15
  Homily 4, 214n.61
  Homily 6, 39, 199n.27, 202n.4,
    203n.17
  Homily 8, 214n.61
  Homily 12, 40, 204n.26

  Homily 21, 200n.28
  Letter to Egyptian Bishops, 38
Clement of Alexandria
  Paedogogus, 210n.53, 227n.49
  Quis dives salvetur, 45,
    210nn.52–54, 214n.61
  Stromateis, 41, 205n.28,
    210nn.52–53
Commodianus
  Explanation of the Psalms,
    232n.91
Cyril of Alexandria
  Homilies on Luke, 220n.102
Didache
  4.8, 45, 196n.8
  13, 208n.48
Epiphanius
  Panarion, 46, 209n.50, 213n.57
Epistle of Barnabas
  19, 45, 208n.47
Eusebius of Caesarea
  De vita Constantini, 200n.32
Gregory Nazianzen
  Oration 3, 200n.33

Gregory Nazianzen (*cont.*)
  Oration 4, 200n.33, 204n.22
  Oration 6, 23, 197nn.13–15
  Oration 14, 71, 214nn.61–62,
    214nn.66–67, 225n.34, 225n.42
  Oration 32, 233n.12
  Oration 33, 197n.15
  Oration 43, 28, 200n.31
  Oration 44, 219n.95
Gregory of Nyssa
  Against the Usurers, 216n.76
  De opificio hominis, 199n.22
  De vita Macrina, 145
  De vita s. Ephraem, 203n.11
  Life of Macrina, 224n.31
  On Virginity, 38, 203n.13
Irenaeus of Lyon
  Against Heresies III, 199n.21
  Against Heresies IV, 45, 208n.49,
    209n.50
  Against Heresies V, 40, 205n.27
Jerome
  Epistle 45, 228n.58
  Homily 86, 56, 80–92, 93, 111–20,
    133–39, 154–58, 163–65, 229–32
    varia, 238–39 *varia*, 242–43
    varia, 249 *varia*
John Chrysostom
  De Anna hom. 5, 206n.36
  Homilies on the Acts of the
    Apostles 5.4, 41, 205n.29
  Homilies on 1 Corinthians, 39,
    203n.19, 214n.66, 214n.70
  Homilies on 2 Corinthians, 214n.69
  Homilies on Genesis, 224n.31,
    225n.42, 232n.91
  Homilies on John, 39, 202n.8,
    203n.20, 214n.61, 214n.71,
    215n.72
  Homilies on Matthew, 47,
    199n.27, 203n.16, 203n.18,
    209n.50, 214nn.66–68,
    218n.87
  Homilies on 1 Timothy,
    202n.8
  Peccata fratrum non evulganda,
    203n.18
  Two Homilies on Those Who Hate
    Riches, 202n.8
Justin Martyr
  Apology I, 197n.17
  Dialogue with Trypho,
    196n.11
Lactantius
  Divine Institutes III, 213n.60
Minucius Felix
  Octavius, 197n.17
Origen
  Contra Celsum VII.59–60, 38,
    203n.12
  On Psalm 36, 232n.91
Palladius
  Lausiac History, 55
(anon.) Pelagian author
  On Wealth, 213n.58
Peter of Alexandria
  On Riches, 46
Pseudo-Chrysostom
  On the Parable of the Prodigal
    Son, 38, 203n.14
Salvian of Marseille
  Concerning the Governance of
    God, 40, 204n.23
Shepherd of Hermas, 45, 196n.8,
  210n.51
Tertullian
  Apology, 196n.11, 197n.17,
    199n.26

Theodoret of Cyrus
  Commentary on Romans 12, 202n.10
  Discourse on Providence 6, 122, 127, 210n.51, 224n.31, 241n.23

Theophilus of Alexandria
  Festal Letters, 224n.31

BRIAN MATZ

is associate professor of the history of Christianity
and the Archbishop Raymond G. Hunthausen Professor of Peace and
Justice at Carroll College. He is author and co-editor of a number
of books, including *Reading Patristic Texts on Social Ethics: Issues and
Challenges for Twenty-First-Century Christian Social Thought*
(co-edited with Johan Leemans and Johan Verstraeten).

www.ingramcontent.com/pod-product-compliance
Lightning Source LLC
Chambersburg PA
CBHW050336230426
43663CB00010B/1885